The Complete Terrorism Survival Guide

How to Travel, Work & Live in Safety

By Juval Aviv

Former Israeli Counterterrorism Intelligence Officer
Security Advisor to Corporations & Senior Executives

JURIS

Copyright © 2003 by Juval Aviv, William P. Kucewicz
and Juris Publishing, Inc.

ISBN:1-57823-130-2

Manufactured in the United States of America

Questions About This Publication

FOR EDITORIAL ASSISTANCE, please call

JURIS PUBLISHING, INC.
71 NEW STREET
HUNTINGTON, NY 11743
TELEPHONE: 1(631)350-0200

Dedications

To Tsila, Atalya, Don, Todd and Zoé for their immeasurable love and support.

Acknowledgements

This book has been in the making for many years. Yet, the events of September 11th underscored the urgent need for it to be written and published. A number of people have shown considerable support for this project. This book would not have been written without their sustained interest and guidance.

I would like to thank Anthony Williams, Esq. of Coudert Brothers for motivating me to put my thoughts down on paper.

I am deeply grateful to Daniel Aharoni, Esq., my friend and General Counsel, for continually getting me out of trouble.

I am indebted to Lawrence Newman, Esq. of Baker and McKenzie for his steadfast support and meaningful insights.

And finally, to my staff at Interfor, Inc. for their tireless efforts. A special thanks to Anna Moody, Esq, and Abby Barasch for taking charge of this project.

Juval Aviv

BIOGRAPHY

Mr. Juval Aviv has an M.A. in Business from Tel Aviv University and served as an officer in the Israel Defense Force (Major, retired) leading an elite Commando/Intelligence Unit. Additionally, Mr. Aviv was selected by the Israel Secret Service (Mossad) to participate in a number of intelligence and special operations in many countries in the late 1960s and 1970s. In 1984, a true account of one mission was published, entitled Vengeance, which was available in 27 countries. The book became a best seller and was later made into an award-winning film, Sword of Gideon, which was broadcast in North America on HBO and in other countries.

Over the past 20 years, Interfor, Inc., founded by Mr. Aviv, has become a leader in corporate intelligence worldwide, working with U.S. and foreign law firms, major banks, insurers and governmental agencies. Interfor's areas of expertise include security and vulnerability assessments, industrial espionage inquiries, due diligence investigations, litigation support and competitor intelligence. Interfor also provides asset searching and corporate fraud investigation services, both in the U.S. and internationally, in cases involving large debts or where assets have been hidden offshore in bank secrecy jurisdictions to avoid judgment creditors.

For over thirty years Mr. Aviv has worked with corporations and other entities, both domestically and internationally, on security measures for the protection of assets and personnel. Mr. Aviv's experience is broad and includes high profile clients such as El Al Airlines. While working as a consultant with El Al, Mr. Aviv surveyed the existing security measures in place and updated and developed El Al's security program, making El Al the safest airlines in business today.

Mr. Aviv is a leading authority on terrorist networks and their inner workings and served as lead investigator for Pan Am

Airways into the Pan Am 103-Lockerbie terrorist bombing. Mr. Aviv has been a speaker and panel participant for many organizations including the International Bar Association, the National Conference of Bankruptcy Judges, the U.S. Department of Justice, the Internal Revenue Service, and the American Bankruptcy Institute.

About Interfor Inc.

Interfor, Inc. is an international firm specializing in U.S. and international corporate investigations. Interfor's investigative and intelligence services encompass corporate due diligence, litigation support and intelligence gathering, asset search and recovery, financial and corporate fraud, physical security assessments and special factual inquiries.

Interfor's clients are U.S. and international law firms, insurers, multinational corporations and financial institutions. With one hundred years of combined experience, Interfor's staff consists of highly skilled investigators and fraud auditors many of whom have been associated with government, defense and intelligence agencies. We are supported by a sophisticated research division using state-of-the-art technology.

For additional information about Interfor that is available in seven languages, please visit us at www.interforinc.com.

Preface

Just as terrorism knows no bounds, the war against it may know no end.

Even though the Taliban were ousted and members of Al Qaeda were sent scurrying for their lives, the victory in Afghanistan doesn't mean that the war against terror is nearing a close. Far from it. If we are to take President George Bush and Prime Minister Tony Blair at their word, the U.S., Britain and their allies will be locked in mortal combat with terrorism for a very long time. Al Qaeda, in turn, has vowed to conduct "guerrilla war," raising the possibility of smaller scale but more frequent attacks in the future, and it has teamed up with the Iranian-supported Hezbollah, the most formidable terrorist group in the world, to provide better logistical support and training for terror operations.

For Americans, Britons, Canadians and the other peoples of the civilized world—ordinary folks like you and me—this means that we will continue to be viewed by terrorists as potential targets, probably for as long as we live. The scourge of terrorism was long in the making. It won't die easy. So be prepared for the worst.

No one, of course, will ever forget Sept. 11. The devastation and loss of life were truly horrific. But as violent and as deadly as that day was, those events—and the lethal anthrax letters that followed—could pale in comparison with what's to come. Terrorists are anxious to get their hands on weapons of mass destruction—be they chemical, biological, radiological or nuclear. At least one group already has. Members of a Japanese cult deployed nerve gas in the Tokyo subway system in 1995, killing a dozen persons and injuring more than 5,000 others, and experimented with biological warfare agents before they were finally caught. Similar mass attacks are bound to occur in the future. Toxic mustard gas, for example, can be manufactured relatively easily in makeshift basement labs, using formulas that are in the public domain and equipment that's available commercially. Researchers at the State University of New York indeed showed how easy it is to create a bioweapon when in 2002 they followed a recipe found on the Internet and purchased mail-order supplies to make a polio virus. Searches of the rubble in Afghanistan turned up countless Al Qaeda documents pertaining to weapons of mass destruction: how to make them, how to use them and where to get them. It's only a matter of time before one of these obscene weapons is used on a grand scale against an unsuspecting people. Where or when, no one knows. But it will happen.

The dangers are many. Commuters might discover to their sorrow that they were exposed to a lethal chemical or biological agent on their way to work. Office or factory workers could die after inhaling radiological dust that spewed, unseen, from their building's air-conditioning ducts. A nuclear bomb the size of a suitcase could level a small city. Then, too, there are the traditional forms of terror: bombings, hijackings, carjackings, executions and kidnappings for ransom.

If Sept. 11 taught us anything, it was this: To rely totally on government for our individual safety is foolish, because it leaves us open to the next catastrophe. Each one of us therefore must become personally responsible for our own security and the safety of our families. To survive terrorism, you have to be a step ahead. Self-preparedness and out-of-the box thinking are essential. Survival depends on outwitting, outfoxing and outsmarting the purveyors of terror. And that's precisely the purpose of this book—to teach you how to survive terrorism by using your head.

This guide teaches you how to protect yourself and your loved ones. You'll be instructed on how to create, in effect, a perimeter defense against terrorism to safeguard your home and office. You'll learn how to travel in safety. You'll be shown how to pick a secure hotel. You'll be able to walk the streets and hail taxis in foreign countries without fear. You'll be told where you can find vital information on the latest terrorism threats and get help should anything untoward happen. And you'll be able to guard your savings and your very identity from theft by terrorists (and ordinary criminals). Protecting your money and identity is important. The international crackdown on the funding of terror organizations will force terrorists to look elsewhere for money, and that could mean stealing your credit card numbers, pilfering your financial accounts, or assuming your identity to apply for credit, take out loans, secure a passport or rent cars and apartments.

As you may be able to tell already, this book leaves no stone unturned. It looks at every conceivable threat and explains the steps you can to take to stay out of harm's way. The guide, in fact, provides the same practical advice that my colleagues and I at Interfor, Inc. give to our corporate clients, many of whom rank among the world's top companies and senior executives. My intention in this book is to help, most especially, those individuals and businesses that can't afford to hire a security professional to advise them. My recommendations, tips and cautions are therefore practical, instructive and easy to follow.

For those wondering whether my advice is any good, allow me to tell you about my counterterrorism credentials. I'm a former member of the Israeli Defense Force, a retired Major. In the 1960s and 1970s, I led an elite commando-intelligence unit and took part in a number of special operations, mostly outside Israel. I also spent time in Israeli airport security. These days, I'm considered by many to be a global leader in counterterrorism and business intelligence. I was, for instance, the lead investigator for Pan American World Airways into the 1988 bombing of Pan Am Flight 103 over Lockerbie, Scotland. And my work has been featured in such publications as The New York Times, Time and Newsweek.

I founded Interfor, Inc. (www.interforinc.com) in 1979 and remain its president and CEO. Based in New York, Interfor has offices around the world and conducts a wide range of intelligence-gathering operations and investigations for the business and financial communities, industrial and service companies, law firms, and governments and agencies in the U.S. and overseas. We also advise clients on terrorism and crime prevention and protection. A number of our staff members previously were associated with various defense and intelligence agencies, including the FBI, CIA, British Secret Service and Israeli intelligence. I indeed own a debt of gratitude to my colleagues at

Interfor and the other professionals who helped to make this guide possible.

My experience with terrorism tells me that people want, most of all, sound, sensible and easy-to-follow advice. Vague suggestions and amateurish tips just won't do. My business clients realize that the dangers can never be eliminated completely, but the odds of becoming a victim of terrorism or crime can be reduced significantly if the proper precautions are taken in advance. This survival guide reflects the sum and substance of my many years in the fields of counterterrorism and investigation. I pray that those who read it and follow its advice may outlive the terrorists and criminals who today mercilessly menace and heartlessly terrorize innocent men, women and children all over the world.

Juval Aviv
New York

TABLE OF CONTENTS

Chapter 1

The Philosophy of Security

September 11 pierced fatally and forever the protections that two oceans had long afforded the United States. No more was the U.S. insulated from the world of terror. No longer was it immune from its violence and horror. Americans learned to their sorrow that a few dedicated fanatics, wielding only knives and box-cutters, could mount a devastating assault on their shores and kill more civilians than in any other act of violence in the nation's history. Even the billions of dollars spent on defense didn't stop it.

How could this have happened?

The terrorists exposed a chink in America's armor. By following a detailed, sophisticated plan, they demonstrated they could evade detection and exploit America's security weaknesses—weaknesses that are inherent in any free and open society. And therein lies part of the problem.

The United States is—or at least was—a terrorist's dream. The very liberties and opportunities that make America so fine a country can be ruthlessly misused by those who would do her harm. As a mobile society, people are on the move around the country all the time on business, vacation or relocation, making it easy for strangers to fit it. Finding apartments, getting cars and opening accounts aren't too difficult. The United States also is a nation of immigrants, so foreign accents and appearance haven't been viewed, until Sept. 11 at least, as anything out of the ordinary. Neither is government or the police overly intrusive. People aren't required to carry official ID cards, as they are in more than 100 other countries, and the police don't check hotel registries nightly as they do in many parts of the world.

Terrorists have found it relatively easy to recede into the American woodwork (as investigators looking into the Sept. 11 and anthrax attacks discovered to their consternation). Usually, they could go about conducting reconnaissance on their intend-

1

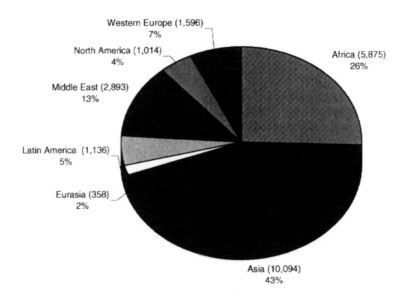

**Civilian Casualties of International Terrorism
Pre-Sept. 11 by Global Region, 1991-2000**

Western Europe (1,596)
7%

North America (1,014)
4%

Middle East (2,893)
13%

Latin America (1,136)
5%

Eurasia (358)
2%

Africa (5,875)
26%

Asia (10,094)
43%

Source: U.S. Department of State

ed targets undisturbed by law enforcement or intelligence services. If they needed equipment to carry out their plan, they normally could find it without raising suspicions. Getting money wasn't very difficult, either. Funds were easily transferred from overseas.

Compounding the problem of terrorism has been the notion of American invulnerability. Prior to Sept. 11, the U.S. had been coddled into a false sense of security. As most of the world battled terrorism on its doorstep, America remained largely immune. From 1991 through 2000, the U.S. experienced only 20 international-terrorist incidents, while the rest of the world suffered nearly 3,800 attacks. New York's World Trade Center was, of course, ravaged in February 1993 by a massive truck bomb that killed six persons and injured 1,000. Excluding those casualties, however, only eight other Americans fell victim to international terrorism conducted within the country's borders in the period 1991-2000. Even when the victims of the 1993 blast are included, all U.S. casualties of international terrorism still represented only four percent of the nearly 23,000 people around the world who were killed or injured by terrorists during that period.

1.01. The End of Innocence

Americans can thank geography for helping to protect them so well for so long. Most anti-U.S. militants reside in the Middle East—and to a lesser extent in Asia and Latin America. The Atlantic and Pacific oceans thus kept many of America's worst enemies more than an arm's length away. Besides logistical difficulties, distance also made assaults on the U.S. prohibitively expensive for most foreign terrorist groups. It's estimated that it cost a half a million dollars to plan, prepare and execute the 2001 aerial attacks on the World Trade Center and the Pentagon.

Nevertheless, some foreign extremists did manage to overcome the geographic and financial hurdles even before Sept. 11. In the 1980s and 1990s, international (as opposed to domestic) terrorists were behind 163 actual, suspected or prevented attacks within the United States, according to the Federal Bureau of Investigation (FBI). That represented more than a third of the 457 terrorist incidents recorded in those two decades. (Various domestic political extremists, special-interest groups and individuals were responsible for the rest.) All told, from 1980 through 1999, terrorism in America injured more than 2,000 people and claimed 205 lives.

Despite these many casualties and attacks, law enforcement and government policymakers continued to view international terrorism primarily as a criminal matter. They failed to appreciate that terrorism is a different breed of animal. International terrorists aren't street thugs lying in wait for a vulnerable passerby or burglars hoping to crack a safe. Neither are they deranged in a clinical sense, as, say, the Unabomber was. Rather, most are fanatics, fiercely wedded to a cause and bent on the destruction of their supposed enemies. For them, a human life is a trophy.

The general failure of U.S. decision-makers to understand the true nature of terrorism led Middle East expert Daniel Pipes to write in *The Wall Street Journal* the day after the Sept. 11 attacks: "The tactical blame falls on the U.S. government, which has grievously failed in its topmost duty to protect American citizens from harm. Specialists on terrorism have been aware for years of this dereliction of duty; now the whole world knows it."

It has since been learned that the Clinton administration had begun to take some praiseworthy antiterrorism steps before it left office. ("Mistakes Made the Catastrophe Possible," *Wall Street Journal*, September 12, 2001) In a lengthy, two-part exposé published in December 2001, the *Washington Post's* Barton Gellman revealed that President Bill Clinton signed three "highly classified" Memoranda of Notification after it was determined that Osama bin Laden's Al Qaeda organization was responsible for the U.S. embassy bombings in Kenya and Tanzania in August 1998. One of the memoranda authorized bin Laden's killing instead of his mere capture. Two U.S. submarines were stationed in waters near enough to Afghanistan to launch cruise-missile strikes if bin Laden were spotted. And the Central Intelligence Agency recruited, trained and paid insurgents in the region to capture or kill the Al Qaeda chieftain. ("Broad Effort Launched After '98 Attacks," *Washington Post*, Dec. 19, 2001; "Clinton's War on Terror," *Washington Post*, Dec. 20, 2001.)

Of course, the Clinton administration did wind up with egg on its face when, 13 days after the embassy bombings, cruise missiles were launched against sites in Afghanistan and Sudan. One strike reportedly missed bin Laden by a few hours, while the other demolished a harmless pharmaceutical plant in Khartoum. The Clinton White House also may have mishandled offers by assorted foreign governments to turn bin Laden over to the United States. Congress, meanwhile, made antiterrorism intelligence gathering harder by restricting the hiring of foreign operatives with records of human-rights violations.

Those weren't Washington's only missteps, however. Gellman reported, for example, that the Treasury Department opposed funding for a National Terrorists Asset Tracking Center

**Total Casualties Caused by International Terrorist
Attacks by Global Region, 2001**

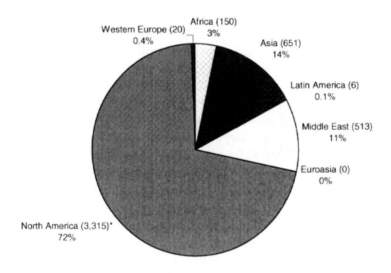

*Includes an estimated 3,000 killed but no estimate of wounded in the World
Trade Center attacks.

Source: U.S. Department of State

and declined to monitor the non-bank money transfers of the
hawala network used by bin Laden's operatives. FBI agents were
prevented from opening cases against domestic fundraisers
supporting foreign terror groups for fear the probes would be
viewed as ethnically "profiling" Islamic charities.

The sum of this antiterrorism activity and inactivity was that
bin Laden and his ilk came to believe that the United States was
a feckless, toothless giant that would never respond decisively to
any attack, no matter how deadly or fearsome. So, bin Laden
and his band set about planning and executing the Sept. 11 plot,
believing they not only could carry the attacks out successfully
but also could conduct them with impunity.

September 11 marked the end of American innocence about
terrorism. No one will ever forget the wooly black smoke that

issued from the upper floors of the World Trade Center, the hellish fireballs that erupted as the planes struck, or the surreal collapse of the two 110-story towers into gray tidal waves of dust and debris. But more was on fire that morning than just the Twin Towers and the Pentagon. Also aflame was the implicit contract Americans have with their government to keep them safe from foreign aggression.

It's impossible to overstate the profound implications of Sept. 11 for the United States. Protection from terrorism was, in an instant, transformed from a distant problem for leaders in Washington to handle to a pressing matter of personal responsibility for each and every American. The government simply could no longer be trusted to keep citizens safe from foreign invaders. Even the people who live and work in Washington, D.C. lost faith in the federal government's ability to protect them. "Some Washingtonians, After the Attacks, Now Have Escape Routes." That telling headline ran in *The Wall Street Journal* following the anthrax outbreaks on Capitol Hill and the attacks on the Pentagon and World Trade Center (*The Wall Street Journal*, Nov. 23, 2001). The newspaper reported that "a growing number of people" in Washington "are planning their escapes, just in case" terrorists strike again. One man told of buying a 12-gauge, pump-action shotgun, fearing a breakdown in public order after another terrorist incident.

What is the rest of the country to make of their government if even the residents of the nation's capital don't feel secure? The public's patience could wear tissue-thin if it reads more stories like the one that appeared in *The New York Times* fully four months after Sept. 11. The U.S. government, the *Times* reported, was still making available hundreds of formerly secret documents explaining how to turn dangerous germs into deadly biological weapons (BW). Experts described the documents as "cookbooks" for terrorists. The biological-weapons studies, written from 1943 to 1969, were declassified and made public over the past three decades, and various federal agencies sell many them over the phone and the Internet for as little as $15 apiece. Others can be obtained by mail through the Freedom of Information Act. One report, titled "Development of 'N' for

Offensive Use in Biological Warfare," concerns the weaponization of the germ that causes anthrax, *Bacillus anthracis*, code-named 'N.' Another report, on "The Stability of Botulinum Toxin in Common Beverages," deals with the most poisonous substance known. And "Selection for Freeze-Drying, Particle Size Reduction and Filling of Selected BW Agents" includes plans for a pilot factory that could produce dried germs in powder form, designed to lodge in human lungs. "It's pretty scary stuff," Raymond A. Zilinskas, a senior scientist at the Monterey Institute of International Studies in California told the *Times*. "There's a whole bunch of literature out there that's really cookbook." ("U.S. Selling Papers Showing How to Make Germ Weapons," *The New York Times, Jan. 13, 2002.)*

Adding insult to injury, the U.S. Army's premiere biowarfare research laboratory at Fort Detrick, Maryland admitted in January 2002 that it lost track of more than two dozen potentially dangerous biological specimens around 1991. Among the missing items were microbes that cause anthrax. Worse, we now know that the FBI mishandled warnings from at least two field agents about suspicious Middle Eastern men getting flight training in the U.S.

1.02. Why Governments Exist

From time immemorial, people have banded together for their mutual protection. There is, after all, safety in numbers. Our primeval ancestors discovered it was easier to safeguard their lives and property when they joined to fashion a common defense against aggressors than to try and go it alone. It was from this native desire for self-preservation that the very first civilized communities, cities and governments sprang. Explaining the process, Niccolò Machiavelli (1469-1527), the famed advisor to Italian nobility and the first great political philosopher of the Modern Age, writes in *The Discourses* that cities are built

> when inhabitants, dispersed in many small communities, find that they cannot enjoy security since no one community of itself, owing to its position and to the smallness of its numbers, is strong enough to resist the onslaught of

**Actual, Suspected and Prevented Terrorist
Incidents in the U.S., 1980-1999**

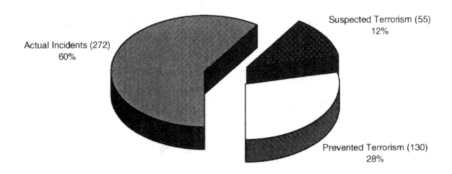

Actual Incidents (272)
60%

Suspected Terrorism (55)
12%

Prevented Terrorism (130)
28%

Source: Federal Bureau of Investigation

an invader, and, when the enemy arrives, there is no time
for them to unite for their defense; or, if there be time,
they have to abandon many of their strongholds, and
thus at once fall as prey to their enemies. Hence, to
escape these dangers, either of their own accord or at the
suggestion of someone of greater authority among them,
such communities undertake to live together in some
place they have chosen in order to live more convenient-
ly and the more easily to defend themselves. This was the
case with Athens and Venice, among many others.

The ancient Athenian philosopher Aristotle (384-322 B.C.), a
student of Plato and a tutor of Alexander the Great, studied the
histories and constitutional makeup of more than 150 cities of
the ancient world and concluded that the state—at first, nothing
more than an "association" of several villages—"came about as
a means of securing life itself." Self-preservation through
mutual defense, in other words, was a primary motivation for
the formation of the world's earliest communities. In *The Politics*,

his masterwork of political philosophy and civic advice, Aristotle tells how to make a Greek city-state "hard for a hostile force to invade." It should be situated in such a way that "the land as well as the inhabitants" can "be taken in at a single view, for a country which is easily seen can be easily protected." Its chief city should be "a convenient center for the protection of the whole country," guarded by a navy and surrounded by "strong walls."

Amazingly, even back in 350 B.C. when *The Politics* was written, Aristotle foresaw that defense technologies would be ever evolving: "Not only should cities have walls, but care should be taken to make them ornamental, as well as useful for warlike purposes, and adapted to resist modern inventions. For as the assailants of a city do all they can to gain an advantage, so the defenders should make use of any means of defense which have been already discovered, and should devise and invent others, for when men are well prepared no enemy even thinks of attacking them."

Two millennia later, noted English political philosopher John Locke (1632-1704) echoed the view that people create governments for their shared protection: "Men being, as has been said, by nature all free, equal, and independent, no one can be put out of this estate and subjected to the political power of another without his own consent, which is done by agreeing with other men, to join and unite into a community for their comfortable, safe, and peaceable living, one amongst another, in a secure enjoyment of their properties, and a greater security against any that are not of it." In his *Second Treatise of Government: An Essay Concerning the True Original, Extent, and End of Civil Government*, Locke explains how fear of invasion and theft led to the organization of societies and the formation of governments: A person living in the "state of nature" before governments were formed was free of all restraints yet "constantly exposed to the invasion of others." This meant "the enjoyment of the property he has in this state is very unsafe, very insecure. This makes him willing to quit this condition which, however free, is full of fears and continual dangers; and it is not without reason that he seeks out and is willing to join in society with others who are already united, or have a mind to unite for the mutual preservation of their lives, liberties and estates, which I call by the general name—property."

Nearly a century later, this passage inspired Thomas Jefferson to write in the Declaration of Independence: "WE hold these Truths to be self-evident, that all Men are created equal, that they are endowed by their Creator with certain unalienable Rights, that among these are Life, Liberty and the Pursuit of Happiness—That to secure these Rights, Governments are instituted among Men." The "Free and Independent States" of America, moreover, were declared to "have full Power to levy War [and] conclude Peace," and Americans volunteered to form an army and navy to expel the British. When the time came for America to create its own brand of government, mutual defense featured prominently. The U.S. Constitution indeed begins: "We the People of the United States, in Order to form a more perfect Union, establish Justice, insure domestic Tranquility, provide for the common defence. . . ."

Today's terrorists mean to break the age-old link between mutual defense and personal safety. Terrorists try to avoid clashing with a nation's military head on; conventional warfare isn't their forte. Instead, they attack a country's cherished symbols, target its businesses and murder its innocent civilians. An 11-volume Al Qaeda training manual found in Afghanistan instructed followers to attack locations with "high human intensity" like skyscrapers and sports stadiums and sites of "sentimental value," such as the State of Liberty, London's Big Ben and Paris's Eiffel Tower. Photographs of Seattle's Space Needle were found in an Al Qaeda computer, and an Al Qaeda "senior operative" debriefed by the FBI told of plans to hijack a U.S. aircraft and smash it into a nuclear power plant.

But it doesn't stop there. An Al Qaeda training videotape showed militants armed with live ammunition practicing to kidnap and assassinate whole groups of world leaders. One scenario had the terrorists attacking a golf tournament attended by a number of international leaders. Another involved an assassination attempt on a motorcade in Washington, D.C. In general, terrorists aim to make targeted governments appear

International Terrorist Attacks, Worldwide Total, 1981-2001

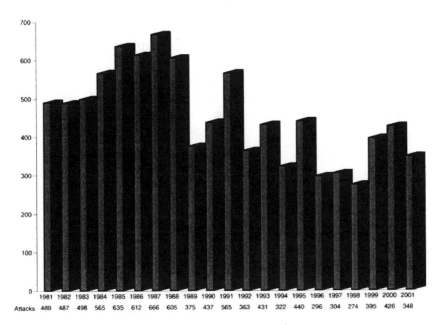

	1981	1982	1983	1984	1985	1986	1987	1988	1989	1990	1991	1992	1993	1994	1995	1996	1997	1998	1999	2000	2001
Attacks	489	487	498	565	635	612	666	605	375	437	565	363	431	322	440	296	304	274	395	426	348

Source: U.S. Department of State

impotent, incapable of protecting citizens, businesses and institutions from foreign aggression. Their hope is to cast doubt on a government's legitimacy by making a terrified people ask: "If our government can't protect us from harm, what good is it? Throw the bums out!"

September 11, of course, produced quite the opposite reaction. While bin Laden was right about his organization's ability to execute the attacks, he was wrong about how America (and its allies) would respond. Instead of being terrified, Americans became resolute. Instead of blaming Washington, they hoisted the flag. And instead of bowing to terrorism, they vowed to destroy it. "A great people has been moved to defend a great nation," President George W. Bush said in a nationally televised address on the evening of Sept. 11. "Terrorist attacks can shake the foundations of our biggest buildings, but they cannot touch the foundation of America."

1.03. The Terrorist Mind

The terrorists' simplistic reasoning evinces a shocking naiveté about the nature of democracy and an utter ignorance of the true character of a free society. Yet they forge on, reveling in every new murder and urging their compatriots to execute even more barbaric feats of terror. As British Prime Minister Tony Blair stated so eloquently the day after Sept. 11, "the world now knows the full evil and capability of international terrorism which menaces the whole of the democratic world. The terrorists responsible have no sense of humanity, of mercy, or of justice. To commit acts of this nature requires a fanaticism and wickedness that is beyond our normal contemplation." (BBC News, September 12, 2001)

What are we to make of such people? This much we know: Leaders of terrorist organization are warped, self-deluded personalities who advocate a cause mainly as a means of attracting pliant, sycophantic followers and achieving personal celebrity. In heading their organizations and sanctioning plots, they gain a personal satisfaction from the exercise of control and power over others. When a scheme of theirs makes headlines, it feeds their sense of self-importance and invincibility, spurring them to contemplate and approve other, more heinous acts.

Terrorist plots aren't necessarily masterminded by a group's leader, however. That's generally left to top lieutenants—typically skilled devotees who have a need to prove themselves but lack the conscience to distinguish right from wrong. Seasoned veterans similarly may act as "wise men," coordinating and directing attacks by less experienced recruits.

Many terrorists begin as poor, ill-educated, often troubled youths who find ersatz identities by becoming members of a group. Others, by contrast, are surprisingly well educated and come from well-to-do families but have taken up terrorism because they've grown disaffected, disheartened and angry over a lack of jobs, ruined dreams or crushed ambitions. Still others may be single-minded religious zealots or uncompromising political extremists, such as Marxist-Leninists, nationalists or separatists. In almost all cases, terrorists develop a fierce group loyalty, and many become psychologically dependent on their membership in a group and its leader.

Edward Walker, who was U.S. Ambassador to Egypt from 1994 to 1997, says that a large number of Middle East terrorists are "out-of-work, educated people," who have formed "resentments" because the economic and education systems in their countries have failed them. "That is why they turn to Islam and why some of them . . . turn to a more radical form," he said in "Looking for Answers," a "Frontline" television documentary. "They feel abused. They feel that there is no hope, and they look for an out, a way out, and they build on each other's disappointment." (PBS Program No. 2002, October 11, 2001)

Ahmed Sattar is example of this phenomenon. "As a young man growing up in Egypt in the '70s, in the '80s, looking around me, [having] no hope, seeing things deteriorating to a level that will not be acceptable by anybody, there was no other way except the Islam ideology—to believe in it and try to change things through it," he explains. Sattar was a former aide to the blind Egyptian cleric Sheik Omar Abdel Rahman. The sheik was convicted, along with nine others, of plotting to blow up the United Nations building, FBI headquarters in Manhattan, two New York underwater tunnels and the George Washington Bridge; a U.S. court sentenced him in 1996 to life imprisonment. As a cleric in Egypt, Rahman gained a large following of students and unemployed college graduates while calling for an armed struggle, or *jihad*, to establish an Islamic state in Egypt. (Public Broadcasting System, Program No. 2002, October 11, 2001)

In recent years, the importance of Islamic fundamentalism has grown in the Muslim regions of world, particularly the Middle East. While not all fundamentalists are terrorists, many, if not most, Middle Eastern terrorists profess a belief in Islamic fundamentalism. The *Encyclopedia of Politics and Religion*, (Robert Wuthnow, ed. 1998) states:

"Most fundamentalists are neither uneducated, back-ward-looking people nor the credulous dupes of silver-tongued preachers. To the contrary, they are medical doctors, nurses, engineers, teachers, businessmen, and college-educated mothers and fathers, who readily use (or even invent) the tools of technology, mass communications, and modern science. Yet they feel strongly that Western societies erred grievously when they replaced God, religion, and divine law with human reason and secular political principles as the basis for the legal and social order. For such people, religiously derived morality is the only acceptable framework for discerning the common good, evaluating human behavior, and governing society."

Fundamentalists believe that the laws of Islam should be accepted universally. Their faith, as they see it, thus grants them incomparable power and authority. *New York Times* writer Edward Rothstein explains: "The fundamentalist does not believe these ideas have any limits or boundaries. Goals are not restricted to a particular place or a particular time. The place is every place; the time is eternity. That is why fundamentalism is often expansionist; it must extend its reach as part of the great battle.... The goals of fundamentalist terror are not to eliminate injustice but to eliminate opposition." ("Exploring the Flaws in the Notion of the 'Root Causes' of Terror," *The New York Times*, November 17, 2001.)

Vice Admiral Thomas R. Wilson, director of the Defense Intelligence Agency, told the Senate Armed Service Committee on March19, 2002 that the Sept. 11 attacks were "the first strategic strikes in a war against the U.S. vision of the future world order." Saying that Islamic "extremists and their allies understand that their desired world cannot coexist with our brand of civilization," he predicted that the next decade may be defined by a "struggle over globalization," pitting the U.S. and its values against the reactionary opponents of openness, democracy, individual rights, economic freedom, scientific rationalism and the rule of law.

The problem of religious zealotry may well be much larger than is widely imagined. Daniel Pipes, writing in the January 2002 issue of *Commentary* magazine, estimates that the U.S. has more than 100 million Islamic enemies around the world. He divides them into three constituencies: 1) an inner core of militants who are active members of terrorist organizations like Al Qaeda and stretch from Afghanistan to Argentina; 2) sympathizers who approve of violent radicalism but don't take part in it, and 3) Muslims who are simply anti-American. An underlying difficulty, Pipes points out, is that "the hard work of adjusting Islam to the contemporary world has yet really to begin—a fact that itself goes far to explain the attraction of militant Islamic ideology."

General Tommy R. Franks, commander-in-chief of the United States Central Command and the officer in charge of day-to-day U.S. military operations in Afghanistan, said at a Department of Defense press briefing on January 18, 2002, that "there is a distinct possibility that terrorists acts can be committed today, tomorrow, in a great number of place around the world—perhaps as many as 60-plus countries—where we see terrorist organizations, cells, operating with great reach, global reach." Indeed, it would be a mistake to focus too much on Al Qaeda, for there are plenty of other dangerous terrorist groups to pick from around the world (as the appendix on terrorist organizations in the back of this book makes plain). Take, for example, the Iranian-backed and Lebanon-based organization Hezbollah. Foreign-policy expert Michael A. Ledeen of the American Enterprise Institute calls Hezbollah "the world's most deadly and dangerous terrorist organization, even more so than Al Qaeda." (Interview, "Special Report with Brit Hume," Fox News Network, July 12, 2002.) In fact, until Sept. 11, it had killed more Americans than all of the other international terrorist groups combined, according to L. Paul Bremer, chairman of the National Commission on Terrorism and former U.S. ambassador-at-large for counterterrorism (quoted in, "Experts Urge Bush to Expand Anti-Terror Campaign," Roxana Tiron, *National Defense Magazine,* January 2002).

It hasn't helped matters that most Islamic terrorists come from countries without democratic traditions or open societies. The authoritarian regimes they live under tend to be repressive, showing little regard for individual liberties and meting out harsh punishment to their opponents. The economies in most of these countries are underdeveloped and largely state-run, offering scant opportunities for individual advancement through economic growth or entrepreneurial ventures. Director of Central Intelligence George J. Tenet noted in testimony before the U.S. Senate Committee on Intelligence in February 2002 that terrorist groups "exploit" the "social, economic and political tensions across the world" by "mobilizing their followers."

Most of the countries that breed terrorists, in fact, are ruled by self-aggrandizing elites or cruel dictators who care little for broad-based prosperity and actually fear the emergence of a vibrant middle class. Were the ranks of well-educated professionals and entrepreneurs to grow substantially, these rulers know that their days would be numbered. A large, thriving middle class would demand sweeping political reform and eventually force out the old regimes. Therefore, it has behooved many of these governments to condone terrorism and anti-Americanism in order to deflect criticism of their own shortcomings and their countries' economic woes. Consequently, many terrorists misunderstand the West. In part, this is because they've never personally enjoyed the benefits of freedom, democracy and free enterprise. There are striking dichotomies, however. While decrying the United States, many America-haters in the Middle East and elsewhere are not-so-secret fans of its pop culture, especially Hollywood movies. One newsman covering the war in Afghanistan reported entering a shop that had wall posters of bin Laden and Clint Eastwood side by side. A penetrating look at the psychology of terrorists has been supplied by Martha Crenshaw, a professor of government at Wesleyan University in Middletown, Connecticut and editor of the book *Terrorism in Context* (Pennsylvania State University Press, 1995).

In an Internet forum a few years ago, she stated:

> "There is no single 'terrorist personality.' Members of such groups often display many different psychological traits. Terrorism is what unites them. What is important is that terrorism is typically a group phenomenon. It is based on membership in an organization that is a 'total institution,' stressing cohesion, loyalty, commitment to the cause, conformity, and identification with the group.

"People who join such groups may do so because they have a psychological need to belong rather than out of political commitment, and once they are in the group they lose the ability to act on their own initiative. Furthermore, it is difficult, if not impossible, to leave. Abandoning the group is treachery. It may be punishable by death or severe penalties such as kneecapping. You might even put your family at risk. Moreover, most 'terrorists' are young men. The leaders of such groups may be older, but the followers are often impressionable adolescents. They may also have few alternatives—no educational or job prospects, for example. Where there is a high level of political dissatisfaction, turning to an extremist political group might have the same attraction as joining a gang in the inner city.

"But at the same time, we have to recognize that people are not equally susceptible to the appeals of extremism. Not all of us would be capable of violence against others or certainly of killing ourselves. Not everyone has the disposition to be a good soldier or perform well under combat conditions. It also happens that people who are prone to violence seek out opportunities to engage in it. If an organization already exists that promises such an opportunity, then they will be motivated to join. Politics will be secondary."

("Understanding Terrorism," The Online NewsHour Forum, Public Broadcasting Service, Aug. 15, 1997.)

Days after the Sept. 11 attacks, Crenshaw offered yet another valuable insight into the terrorist mind, explaining that "'suicide' terrorists may not be in the least suicidal in the clinical sense." Rather, she said, "these individuals feel honored and proud to be chosen. They form an elite. They anticipate that their death will ensure that they are never forgotten. Faith in an afterlife often reinforces their conviction in the power of martyrdom." ("The Attack on America; Know the Enemy Mind," Martha Crenshaw, *New York Newsday*, Sept. 16, 2001.)

1.04. What the Future Holds

The truth be told, America hasn't seen terrorism yet. "Let there be no doubt," U.S. Defense Secretary Donald H. Rumsfeld said at the end of January 2002, "in the years ahead, it is likely that we will be surprised again—by new adversaries who may also strike in unexpected ways. And as they gain access to weapons of increasing power, these attacks could grow vastly more deadly than those we suffered September 11th." (Donald Rumsfeld, speech at the National Defense University, Washington, D.C., Department of Defense transcript, Jan. 31, 2002)

As ghastly as the devastation was at the World Trade Center and the Pentagon, Sept. 11 doesn't come close to the damage and loss of life that a weapon of mass destruction would cause. Biological agents, toxic chemicals, radiological exposure and nuclear detonations could kill many thousands, if not millions, in one stroke. International terrorists are seeking to acquire these weapons, and some may already possess them.

President Bush, in his State of the Union address of January 2002, said that states like Iraq, Iran and North Korea, along with their "terrorist allies," constitute "an axis of evil, arming to threaten the peace of the world. By seeking weapons of mass destruction, these regimes pose a grave and growing danger. They could provide these arms to terrorists, giving them the means to match their hatred. They could attack our allies or attempt to blackmail the United States. In any of these cases, the price of indifference would be catastrophic." Central Intelligence Director Tenet echoed those remarks days later, saying: "Terrorist groups worldwide have ready access to information on chemical, biological, and even nuclear weapons via the Internet, and we know that Al Qaeda was working to acquire some of the most dangerous chemical agents and toxins." Documents recovered in Afghanistan showed that bin Laden was pursuing "a sophisticated biological weapons research program," he said, adding: "We also believe that bin Laden was seeking to acquire or develop a nuclear device. Al Qaeda may be pursuing a radioactive dispersal device—what some call a 'dirty bomb.' Alternatively, Al Qaeda or other terrorist groups might also try to launch conventional attacks against the chemical or nuclear industrial infrastructure of the United States to cause widespread toxic or radiological damage."

"Al Qaeda and other terrorist groups will continue to plan to attack [the United States] and its interests abroad," Tenet said. "Their *modus operandi* is to have multiple attack plans in the works simultaneously, and to have Al Qaeda cells in place to conduct them." Tenet extended his remark in March 2002 testimony before the U.S. Senate Armed Services Committee, saying that Al Qaeda and "other like-minded groups remain willing and able to strike us." ("Worldwide Threat: Converging Dangers in a Post 9/11 World," U.S. Senate Select Committee on Intelligence testimony, Feb. 6, 2002.)

It's almost inevitable that terrorists somewhere someday will successfully use a weapon of mass destruction. "Proliferation of the weapons of mass destruction does not mean that most terrorist groups are likely to use them in the foreseeable future, but some almost certainly will," terrorism expert Walter Laqueur of the Center for Strategic and International Studies in Washington, D.C. wrote in a prescient 1996 article in *Foreign Affairs* entitled "Postmodern Terrorism." Future terrorists, he said, will be "individuals or like-minded people working in very small groups," who "will be less ideological, more likely to harbor ethnic grievances, harder to distinguish from other criminals, and a particular threat to technologically advanced societies." As far as weapons of mass destruction are concerned, he concluded that individual terrorists and small militant groups "will not be bound by the constraints that hold back even the most reckless government."

"An individual," he warned, "may possess the technical competence to steal, buy, or manufacture the weapons he or she needs for a terrorist purpose; he or she may or may not require help from one or two others in delivering these weapons to the designated target. The ideologies such individuals and mini-groups espouse are likely to be even more aberrant than those of larger groups. And terrorists working alone or in very small groups will be more difficult to detect unless they make a major mistake or are discovered by accident." Middle East expert Pipes is even more emphatic, saying: "Future attacks are likely to be biological, spreading germs that potentially could threaten the whole country. When that day comes, [the U.S.] will truly know what devastation terrorism can cause." ("Mistakes Made the Catastrophe Possible," Pipes, *The Wall Street Journal*, December 12, 2001.)

Recognizing the dangers posed by biological agents, a team at the Center for Nonproliferation Studies at California's respected Monterey Institute of International Studies compiles information from around the world on terrorism and criminality relating to weapons of mass destruction—specifically, biological, chemical, radiological and nuclear weapons. Its findings are chilling. Although many of what the center calls "incidents" are nothing more than hoaxes, a startlingly large number of cases actually involve weapons with genuine mass-destruction capability. Moreover, of the 703 weapons-of-mass-destruction incidents—actual (75) and hoaxes (628)—recorded in 2000-2001, six of every seven occurred in the U.S. or Canada.

Beyond the weaponry of terror, the civilized world has another worry—that is, the thousands of Al Qaeda alumni, trained over the years at terrorist camps in Afghanistan, who are now waiting in "sleeper cells" in the U.S. and other countries around the world. "There may no longer be a command headquarters like there was in Afghanistan," French terrorism expert and United Nations Security Council advisor Roland Jacguard told *The Wall Street Journal* in late 2001. "But now smaller, more numerous, more cloistered sleeper cells are likely to multiply across the world." ("Moving Targets: Now, It's the Alumni of bin Laden's Camps Giving Cause for Fear," by Jay Solomon, et al., *The Wall Street Journal*, Dec. 13, 2001)

In his first State of the Union address in January 2002, President Bush said:

> "What we have found in Afghanistan confirms that, far from ending there, our war against terror is only beginning. Most of the 19 men who hijacked planes on September the 11th were trained in Afghanistan's camps, and so were tens of thousands of others. Thousands of dangerous killers, schooled in the methods of murder,

Weapons of Mass Destruction Incidents
by Region, Actual and Hoaxes, 2000-2001

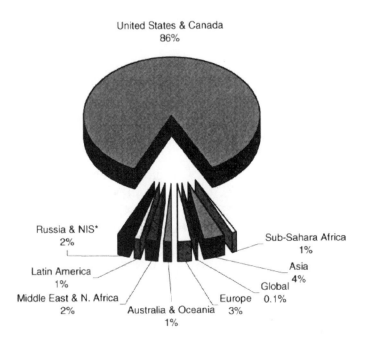

United States & Canada
86%

Russia & NIS*
2%

Sub-Sahara Africa
1%

Latin America
1%

Asia
4%

Middle East & N. Africa
2%

Global
0.1%

Europe
3%

Australia & Oceania
1%

*Newly Independent States (NIS) of the former Soviet Union.

Source: Center for Nonproliferation Studies, Monterey Institute of International Studies

often supported by outlaw regimes, are now spread throughout the world like ticking time bombs, set to go off without warning." It's believed that Al Qaeda's Afghan camps trained 15,000 to 20,000 terrorists all told.

U.S. intelligence and law enforcement are only beginning to grasp the magnitude of the problem. It now appears that sleepers (i.e., terrorists who enter a country under false pretexts, such as attending school or taking jobs, and who may appear as

wholesome as apple pie) have been recruiting and training new
members while they've been in the U.S. To elude the post-Sept.
11 dragnet, moreover, the sleepers have gone under deep cover,
hoping to make themselves harder to find. By latest count, there
may be as many 5,000 people in the U.S. with links to the Al
Qaeda network, and there are even reports that Al Qaeda
scouted an Oregon ranch for use as a possible terrorist training
camp.

"There is no question in my mind . . . we will be attacked
again," the FBI's chief of counterterrorism, Dale Watson, told a
law-enforcement conference in July 2002. The terrorist "fleas"
infesting the U.S., he added, "want to kill you. They could be in
your neighborhood." (quoted in, "FBI Boss Thinks bin Laden Is
Dead," by Christopher Newton, Associated Press, July 17, 2002.)

Two months earlier, FBI Director Robert S. Mueller III said
in a speech: "Terrorists can and will strike virtually anyone,
anywhere, at any time. Right now, Al Qaeda alone has roots in
more than one out of four nations. Their pockets are deep and
their financial supporters are all over the world, including right
here in our own backyard. And yet, terrorists are more invisible
than ever. They don't wear military uniforms. They blend into
society. They can be a businessman in a three-piece suit. They
can be the shopper in line at the local Wal-Mart. They can even
be—as we have seen so tragically—the person sitting next to you
on an airplane." (Remarks Prepared for Delivery at the Anti-
Defamation League's 24th Annual National Leadership Conference in Washington, D.C.," Federal Bureau of Investigation,
May 7, 2002.)

The governments of Singapore, Malaysia and the Philippines
have had some success in uncovering sleepers in their midst.
One of several suspects arrested in January 2002 was a 30-year-
old Indonesian who slipped into Singapore using a fake Filipino
passport in October 2001, shortly after the U.S. commenced its
bombing raids against the Taliban and Al Qaeda in Afghanistan.
His mission, said Singapore authorities, was to activate an Al
Qaeda sleeper cell that had been in place for years awaiting
orders from Afghanistan. For eight years, the sleepers assiduously avoided arousing suspicion; they didn't contact other

terrorists and even eschewed joining local mosques. The terrorists, it was discovered, planned to bomb the embassies of the U.S., Australia, Britain and Israel and commercial buildings housing U.S. companies in Singapore.

"I am very anxious" about the dangers of sleep cells, confided Jean-Louis Bruguière, a French magistrate and noted expert on Islamic terrorism who heads a special counterterrorism office of the French police. "There are many autonomous cells in Europe and North America we do not know about. They do not need orders from Osama bin Laden or the *jihad*. They finance their own operations with credit card fraud and theft. The threat, even with bin Laden gone, is very high," he said in a November 2001 *New York Times* interview. "These groups are protean; they change their shape like the AIDS virus. The way they communicate or carry out one operation is not the way they carry out the next one. And many of them, especially those with the group known as Takfiris [a radical Egyptian sect devoted to the destruction of Islam's enemies], are so integrated into Western society, even eating pork, drinking [alcohol] and wearing Western clothes as a cover, that they are almost impossible to discover beforehand." (Quoted in "A Nation Challenged: Intelligence; A Powerful Combatant in France's War on Terror," by Chris Hedges, *The New York Times*, Nov. 24, 2001.)

Bruguière also touched upon a problem that continues to confound law enforcement—namely, the seeming ease with which terrorists can get hold of money to fund individual operations. Terrorism can be a "low-budget enterprise," *The Wall Street Journal* found after conducting an extensive, post-Sept. 11 review of terrorist-related court documents. ("Terror on a Budget: Bin Laden's Network, Despite Rich Image, Runs on a Shoestring," by Jerry Markon, et al., *The Wall Street Journal*, Sept. 20, 2001.) Even though the costs of maintaining a large, international network may be high, individual terrorist cells can operate on a shoestring. The Sept. 11 hijackers, for instance, stayed in cheap hotels and haggled over bills; one lived off money from his parents.

The ability of terrorists to find easy money is well known in Europe and the Middle East. "Islamic terrorism in Europe is a deeply rooted phenomenon that regenerates itself continuously," according to Italian magistrate Stefano Dambruoso, who has uncovered Islamic terrorist networks in his own country. He cites, in particular, the ability of terrorist groups to gain funding from voluntary donations and criminal activity. "It may seem strange," he observes, "but apart from proceeds from illegal activity, such as drug trafficking, one of the main sources of income for the groups is contributions." (quoted in "The New Global Threat," by Daniel Pipes, *Jerusalem Post*, April 11, 2001.) Indeed, U.S. investigators found it harder to track down the sources of terrorist funding than they initially expected. The money transfers often are small, originate from a variety of sources and flow through non-banking channels. What's more, an FBI official has told Congress that international terrorists continue to resort to "traditional fraud schemes," such as credit card fraud, identity theft and "credit card bust-out schemes," to finance their activities.

Such scams aren't new. A U.S. Secret Service official told a congressional hearing in 1998 of a notorious credit card "bust-out" scheme perpetrated by at least 31 suspects with "affiliations to known Middle Eastern terrorist groups." Organized into cells "throughout the United States," he said that members of the group applied for and received as many as 40 credit cards each. They then systematically "boosted" the credit limits to the maximum by submitting worthless checks as payments made in advance of any purchases. In most cases, the check amounts exceeded the cardholders' credit limits and sometimes were double a card's limit. In keeping with U.S. banking regulations, the payments were credited to the card accounts before the checks cleared. Even though the checks were worthless, the cardholders were able to purchase merchandise and obtain cash advances up to and exceeding their credit limits, thereby "busting out" the accounts.

Now, the very action of rounding up terror suspects in the U.S. and elsewhere and then trying them in courts could create a new set of difficulties. What if citizens of these countries are taken hostage by terrorists demanding the release of their jailed compatriots? Sadly, it has already begun. A group calling itself

The National Movement for the Restoration of Pakistani Sovereignty seized *Wall Street Journal* reporter Daniel Pearl in Karachi in January 2002, demanding that all Pakistanis being "illegally" detained by the FBI inside the U.S. merely on suspicion must be given access to lawyers and allowed to see their families. Pearl's beheaded body was found weeks later.

Even Secretary of Defense Rumsfeld had to concede in late 2001 that "there isn't any way to defend against terrorists at every spot on the face of the globe or in a country, against every technique, at every moment of the day or night." (from interview transcript, "Meet the Press," NBC News, Dec. 2, 2001.) Rumsfeld's admission bears a striking similarity to an all-too-prescient warning issued in February 2001 by Director of Central Intelligence Tenet. In testimony on "The Worldwide Threat in 2001: National Security in a Changing World," he told the Senate Armed Services Committee that terrorists are "becoming more operationally adept and more technically sophisticated in order to defeat counterterrorism measures. For example, as we have increased security around government and military facilities, terrorists are seeking out 'softer' targets that provide opportunities for mass casualties. Employing increasingly advanced devices and using strategies such as simultaneous attacks, the number of people killed or injured in international terrorist attacks rose dramatically in the 1990s, despite a general decline in the number of incidents. Approximately one-third of these incidents involved U.S. interests." (Senate Select Committee on Intelligence, Central Intelligence Agency transcript, Feb. 7, 2001).

As governments around the world made it harder for terrorists to operate, the terrorists responded by identifying new, headline-grabbing targets that offered greater potential for inflicting large numbers of casualties in a single or coordinated multi-site attack. There's no reason to believe now that they won't respond to the latest crackdown on international terrorism in the same way—that is, by picking targets and employing weapons that will produce even larger numbers of deaths and injuries. The U.S. Nuclear Regulatory Commission sent the following ominous memo to the operators of America's more

than 100 nuclear reactors in late January 2002: "FBI headquarters
has provided the following information to all field offices.
During debriefings of an al Qaeda senior operative, he stated
there would (be) a second airline attack in the U.S. The attack
was already planned and three individuals were on the ground
in the U.S. The attack was already planned and three individuals
were on the ground in the states recruiting non-Arabs to take
part in the attack. The plan is to fly a commercial aircraft into a
nuclear power plant to be chosen by the team on the ground.
The plan included diverting the mission to any tall building if a
military aircraft intercepts the plane. No specific timeline or
location was given for the attack." ("Nuclear Regulatory Commission Memo Warning Of Terror Attacks," text of memo titled
"Information Assessment Team Advisory Update For Power
Reactors, Non-Power Reactors, Decommissioning Reactors, Category I And Iii Fuel Facilities, Independent Spent Fuel Storage
Installations, And Large Material Licensees" published by
CNN.com, Jan. 31, 2002).

In his post-Sept. 11 address to a Joint Session of Congress,
President Bush pledged that "this country will define our times,
not be defined by them. As long as the United States is
determined and strong, this will not be an age of terror; this will
be an age of liberty, here and across the world." However,
unless the United States and civilized peoples everywhere
subscribe to a new, more stringent philosophy of security,
terrorists will find the gaps. They always do. "Terrorists are
strategic actors. They choose their targets based on the weaknesses they observe in our defenses and our preparedness,"
says the Office of Homeland Security in its July 2002 report "The
National Strategy For Homeland Security."

1.05. Proactive Security

Since 1983, the U.S. law has defined terrorism as "premedi-
tated, politically motivated violence perpetrated against non-
combatant targets by subnational groups or clandestine agents."
(Title 22, United States Code, Chapter 38, Sec. 2656f)

The Defense Department has its own definition, calling
terrorism "the calculated use of violence or threat of violence to

inculcate fear [and is] intended to coerce or to intimidate governments or societies in the pursuit of goals that are generally political, religious or ideological." (DOD Dictionary of Military and Associated Terms, compiled by Joint Chiefs of Staff, Publication 1-02, as amended through 14 August 2002, U.S. Department of Defense)

These definitions aren't all that different from the classic definition of war. Renowned Prussian military strategist Karl von Clausewitz famously said that war is a continuation of politics by other means (or, to quote him correctly, "War is not merely a political act, but also a real political instrument, a continuation of political commerce, a carrying out of the same by other means"). In *On War* (1832), Clausewitz further notes that war "is an act of violence intended to compel our opponent to fulfil our will." That, too, sounds very much like a goal of terrorism. (The term "terrorism" was coined in the 1790s and referred to the French Revolution's Reign of Terror, which made famous the guillotine.)

One key difference between war and terrorism is that wars are waged between nations, and terrorists and their organizations aren't nations (although they may have state sponsors). Terrorists neither wear uniforms nor do they always carry their arms openly. These two conditions are enumerated in the Geneva Convention of 1949 pertaining to the treatment of prisoners of war—a convention that also bars hostage-taking. Still, terrorists believe they're soldiers engaged in a mighty conflict, and this presents a unique challenge to their targets— the peoples of the free world—for it means that individual citizens must assume large part of the responsibility of self-defense normally relegated to the military and law enforcement. This, in turn, requires a rethinking of traditional concepts of security.

In essence, security is determined by the barriers that are in place. These include physical barriers (e.g., doors and locks) but also encompass behavioral barriers (e.g., personal habits and routines) and systems barriers (e.g., security personnel and computer firewalls). The aim of security is to design a combination of systems, procedures and physical roadblocks that minimize risk and exposure to terrorism. Security thus is a function of logic. Moreover, a belief in security is an essential prerequisite. People must believe that it can work in preventing the untoward from happening and that it's doable. But believing in security is only half the battle, for security also entails keeping an open mind and planning ahead. Here, knowledge is essential. Travelers, for example, have to learn more about their destinations prior to departure and plan accordingly. An ounce of prevention, as the saying goes, is worth a pound of cure.

Security planning must be done with the goal of prevention. The more sophisticated the barriers erected, the harder and longer it will take an intruder to get past them. A terrorist may give up after deciding his intended target is too hard to attack and go on to someone or someplace else. What individuals and companies need to do, therefore, is to put enough barriers in place so a terrorist will say, "This guy (or business) is too protected, too professional, too difficult to get to; I'm moving on to something else." The philosophy of security also means planning for the unexpected. Israel, for instance, has had contingency plans in place for decades to deal with hijacked-aircraft attacks on tall buildings and city centers. Its security forces are prepared for such an emergency. Who knows how Sept. 11 might have turned out had the U.S. had similar contingency plans in place.

Israeli air-travel security, in fact, makes an excellent case study in counterterrorism procedure. El Al, the Israeli national carrier, is the most secure of all the world's airlines because of its adherence to a well-thought-out philosophy of security. Every member of its security force is handpicked and trained (or trainable), and redundancy is built into the system. El Al creates concentric rings of defense. If a terrorist somehow manages to penetrate an outer ring, he'll be caught by one of the inner ones. Security breaches and system failures are bound to happen. But by erecting ring after ring of defense, El Al minimizes the damage that a security lapse may cause. Sky marshals are aboard El Al flights, but a plane flying at 30,000 feet is the last place to conduct a war against terrorism. The danger to passengers and crew is too great. The battle against hijacking, therefore, needs to be fought primarily on the ground—that is, in air-terminal security checks that prevent hijackers from boarding planes and with intelligence that rounds up suspected plotters long before they get near an airport.

El Al's extensive pre-boarding questionnaire is a vital tool in hijacking prevention. It may come as a surprise to learn that Israeli airport security personnel rarely care about the answers passengers give to their specific questions. The answers aren't all that important. The reason: Getting answers isn't the purpose of asking the questions. That's not the point of the exercise. Rather, Israeli airport security personnel ask a long list of questions in order to gauge travelers' physical and emotional responses, their body language, their tone of voice and the look in their eyes. These indicators provide a more accurate reading of a traveler's true intentions than the specific answer to any given question.

Throughout Israel, in fact, most everyone subscribers to a strict philosophy of security. A bag left on the street for only a few seconds will get an immediate response. The item will be moved to a safer location, and the person who left it unattended will by questioned—not by the police, necessarily, but by civilian passersby. Israelis consider security a personal responsibility, and they take that responsibility seriously.

One lesson of Sept. 11 is that no one should depend solely on government for his personal protection. Security is now a matter of personal initiative. To be protected against terrorism—or other forms of violence—means that individuals must become proactive, taking steps to prevent attackers from getting to them and developing a mindset that makes security precautions a habit, as much a part of daily life as brushing your teeth.

Businesses, too, have to make security a higher priority. According to the latest U.S. State Department data, commercial facilities around the world accounted for more than two-thirds of all the targets struck by international terrorists in 1995-2001. Yet barely two months after Sept. 11, it was striking how many firms didn't want to think about terrorism any more—much less incur the costs of antiterrorism safeguards. All too often, business executives think only of dollar signs after hearing the

Annual International Terrorist Attacks by Global Region, 1996-2001

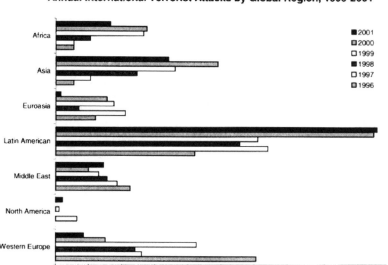

Source: U.S. Department of State

words "antiterrorism protection." The interesting thing is, many security measures can be implemented without spending a penny. Changes in procedures and lifestyles, for instance, are cost-free, yet effective.

After Sept. 11, alas, some U.S. companies decided that they'd simply fall back on their insurance coverage in the event a catastrophe occurred. They're insured for every contingency, they reasoned, so why spend money on added security? One item that such shortsighted firms overlook is the value of the intellectual property embodied their workforces. Insurance doesn't cover that type of loss. Besides, any act of terror, however minor, causes disruption, delay and unwanted publicity. These intangibles carry costs, too. In contrast, there are the wise companies that believe in prevention and accept that it costs money. Knowing not to overdo it, they take an even-keel approach, doing what it takes to provide adequate security—no more, no less. Firms such as these often hire professional security consultants to advise them. They're the smart ones; they recognize that security requirements change over time. Whereas a few solid locks and some well-placed lighting once were sufficient safeguards, these may no longer be adequate today. Professional security advisors evaluate each situation on its merits and impartially recommend what ought to be done.

Security is as much an attitude as it is investment. Management from top to bottom has to subscribe to a philosophy of security for it to be effective. A view toward terrorism prevention must infuse a company. Additionally, it isn't enough merely to protect a few senior executives from kidnapping, assassination and the like. Rank-and-file personnel also must be protected. And that doesn't mean giving them keys to newly locked washrooms. Frankly, if management doesn't subscribe to the whole package and doesn't embrace a proactive philosophy of security, it oughtn't to take any precautions at all. There's no such thing as being half-pregnant. Businesses can't cherry pick security measures and expect to be safe.

Nationally, enhanced security doesn't mean just better airport checks, sky marshals or more money for antiterrorism programs. Real security requires the personal commitment of individuals. It means everyone, each of his or her own accord, taking protective measures and, in so doing, protecting others and protecting the countries they live in. The more counterterrorism barriers that are erected, the harder the terrorists' task will become and the easier it will be to uncover their vicious plots beforehand. That said, the threat of terrorism needs to be put into perspective. What are the chances that any one person will become a victim of terrorism? The answer is, very low. A person is more likely to be killed by a street thug or to die from a disease contracted on a trip overseas than to be murdered by a terrorist. This isn't to say that the threat of terrorism is to be ignored or treated lightly. No, absolutely not. Unless and until counterterrorism becomes a way of life in the U.S. and elsewhere around the globe, the odds of further assaults will increase dramatically. Recognizing that the risk of injury or death from violent crime is higher than the danger of terrorism for any one individual, this book opts to cover all bases. Later chapters deal with the dangers of both terrorism and everyday crime, for as far as one's own safety is concerned, to separate terrorism from crime is to make a distinction without a difference. Surviving terrorism, for all practical purposes, means surviving crime, and surviving crime means staying alive.

1.06. Recommended Online Reading

"Fundamentalism," *Encyclopedia of Politics and Religion*, edited by Robert Wuthnow, Congressional Quarterly Press, www.cqpress.com/context/articles/epr_fund.html.

"Global Threats and Challenges," Vice Admiral Thomas R. Wilson, Defense Intelligence Agency, U.S. Senate Armed Services Committee testimony, March 19, 2002, www.dia.mil/.

"Homeland Defense," Center for Strategic and International Studies, www.csis.org/burke/hd/index.htm.

"Inside Terrorism," by Bruce Hoffman, www.nytimes.com/ books/first/h/hoffman-terrorism.html

"Looking for Answers," "Frontline" transcript, Public Broadcasting Service, *www.pbs.org/wgbh/pages/frontline/shows/terrorism/etc/script.html*.

"Mistakes Made the Catastrophe Possible," "Who Is the Enemy?" and "The New Global Threat," by Daniel Pipes, www.danielpipes.org.

"The National Strategy For Homeland Security," U.S. Office of Homeland Security, July 2002, www.whitehouse.gov/homeland/book/index.html.

"Patterns of Global Terrorism," U.S. Department of State, www.state.gov/s/ct/rls/pgtrpt/.

"Postmodern Terrorism," by Walter Laqueur, *Foreign Affairs*, September/October 1996, http://usinfo.state.gov/journals/itgic/0297/ijge/gj-3.htm.

"Remarks Prepared for Delivery at the Anti-Defamation League's 24th Annual National Leadership Conference," Robert S. Mueller III, Federal Bureau of Investigation, May 7, 2002, www.fbi.gov/pressrel/speeches/speeches.htm.

"Terrorism in the United States," Federal Bureau of Investigation, www.fbi.gov/publications/terror/terroris.htm.

"Worldwide Threat: Converging Dangers in a Post 9/11 World," Director of Central Intelligence George J. Tenet, U.S. Senate

Select Committee on Intelligence testimony, Feb. 6, 2002, www.cia.gov/cia/public_affairs/speeches/speeches.html.

Chapter 2

The Nature of the Threat

Simplicity can be deceiving. Nineteen hijackers, armed with primitive weapons, brought down the Twin Towers of the World Trade Center, punched a hole in the Pentagon and slaughtered more people than died in the Japanese raid on Pearl Harbor. They accomplished these horrendous feats by doing the unthinkable—by turning four passenger jetliners into missiles. This monstrous innovation refutes a heretofore commonly held view about international terrorists—namely, that their backwardness, lack of sophistication and crudity of weapons posed no real threat to a country as advanced as the United States. Sept. 11 put an end such thinking. The coordination and complexity of the aerial attacks on New York and Washington revealed just how ingenious terrorists have become in devising new, murderous schemes—and the insane lengths to which they're willing to go.

Almost each passing day now brings some new revelation about the obscene ambitions of the world's terrorists organizations and the horrendous weapons they mean to employ. Searches of Al Qaeda facilities in Afghanistan "found a number of things that show an appetite for weapons of mass destruction—diagrams, materials, reports that things were asked for, things were discussed at meetings, that type of thing," Defense Secretary Rumsfeld told a mid-January 2002 press briefing. (News Briefing transcript, Department of Defense, Jan. 16, 2002.) Four months later, he offered this ominous warning: "Let there be no doubt, it is only a matter of time before terrorist states armed with weapons of mass destruction develop the capability to deliver those weapons to U.S. cities, giving them the ability to try to hold America hostage to nuclear blackmail." (Transcript, Defense Subcommittee of Senate Appropriations Committee, May 21, 2002).)

Caches of documents and computers unearthed in Afghanistan revealed that Osama bin Laden and his henchmen sought to obtain every type of weapon of mass destruction imaginable—from chemical and biological agents to radiological devices and nuclear bombs. What this has told the governments and the peoples of the civilized world is that this new breed of terrorist, fiendishly callous and all-too-well versed in the modern technology of war, is capable of attempting anything. It also has sent another message—that the nature of today's terrorism threat has become an all-encompassing one. "The threat of terrorists using chemical, biological, radiological, and nuclear (CBRN) materials appears to be rising—particularly since the 11 September attacks. Several of the 30 designated foreign terrorist organizations and other non-state actors worldwide have expressed interest in CBRN—although terrorists probably will continue to favor proven conventional tactics such as bombings and shootings," the Central Intelligence Agency (CIA) said in an unclassified report submitted to Congress in January 2002.

Terror weapons needn't be complicated or difficult to make to be effective. The FBI has warned of both truck bombs and belt bombs, and Director Robert S. Mueller III has said that a walk-in suicide bombing like those that have hit Israel are "inevitable" in the U.S. Poisoning by some insecticides would have physiological effects similar to nerve gas. A basement-laboratory terrorist employing 1960s technology and working from published scientific literature could produce life-threatening mustard gas. Actually, a lot of commercially available equipment and supplies have dual-use capabilities, meaning they can be used for either peaceful or hostile purposes. Matter of fact, the CIA report even warns that "terrorist groups are most interested in chemicals such as cyanide salts to contaminate food and water supplies or to assassinate individuals. Terrorist groups also have expressed interest in many other toxic industrial chemicals—most of which are relatively easy to acquire and handle—and traditional chemical agents, including chlorine and phosgene and some groups have discussed nerve agents." In 1988, Iraq's Saddam Hussein used cyanide and mustard gas to kill 5,000 Kurds and injure 10,000 more. More recently, the Bush administration accused Cuba of involvement in germ warfare research and manufacture and also said that Libya and Syria were making biological and chemical weapons.

2.01. A Perilous Future

What we now know of today's terrorists can lead to only one conclusion: If we rule out the possibility of more barbaric attacks in the future, we do so at our peril. Consider the nerve-gas assault on the Tokyo subway system in March 1995. Carried out by five members of the Japanese doomsday cult Aum Shinrikyu, the gas killed 12 persons and injured 5,700 others. Until that happened, few thought the deployment of nerve gas by terrorists was really possible. "The Aum Shinrikyu incident provides a poignant example of how old notions of threats can restrict our scope of vision, causing us to miss important new threats," observed John V. Parachini, a senior associate at the Monterey Institute of International Studies Center in California. (Statement: "Combating Terrorism: Assessing the Threat," Center for Nonproliferation Studies, Monterey Institute of International Studies before U.S. House of Representatives Committee on Government Reform, Subcommittee on National Security, Veterans Affairs, and International Relations, Oct, 20, 1999). The institute's Center for Nonproliferation Studies has been keeping track of all of sorts of incidents involving weapons of mass destruction (WMD) worldwide. These include WMD use, possession, threatened use with possession, acquisition attempts, plots, hoaxes, pranks and threats. In 2000-2001, it recorded 703 such incidents, of which 75 involved actual weapons. The incidents included 628 WMD hoaxes, most of which were related to the controversy over abortion in the U.S.

"What makes a WMD terrorist incident unique is that it can be a transforming event. A terrorist attack involving weapons of mass destruction would have catastrophic effects on American society beyond the deaths it might cause," Frank J. Cilluffo, co-director of the Terrorism Task Force at the Center for Strategic and International Studies in Washington, D.C., advised a House panel in October 1998. "Aside from the actual physical effects

**Weapons of Mass Destruction Incidents
by Type of Event, 2000-2001**

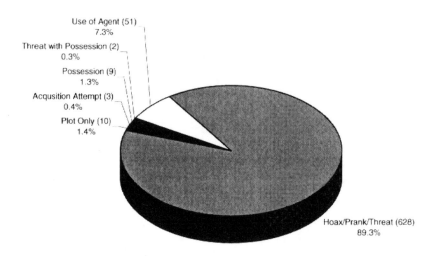

Use of Agent (51)
7.3%

Threat with Possession (2)
0.3%

Possession (9)
1.3%

Acqusition Attempt (3)
0.4%

Plot Only (10)
1.4%

Hoax/Prank/Threat (628)
89.3%

Source: Center for Nonproliferation Studies, Monterey Institute of International Studies

and human suffering resulting from a WMD event, the psychological impact would be enormous, shaking the nation's trust and confidence in its government to its core."

Terror organizations, meanwhile, are scouring the globe for technical experts and collaborators to assist them. Russia, in particular, is a repository of underused expertise. Besides its trove of weapons and warfare technology, Russia has innumerable personnel skilled in the modern art of war, and terrorist groups and their state sponsors are trying desperately to win them over. Russia's lousy economy is raising fears that unemployed or underpaid military scientists will sell their expertise to the highest bidder and that "loose nukes" and biological weapons will reach the international black market. Some Russians experts are believed to be assisting state sponsors of terrorism already.

"Despite improvements in Russia's economy, the state-run defense, biotechnology, and nuclear industries remain strapped for funds, even as Moscow looks to them for badly needed foreign exchange through exports. We remain very concerned about the proliferation implications of such sales in several areas," the CIA told Congress in January 2002. "Russian entities during the reporting period continued to supply a variety of ballistic missile-related goods and technical know-how to countries such as Iran, India, China, and Libya." Moreover, the CIA said that in the first half of 2001, "Russian entities remained a significant source of dual-use biotechnology, chemicals, production technology, and equipment for Iran. Russia's biological and chemical expertise makes it an attractive target for Iranians seeking technical information and training on BW [biological warfare] and CW [chemical warfare] agent production processes." And CIA Director Tenet told the Senate Armed Service Committee in March 2002 that "Russian entities continue to provide other countries with technology and expertise applicable to CW, BW, nuclear, and ballistic and cruise missile projects. Russia appears to be the first choice of proliferation states seeking the most advanced technology and training. These sales are a major source of funds for Russian commercial and defense industries and military R&D [research and development]."

The Soviet biowarfare program, which once employed 60,000 people, was so immense and so far advanced that it may have produced more than 50 different biological warfare agents. "Over a twenty-year period that began, ironically, with Moscow's endorsement of the Biological Weapons Convention in 1972 [banning such weapons], the Soviet Union built the largest and most advanced biological warfare establishment in the world," Kenneth Alibek writes in his autobiographical book *Biohazard: The Chilling True Story of the Largest Covert Biological Weapons Program in the World—Told from Inside by the Man Who Ran It*. (Dell Publishing, New York 1999). Alibek was deputy director of the Soviet program, known as Biopreparat, from 1988 until his defection to the U.S. in 1992. "Biopreparat claims that it no longer conducts offensive research, and Russia's stockpile of germs and viruses has been destroyed," he says. "But the threat of a biological attack has increased as the knowledge developed in our labs—of lethal formulations that took our scientists years to discover—has spread to rogue regimes and terrorist groups."

Even more unconventional is the looming danger of cyberterrorism—that is, attacks on critical infrastructure, financial institutions and government operations, using the modern skills of information technology. At worst, cyberterrorism would bring an economy to its knees. At best, it would only rob people of their money and identities. The CIA is "alert to the possibility of cyber warfare attack by terrorists," Director of Intelligence George J. Tenet testified in February 2002. "September 11 demonstrated our dependence on critical infrastructure systems that rely on electronic and computer networks. Attacks of this nature will become an increasingly viable option for terrorists as they and other foreign adversaries become more familiar with these targets, and the technologies required to attack them." ("Worldwide Threat: Converging Dangers in a Post 9/11 World," U.S. Senate Select Committee on Intelligence testimony, Feb. 6, 2002.)

The Bush administration, along with its global coalition partners, means to eradicate the scourge of terrorism from the face of the Earth. While a wholly admirable ambition, the effort likely will achieve an asymptotic result—nearing but never reaching its goal. Terrorists do what works and are emboldened by success. They learn from others. Their weapons and tactics evolve. Their targets change. Any new twist in the art of terror provides fresh ideas for terrorist masterminds all over the world. Copycats proliferate, and the more daring and fanatical conceive of ever more atrocious acts.

William Church, a former U.S. Army Intelligence officer and an expert in infrastructure warfare, gave a telling interview to TechWeb News in 1998 that has special relevance today. In explaining why terrorists had yet to shift into wholesale cyber combat, he said: "For terrorists to make this transition, there have to be a number of factors brewing or building. First, they must understand the use of the weapon, and they must trust the use of the weapon. Normally, terrorists only make that trust or that leap if they've built it themselves, they've experimented

International and Irish Terrorists Detained in Britain
Under Prevention of Terrorism Legislation

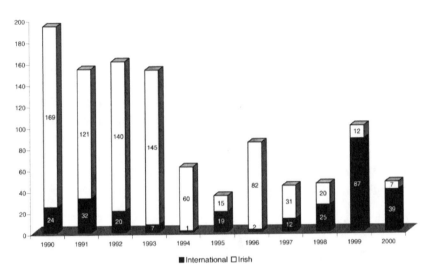

Source: U.K. Home Office

with it, and they know for a fact it will work. Then they're willing try their one-time shot at using this type of weapon. They normally don't like to experiment. That's why, overall, weapons proliferate from states to terrorists. They get to see how it actually works."

"The other transition point," he continued, "is mentality, or mental mindset, you might say. They must know it; they must trust it. But more importantly, it has to feel right to them. If you look at the Irish Republican Army, which was probably the closest [to cyberwar capability] before they made peace, they were on the verge of it. They had computer-oriented cells. They could have done it. They were already attacking the infrastructure by placing real or phony bombs in electric plants to see if they could turn off the lights in London. But they were still liking the feel of physical weapons and trusting them." (Interview, "Analyzing The Threat Of Cyberterrorism," by John Borland, *TechWeb News*, Sept. 25, 1998.)

Church's comments underscore the fact that the United States isn't the only country at risk from terrorism. There's scarcely a free society in the world that isn't threatened. The British Home Office came to the horrifying conclusion near the end 2001 that the "presence of extremists in the United Kingdom at this time and for the foreseeable creates a situation of public emergency threatening the life of the nation." What follows is our appraisal of the entire spectrum of terrorist threats that the civilized world faces today—from hijackings and bombings to chemical-biological warfare and cyberterrorism. It's intended to provide a base of knowledge upon which any good antiterrorism program, implemented by individuals or businesses, must be founded.

2.02. Hijackings, Carjackings, Etc.

Despite stepped up security, airplane hijackings will remain a favorite terrorist tactic. Terrorists needn't succeed in taking over an aircraft to accomplish their mission. That's because terrorists are publicity-seekers who aim to sow fear and panic. Any hijacking, even a failed one, makes headlines. In that respect, all attempted hijackings are viewed as successful in the eyes of radicals. The ripple effect usually is more damaging than a hijacking itself. Business travelers and tourists think twice about their plans and cancel trips, playing into the terrorists' hands. While the airline and travel industries get hit the hardest, the entire economy suffers. Face-to-face meetings are postponed, slowing the pace of business decisions and new contract signings.

Certainly, increased airport security will make it more difficult for terrorists to board planes—or to plant bombs on board. Nonetheless, the case of shoe-bomber Richard Reid, the British citizen linked to the Al Qaeda network, makes clear that terrorists will continue to devise novel ways of getting past security. Reid was subdued over the Atlantic by flight attendants and passengers on an American Airlines jet in December 2001 after he tried to ignite his sneakers, which contained explosives. British and U.S. investigators think Reid's foiled bombing may have been a trial run for future, simultaneous assaults on passenger planes. Additionally, a *Wall Street Journal* reporter in Afghanistan purchased a discarded Al Qaeda computer and discovered stored and encrypted documents indicating that Reid may have scouted Egypt and Israel for new targets, including airplanes and tall buildings.

Israel's experience with terrorism offers a glimmer of what the future may hold for the United States and other nations. Following a rash of hijackings in the late 1960s and early 1970s, El Al, the Israeli airline, beefed up security and the incidence of hijacking attempts fell dramatically. But, as Sir Isaac Newton says, "For every action there is an equal and opposite reaction." And that's what happened in Israel. Terrorists, finding it nearly impossible to board an El Al flight, switched their *modus operandi* and turned to suicide bombings—a scourge that continues to plague Israel to this day.

The point is that something similar could occur in the United States and elsewhere. If their path to commercial airplanes is blocked, terrorists will look for other ways of carrying out their plots. Missile attacks against commercial airliners would be one way around tightened airport security. Handheld anti-aircraft missiles, costing $50,000 and up on the black market, are in plentiful supply in the Middle East and other parts of the world, making it relatively simple for terrorists to get hold of them. It probably wouldn't take much to get a batch of weapons into any country. If large quantities of drugs can be smuggled across borders on a regular basis, surely terrorists could find ways of getting a few missiles into a country. In fact, in November 2002, two shoulder-launched rockets were fired at an Israeli airliner as it took off from the coastal resort city of Mombassa Kenya; the missiles just missed hitting the plane.

Alternatively, militants might pick a foreign country where security is lax and target a U.S., Canadian, British or other airliner on an international flight. In 1976, Israel captured five terrorists (three Palestinians and two Germans) armed with a Soviet-made anti-aircraft missile just hours before the men planned to fire on an Israeli jetliner during takeoff from Kenya's Nairobi Airport. Italian police in 1979 arrested a Palestinian terrorist in Rome who had several anti-aircraft missiles in his

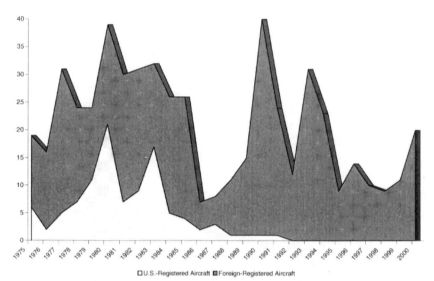

Source: Federal Aviation Administration, Office of Civil Aviation Security

possession. In addition, German officials have warned of possible passenger-ship hijackings in Europe by Islamic terrorists. Palestinian terrorists in 1985 took over the cruise ship *Achille Lauro* in the Mediterranean and murdered Leon Klinghoffer, a U.S. citizen, and in 1988 Abu Nidal extremists attacked a day-excursion ship in Greece.

Yet another worry for travelers, notably those going abroad, is carjackings. Carjackings are more common than many people realize. In the U.S., successful and attempted carjackings averaged about 49,000 a year in the mid-1990s (the latest period for which data are available). About six-in-ten took place in public parking lots, at airports and near bus or train stations. Overseas, the problem is worse, for in many countries, carjackings aren't perpetrated only by criminals but also by terrorists. The terrorist carjacker is a breed apart in that he isn't just after the car but the driver, too. His aim is kidnapping for ransom. This is an especially serious problem in Colombia, where the National Liberation Army of Colombia (ELN) and the Revolutionary

Armed Forces of Colombia (FARC) have turned kidnapping-for-ransom into a business. But carjackings also are rife in other parts of Latin America, areas in Africa and a few European nations. (See the Chapter 5 on foreign travel for more country-specific information.)

Executive jets pose another hazard. While too small to inflict much damage on a large building, a hijacked private jet—especially if packed with explosives—could severely damage or destroy historic sites (e.g., the Statue of Liberty). Historic sites of patriotic significance indeed already are on the extremists' hit list. Four Algerian terrorists who commandeered a Paris-bound Air France jet on Christmas Eve 1994 planned to crash into the Eiffel Tower; the scheme was foiled when French commandos raided the plane after it landed in Marseilles for refueling, killing the hijackers. Even a small, explosives-filled plane could so damage a critical infrastructure facility (e.g., a hydroelectric dam or nuclear power plant) that such an attack might precipitate a mass evacuation and extensive power outages. The U.S. Nuclear Regulatory Commission (NRC), as noted in the previous chapter, issued a startling warning in January 2002 to reactor operators that the FBI had information from an Al Qaeda "senior operative" that an attack on a nuclear plant was planned using a hijacked aircraft. In September 2000, an NRC report said that breaching a cask used to hold spent fuel rods from a nuclear power plant would disperse a lethal dose of radiation over an area many times larger than would be caused by a 10-kiloton nuclear weapon. Moreover, the U.S. Environmental Protection Agency earlier warned that power outages and subsequent equipment restarts at chemical-handling facilities can trigger major chemical accidents.

Then, too, there is always the danger that crop dusters could be used to disseminate chemical or biological weapons over population centers. Other small planes could be used to drop a conventional, radiological or nuclear bomb on a metropolitan area.

2.03. Conventional Explosives

Bombings will be an ever-present terrorist threat, primarily because they are low-cost and relatively easy to plan and execute. "Explosives strike the enemy with sheer terror and fright," says a terrorist manual seized in Manchester, England. Bombs, it adds, are "the safest weapons" because they allow terrorists to "get away from enemy personnel and to avoid being arrested." Acquiring bomb-making materials isn't very difficult, and the bomb-construction techniques have become almost common knowledge. The truck bombs that wrecked the U.S. embassies in Kenya and Tanzania in 1998, inflicting more than 5,000 casualties, contained TNT and the fertilizer aluminum nitrate and were hooked up to heavy-duty vehicle batteries. Terrorists even know how to plant bombs in such innocuous items as desks, books and tobacco pipes, according to Al Qaeda documents retrieved in Afghanistan. Moreover, terror organizations always seem to manage to find some pliant recruit willing to go to his death in the name of a cause.

The U.S. itself has had a surprisingly long history of terror bombings (as the chronology near the back of this book makes clear). What was perhaps the first incident of its kind in the United States. took place on Sept. 16, 1920 only blocks away from what became the site of the World Trade Center. A bomb left in an unattended, horse-drawn wagon exploded at Wall and Broad streets in lower Manhattan, near the New York Stock Exchange and J. P. Morgan & Co. The explosion killed three dozen persons and injured hundreds. Bolsheviks or anarchists were suspected, though no one was ever charged with the crime. More recently, Puerto Rican nationalists with the FALN began a bombing spree in 1974 that struck government buildings, businesses and historic landmarks, including Fraunces Tavern near Wall Street. The FALN ultimately was tied to more than 130 bombings in the U.S.

From 1980 to 1999, according to the FBI, there were 321 terrorist bombings in the U.S. That represented 70 percent of all U.S. terror incidents, which ranged from assassinations to rocket attacks. The most infamous bombing by international terrorists occurred in February 1993, when Islamic extremists came close to toppling the World Trade Center's south tower using conventional explosives. A truck bomb equivalent to a ton of TNT detonated in the underground garage, ripping apart several floors and leaving a massive crater. Had the vehicle been parked slightly closer to a crucial support column, the 1,360-foot, 500,000-ton tower might have fallen over. As it was, the explosion killed six persons and injured 1,000 others. The FBI, in fact, has warned shopping centers and supermarkets to be on the lookout for belt bombers and has told city officials around the country to be on the alert for possible truck bombings.

Foreign terrorists aren't the only worry when it comes to bombings. In April 1995, Americans Timothy McVeigh and Terry Nichols destroyed the Alfred P. Murrah Federal Building in Oklahoma City with a massive truck bomb that killed 166 people and injured hundreds more. At the time, it was the worst terror attack ever carried out within the United States. Two years later, the FBI foiled an attempt by four Ku Klux Klan members to place an improvised explosive devise on a hydrogen sulfide tank at a gas processing plant near Dallas, Texas. The FBI was able to infiltrate the group prior to the attack. A surveillance tape showed two of the bombers discussing the potential death of hundreds of area residents. When the discussion turned to the children who might die, one plotter looked at her husband and said, "If it has to be . . . it has to be." The explosion was intended as a diversion for an armored car robbery the group planned to commit on the other side of town.

International terrorists also have had their sights on critical infrastructure and information systems, which could be wrecked by conventional bombs. "While attention is focused on computer-based 'cyber' attacks, we should not forget that key nodes and facilities that house critical systems and handle the flow of digital data can also be attacked with conventional high-explosives," then-Director of Central Intelligence John M. Deutch warned in congressional testimony in 1996. "These information attacks, in whatever form, could not only disrupt our daily lives, but also seriously jeopardize our national or economic security. Without sufficient planning as we build these systems, I am also concerned that the potential for damage could grow in the years ahead." ("Foreign Information Warfare Programs and Capabilities," Senate Governmental Affairs Committee, Permanent Subcommittee on Investigations, June 25, 1996.)

In March 2002, U.S. authorities arrested a Pakistani immigrant, saying he was plotting to blow up power plants and other sites in South Florida.

2.04. Chemical Weapons

Chemical munitions are among the most feared weapons in the world, especially because the body's reaction to them can be so acute, with death often coming in minutes. During the Gulf War of 1991, Israelis donned gas masks every time an Iraqi-launched Scud missile appeared overhead. None of the 39 Scuds lobbed at Israel contained chemical munitions, as it turned out. Still, the public's response shows how seriously Israelis treat the possibility of chemical warfare.

Iraqi leader Saddam Hussein had plenty of chemical weapons at his disposal (and has them still). In the late 1980s, he had used hydrogen cyanide and mustard gas in the Anfal campaign against the Kurds, most notably in the Halabja Massacre of 1988 in which an estimated 5,000 civilians were killed and more than 10,000 were injured. Around the same time, Iraq also developed an offensive biowarfare capability, weaponizing anthrax, botulinum toxin and aflatoxin (a naturally occurring mycotoxin produced by mold). What stopped Hussein from deploying these weapons, apparently, were warnings from both Israel and the U.S. that if he used chemical (or biological) weapons, he could expect a nuclear strike in retaliation. General Avihu Ben-Nun, commander of the Israeli Air Force, said after the Gulf War that "the fact that he didn't launch chemical weapons against us was only because [Hussein] feared our retaliatory response." (Quoted in, "Israel Debates Lasting Effects of Nonretaliation in Gulf War," by Barbara Opall, *Defense News*, Sept. 9, 1991, page 38.)

Chemical munitions were first used in World War I against the Allied salient at Ypres, Belgium. German troops released thousands of canisters of chlorine gas at sunrise on April 22,

Weapons of Mass Destruction, Actual Incidents
Worldwide by Type of Agent, 2000-2001

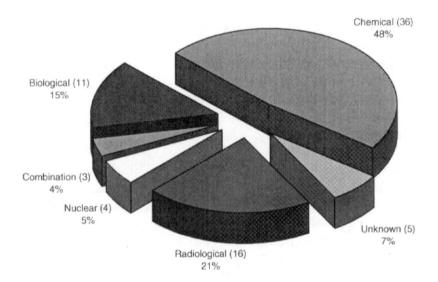

Chemical (36)
48%

Biological (11)
15%

Combination (3)
4%

Nuclear (4)
5%

Unknown (5)
7%

Radiological (16)
21%

Source: Center for Nonproliferation Studies, Monterey Institute of International Studies

1915. The gas debilitated some 10,000 Allied soldiers—mostly French Algerians—half of whom died within ten minutes of the chlorine cloud reaching the front line. Later in the war, the Germans also deployed phosgene and mustard gas, and the Allies replied with their own chemical barrages. Chemical munitions quickly became the most dreaded of all the new weapons employed in what was thought to be "The War to End All Wars."

Toxic chemical weapons fall into four categories: nerve agents, blister or vesicant agents, blood agents and pulmonary agents. Nerve agents, such as sarin, soman, tabun and VX gas, can incapacitate a victim in an instant and kill within 15 minutes. Blister agents, such as mustard gas, are slower acting and less deadly. Blood agents, such as hydrogen cyanide, rapidly cause seizures, respiratory failure and cardiac arrest. And pulmonary agents, such as chlorine and phosgene, vary in effect but are often lethal. Heavy metals such as arsenic, lead and mercury also have weapons potential.

Terrorist interest in chemical weapons is growing. Subway riders in Tokyo in 1995 succumbed to sarin, the odorless, colorless nerve agent first developed by Nazi Germany. The Aum Shinrikyu cult that released the gas previously had conducted 10 chemical attacks in Japan, using sarin, phosgene, hydrogen cyanide and VX gas. (It also tried biological weapons on several occasions, but the attacks failed.) Japanese courts have sentenced a number of the convicted conspirators to death by hanging or life imprisonment.

Documents retrieved in Afghanistan revealed that Osama bin Laden sought chemical munitions. Bin Laden himself maintained that he already had offensive chemical and nuclear weapons, telling a Pakistani newspaper in November 2001: "If America used chemical and nuclear weapons against us, then we may retort with chemical and nuclear weapons. We have the weapons as a deterrent." (Quoted in, "Israel Debates Lasting Effects of Nonretaliation in Gulf War," by Barbara Opall, *Defense News*, Sept. 9, 1991, page 38.) In a 1998 *Time* magazine interview, he said that acquiring chemical and nuclear weapons is a "religious duty," adding: "If I have indeed acquired these weapons, then I thank God for enabling me to do so." (Interview with Osama bin Laden, *Time*, Dec. 23, 1998.)

By 1999, the Pentagon had become so concerned about the risk of chemical-biological attack that it started the Family and Force Protection Initiative to provide enhanced protection for the dependents of U.S. military personnel and civilian Defense Department employees and their families around the world. The program was first implemented for U.S. Forces Korea.

A chemical attack typically is envisioned as the release of gas canisters, but that's not the only way of dispensing poison gas. One weapons expert has postulated that terrorists dressed as a maintenance crew might enter a train station, subway, large building or airport with drums labeled as cleaning fluid. The drums would, in fact, contain a deadly poison, which if unleashed at rush hour could cause tremendous casualties. The U.S. also faces a potential chemical threat from offshore. Terrorists aboard a ship in international waters could fire, for example, a Scud missile filled with chemical (or biological or nuclear) munitions and hit a city near the coast or slightly inland. Potential targets include Boston, Houston, Los Angeles, Miami, New Orleans, New York, Norfolk, Philadelphia, Portland (Maine and Oregon), Richmond, San Diego, San Francisco, Seattle, Tampa and Washington, D.C.

Finally, an indirect way of attacking a country with lethal chemicals would be to blow up a chemical factory or chemical-filled railcar. Deadly chemicals produced commercially in the U.S. and most industrial economies include chlorine and hydrogen fluoride, among others. Even phosgene, the deadly gas first used in combat in World War I, can be found at more than 30 U.S. chemical plants. All told, approximately 850,000 facilities in the U.S. use hazardous chemicals. The U.S. Environmental Protection Agency estimates that a terrorist attack on a chemical plant or railcar could endanger tens of thousands to over a million people, depending on the chemical involved, the amount released and the proximity to population centers. ("Chemical Plants Are Feared as Targets," by James V. Grimaldi and Guy Gugliotta, *Washington Post*, Dec. 16, 2001. See also "Chemical Accident Prevention: Site Security; A Chemical Safety Alert," Environmental Protection Agency, February 2001.)

2.05. Bioterrorism

Of all the weapons of mass destruction, biological agents pose the worst terrorist threat. Our assessment is based on the ease with which a determined terrorist organization could acquire biological-weapons technology, materials and expertise and the impact a large-scale attack would have on a nation's population and economy. A nuclear blast might kill and injure more people in a single incident, but bioterrorism presents the frightening prospect of a virtually nationwide—or even a multi-nationwide—barrage that could inflict innumerable casualties. As early as 1984, in fact, terrorism experts Neil C. Livingstone and Joseph D. Douglass, Jr. warned that chemical-biological weapons (CBW) were "the poor man's atomic bomb. "CBW: The Poor Man's Atomic Bomb," National Security Paper 1, Institute for Foreign Policy Analysis, Inc., February 1984.)

A bioweapon, significantly, needn't contain only one infectious agent. It could be concocted of a witch's brew of germs, which when dispersed in combination might be murderously lethal and impossible to treat medically. Biological agents also could be genetically re-engineered, making existing vaccines and other medical treatments ineffective. In addition, terrorists handling a bio-agent could be vaccinated beforehand, making them immune to the weapon's deadly effects. U.S. scientists, moreover, have expressed concern that information published in scientific journals on DNA primers—the bits of DNA used to extract genes from an organism and also used to detect biological warfare agents—could be exploited by terrorists to foil biowarfare sensors, according to *The New York Times*. ("Traces Of Terror: Bioterrorism; Scientists Worry Journals May Aid Terrorists," by Nicholas Wade, *The New York Times*, July 26, 2002.)

There is "a significant risk within the next few years" that the U.S. could confront an adversary—"either terrorists or a rogue state"—that possesses chemical and biological weapons (CBW), CIA Director Tenet said in February 2002. "The CBW threat continues to grow for a variety of reasons, and to present us with monitoring challenges. The dual-use nature of many CW and BW agents complicates our assessment of offensive programs. Many CW and BW production capabilities are hidden in plants that are virtually indistinguishable from genuine commercial facilities. And the technology behind CW and BW agents is spreading." ("Worldwide Threat: Converging Dangers in a Post 9/11 World," U.S. Senate Select Committee on Intelligence testimony, Feb. 6, 2002.) Western intelligence in late 2001 got hold of an Al Qaeda bioterrorism manual distributed on CD-ROMs. According to a CNN report, the handbook included precise formulas for manufacturing biological and chemical weapons, made from readily available ingredients. One chapter was tiled "The Poisonous Letter." ("Evidence Suggests Al Qaeda Pursuit of Biological, Chemical Weapons," by Mike Boettcher, CNN, Nov. 14, 2001.) Newsweek, meanwhile, reported that dozens of rabbits and dogs were found fatally poisoned near bin Laden's Jalalabad training camps. ("Unmasking Bioterror," by Sharon Begley, *Newsweek*, Oct. 1, 1998.)

"The interest of terrorist groups in biological weapons is no surprise. Biological weapons have a number of very attractive features for terrorists uses," Alibek, the former Soviet bioweapons expert, told a congressional hearing in May 2000. "The killing power can approach that of nuclear weapons. They are relatively inexpensive to make. . . . And the techniques and equipment that are used in ordinary biotechnology research and production can be used for biological weapons." In fact, he said, "primitive versions can be produced in a small area with minimal equipment by someone with limited training." (Kenneth Alibek, testimony before the House Armed Services Committee, May 23, 2001.)

The ease with which terrorists could produce germ weapons was borne out in 2002 when researchers at the State University of New York downloaded a genetic blueprint from the Internet and ordered supplies by mail to synthesize a polio virus. "It was very easy to do," said Dr. Eckard Wimmer, leader of the research team. "The world had better be prepared." (Quoted in "First Synthetic Virus Created," by David Whitehouse, BBC News, July 11, 2002.)

Terrorists, alternatively, could turn to a sympathetic country or bribable scientist for help. There are plenty to choose from. At least 14 "countries of concern" are believed by the U.S. government to have bioweapons programs. They are: Bulgaria, China, Cuba, Egypt, India, Iran, Iraq, Laos, Libya, North Korea, Russia, South Africa, Syria and Vietnam. In late 2001, an Iraqi defector told *The New York Times* of at least 20 hidden Iraqi sites for the production and storage of biological, chemical and nuclear weapons. ("An Iraqi Defector Tells of Work on at Least 20 Hidden Weapons Sites," by Judith Miller, *The New York Times*, Dec. 20. 2001)

Chemical and biological weapons, as well as toxins, are outlawed by the 1925 Geneva Protocol, the 1972 Biological Weapons Convention and the 1993 Chemical Weapons Convention. U.S. Undersecretary of State John R. Bolton said in a May

2002 speech that the terrorist-friendly governments of Cuba, Libya and Syria are violating these arms-control agreements by engaging in the research and development of biochemical warfare agents. "The United States believes that Cuba has at least a limited offensive biological warfare research and development effort," he said, adding that Cuba has "provided dual-use biotechnology to other rogue states." The U.S., he noted, is "concerned that such technology could support biological warfare programs in those states." Libya, Bolton said, "may be capable of producing small quantities of biological agent," and Syria has a "stockpile of the nerve agent sarin" and is "engaged in research and development of the more toxic and persistent nerve agent VX." (Quoted in "Washington Accuses Cuba of Germ-Warfare Research," by Judith Miller, *The New York Times*, May 7, 2002.) During a trip to Iran, Syria and Libya in 2001, Cuban leader Fidel Castro claimed in Tehran that Iran and Cuba together could "bring America to its knees."

Biowarfare has a long pedigree. One of the very first instances took place in the 6th century B.C. when Assyrians tainted an enemy's wells with rye ergot, a convulsion-causing fungus. In 1346, the Tartar Mongols started an epidemic in the besieged Crimean town of Kaffa by hurling the corpses of plague victims over the city's walls. In North America, during the French and Indian Wars of 1754-1767, British troops were suspected of distributing smallpox-infected blankets to Native American Indians. And the Japanese used biological agents in World War II against the Chinese and in grisly experiments on prisoners of war. More recently, an Ohio microbiologist, said to have suspect motives, was arrested in 1995 after fraudulently acquiring by mail the bacterium responsible for pneumonic plague (i.e., the Black Death). Also in 1995, Japan's Aum Shinrikyu cult, besides disbursing sarin gas in the subway, made at least nine attempts—all of which were unsuccessful—to infect central Tokyo with aerosolized anthrax and botulism. The cult further tried to obtain the deadly Ebola virus.

Bioweapons can be deployed by direct contamination (e.g., poisoning of food or water), vectors (e.g., mosquitoes, fleas or mailed letters) and aerosols (e.g., sprays or bombs). Of the three, aerosols generally are considered the most efficacious means of dissemination. "The primary result of an effective aerosol cloud is simultaneous infections among all those who were exposed to a sufficiently dense portion of the cloud," explains Alibek. "If the agent is contagious, the disease will then spread. In addition, agents that can survive for a long time in the environment will eventually settle, contaminating the ground, buildings, water and food sources, and so on. In some cases, these sediments can form another dangerous aerosol cloud if they are disturbed."

The poisoning of food and the disruption of agriculture are other possibilities. Salmonella, *E. coli* and botulism, among others, could be used to infect foodstuffs. In fact, this already has happened. The Rajneeshee religious cult contaminated restaurant salad bars and water glasses in The Dalles, Oregon with salmonella bacteria in 1984. Although no one died, 751 persons fell ill with food poisoning. The cultists hoped to affect the results of a local election by incapacitating voters. "We are not even scratching the surface as far as monitoring and inspecting foods" for bioterrorism, Health and Human Resources Secretary Tommy G. Thompson told a congressional subcommittee in October 2001. "We have to do a much better job. I am more fearful about this [bioterrorism] than anything else." (Remarks before House Committee on Government Reform, Subcommittee on National Security, Veterans Affairs and International Relations, October 23, 2001.)

Actually, public-health officials may have a bigger job on their hands than even Secretary Thompson realizes. In March 2002, California's *Sacramento Bee* reported that government-mandated tests for *E. coli* contamination in ground beef miss varieties of the bacteria responsible for one out of three potentially deadly food-borne illnesses caused by the germ. Scientists at California State University tested 200 samples of meat obtained from local stores and found that 22, or 11 percent, contained genes that make a variety of *E. coli* pathogens. Of these positive results, at least four samples, or 2 percent of the total tested, had *E. coli* varieties that are typically overlooked under current screening procedures. ("Some Harmful E. Coli

Overlooked in Testing," by Edie Lau, The Sacramento Bee, March 8, 2002.)

"Historically, anti-animal, anti-plant biological warfare (BW) has been a substantial component of many state BW programs," Jonathan Ban of the Chemical and Biological Arms Control Institute said in a June 2000 study. ("Agricultural Biological Warfare: An Overview," Jonathan Ban, Chemical and Biological Arms Control Institute, Paper Number 9, June 2000.) In World War I, German agents used anthrax and the equine disease glanders to infect livestock and feed destined for Allied forces. Russia-bound Romanian sheep were infected with anthrax; Argentine mules intended for Allied troops were poisoned with anthrax, and American horses and feed for expert to France were infected with glanders.

There are other examples. The apartheid-era government of South Africa may have weaponized anthrax to poison animals. Iraq has tested plant pathogens to determine their effects on crops such as wheat. And Soviet biowarfare scientists succeeded in weaponizing wheat stem rust, rice blast, rinderpest (a deadly bovine disease) and possibly other blights. (Statement of Floyd P. Horn, administrator, Agricultural Research Service, U.S. Department of Agriculture, before Senate Emerging Threats and Capabilities Subcommittee, Armed Services Committee, Oct. 27, 1999.

Terrorists, too, have targeted agriculture. In 1978, Arab Revolutionary Army Palestinian Commandos contaminated Israeli citrus exports to Europe with mercury. What's more, a U.S. Department of Agriculture official has speculated that terrorists might try to make money in a food crisis. If a terrorist group knew of an impending agricultural attack, it could turn a hefty profit in the commodities futures market, for instance. Just look at what happened to the British meat industry after the recent outbreaks of foot-and-mouth and "mad cow" disease.

The U.S., unlike many countries, is fortunate in that its agriculture and food industries are decentralized, making it harder for terrorists to wipe out large numbers of consumers. Yet even one biological attack employing food as a vector would touch off a national crisis, with the public fearing that anything they ate or drank might kill them. In response to the danger of terrorist "sleepers" taking food-handling or food-processing jobs, the U.S. Food and Drug Administration in January 2002 issued voluntary guidelines to the food and farm industries urging them to conduct criminal background checks on workers and job applicants.

Because few physicians have ever seen a case, say, of plague, smallpox or tularemia, a bioterrorism attack could take time to detect. Normal public health checks sooner or later would show an increased incidence of a disease—particularly a rare infection—and would alert authorities to the possibility of a bioterrorism incident. Still, a sneak bio-attack with an invisible substance might go unnoticed for days or weeks, depending on the disease's incubation period.

A congressional report concluded in June 2000 that the outbreak of mosquito-borne West Nile virus in New York a year before, which killed seven persons, exposed gaping holes in the nation's preparedness to deal with biowarfare. ("West Nile Virus: Preliminary Information on Lessons Learned," General Accounting Office (GAO/HEHS-00-142R), June 23, 2000.) U.S. Senator Charles E. Schumer of New York said the natural outbreak was "the closest example of a dry run for a bioterrorist attack" that the United States has yet had. ("Preliminary Government Report On West Nile Virus: U.S. Labs Are Unprepared For Bioterrorist Attack; Lab Capacity Insufficient To Handle Major Viral Outbreak," Office of Senator Charles E. Schumer, press release, June 25, 2000.)

The first tip off to a bio-attack, oddly enough, might come from a rather mundane source: drug-store sales. *The Wall Street Journal* has reported that major chains such as CVS, Rite Aid and Walgreens use sophisticated technology to monitor sales of everything from flu medications to cough drops. Public-health officials now are looking at ways of tapping into the data. The reason: Drug-store sales data could aid in the early detection of a bioterrorist attack "because people almost always try over-the-counter remedies before going to the doctor," the *Journal* said. ("Drugstore Data Could Be Tip-Off to Bioterrorism," by Jonathan Eig and Thomas M. Burton, *The Wall Street Journal*, Nov. 13,

2001.) There's a problem, though. One in ten U.S. public-health agencies has no Internet access. The ratio is likely lower in most other countries of the world.

Foreign terrorists surely learned a great deal from the U.S. anthrax outbreaks of 2001, which claimed five lives and affected hundreds. Anthrax spores, it was discovered to most everyone's amazement (scientists included), can be so finely milled that they can seep through the pores of a paper envelope and contaminate not only the letter's recipient but also the machinery that handles the nation's mail. The results were both scary and deadly. Two U.S. Postal Service workers in Washington, D.C. died from indirect exposure to the anthrax-tainted letters sent to members of Congress. Most probably, the machinery and air in the mail-sorting facility became contaminated, and the two postal employees were so sensitive to the germ that even a small number of spores were lethal. A woman in New York and another in Connecticut also seem to have died from trace amounts of anthrax that attached to mail addressed to them. Other spores wended their way through the postal system and contaminated mail-sorting and letter-opening machines in Washington, D.C., southern New Jersey and New York City. An anthrax-tainted diplomatic mailbag even turned up at the U.S. Embassy in Vilnius, Lithuania. Imagine what would happen if terrorists simultaneously posted hundreds of anthrax-laced letters at mail boxes across the United States. The casualties would be many, and public panic could be rife.

Johns Hopkins University's Center for Civilian Biodefense Studies staged a mock bioterrorism exercise called Dark Winter in June 2001 simulating meetings of the National Security Council in reaction to a fictional, covert smallpox attack. The results weren't pretty. Among the findings were: U.S. leaders are unfamiliar with the character of bioterrorist attacks and the available policy options; the lack of sufficient vaccine or drugs to prevent the spread of disease severely limits management options, and the U.S. healthcare system doesn't have the surge capacity to deal with mass casualties.

It's no wonder the medical community is worried. In the late 1990s, Johns Hopkins established the Working Group on Civilian Biodefense (WGCB), comprised of about two dozen experts, to investigate the bioterrorism problem. The results of its work, quoted below, have been published in the Journal of the American Medical Association and are available on the Internet. The series of articles is the single-best, independent source of medical information on the potency and lethality of germ weapons to be found anywhere. A terrorist attack using bioweapons, the panel says, "would be especially difficult to predict, detect, or prevent, and thus, it is among the most feared terrorist scenarios." It further notes that the dispersal of biological agents in aerosol form would be "most likely to inflict widespread disease." ("Anthrax as a Biological Weapon: Medical and Public Health Management," Working Group on Civilian Biodefense, Center for Civilian Biodefense Strategies, The Johns Hopkins University, *Journal of the American Medical Association*, May 12, 1999, Vol. 281, No. 18, p.1735.)

The WGCB has thus far identified at least six bioterrorism agents—anthrax, botulinum toxin, hemorrhagic fever viruses, plague, smallpox and tularemia—that "could cause disease and deaths in sufficient numbers to cripple a city or region."

Anthrax is "one of the most serious of these diseases," it says in a 1999 report. ("Anthrax as a Biological Weapon: Medical and Public Health Management," Working Group on Civilian Biodefense, Center for Civilian Biodefense Strategies, The Johns Hopkins University, Journal of the American Medical Association, May 12, 1999, Vol. 281, No. 18, p.1735.) A 1979 analysis by the World Health Organization found that the release of aerosolized anthrax spores upwind of a city of five million people could result in 250,000 casualties, of whom as many as 100,000 would die. The U.S. Office of Technology Assessment later reported that the release of 100 kilograms of aerosolized anthrax over Washington, D.C. would kill 130,000 to three million people. That's equivalent to the death toll that could be expected from the detonation of a hydrogen bomb.

Anthrax (derived from the Greek word for coal, *anthrakis*, because of the black, coal-like sores the disease can cause) occurs in three different forms—cutaneous (or skin), gastrointestinal and inhalation—depending on the mode of exposure.

Without treatment with antibiotics, says the U.S. Food and Drug Administration, the mortality rates are about 20 percent for cutaneous anthrax, 25 to 75 percent for the gastrointestinal form, and 80 percent and above for inhalation anthrax. The disease can be so dangerous, say the Johns Hopkins experts, that "proper burial or cremation of humans and animals who have died because of anthrax infection is important in preventing further transmission of the disease." The economic cost of an anthrax attack is estimated at more than $26 million for every 100,000 people exposed to the disease.

In 1979, an explosion at a Soviet military compound that was manufacturing anthrax weapons sent up a cloud of spores that blanketed the neighboring city of Sverdlovsk. A reported 79 persons were infected, and 68 died of inhalation anthrax. Although the Kremlin at first insisted that the fatalities were caused by the consumption of tainted meat, officials later admitted that the accidental release of weaponized anthrax spores was to blame.

As for terrorists getting hold of anthrax, the WGCB found in its 1999 assessment: "Most experts concur that the manufacture of a lethal anthrax aerosol is beyond the capacity of individuals or groups without access to advanced biotechnology. However, autonomous groups with substantial funding and contacts may be able to acquire the required materials for a successful attack." In a follow-up report, publish in May 2002, the group said: "The anthrax attacks of 2001 have heightened concern about the feasibility of large-scale aerosol bioweapons attacks by terrorist groups." ("Anthrax as a Biological Weapon, 2002: Updated Recommendations for Management," Working Group on Civilian Biodefense, Center for Civilian Biodefense Strategies, The Johns Hopkins University, *Journal of the American Medical Association*, May 1, 2002, Vol. 287, No. 17.)

The U.S. discovered a laboratory under construction near Kandahar, Afghanistan, where Al Qaeda planned to develop biological weapons, including anthrax. No actual bio-agents were found, however. Anthrax, of course, needn't be aerosolized to become an effective terrorist weapon, as the lethal letter campaign of the fall of 2001 that claimed five lives made clear.

U.S. investigators have since found that the anthrax in those letters was freshly made—produced no more than two years before—and grew more potent with each new letter. Tests revealed that last discovered letter, which as sent to U.S. Senator Patrick K. Leahy of Vermont, was the deadliest of all. This suggests the maker of the deadly germ was no amateur, and there are lingering suspicions that the anthrax was produced by a state-sponsor of terrorism, most likely Iraq. The good news is that researchers have found that the quick use of antibiotics probably prevented nine or more cases of serious infection from the inhalation of the anthrax spores and likely saved at least five lives. The bad news is that the survivors of the anthrax-tainted letters have been slower to recover than had been expected, indicating just how little doctors and scientists know about anthrax contamination and the long-term health effects of all biological-warfare agents.

Perhaps more significant is the possibility that anthrax could be genetically re-engineered, rendering existing vaccines useless. According to the Johns Hopkins biodefense group, a Russian study published in 1997 indicated that "genes transferred from the related *B cerise* can act to enable *B anthracites* to evade the protective effect of the live attenuated Russian vaccine in a rodent model. Research is needed to determine the role of these genes with respect to virulence and ability to evade vaccine-induced immunity."

Anthrax isn't the only deadly germ that could be genetically altered to create an even more potent biological weapon against which current vaccines would be ineffective. There are dozens of lethal bacteria, viruses and toxins that could be genetically reconfigured using the modern techniques of biotechnology. In fact, the former Soviet Union was engaged in a massive effort to do precisely that, thus presenting the worrisome possibility that the technology could find its way into terrorist hands.

Botulinum toxin, the most poisonous substance known, poses another significant bioterrorism threat because of its extreme potency and lethality. A single gram of crystalline toxin, properly distributed and inhaled, would kill more than a million people. The toxin, cautions the WGCB, is easy to produce and transport, making the risk of its misuse high. Despite its extreme potency, however, scientists say that botulinum toxin is "easily destroyed." Detoxification of contaminated food or drink requires heating to an internal temperature of 185°F (85°C) for at least five minutes. Terrorists already have used botulinum toxin, thankfully without success. Aum Shinrikyu, the Japanese cult, obtained *C botulinum* from soil collected in northern Japan. Then, on at least three occasions between 1990 and 1995, it dispersed aerosolized botulinum toxin at a number of sites in downtown Tokyo and at U.S. military installations in Japan. The attacks failed, apparently because of faulty microbiological technique, deficient aerosol-generating equipment or internal sabotage, the WGCB reports.

"Development and use of botulinum toxin as a possible bioweapon began at least 60 years ago," notes the biodefense panel. "The head of the Japanese biological warfare group (Unit 731) admitted to feeding cultures of *C botulinum* to prisoners with lethal effect during that country's occupation of Manchuria, which began in the 1930s. The U.S. biological weapons program first produced botulinum toxin during World War II. Because of concerns that Germany had weaponized botulinum toxin, more than 1 million doses of botulinum toxoid vaccine were made for Allied troops preparing to invade Normandy on D-Day. The U.S. biological weapons program was ended in 1969-1970 by executive orders of Richard M. Nixon, then president. Research pertaining to biowarfare use of botulinum toxin took place in other countries as well." ("Botulinum Toxin as a Biological Weapon: Medical and Public Health Management," Working Group on Civilian Biodefense, Center for Civilian Biodefense Strategies, The Johns Hopkins University, Journal of the American Medical Association, February 28, 2001, Vol. 285, No. 8, p.1059.)

Four state sponsors of terrorism—Iran, Iraq, North Korea and Syria—either have developed or are developing botulinum toxin as a weapon. Some of these countries have enlisted the help of Russian scientists versed in the art of bioweaponry. And documents turned up in Afghanistan included a step-by-step guide to making botulinum toxin.

Hemorrhagic fever viruses (HFVs), including deadly the Ebola virus, are also known to interest terrorists, among others. Japan's Aum Shinrikyu cult tried to acquire the Ebola virus, and the Soviet Union's biowarfare scientists worked on turning Ebola, as well as the related Marburg virus, into a weapon. The Ebola virus, named after a river in the Democratic Republic of the Congo (formerly, Zaire) in Africa, was first recognized in 1976.

Infection with Ebola virus in humans is "incidental"—meaning that while the disease can be spread from person to person, it isn't contagious is the typical sense. "People can be exposed to Ebola virus from direct contact with the blood and/or secretions of an infected person," explains the Centers for Disease Control (CDC). "This is why the virus has often been spread through the families and friends of infected persons: in the course of feeding, holding, or otherwise caring for them, family members and friends would come into close contact with such secretions. People can also be exposed to Ebola virus through contact with objects, such as needles, that have been contaminated with infected secretions." ("Viral Hemorrhagic Fevers: Fact Sheets; Ebola Hemorrhagic Fever," Centers for Disease Control and Prevention, 2001.) Other routes of infection include the bite of an infected arthropod, aerosol generated from infected rodent excreta, or by direct contact with infected animal carcasses.

The World Health Organization describes Ebola as "one of the most virulent viral diseases known to humankind," causing death in 50 to 90 percent of all clinically ill cases. Most people infected with Ebola die within a week after suffering debilitating symptoms, including blindness and profuse bleeding from major body openings. The CDC says researchers don't understand why some people are able to recover from Ebola and others aren't.("Ebola Hemorrhagic Fever," Fact Sheet No. 103, World Health Organization, Revised December 2000.) The very gruesomeness of the disease, however, makes it a candidate terror weapon. In a May 2002 report, the Johns Hopkins biodefense group said the use of an HFV weapon would manifest itself in physical symptoms 2 to 21 days later. It also noted that there are no licensed vaccines to treat the diseases caused by HFVs. ("Hemorrhagic Fever Viruses as Biological Weapons: Medical and Public Health Management," Working Group on Civilian Biodefense, Center for Civilian Biodefense Strategies, The Johns Hopkins University, *Journal of the American Medical Association*, May 8, 2002, Vol. 287, No. 18.)

Plague, too, represents a serious bioterrorism hazard, especially because it's so highly contagious. The disease is caused by the *Yersinia pestis* bacterium. Because the bacterium is available around the world, experts say it's hard to prevent its mass production and aerosol dissemination. Moreover, pneumonic plague's high fatality rate and the potential for the secondary spread of the disease in an epidemic make the use of plague as a biological weapon of "great concern," says the WGCB. ("Plague as a Biological Weapon: Medical and Public Health Management." Working Group on Civilian Biodefense, Center for Civilian Biodefense Strategies, The Johns Hopkins University, Journal of the American Medical Association, May 3, 2000, Vol. 283, No. 17, p. 2281.)

Outbreaks of plague have cost tens of millions of lives over the centuries. The first recorded pandemic began in Egypt and swept across Europe in 541. The affected regions saw their populations cut by 50 percent or more. The most famous plague pandemic, the Black Death, began in 1346 and was spread by infected rats and humans. It eventually killed 20 to 30 million people, or one-third of Europe's population, over a period of more than 130 years. A third plague pandemic rolled across China in 1855 and eventually infected all of the then-inhabited continents, killing more than 12 million in India and China alone. Interestingly, the Great Fire of London of 1666 had the salutary effect of eradicating the Great Plague that had killed nearly one-fifth of the city's population; the fire not only burned down most of medieval London but also consumed the city's plague-infected rats.

"Advances in living conditions, public health, and antibiotic therapy make future pandemics improbable," the Johns Hopkins group notes. "However, plague outbreaks following use of a biological weapon are a plausible threat." In 1970, the World Health Organization calculated that if 50 kilograms of aerosolized *Y pestis* were released over a city of five million people, pneumonic plague could afflict as many as 150,000 persons and kill 36,000 of them. Symptoms would begin to appear one to six days after exposure, and victims would die quickly. Making the crisis worse, large numbers of inhabitants could be expected to flee an infested city, further spreading the disease. (Health Aspects of Chemical and Biological Weapons (Geneva, Switzerland: World Health Organization, 1970), pp.98-109, cited in "Plague as a Biological Weapon: Medical and Public Health Management." Working Group on Civilian Biodefense, Center for Civilian Biodefense Strategies, The Johns Hopkins University, Journal of the American Medical Association, May 3, 2000, Vol. 283, No. 17, p. 2281.)

Weapons of Mass Destruction Incidents Yearly by Type of Agent, 2000-2001

| | 2000 | | 2001 | | |
	Actual	Hoaxes	Actual	Hoaxes	Total
Biological	4	22	7	600	633
Chemical	25	0	11	1	37
Nuclear	2	0	2	2	6
Radiological	14	3	2	0	19
Combination	0	0	3	0	3
Unknown	5	0	0	0	5
Total	50	25	25	603	703

Source: Center for Nonproliferation Studies, Monterey Institute of International Studies

Smallpox is yet another disease that could inflict massive casualties if turned into a terrorist weapon. It's a communicable disease that's spread from person to person. It's usually transmitted through direct contact and via droplets or aerosols exhaled by an infected person. "If used as a biological weapon, smallpox represents a serious threat to civilian populations because of its case-fatality rate of 30 percent or more among unvaccinated persons and the absence of specific therapy," the

WGCB warns. "Although smallpox has long been feared as the most devastating of all infectious diseases, its potential for devastation today is far greater than at any previous time. Routine vaccination throughout the United States ceased more than 25 years ago. In a now highly susceptible, mobile population, smallpox would be able to spread widely and rapidly throughout this country and the world."

Smallpox spreads like wildfire. A clandestine aerosol release of smallpox, even if it infected only 50 to 100 persons at first, would rapidly spread in a highly susceptible population, expanding by a factor of 10 to 20 times or more with each generation of cases, the biodefense panel says. Between the time of an aerosol release of smallpox virus and diagnosis of the first cases, an interval as long as two weeks or more is apt to occur. The good news is that by that time there would be no risk of further environmental exposure from the original aerosol release, because the virus is fully inactivated within two days.

A public-health effort began in 1967 to eradicate smallpox worldwide, and victory was declared 10 years later. "The deliberate reintroduction of smallpox as an epidemic disease would be an international crime of unprecedented proportions," says the Johns Hopkins panel, adding that this is "now regarded as a possibility" because of bioterrorism. ("Smallpox as a Biological Weapon: Medical and Public Health Management," Working Group on Civilian Biodefense, Center for Civilian Biodefense Strategies, The Johns Hopkins University, *Journal of the American Medical Association*, Vol. 281, No. 22, p. 2127.)

The former Soviet Union, alas, did purposely manufacture and test weaponized smallpox. The Center for Nonproliferation Studies of the Monterey Institute of International Studies in June 2002 released the first authoritative English translation of an official Soviet report describing a previously unknown outbreak of smallpox in 1971 in the city of Aralsk, Kazakhstan, then located on the northern shore of the Aral Sea. A retrospective analysis of the Soviet report, which was written shortly after the incident by a Soviet public-health official, indicates that the outbreak may have originated in an open-air test of a smallpox biological weapon on Vozrozhdeniye Island, a top-secret biowarfare testing ground in the middle of the Aral Sea. Seven persons became ill in the outbreak, and three died; the city of Aralsk was quarantined, and its more than 50,000 inhabitant were vaccinated. "If the analysis is correct," the Monterey experts say, "it provides the first evidence that the Soviet Union field-tested a smallpox weapon and that such testing caused civilian deaths." Former Soviet bio-warfare expert Alibek has confirmed that the Soviet Union succeeded in transforming smallpox into a bioweapon, which could be used in bombs or missiles. The U.S.S.R. developed sufficient capacity to turn out tons of smallpox virus every year, he says, maintaining that Russia still has a genetic-engineering research program aimed at producing more virulent and contagious recombinant strains of the disease.

Tularemia is the sixth and last disease that thus far concerns the WGCB experts. Indeed, tularemia may already have been used in warfare. The causative agent of tularemia, *Francisella tularensis*, is "one of the most infectious pathogenic bacteria known," the group points out. The inhalation of just 10 organisms can cause the disease, resulting in severe and sometimes fatal illness. Tularemia, however, isn't contagious. Still, the biodefense experts consider *F tularensis* to be "a dangerous potential biological weapon because of its extreme infectivity, ease of dissemination and substantial capacity to cause illness and death."

Although *F tularensis* could be used as a weapon in various ways, the working group at Johns Hopkins believes that an aerosol release would have the greatest adverse public-health effect. "Release in a densely populated area would be expected to result in an abrupt onset of large numbers of cases of acute, nonspecific febrile illness beginning 3 to 5 days later (incubation range, 1-14 days), with pleuropneumonitis developing in a significant proportion of cases during the ensuing days and weeks." ("Tularemia as a Biological Weapon: Medical and Public Health Management," Working Group on Civilian Biodefense, Center for Civilian Biodefense Strategies, The Johns Hopkins University, Journal of the American Medical Association, June 6, 2001, Vol. 285, No. 21, p. 2763.)

A World Health Organization study in 1969 estimated that the aerosol dispersal of 50 kilograms of virulent *F tularensis* over a city of five million would result in 250 000 casualties, including 19 000 deaths. Illness from the disease, it said, would persist for several weeks, and disease relapses could occur over ensuing weeks and months. Alibek says that Soviet research resulted in weapons production of *F tularensis* strains engineered to be resistant to antibiotics and vaccines. He also suspects that "a tularemia outbreak among German troops in southern Russia in 1942 indicates that this incident was very likely the result of the U.S.S.R.'s use of biological weapons."

In addition to the six biological agents of greatest concern to the John Hopkins panel, another potential bioterrorism weapon deserves mention. Ricin, one of the most lethal naturally occurring toxins known, is derived from the beans of the castor plant. Castor beans are available worldwide and are used, for instance, to make castor oil. Ricin is fairly easy to manufacture, making the toxin another potential bioterrorism weapon. Just one milligram is enough to kill an adult. After inhalation, symptoms set in 18 to 24 hours, and death typically comes in 36 to 72 hours. If death hasn't occurred in three to five days, the victim usually survives. An Al Qaeda compound near Kabul, Afghanistan, which included a makeshift laboratory, held documents on the production of ricin. The London *Times* reported in November 2001 that among the papers recovered from the site was one that read: "A certain amount [of ricin], equal to a strong dose, will be able to kill an adult, and a dose equal to seven [castor] seeds will kill a child." ("Laden Had Plans to Make Biological Poison," by Anthony Loyd and Martin Fletcher, *The Times*, London, Nov. 16, 2001.) Other pages listed ricin's properties and medical symptoms. In 1978, an assassin used ricin to murder the exiled Bulgarian dissident Georgi Markov. Markov was stuck in the leg with a specially made umbrella while walking across a London bridge. The umbrella implanted a small, ricin-laced pellet under his skin. Markov died soon after; an autopsy turned up the deadly pellet. The communist Bulgarian government of the time, irked by Markov's radio broadcasts from London, was said to be behind the assassination.

2.06. Nuclear and 'Dirty' Bombs

After biological weapons, nuclear devices in the hands of terrorists pose the next-greatest threat of mass destruction. In weighing these two types of weaponry, nuclear devices are probably more difficult for terrorists to obtain than biological agents, and a small nuclear explosion would likely inflict fewer casualties than a well-orchestrated, multi-site biological attack.

The British Home Office disagrees. It puts the threat of nuclear attack at the top of its list of terrorist risks. In a rare public disclosure, the Home Office in December 2001 submitted a detailed, 20-page account of the United Kingdom's vulnerabilities to terrorist attacks to a court hearing a case involving a Moroccan man arrested in London under Britain's antiterrorism laws. Heading the list of risks was a nuclear blast, "which would have a devastating effect on the U.K." Biological or chemical attacks, it said, would be "potentially less devastating" but still "would lead to widespread public alarm and potentially many fatalities." ("New Terror Threat to Britain," by Jeevan Vasagar, *The Guardian*, London, Dec. 22, 2001.)

Either way, nuclear weapons may be a bigger danger to humanity now than they were during the Cold War. Instead of nuclear-tipped missile strikes, today's nuclear devices could easily enter a country undetected. Some nuclear bombs are as small as a suitcase or knapsack; others could be concealed in nondescript shipping crates sent via ship from overseas by persons unknown. To illustrate the problem, more than 16,000 cargo containers arrive by ship at U.S. ports every day. They then are transported by truck or rail to their final destinations. Although technology is being dispatched to scrutinize arriving containers for radioactivity, skilled terrorists could still plant a nuclear device in a shipping crate, setting it to detonate at a predetermined time, by radio signal or when the container is opened. Even a modest-sized devise could level a small city, inflicting tens of thousands of casualties. A 12.5-kiloton device, for example, would kill an estimated 23,000 to 80,000 people in an average-sized city and injure countless more.

Terrorist groups and their state sponsors already have put a great deal of effort and emphasis on acquiring nuclear weapons, related technologies and radioactive materials. For example, the U.S. has evidence of contacts between Pakistani nuclear-weapons scientists and the Taliban in Afghanistan and Osama bin Laden's Al Qaeda terrorist network. Captured Al Qaeda documents and interrogations obtained in Afghanistan revealed that bin Laden dearly wanted to lay his hands on nuclear technology and materials.

Al Qaeda indeed has been trying to acquire fissible materials since the early 1990s. And the CIA reported in January 2002 that it "uncovered rudimentary diagrams of nuclear weapons inside a suspected Al Qaeda safehouse in Kabul. These diagrams, while crude, describe essential components—uranium and high explosives—common to nuclear weapons." Bin Laden's terrorist organization apparently had detailed plans for a nuclear bomb similar to "Fat Man," the nuclear bomb dropped on Nagasaki, Japan in 1945. *The Times* of London reported in November, 2001 that one of its correspondents discovered partly burned documents describing nuclear bombs and other explosive devices in a hastily abandoned safe house in Kabul, Afghanistan. The papers included studies on a kinetic-energy super-gun capable of firing chemical or nuclear warheads, preliminary research on thermonuclear devices and instructions for making smaller bombs.

"There were descriptions of how the detonation of TNT compresses plutonium into a critical mass, sparking a chain reaction, and ultimately a thermonuclear reaction," The *Times* said. "The discovery of the detailed bomb-making instructions, along with studies into chemical and nuclear devices, confirms the West's worst fears and raises the spectre of plans for an attack that would far exceed the September 11 atrocities in scale and gravity. . . . While the terrorists may not yet have the capability to build such weapons, their hopes of doing so are clear." ("Bin Laden's Nuclear Secrets Found," by Anthony Loyd, The *Times*, London, Nov. 15. 2001.)

A less conventional radioactive device is a so-called "dirty bomb"—that is, a conventional explosive around which is wrapped highly radioactive material, such as uranium or plutonium. The radioactive material might be weapons-grade or could come from spent nuclear-reactor fuel rods or even hospital waste (i.e., materials used in radiation therapy). When the device explodes, the radioactive material is blasted into the air and strewn across the neighboring landscape. A dirty bomb doesn't cause an atomic chain reaction like a nuclear warhead. Instead, it merely scatters radioactive debris, much as a hand grenade sends out shrapnel. In fact, a radiological weapon needn't explode at all. Radioactive powder could be introduced, say, into a building's air-conditioning system.

Exposure to a radiological weapon can lead to acute reactions, including death or chronic, lifelong ailments. Still, experts are careful not to over-dramatize the effects of a dirty bomb. "To actually kill any significant number of people with [radiation from] such a device would be hard," Matthew Bunn of Harvard's Kennedy School of Government told the New York *Daily News*. "To cause terror—just enough material to make sure the word 'radioactive' gets on the news—might be enough." Nikolai Sokov of Center for Nonproliferation Studies agrees, saying that the "greatest consequence will be psychological—people will be scared." Bunn and Sokov quoted in "Tests Predict Toll of Terror Attacks," by Bob Port, *New York Daily News*, March 3, 2002.) Nonetheless, the clean up after a dirty-bomb blast would be tremendously costly and could take years, perhaps making a vital city district—such as midtown Manhattan, Wall Street, Chicago's Loop or Capitol Hill—uninhabitable for a very long time.

Analogous to a dirty bomb would be a terrorist attack on a nuclear power plant. Although these reactors are encased in protective shells, it's possible that a large plane loaded with explosives could penetrate a plant and release radioactive material into the atmosphere. Terrorists otherwise might somehow enter a nuclear power plant and disable its safety mechanisms. This could cause a nuclear meltdown like the one that occurred at Chernobyl in the Ukraine in 1986, which killed more than 30 people immediately and disbursed radiation over a 20-mile radius, necessitating the evacuation of 135,00 people. At Chernobyl, though, an explosion had rocked the plant, destroying its protective covering, which allowed radioactive material to

Nuclear Reactors Worldwide

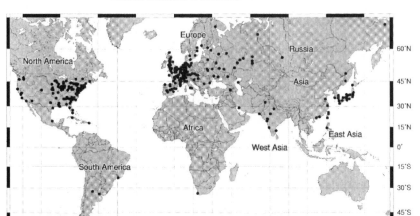

Source: International Nuclear Safety Center, Argonne National Laboratory

escape. Ukraine's Ministry of Health now says that 125,000 people have died and 3.5 million others have become ill as a result of the Chernobyl accident.

Nuclear Reactors Worldwide

There are two principal sources from which terrorists might acquire readymade nuclear weapons, bombing-making know-how or radioactive material: a sympathetic country that either already has nuclear devices or is on the road to developing them, or the international black market. In June 2002, the International Atomic Energy Agency, the world's nuclear non-proliferation watchdog, warned that terrorists could find key materials to build a dirty bomb in almost any country in the world and that more than 100 nations may not be keeping close track of such radioactive substances as cobalt-60, strontium-90, caesium-137 and iridium-192.

CIA chief Tenet testified in February 2002 that "we are concerned about the possibility of significant nuclear technology transfers going undetected. This reinforces our need to more closely examine emerging nuclear programs for sudden leaps in capability. Factors working against us include the difficulty of monitoring and controlling technology transfers, the emergence of new suppliers to covert nuclear weapons programs, and the possibility of illicitly acquiring fissile material. All of these can shorten timelines and increase the chances of proliferation surprise." Worse, terrorists may soon be able to launch nuclear strikes against Western nations using short-range missiles. "Several countries of concern are also increasingly interested in acquiring a land-attack cruise missile (LACM) capability," Tenet noted. "By the end of the decade, LACMs could pose a serious threat to not only our deployed forces, but possibly even the U.S. mainland." ("Worldwide Threat: Converging Dangers in a Post 9/11 World," U.S. Senate Select Committee on Intelligence testimony, Feb. 6, 2002.)

As the only Muslim nation known to possess nuclear weapons, Pakistan is always a potential source of an "Islamic bomb." It detonated its first nuclear device in May 1998 and currently is believed to have around 20 nuclear weapons, with the ability to make more. Islamabad has enough highly enriched uranium (i.e., 585 to 800 kilograms) to build 30 to 52 fission bombs, experts say. The hub of Pakistan's nuclear weapons program is in Kahuta at the Khan Research Laboratories, which produces enriched uranium using technology reportedly stolen from the Netherlands a year after India's first nuclear test in 1974. Besides its Kahuta plant, Pakistan also has a research reactor at Khushab capable of supplying weapons-grade material. Built with Chinese assistance, the reactor became operational in March 1998 and is capable of producing 10 to 15 kilogram of weapons-grade plutonium annually—or just about enough to build one or two new nuclear bombs every year. Other Pakistani plants also may produce weapons-grade material.

Among the state sponsors of terrorism seeking nuclear-weapons capability are Iraq, Iran and Libya. The most dangerous of the three is Iraq. "All other things being equal, the current leadership in Baghdad will eventually achieve a nuclear weapon in addition to their current inventories of other weapons of mass destruction," Charles Duelfer, former deputy executive chairman of the U.N. Special Commission on Iraq, or

UNSCOM, warned the U.S. Senate Foreign Relations Committee in July 2002.

Prior to the 1991 Gulf War, Iraq was thought to be just two years away from producing a nuclear weapon. U.S. bombing raids destroyed many of Iraq's suspected nuclear sites. However, Iraqi leader Saddam Hussein, who has been called "one of the most ruthless people that the world has ever seen," has fended off United Nations' nuclear-weapons inspectors since 1991. "With sufficient black-market uranium or plutonium, Iraq probably could fabricate a nuclear weapon," warned the Center for Nonproliferation Studies in a September 2001 assessment. "If undetected and unobstructed, [it] could produce weapons-grade fissile material within several years." Iraq has design plans for the construction of nuclear weapon and is engaged in the "clandestine procurement of special nuclear weapon-related equipment," the center says. Iraq also has a "large and experienced pool" of nuclear scientists and may possess key components and software.

Iraqi nuclear scientist Hussein al Shahristani told the London-based Arabic magazine *Al-Majallah* in January 1996 that Saddam Hussein changed the peaceful nature of Iraq's nuclear program when he took power in 1979, instructing all scientific facilities to begin developing nuclear weapons. During the 1980s, Iraq established 15 major nuclear installations capable of enriching uranium. Al Shahristani described how Iraq came close to enriching uranium to 93 percent with the assistance of Western companies. Western firms also apparently helped Iraq develop complex detonation devices crucial to the successful explosion of a nuclear weapon.

"Saddam never abandoned his nuclear weapons program," CIA chief Tenet stated in his 2002 Senate testimony. "Iraq retains a significant number of nuclear scientists, program documentation, and probably some dual-use manufacturing infrastructure that could support a reinvigorated nuclear weapons program. Baghdad's access to foreign expertise could support a rejuvenated program, but our major near-term concern is the possibility that Saddam might gain access to fissile material." Fear of an Iraqi nuclear bomb led Israel to conduct in a preemptive air strike against a newly built French nuclear reactor near Baghdad in June 1981, destroying the facility.

Elsewhere, Iran, which has sought to recruit Russian scientists for its arms program, is probably at least a decade away from completing a nuclear weapon. As a possible prelude to nuclear-weapons development, Iran has a large program to construct reactors for generating electricity. Tenet has warned that "Iran remains a serious concern because of its across-the-board pursuit of WMD [weapons of mass destruction] and missile capabilities. Tehran may be able to indigenously produce enough fissile material for a nuclear weapon by late this decade. Obtaining material from outside could cut years from this estimate. Iran may also flight-test an ICBM [intercontinental ballistic missile] later this decade, using either Russian or North Korean assistance."

In January 1995, after years of searching for a supplier to complete its first nuclear power plant, Iran signed an $800 million deal with the Russian Ministry of Atomic Energy to finish work on a reactor at Bushehr. The plant, due for completion in 2003, is supposed to conform to International Atomic Energy Agency regulations barring the use of materials and technology for nuclear-weapons development. In December 2001, Russia's parliament ratified a new partnership treaty with Iran, which calls for joint cooperation in the development of nuclear energy for peaceful purposes. CIA Director Tenet testified ominously in March 2002: "Russia continues to supply significant assistance on nearly all aspects of Tehran's nuclear program. It is also providing Iran assistance on long-range ballistic missile programs." That oil-rich Iran would want nuclear power plants has raised eyebrows. U.S. and Israeli officials believe that Iran hopes to build nuclear weapons. The U.S. has opposed the Iranian nuclear energy program, arguing that Iran has sufficient oil and gas reserves for power generation and that expensive nuclear reactors are unnecessary and could be used for military purposes.

Libya has made numerous attempts to obtain nuclear weapons and technology since the early 1970s. It has approached both China and Pakistan to obtain nuclear technology. Libya's efforts are believed to have been largely unsuccessful, and its nuclear research program remains at a rudimentary stage. Libya, however, does have a small, Soviet-supplied research reactor at Tajura. Built in 1979, it's said to comply with international nonproliferation safeguards.

Russia is the largest black-market source of nuclear weaponry, materials and expertise. When the U.S.S.R. broke up in 1991, it had more than 40,000 nuclear weapons and thousands of tons of fissionable material. Especially troubling is the fact that Russia hasn't had the financial wherewithal or controls needed to ensure that parts of its massive nuclear arsenal don't fall into the wrong hands. There's also the fear that impoverished Russian nuclear scientists and technician could be enticed to sell their expertise to a terrorist organization.

"The most urgent unmet national security threat to the United States today is the danger that weapons of mass destruction or weapons-usable material in Russia could be stolen and sold to terrorists or hostile nation states and used against American troops abroad or civilians at home," warned a U.S. Energy Department advisory panel in January 2001. The group, co-chaired by former U.S. Senator Howard Baker and former White House Counsel Lloyd Cutler, stated: "This threat is a clear and present danger to the international community as well as to American lives and liberties." It added that Iraq, Iran and "other countries" have sought weapons-grade materials from the Russian stockpile. The report posited a "worst-case scenario" in which a nuclear engineer with a grapefruit-sized lump of highly enriched uranium or an orange-sized lump of plutonium and commercially available components fashioned a nuclear device small enough to fit into a van. "The explosive effects of such a device," it said, "would destroy every building in the Wall Street financial area and would level lower Manhattan." In fact, worries about a briefcase bomb or a radiological dispersal device led then-New York City Mayor Rudolph Giuliani to implement special precautions at the 2002 New Year's Eve celebrations in Times Square. Most notably, police units carried radiation-detection devices.

"The former Soviet Union produced over 1,300 tons of nuclear weapons-grade plutonium and uranium, most of which is now vulnerable to theft or diversion," cautions an analysis by the Carnegie Endowment for International Studies. "Of even greater concern is the fact that Russia itself doesn't even know how much material it produced or where all of its is, and the world has to confront the very real possibility that some of this material may already be missing. We know that terrorist groups, including Al Qaeda, have shown interested in getting such material from Russia in the past."

Weapons-usable materials indeed may be on the black market already. "Since the collapse of the Soviet Union in 1991, there have been frequent reports of illicit trafficking in fissile materials from the NIS [Newly Independent States]. Especially since the events of September 11, 2001, there has been widespread concern that terrorist organizations or proliferant states may illicitly obtain fissile material from the NIS," notes the Center for Nonproliferation Studies. "Looking closely at the available open-source evidence," it says, "one can identify 13 confirmed cases in which more-than-minuscule quantities of highly enriched uranium (HEU) or plutonium have been stolen or diverted from nuclear facilities in NIS. In five of these cases, the material was exported beyond the NIS before it was recovered. In seven other cases, the material was seized before it left the NIS. In one case, the whereabouts of the stolen material remain unknown. Aside from these 13 cases, in one additional case, an attempted theft at a Russian nuclear facility was thwarted before the conspirators removed the material involved from the site. All of these incidents are of proliferation concern because of the type and quantity of material involved and/or because of the circumstances surrounding them."

Several Russians have been caught attempting to purloin weapons-related materials. In late 1998, conspirators at a Ministry of Atomic Energy facility in Chelyabink were arrested for trying to steal fissible material; the amount was nearly enough to make one nuclear bomb. At about the same time, an employee at Russia's premier nuclear weapons laboratory in Sarov was arrested for espionage and charged with attempting to sell documents on nuclear weapons designs to agents of Iraq and Afghanistan for $3 million. In January 2000, four sailors at a naval base on the Kamchatka Peninsula were arrested with a stash of stolen radioactive material.

Finally, a nuclear wildcard is North Korea. It has been trying to develop nuclear bombs since the 1980s and reportedly could have at minimum two warheads. The secretive leaders of that impoverished country might be persuaded by offers of large amounts of cash to part with any nuclear bombs, technology or fissionable material in their possession. Activity at North Korea's Yongbyon nuclear research center was frozen under a 1994 agreement with the U.S. A subsequent examination of nuclear waste revealed that North Korea had extracted about 24 kilograms of plutonium. A standard 20-kiloton nuclear warhead contains eight kilograms of critical mass. Thus, North Korea seems to have produced enough fissionable material for three nuclear warheads.

"North Korea," cautioned Tenet in February 2002, "continues to export complete ballistic missiles and production capabilities along with related raw materials, components, and expertise. Profits from these sales help P'yongyang to support its missile—and probably other WMD—development programs, and in turn generate new products to offer to its customers—primarily Iran, Libya, Syria, and Egypt. North Korea continues to comply with the terms of the Agreed Framework that are directly related to the freeze on its reactor program, but P'yongyang has warned that it is prepared to walk away from the agreement if it concluded that the United States was not living up to its end of the deal."

2.07. Cyberterrorism

Cyberterrorism has been called "the threat of the new millennium." That's because today's advanced economies are information-dependent, and most information and data now travel via the Internet. Cyberspace thus represents an enticing target for terrorists. Within days of the terrorist attacks of Sept. 11, in fact, groups of Pakistani computer hackers declared a "cyber jihad" (or "holy war") against the United States and

U.S. Poll: Threat of Cyberterror Attacks Against
Critical Infrastructure, December 2001

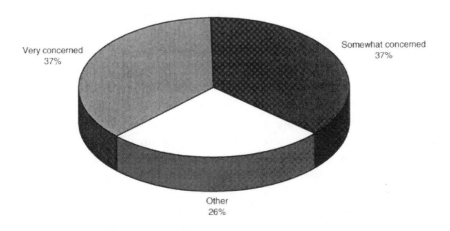

Source: Information Technology Association of America

called on all hackers of Muslim faith to take part. A series of cyber attacks followed, compromising thousands of websites and disrupting Internet traffic and e-commerce. Among the targets were websites of the U.S. Department of Defense and Aon Corp., an insurance company that had an office in the World Trade Center and lost some 200 employees when the towers collapsed.

"We are in a race with technology itself," Tenet told a Senate committee in March 2001. "No country in the world rivals the U.S. in its reliance, dependence, and dominance of information systems. The great advantage we derive from this also presents us with unique vulnerabilities." He noted that cyber attacks on U.S. military, economic or telecommunications infrastructure "can be launched from anywhere in the world" and "can be used to transport the problems of a distant conflict directly to

America's heartland." ("Worldwide Threat 2001: National Security in a Changing World," statement before the Senate Select Committee on Intelligence, Central Intelligence Agency transcript, Feb. 7, 2001.)

"Terrorists and other non-state actors are beginning to recognize that information warfare offers them new, low cost, easily hidden tools to support their causes," Tenet previously informed a Senate committee back in 1998. "Established terrorist groups are likely to view attacks against information systems as a means of striking at government, commercial, and industrial targets with little risk of being caught. Global proliferation of computer technology and the open availability of computer tools that can be used to attack other computers make it possible for terrorist groups to develop this capability without great difficulty." He said, "It may even be possible for terrorists to use amateur hackers as their unwitting accomplices in a cyber attack." (Testimony before the Senate Committee on Government Affairs, Central Intelligence Agency transcript, June 24, 1998.)

The Internet incidents of September 2001 weren't the first cyberspace attacks. A group called the Internet Black Tigers took responsibility in the late 1990s for assaults on the e-mail systems of Sri Lankan diplomatic posts around the world. Italian sympathizers of Mexico's Zapatista rebels crashed Web pages belonging to Mexican financial institutions. Another group known as the Electronic Disturbance Theater (EDT), which promotes online civil disobedience in support of the Zapatista movement, began conducting Internet "sit-ins" in 1997 against various websites; at designated times, thousands of protestors pointed their browsers at preselected sites using software that flooded the targets with rapid and repeated download requests. Animal-rights groups have even used EDT's software against organizations said to abuse animals.

The Electrohippies conducted similar Web sit-ins against the World Trade Organization in late 1999. And NATO computers were hit in 1999 with virus-infected e-mail bombs and denial-of-service attacks by politically motivated hackers known as "hacktivists" protesting the NATO bombings in Kosovo. Businesses, public organizations and academic institutes, too, received virus-laden e-mails from anti-NATO protestors in Eastern Europe. In February 2002, hacktivists took credit for a "virtual sit-in" that crashed the Web site of the World Economic Forum, which at the time was holding its annual meeting in New York.

A British government study, published in April 2002, found that while cyber attacks on U.K. businesses had nearly doubled during 2001, relatively few companies had spent enough on security to safeguard their websites and data systems. The Information Security Breaches survey found that 44 percent of all U.K. businesses questioned had suffered a malicious security incident or breach in 2001, up from a rate of 24 percent in 2000. Even though the cost of each incident averaged more than $45,000—and $750,000 or more in serious cases—only 27 percent of the surveyed firms reported spending more than 1 percent of their technology budgets on security. The problem, said one expert involved in the survey, is that many British companies "take a fairly narrow information-technology view of security rather than as a part of a strategy to embed a security culture within an organization."

Cybernetic assaults pose much greater dangers than mere website meddling and infected e-mails. Barry C. Collin, who coined the term "cyberterrorism" in 1996, has warned that the "cyberterrorist will make certain that the population of a nation will not be able to eat, to drink, to move, or to live." What's more, he said, "the people charged with the protection of their nation will not have warning, and will not be able to shut down the terrorist, since that cyberterrorist is most likely on the other side of the world."

The threat of cyberterrorism first came to the fore in the Clinton administration. "International terrorist groups clearly have the capability to attack the information infrastructure of the United States, even if they use relatively simple means," then-CIA Director John M. Deutch told a congressional subcommittee in 1996. "Since the possibilities for attacks are not difficult to imagine, I am concerned about the potential for such attacks in the future. The methods used could range from such

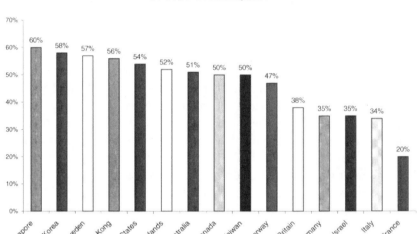

Percentage of Households with Internet Access via Home PC,
Selected Countries, 2001

Source: Nielsen//Net Ratings

traditional terrorist methods as a vehicle-delivered bomb—directed in this instance against, say, a telephone switching center or other communications mode—to electronic means of attack. The latter methods could rely on paid hackers. The ability to launch an attack, however, are [sic] likely to be within the capabilities of a number of terrorist groups, which themselves have increasingly used the Internet and other modern means for their own communications. The groups concerned include such well-known, long-established organizations as the Lebanese Hizballah, as well as nameless and less well-known cells of international terrorists, such as those who attacked the World Trade Center [in 1993]."

"Virtually any 'bad actor,'" he said, "can acquire the hardware and software needed to attack some of our critical information-based infrastructures. Hacker tools are readily available on the Internet, and hackers themselves are a source of expertise for any nation or foreign terrorist organization that is interested in developing an information warfare capability. In fact, hackers, with or without their full knowledge, may be supplying advice and expertise to rogue states such as Iran and Libya." Deutch said his "greatest concern" was that hackers, terrorists or hostile governments would use information warfare as part of a coordinated attack designed to disrupt 1) infrastructure, such as electric power distribution, air traffic control or financial sectors, 2) international commerce, and 3) deployed military forces in time of peace or war. ("Foreign Information Warfare Programs and Capabilities," John M. Deutch, Director of U.S. Central Intelligence, Senate Governmental Affairs Committee, Permanent Subcommittee on Investigations, June 25, 1996.)

U.S. government tests have, in fact, shown that the Pentagon's information network, which you'd think would be the most secure computer system in the world, is extremely vulnerable to cyber attack. In an information-warfare exercise conducted in 1997 code-named Eligible Receiver, teams from the National Security Agency, which operates the nation's spy satellites, used publicly available techniques to hack into Pentagon computers. By the time they were done, the hackers were able to intercept, erase and change messages on the classified Department of Defense network, denying the generals in charge the ability to control their own forces. (A subsequent exercise revealed that 63 percent of the test attacks on the Pentagon's computer systems went undetected.)

The dangers of cyber attacks against the U.S. military are more the mere conjecture. Hackers based in Russia systematically broke into U.S. Defense Department computers for more than a year in 1998-99, taking vast quantities of materials that were later described as "sensitive" but not classified. The "coordinated, organized" attacks averaged 60 to 80 a day, a U.S. official said.

Many hostile governments, not surprisingly, are embarked on intensive information-warfare efforts. Citing a classified intelligence report, Deutch revealed in 1996 that the U.S. had "evidence that a number of countries around the world are developing the doctrine, strategies, and tools to conduct information attacks." Five years later, Deutch's successor at the CIA, George Tenet, reportedly told a closed-door congressional meeting that "at least a dozen" countries are working on information-warfare programs intended to disable an opponent's computer systems. And the *Los Angeles Times* in April 2002 reported a classified CIA study had concluded that the Chinese military is working on plans to launch wide-scale cyber attacks on U.S. and Taiwanese computer networks, including Internet-linked military systems considered vulnerable to sabotage. ("CIA Warns of Chinese Plans for Cyber-Attacks on U.S.," by Eric Lichtblau, April 25, 2002.)

Beyond military systems, Tenet warned in 1998 that "an adversary capable of implanting the right virus or accessing the right terminal can cause massive damage" to computer-controlled financial, water, sewage, power and telecommunications networks. (Testimony by Director of Central Intelligence George J. Tenet before the Senate Committee on Government Affairs, Central Intelligence Agency transcript June 24, 1998.)

The Eligible Receiver teams indeed found that the U.S. electric power grid and emergency 911 systems had weaknesses that could be exploited by an adversary simply by using tools that are publicly available on the Internet.

The spectrum of potential cyber attacks is mind-boggling. In a groundbreaking 1996 paper titled "The Future of Cyberterrorism: Where the Physical and Virtual World Converge," Barry C. Collin noted that the "face of terrorism is changing." Instead of deploying explosives-laden trucks, suicide bombers or even poison gas, he said that an Information Age enemy using the binomial language of computers will attack us "with ones and zeros at a place we are most vulnerable: the point at which the physical and virtual worlds converge." Among his alarming list of possible attacks, he hypothesized that cyberterrorists could infiltrate air-traffic control systems, causing airplanes to collide, or remotely access the processing control systems of cereal manufacturers, changing the levels of iron supplement, and thus sicken or kill children. He further warned that cyberterrorists might remotely alter the formulas of medications produced at pharmaceutical manufacturing plants or change the pressure in natural gas lines, causing values to fail and lines to explode in massive fireballs. Collin concluded that "these examples are not science fiction. All of these scenarios can be executed today. As you may know, some of these incidents already have occurred in various nations. More of such acts will take place tomorrow."

Here are a few examples of what cyberterrorists have already accomplished: Hackers successfully raided Russia's state-run natural-gas monopoly, Gazprom, in 1999. The hackers, who had the help of a collaborator inside Gazprom, bypassed the company's cyber security barriers and used a Trojan horse to take over the central switchboard that controls gas flows in pipelines. Whether the incident caused any damage has never been revealed. In Northern Ireland, the Provisional Irish Republican Army employed the services of contract hackers to penetrate U.K. government computers to acquire the home addresses of law enforcement and intelligence officers. Japan's Metropolitan Police Department reported in March 2000 that a software system it had purchased to track police vehicles, including unmarked cars, had, in fact, been developed by the Aum Shinrikyu cult, the same group that gassed the Tokyo subway in 1995. By the time authorities discovered the security breach, the cult already had received classified tracking data on 115 police vehicles. Making matters worse, the cult also had developed software for at least 80 Japanese firms and 10 other government agencies.

The U.S. government, too, may have exposed itself unwittingly to a cyber attack by nefarious software writers who may have helped to remedy Y2K computer bugs. In February 2000, the State Department, fearing a Trojan horse might have been planted in its computers, sent an urgent cable to all U.S. embassies around the world, instructing them to remove software that had been written, as it turned out, by citizens of the former Soviet Union. Other malicious bugs may be lying in wait in the computer systems of governments and companies around the world that employed outsider contractors to work on year 2000 compliance issues. Only time will tell if the *real* Y2K problem turns out to be malicious activity carried out by scurrilous contractors hired to fix the millennium computer bug.

A larger worry is the ever-present danger that a concerted cyber attack could bring down the Internet, turn off electricity, contaminate drinking water and even cause telephones to go dead. A hacker group that goes by the name LOpht told a Senate committee in 1998 that hackers "could very trivially make the Internet unusable for the entire nation." LOpht also testified that given enough resources, a very small group of skilled hackers could wreak havoc on the country, shutting down communications and utilities and even causing instability in financial markets. "In about 20 minutes," one hacker boasted, "any one of us can cause serious disruption to the entire Internet, transfer funds from the Federal Reserve or re-route planes from our home PCs." (Quoted in "Cyber Attack: Is the Nation at Risk?" statement by Senator Fred Thompson before the Senate Governmental Affairs Committee, June 24, 1998.)

Perhaps he could; perhaps he couldn't. But one unnamed U.S. intelligence official has claimed that with $1 billion and 20 capable hackers, he could shut down America. ("Postmodern Terrorism," by Walter Laqueur, *Foreign Affairs*, September/October 1996.) "What he could achieve, a terrorist could too," says terrorism expert Walter Laqueur of the Center for Strategic and International Studies in Washington, D.C.(same) Peter Neumann, a researcher at SRI International of Menlo Park, Calif., told a Senate committee: "Massive coordinated attacks on our infrastructure are possible; however, it may take a Chernobyl-scale event to raise awareness levels adequately, perhaps bringing several of the national infrastructures to their knees simultaneously." (Quoted in "Cyber Attack: Is the Nation at Risk?" statement by Senator Fred Thompson before the Senate Governmental Affairs Committee, June 24, 1998.) To which U.S. Senator Fred Thompson of Tennessee later added: "We cannot wait for an electronic Pearl Harbor or Oklahoma City to recognize there is a problem. At risk are the systems that control national security, air traffic, finances, power, and communications." ("Cyber Attack: Is the Nation at Risk?" statement before the Senate Governmental Affairs Committee, June 24, 1998.)

Thankfully, many governments around the globe are taking the danger of cyberterrorism seriously. In 1998, the Clinton administration formed the National Infrastructure Protection Center—an FBI-led partnership of private-sector companies and federal, state and local agencies—to defend against cyber attacks. A year later, the White House requested nearly $1.5 billion to fund the Critical Infrastructure Applied Research Initiative to protect the nation's computer systems and critical infrastructure from cyberterrorism. "The most critical sectors of our economy—power-generation, telecommunications, banking, transportation and emergency services—are potentially vulnerable to disruptions from computer attack," the White House said in announcing the plan. By fiscal year 2001, the Clinton administration had budgeted more than $2 billion for infrastructure protection.

President Bush redoubled the federal effort to safeguard the nation's infrastructure from cyber weapons following the terrorist assaults on the World Trade Center and the Pentagon. On Oct. 16, 2001, he issued an executive order establishing the President's Critical Infrastructure Protection Board, comprised of 19 cabinet-level officials charged with combating cyberterrorism. "The information technology revolution has changed the way business is transacted, government operates, and national defense is conducted," the executive order stated. "Protection of these systems is essential to the telecommunications, energy, financial services, manufacturing, water, transportation, health care, and emergency services sectors. It is the policy of the United States to protect against disruption of the operation of information systems for critical infrastructure and thereby help to protect the people, economy, essential human and government services, and national security of the United States, and to ensure that any disruptions that occur are infrequent, of minimal duration, and manageable, and cause the least damage possible."

The threat of cyberterrorism also is attracting international attention. In November 2001, the U.S. and 29 other nations signed a treaty establishing new tools and rules for fighting Internet crime. The Convention on Cybercrime, first initiated by the Council of Europe, is designed to streamline laws and harmonize civil and criminal penalties around the world for crimes committed via the Internet. Significantly, the convention was amended in the wake of the Sept. 11 attacks to give the 30 signatory countries common powers to search and intercept the Internet communications of suspected terrorists.

Nonetheless, critical infrastructure cannot be made 100-percent safe from cyber assault. "Although many of the weaknesses in computerized systems can be corrected, it is effectively impossible to eliminate all of them," Dorothy E. Denning, a professor of computer science at Georgetown University in Washington, D.C., told a House panel on terrorism in 2000. Cyberspace could become a valuable terrorist target because attacks get so much publicity. Cyberterrorism, noted Denning, "could be conducted remotely and anonymously, and it would not require the handling of explosives or a suicide mission. It would likely garner extensive media coverage, as journalists and the public alike are fascinated by practically any kind of computer attack. Indeed, cyberterrorism could be immensely appealing precisely because of the tremendous attention given to it by the government and media."

2.08. Thieves and Impostors

Infrastructure isn't the only potential target of cyberterrorists. Individuals, too, may become victims. Noting that "the next generation of terrorists will grow up in a digital world, with ever more powerful and easy-to-use hacking tools at their disposal," one computer expert has theorized that terrorists might, for instance, target robots used in Internet-enabled telesurgery to cause serious harm to patients. An alarm was sounded in late 2000 when a hacker used the Internet to break into the University of Washington Medical Center's computerized database. The hacker downloaded confidential information on thousands of patients—and, in the process, learned a lot more about these people than just their blood types.

"Medical information contains your Social Security number, date of birth and even a physical description," explained Betsy Broder, who tracks identity theft for the Federal Trade Commission. "All of those are keys that people could use to exploit someone's financial identity, as well as their personal identity." *USA Today* reporter Greg Farrell, reporting on the University of Washington incident, added: "The most pernicious use of

**U.S. Poll: Theft of Personal Information
on the Internet, December 2001**

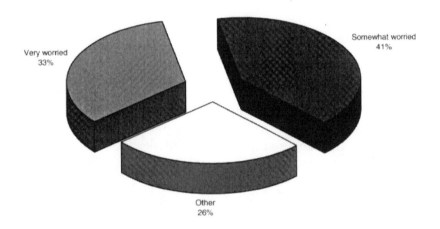

Very worried
33%

Somewhat worried
41%

Other
26%

Source: Information Technology Association of America

medical information involves the elderly or extremely ill. If an
identity thief knows an individual is close to death, he or she
could take out a life insurance policy in the victim's name,
naming themselves or an accomplice as the beneficiary."
("Medical records vulnerable to ID theft," by Greg Farrell, USA
Today, Dec. 12, 2000.)

Unfortunately, the new global war on terrorism could
exacerbate the problem of cybercrime. The multi-nation antiterrorism coalition organized by President Bush following the
horror of Sept. 11 plans to separate the world's terrorists from
their money. Putting the financial squeeze on terrorist organizations, however, could have an unintended consequence: It could
induce terrorists to try and separate individuals and institutions
from *their money*. There already is a vast black market in stolen
credit cards, which cost financial institutions an estimated $1

billion or more a year, and many of the sales of purloined card numbers take place over the Internet. It's only a matter of time before terrorist organizations enter this market in a big way.

While it's all well and good that governments far and wide have frozen terrorist-related bank accounts, shut down businesses serving as terrorist fronts, clamped down on international money- laundering operations and continue to investigate the financial backers of terrorism, don't think for a minute that this defunding effort alone will put terrorists out of business. The dedicated extremists among them won't be stopped merely because their money has been cut off. Instead of abandoning their violent ways for lack of funds, terrorists will seek money elsewhere—and that doesn't mean taking jobs at the local supermarket. They'll go about looking for surreptitious ways to steal money from you and me. As a result, the line between criminality and terrorism will become blurred. Terrorist cells and their parent organizations increasingly will come to depend on common crime as a means of financial support. Two of the most likely methods will be financial fraud and identity theft. Although similar, the two crimes aren't same. In general, financial fraud concerns theft utilizing stolen credit and bank cards, while identify theft occurs when an imposter sets up new bank accounts, takes out loans or applies for credit cards—all in another person's name.

There is precedence for cross-border financial heists and grand-scale credit card theft. In 1994-95, for example, an organized crime group headquartered in St. Petersburg, Russia transferred $10.4 million from Citibank into accounts all over the world. After surveillance and investigation by the FBI's New York field office, all but $400,000 of the funds was recovered. In January 2000, an extortionist in Russia demanded $100,000 from an Internet music retailer after posting online a bunch of credit card numbers stolen from the company's database. In another case, a hacker in San Francisco gained unauthorized access to several California Internet Service Providers and stole 100,000 credit card numbers with a combined credit limit of more than $1 billion. The FBI arrested the man at the San Francisco International Airport when he tried to sell the card numbers to a

Canadian Credit Card Fraud by Type, June 2000 - June 2001

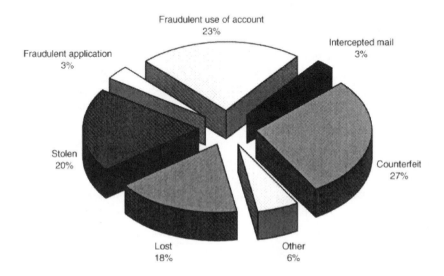

Source: Royal Canadian Mounted Police/Payment Card Partners Committee

cooperating witness for $260,000. Most significantly, investigators probing the finances of the 19 terrorists involved in the Sept. 11 attacks found that part of the $500,000 spent on the operation came from credit card fraud.

The Privacy Rights Clearinghouse estimates that between 500,000 and 700,000 Americans become identity-theft victims every year. The U.S. Federal Trade Commission (FTC) reports that 69 percent of the calls it has received on its fraud hotline have come from identity-theft victims. But don't assume that these were mostly elderly victims, fooled by con artists. The average victim was, in fact, 41 years old.

Identity thieves operate in most ingenious ways. An imposter, for instance, will call a credit card issuer pretending to be someone else and ask that an account's mailing address be changed. He'll then run up charges on that person's account. Because the bills are being sent to the new address, it usually takes time before the victim catches on to the scheme. The FTC says that on average identity theft goes unnoticed for twelve and a half months. An identity thief alternatively might open a new credit card account, using another person's name, date of birth and Social Security number. After the bill goes unpaid, the delinquency is entered into the credit history of the victim, who may remain wholly unaware of the crime until, say, he applies for a loan and is rejected because of bad credit. Imposters have been know even to use another person's name to open bank accounts, take out auto loans and apply for jobs. An identity thief might go so far as to file for bankruptcy *under another person's name.* That way he can avoid paying debts he has incurred in the other person's name or forestall eviction from a home rented, again, using someone else's identity.

However much Osama bin Laden may have inherited (and the numbers vary), foreign terrorists could certainly get their hands on a lot more money by arranging to steal credit cards and personal identities on a grand scale than they ever could from him. Terrorists are already engaged in such schemes to the extent that they regularly use stolen passports and other purloined documents to travel the world. It would, therefore, be a natural extension of their activities if they were to expand into wholesale fraud and identity theft.

To gauge the magnitude of the potential sums involved, consider this warning made to the credit industry by Experian, a credit-rating service: "Most of today's fraud is the work of highly organized and sophisticated international crime organization that operate with little fear of getting caught. . . . Application fraud is a magnet for the criminal mind, involving little risk and big rewards. The 'take' from American businesses is more than $35 billion annually and growing. Far more damaging than delinquent or bankrupt accounts, fraud losses average three times higher than normal charge-offs." ("The Problem of Fraud," Experian, 2001.) If international terrorist organizations could steal just one percent of that amount, they'd have $350 million a year to conduct their dirty work. That's roughly four times as much as the highest estimate of bin Laden's entire inheritance, said to be worth up to $80 million. Moreover, the $35 billion that Experian says is the "take" from credit fraud covers only the United States. So you can see that if terrorists put their minds to it and began ripping off credit cards and identities around the world, the amount of money at their disposal would be enormous.

The U.S. Justice Department under Attorney General John Ashcroft has launched a major crackdown on identity theft, bringing about 100 criminal prosecutions by May 2002 and seeking stiffer penalties for ID theft. It's nevertheless reasonable to assume that the problem of credit card and identity theft will get worse before it gets better. Unless terrorism is expunged completely, it's entirely probable that terrorist organizations worldwide increasingly will tap into these fraudulent schemes to raise money. This means, of course, that each of us must become more vigilant in protecting our money and our very identities.

2.09. Recommended Online Reading

"Al Qaeda Training Manual," U.S. Department of Justice, www.usdoj.gov/ag/trainingmanual.htm.
"America Responds to Terrorism," The White House, www.whitehouse.gov.
"Anthrax as a Biological Weapon: Medical and Public Health Management," Working Group on Civilian Biodefense, Center for Civilian Biodefense Strategies, The Johns Hopkins University, *Journal of the American Medical Association*, May 12, 1999, Vol. 281, No. 18, p.1735, http://jama.ama-assn.org/issues/v281n18/ffull/jst80027.html.
"Anthrax as a Biological Weapon, 2002: Updated Recommendations for Management," Working Group on Civilian Biodefense, Center for Civilian Biodefense Strategies, The Johns Hopkins University, *Journal of the American Medical Association*, May 1, 2002, Vol. 287, No. 17, http://jama.ama-assn.org/issues/v287n17/ffull/jst20007.html.
"Botulinum Toxin as a Biological Weapon: Medical and Public Health Management," Working Group on Civilian Biode-

fense, Center for Civilian Biodefense Strategies, The Johns Hopkins University, *Journal of the American Medical Association*, February 28, 2001, Vol. 285, No. 8, p.1059, http://jama.ama-assn.org/issues/v285n8/ffull/jst00017.html.

"Congressional Material: Intelligence in Congress," Intelligence Resource Program, Federation of American Scientists, www.fas.org/irp/index.html.

"Convention on Cybercrime," Council of Europe, http://conventions.coe.int/.

"Critical Infrastructure Protection in the Information Age," Critical Infrastructure Assurance Office, The White House, www.ciao.gov.

"Cyber Protests Related to the War on Terrorism," National Infrastructure Protection Center, www.nipc.gov.

"Cyberterrorism Hacking and Info Warfare," FindLaw, http://cyber.lp.findlaw.com/criminal/cyber_ter.html.

"Cyber Threat," Overseas Security Advisory Council, www.ds-osac.org.

"Foreign Information Warfare Programs and Capabilities," John M. Deutch, Central Intelligence Agency Archives, www.odci.gov/cia/public_affairs/speeches/archives/1996/dci_testimony_062596.html.

"The Future of Cyberterrorism: Where the Physical and Virtual World Converge," Barry C. Collin, Institute for Security and Intelligence, http://afgen.com/terrorism1.html.

"Hemorrhagic Fever Viruses as Biological Weapons: Medical and Public Health Management," Working Group on Civilian Biodefense, Center for Civilian Biodefense Strategies, The Johns Hopkins University, *Journal of the American Medical Association*, May 8, 2002, Vol. 287, No. 18, *http://jama.amaAssn.org/issues/v287n18/ffull/jst20006.html.*

"Iraq's Weapons of Mass Destruction: The Assessment of the British Government," U.K. Stationary Office, September 2002, www.pm.gov.uk or *www.fco.gov.uk*

"A Nation Online: How Americans Are Expanding Their Use of the Internet," Economics and Statistics Administration, U.S. Department of Commerce, *www.esa.doc.gov/508/esa/nationon-line.htm.*

"The 1971 Smallpox Epidemic in Aralsk, Kazakhstan, and the Soviet Biological Warfare Program," Jonathan B. Tucker and Raymond A. Zilinskas, eds., Center for Nonproliferation Studies, Monterey Institute of International Studies, http://cns.miis.edu/pubs/opapers/op9/index.htm.

"Patterns of Global Terrorism: Background Information on Terrorist Groups," U.S. Department of State, www.state.gov/s/ct/.

"Plague as a Biological Weapon: Medical and Public Health Management." Working Group on Civilian Biodefense, Center for Civilian Biodefense Strategies, The Johns Hopkins University, *Journal of the American Medical Association*, May 3, 2000, Vol. 283, No. 17, p. 2281, http://jama.ama-assn.org/issues/v283n17/ffull/jst90013.html.

"A Report Card on the Department of Energy's Nonproliferation Programs with Russia," Howard Baker and Lloyd Cutler, Secretary of Energy Advisory Board, www.ceip.org/files/events/energyreportcard012401.asp.

"Radiation Emergencies," Centers for Disease Control and Prevention, www.bt.cdc.gov.

"Research on Bioterrorism," National Institute of Allergy and Infectious Diseases, National Institutes of Health, www.niaid.nih.gov.

"Russian WMD as a Terrorist Threat," Jon Wolfsthal, Carnegie Endowment for International Peace, Oct. 8, 2001, www.ceip.org/files/news/sept11home.asp.

"Smallpox as a Biological Weapon: Medical and Public Health Management," Working Group on Civilian Biodefense, Center for Civilian Biodefense Strategies, The Johns Hopkins University, *Journal of the American Medical Association*, Vol. 281, No. 22, p. 2127, http://jama.ama-assn.org/issues/v281n22/ffull/jst90000.html.

"Status Report: Nuclear Weapons, Fissile Material, and Export Controls in the Former Soviet Union," edited by Jon Brook Wolfsthal, et al., Center for Nonproliferation Studies, Monterey Institute of International Studies, http://cns.miis.edu/pubs/print/nsr.htm.

"Tularemia as a Biological Weapon: Medical and Public Health Management," Working Group on Civilian Biodefense, Center for Civilian Biodefense Strategies, The Johns Hopkins University, *Journal of the American Medical Association*, June 6, 2001, Vol. 285, No. 21, p. 2763, http://jama.ama-assn.org/issues/v285n21/ffull/jst10001.html.

"2000 WMD [Weapons of Mass Destruction] Terrorism Chronology: Incidents Involving Sub-National Actors and Chemical, Biological, Radiological, or Nuclear Materials," Center for Nonproliferation Studies, Monterey Institute of International Studies, http://cns.miis.edu/pubs/reports/cbrn2k.htm

"Unclassified Report to Congress on the Acquisition of Technology Relating to Weapons of Mass Destruction and Advanced Conventional Munitions, 1 January Through 30 June 2001" U.S. Central Intelligence Agency, www.cia.gov/cia/publications/bian/bian_jan_2002.htm.

"The War Against Terrorism," Federation of American Scientists, www.fas.org.

"Weapons of Mass Destruction in the Middle East," Center for Nonproliferation Studies, Monterey Institute of International Studies, http://cns.miis.edu/index.htm.

"Worldwide Threat: Converging Dangers in a Post 9/11 World," Director of Central Intelligence

George J. Tenet, U.S. Senate Select Committee on Intelligence testimony, Feb. 6, 2002, html.

Chapter 3

How to Protect Yourself and Your Family

Terrorism survival is largely a matter of personal choice.

At first blush, it may seem ridiculous to say that. How, you might be asking, could the victims of Sept. 11 have averted their fate?

Well, let's first consider the workers who died in the World Trade Center. They would have saved themselves if they'd taken a cue from the 1993 bombing of the Twin Towers. Islamic extremists parked a truck bomb in the trade center's underground garage. The explosion, equivalent to a ton of TNT, left six persons dead and 1,000 injured. The fact that a bombing had occurred didn't consequently make the World Trade Center a safe place to work. Just because the perpetrators were captured and convicted didn't remove the buildings from the terrorists' hit list. The permanent closing of the underground parking garage and the installation of crash barriers around the 16-acre complex didn't mean that terrorists wouldn't find another way to attack the buildings. As we now know, Osama bin Laden planned to strike the World Trade Center again—this time from the air.

Some occupants of the towers recognized the unmitigated danger and left after the 1993 bombing, with companies opting to rent office space in less prominent buildings and workers departing to take jobs elsewhere. Then, too, we'll never know the number of people who thought it best after the 1993 bombing never to apply for employment in the Twin Towers. There are, doubtless, thousands of individuals who were counting their blessings on the morning of Sept. 11.

Next, let's consider the people who died aboard the four planes that were hijacked on Sept. 11. After news had spread of the World Trade Center disaster, passengers on hijacked United Airlines Flight 93 responded by trying to subdue the terrorists.

Although they weren't successful in saving themselves, they most probably did save Washington, D.C.—the hijackers' intended target—from being struck by a second aircraft. If the United Flight 93 passengers, along with those on the other three hijacked jetliners, knew then what we know now, their initial responses to the take-over would have been very different. They would have acted more quickly and forcefully to subdue the hijackers. There's a good chance, in fact, that the terrorists would never have made their way into the cockpits of any of those planes if people knew what was in store.

The problem was that the passengers and crews on three of the fatal flights didn't possess sufficient information about the nature of the terrorist threat to make informed decisions. They underestimated the danger, erred on the side of cautious inaction and turned out to be wrong. In the case of the fourth jet, United Flight 93, which crashed into a field in Somerset County, Pennsylvania, the information about the attacks on the World Trade Center and the Pentagon arrived too late to save them, although the brave actions of several passengers and crew did prevent further death and destruction in the nation's capital.

This analysis isn't meant to be unkind to the dead or unfeeling toward their survivors. It's merely intended to show that the proposition that terrorism survival largely reflects personal choice isn't silly or misinformed. Rather, it's a perfectly valid assertion.

The decisions you make and the actions you take will affect your odds of survival. If you do nothing, you leave things totally to chance. If, however, you develop a personal philosophy of security, take precautionary steps, alter your conduct and lifestyle, institute new procedures and stay informed about the nature of the threat, your chances of falling prey to terrorism will diminish. While the dangers of international and domestic terrorism (or crime, for that matter) can never be eliminated completely, your personal risk of becoming a victim can be lessened. Whether it's reduced in your case is entirely up to you.

3.01. How to Assess Your Risk

The best way to assess your personal risk of becoming a terror victim is to use a proven methodology employed by statisticians, economists and others in organizing data. Information is sorted in five different ways: by location, time, category, hierarchy and the alphabet. Four of these five ways of organizing information can be applied to terrorism risk assessment. The fifth, using the alphabet, isn't applicable (unless terrorists someday decide to pick their targets out of the phone book and start with the letter A).

Here's how to go about the sorting process. And don't worry if you find overlaps; they're to be expected.

- Ask yourself whether you work or live in a geographic location, or frequent places, likely to be targeted by terrorists.

The first location to consider is the country in which you reside. Unless you happen to live on some remote island, you probably can consider yourself a potential target from the start. Then, look at the history of terrorism in your part of the country. In the U.S., for example, the Northeast has experienced twice as many incidents of terror—by both foreign and domestic terrorists—as has the South. Next, look more specifically at the city (or cities) in which you live and work or travel to often. Is it a large, internationally known city? Is the name of your city synonymous with "America," say, or "Canada"? Is your city an important center of government, finance or business? Is it located near an ocean port? Now be even more specific. Is the street on which you live or work internationally recognized? Is your neighborhood normally jammed with people?

The pattern has been for terrorists to go after either high-profile targets or places where lots of people congregate. The World Trade Center, for example, was attacked because it represented Wall Street and American capitalism. London has been a frequent target of Irish republican terrorism because it's the capital of the United Kingdom. And London's Oxford Street has been bombed because it's a main shopping thoroughfare.

Terrorism Activity by U.S. Region, 1980-1999

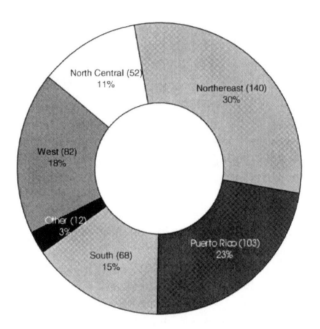

Source: Federal Bureau of Investigation

This isn't to say that terrorists won't change their habits. They might eventually find it easier to conduct attacks in suburban towns or other out-of-the-way locales where police surveillance is comparatively lax and the public is less inclined to believe that terrorists would ever strike there.

- Categorize the places you live, work, and frequent or stay while traveling.

It's easy to confuse category with location, but the two aren't the same (although they may overlap). A category site represents a tempting target no matter where it's situated. Many categories of targets have symbolic importance. Others are merely densely populated. It could even be that an event, such as dedication or award ceremony, is the target.

Take, for example, the Olympic Games. In 1996, a bomb detonated in Centennial Olympic Park in Atlanta, Georgia, where around 70,000 people were celebrating the Summer Olympics. One woman died, and 110 people were wounded. It likely wasn't important that the event was held in Atlanta, for what probably attracted the bomber were both the symbolism of the Olympics and the large crowds associated with the games. At the Munich Olympics in 1972, eight Palestinian Black September terrorists seized 11 Israeli athletes. A rescue attempt by West German authorities left nine hostages and five terrorists dead.

Other categories also are based a high concentration of people, such as shopping malls, big department stores, and entertainment spots (e.g., restaurants, sports stadiums, discos and movie theaters), as well as airports, rail stations, subways and bus terminals. Parades, outdoor concerts and large rallies are other examples. Fame, too, can be a category as in luxury apartments, swanky hotels and national symbols.

Still other categories include: government buildings; headquarters of large, internationally known corporations; sites reflective of key industries (e.g., oil refineries and chemical plants), infrastructure sites (e.g., electric power plants and telephone switching centers) and seaports. Do you, for instance, live near a facility like a nuclear reactor or chemical plant, which, if attacked by terrorists, could pollute its surroundings with radioactive materials or toxic fumes? Do you work near a shipping facility that handles containers from overseas that potentially could contain a hidden nuclear device? Does your job regularly take you to federal courthouses or other government facilities?

Yet another category involves your source of drinking water. Do you have a well, or do you get water from a municipal service? Although the danger from a poisoned reservoir is low (because the contaminant would be too dispersed and would deteriorate rapidly), a pump station could conceivably become a target of chemical or biological terrorism.

- Review your daily schedule and other routines to see if the times are associated with typical terror attacks.

Do you commute to work or school almost invariably at rush hour? Similarly, do you have a transportation-related job, such as a subway police officer, train conductor, bus driver or rail ticket agent, that places you near large numbers of commuters at rush hour? Terrorists frequently do their dirty work at rush hours for the obvious reason that a bomb or other device detonated at such times is likely to kill or injure the largest number of people possible. The nerve-gas attack on the Tokyo subway in 1995 took place at the height of the morning commute. Bombings of commuter trains and subways in France and Britain, too, have been timed for rush hours.

Other time-specific terrorist incidents might take place at large holiday gatherings (e.g., Fourth of July fireworks displays, tree- or menorah-lighting ceremonies and New Year's celebrations), on Election Days or on peak travel days (e.g., immediately before and after Thanksgiving and Christmas). Holiday sales at department stores are another time-related example. Yet other specifically timed attacks could relate to terrorism anniversaries of one sort or another—say, the date Sept. 11 in the years to come, or August 7, the date of the 1998 U.S. embassy bombings in Africa.

And don't forget the time factor when it comes to matters of everyday violent crime. Do you often travel alone at night along deserted streets or wait at empty stations for infrequent trains? There's no sense in protecting yourself from terrorism only to be murdered by a street thug.

- Ask yourself where you stand in the hierarchy of terrorist targets.

The single most important question you have to answer is: Have other people in your line of work been victimized by terrorism because of what they did for a living? The answer says a lot about your odds of being victimized, too.

Well-known business executives especially need to be concerned as a number of assassinations of chief executives have occurred in Europe over the years. Then, there are also the ever-present worries about kidnappings, extortion and ransom demands. But you needn't be a celebrity to be listed as a target. It

Terrorism Risk Scorecard

Fill in points on all applicable lines; multiply where required, and add up score.

1. Location

Live in
Northeast U.S. (9) _____
West or South U.S. (5) _____
North Central U.S. (3) _____
Other U.S. area (2) _____
Other coalition nation (6) _____
Other nation (2) _____

Live in/on
Large city (10) _____
Small city (3) _____
Town/country (1) _____
Downtown/financial district (6) _____
Shopping district (5) _____
Important city street (6) _____
Seaport/military base (10) _____

Work in/on
Large city (10) _____
Small city (3) _____
Town/country (1) _____
Downtown/financial district (6) _____
Shopping district (5) _____
Important city street (6) _____
Transport system (9) _____
Seaport/military base (10) _____
Military stationed overseas (75) _____

2. Category

Live in/on
Luxury building (5) _____

Live in/on (continued)
Tall building (4)
Landmark building (5) _____
Building with underground
   garage (7) _____
Military base (4) _____

Work in/at
Government building (10) _____
Infrastructure site (10) _____
Transport system (10) _____
Landmark site (10) _____
Tall building (7) _____
Office building (4) _____
Large factory (5) _____
Small factory (2) _____
Large store/shopping mall (10) _____
Small store (3) _____
Restaurant/bar/hotel (7) _____
Bank/brokerage (7) _____
Seaport/military base (9) _____

Work for/in
Government (10) _____
Transportation (10) _____
Name company (8) _____
Infrastructure (9) _____
Vital industry (e.g., oil) (8) _____
Retailing/food/hotel (6) _____
Bank/brokerage (6) _____
Police/fire/security (20) _____
Emergency services (15) _____
Military (50) _____
Education/health (2) _____

Subtotal _____   Subtotal _____

Work as
Senior executive (10) _____
Middle manager (5) _____
Office/factory worker (3) _____
Mail Handler (15) _____
Transport worker (15) _____
Banker/retailer (10) _____
Food/hotel service (6) _____
Police/fire/security (20) _____
Emergency services (15) _____
Active duty military (50) _____

Drive to work (1) _____
Use major bridge/tunnel
    (1 per day per week) _____
Train/bus/subway travel
    (1/2 per trip per week) _____

Domestic flights
    (1 per trip per yr) _____
International flights
    (3 per trip per yr) _____
Hotel stays - domestic
    (1 per stay per yr) _____
Hotel stays - abroad
    (2 per stay per yr) _____

Regularly shop in large
    stores/malls (5) _____
Heavy shopper (5) _____
Moderate shopper (2) _____
Dine out often (3) _____
Regular moviegoer (3) _____
Attend sporting events
    (1 per event per yr) _____
Attend other public events
    (1 per event per yr) _____

                Subtotal _____

Visit historic sites
    (1 per visit per yr) _____

3. Time

Work 9-to-5 (7) _____
Work off-hours (3) _____
Large-city commute
    Rush hour (20) _____
    Non-rush hour (10) _____
Other commute
    Rush hour (5) _____
    Non-rush hour (2) _____

4. Hierarchy

Travel abroad (10) _____
Frequent flyer (7) _____
Mass-transit commuter (6) _____
Often in crowds (5) _____
Security-related job (10) _____
Other high-profile job (7) _____

In relation to prior terrorist attacks:
Work in vicinity (10) _____
Live in vicinity (10) _____
Visit attacked cities (5) _____
Work in same job
    category (8) _____

                Subtotal _____

                TOTAL _____

Risk of Terrorist Attack

Low risk: Below 75
Moderate Risk: 75-175
High risk: Above 175

could be that the widely recognized company you work for is the name that the terrorists prize. You just might be your firm's unlucky representative.

Employees also need to give the following questions some thought: Do you handle mail routinely? Do you work in the lobby of your building or near windows exposed to the street? Do you work at a critical infrastructure site, such as a power plant? Do you work for a major industry of national significance, such as oil or computers? One infamous bombing by the FALN, the violent Puerto Rican nationalist group, took place in 1978 at the headquarters of the Mobil Oil Company in midtown Manhattan; the device exploded in the street-level employment office, killing one man and injuring several other passersby on the sidewalk.

Other hierarchical employment profiles include workers at facilities handling large volumes of people (e.g., airports, major subways stations or railheads), sports arenas and large retail stores. Then, too, there are those at greatest risk from hijackings, such as pilots and flight attendants, or assassination, such as law enforcement. Cargo handlers at airports and seaports are similarly at risk from bombs and other concealed devices.

Hierarchical selection also applies to geographic location and travel habits: Do you live or work in a city high on the terrorist list? Do you often visit those cities on business or for pleasure? Do you travel often, particularly by air? Do you go overseas frequently, notably to countries where the incidence of terrorism is high?

- Put two and two together and see how you can change your ways so as to reduce your exposure to terrorism.

In making this personal risk assessment, you want to see how exposed you and members of your family are to possible terrorist assault. The more slots you fit into, the higher the chances are of becoming a victim. If you find a lot of overlap, say in terms of the city you work in and the time of your daily commute, you need to be especially concerned. What you want to do next is try to lessen your risks by changing times, routines, habits, locations, and so on—and perhaps even moving or switching jobs. Instead of being in the wrong place at the wrong time, simply don't be there. A bridge might be destroyed at rush hour by a truck bomb, but you don't have to be on it. A suicide bomber could kill dozens of holiday shoppers at your favorite store, but you don't have to be among them. Subway riders on the way home from work may be overcome by deadly gas, but you don't have to be on that train. You get the idea.

- As a case study, consider the predicament of New Yorkers living above underground public parking garages.

Manhattan is without doubt one of the world's costliest places to live. Housing is not only expensive but also can be difficult to find. Against this backdrop, consider the plight of New Yorkers who reside in buildings with underground public parking facilities. Their predicament presents an ideal example of how to assess personal risk. Manhattan apartments with underground parking are typically among the finest residential buildings in the city. They tend to be modern, well located and filled with amenities, and they often offer spectacular views. But living above a public parking facility in a city that has many times been a target of terrorism presents a serious problem, especially because underground garages have been used before by terror-ists to plant truck and car bombs in expectation of destroying the structures above. Residents of such New York apartment buildings have only three clear options: 1) Move. 2) Get the parking garage closed to the public (and also install security doors and video surveillance to ensure that only tenants can get access, although a terrorist could conceivably rent or buy an apartment in the building and gain entry to the garage that way). 3) Do nothing but cross their fingers. We leave it to you to draw your own conclusion.

3.02. Becoming Security-Minded

Whether we realize it or not, we're all security-minded and safety-conscious to one degree or another. Most of us lock our doors, bypass crime-ridded neighbors, don't unfurl billfolds in public, and stop mail and newspaper deliveries when we're away on vacation. We also look first before we cross streets, drive defensively and know how to dial 911. Terrorism prevention and protection means adding a new set of procedures and routines to the list of precautions we already take. It's easier said than done, however. Think of heart-attack victims. If they're lucky enough to survive their first attack, they almost immediately become health- and fitness-conscious. They start taking care of themselves by going on diets, losing weight and watching what they eat. Some stop smoking and drinking, and many join heath clubs and begin exercising regularly. The intriguing question is: How would these heart-attack victims have fared if they had followed this lifestyle in the first place? Many of them, most probably, would have averted the early onset of heart disease. Our personal health, safety and security, in other words, begin in the mind. Antiterrorism, too, must become a fixture in our thinking before it can become part of our daily lives. The aim is to build concentric rings of defense, which increase your security and safety by making it harder for terrorists to victimize you. Think of the rings as encompassing both the locations at which you spend a good deal of time and the activities you engage in that could bring you in contact with terrorists. Then, it's a matter of instituting security measures and changes in routines that will lessen your chances of falling prey to terror.

- Know the five means of terrorism survival.

In general, there are five ways of surviving terrorism: avoidance, prevention, escape, assistance and time. All of your preplanning, your thinking and your strategies should revolve around those five means of survival. Avoidance means not being in the wrong place at the wrong time. Prevention is the erection of barriers that make it hard for terrorists to get at you and your possessions. Escape is the recognition that you don't have to take your fate at the hands of terrorists lying down. Assistance requires knowledge of how and when to seek outside help. And time is that precious commodity that keeps you alive long enough for help to arrive.

Five Means of Terrorism Survival

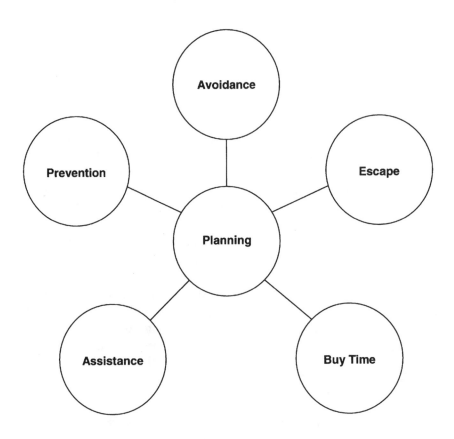

Tip   If you frequently travel around town alone, particularly at night, invest in a personal attack alarm or, at the very least, a loud-sounding whistle.

- Stay away from crowds.

That's the single-best piece of advice that anyone seeking to avoid terrorism can follow. Terrorists most often strike at crowded locations and events, such as shopping malls, large department stores, sporting events, discotheques, historic landmarks, tourist spots, airports, commuter hubs, movie theaters, fashionable restaurants, bars and trendy resorts. By avoiding these events and locations, you avoid the terrorists.

Caution Dark, deserted streets are other places to avoid.

- Think of security as a lock that buys you time.

Security, like a lock, can never be 100-percent perfect. It's not meant to be. The purpose of security measures is to buy time to escape, get assistance or wait for help to arrive. Once you drop the fictitious ideal of perfection, your imagination will be free to conceive of a security plan that's unique to you and your loved ones.

- Adapt your planning to your circumstances.

Everyone's circumstances are different, so adapt security measures to your particular situation. Put each contemplated security step in context. Ask yourself: Why am I doing this? The answers should be, survival. So, again, engineer all of the security measures you take with the goals of avoidance, prevention, escape, getting help or buying time.

- Get informed about potential terrorist targets in your area.

Begin by looking at a map and drawing radii of 10 to 20 miles around your home and workplace. Then, investigate the potential terrorist targets within those zones. Ask your electric utility the location, if any, of the nearest nuclear power plant and repositories of spent nuclear fuel. Ask you local emergency management office, including police and fire departments, if there are other critical infrastructure sites (e.g., dams, chemical plants, telephone switching centers, etc.), hazardous or radioactive waste dumps, or major industrial complexes handling hazardous materials in the vicinity. Ask if any local or state emergency plans are available to the public.

Tip Know how to shut off the gas, water and electricity in the event utility lines are damaged in a major attack (or in an earthquake).

Nuclear Reactors in North America

Source: International Nuclear Safety Center, Argonne National Laboratory

Caution   Note that such hazards as radiation pose particular risks to young children, pregnant women and the elderly.

• Map assorted evacuation routes.

Most local authorities have contingency plans for the evacuation of nearby residents and workers in the event, say, of an emergency at a hazardous chemicals facility or a nuclear power plant. Traffic flow, supposedly, would be directed away from the site. However, at least half the residents and workers within 10 miles of the facility probably would flee, creating chaos on the roads—particularly on highways and other major thoroughfares. So, ask local emergency managers for copies of official evacuation arteries and then review your road maps in search of alternative avenues of evacuation, routes likely to be less traveled in an emergency.

Tip   Weigh the option of staying put in such an emergency. Road rage, traffic jams and outdoor exposure to toxic materials may be pose more danger than simply staying in your home or workplace. Stay tuned to your local television and radio emergency stations for official information and instructions in a crisis.

- Don't return home with a fuel tank that's less than half full.

In an emergency evacuation, because of, say, a chemical or nuclear attack, you may have to travel a long way to reach safety. The roads will, of course, be jammed, and traffic may crawl. The last thing you want to happen is to run out of gas. So, keep your fuel tank at least half fuel.

Gassing up before coming home will serve another, perhaps more important purpose: It will test your antiterrorism vigilance. Everyone has a tendency to let his guard down in times of peace and tranquility. Terrorists count on that. It may indeed be one reason why they often let considerable time to elapse between attacks. Your gas gauge is an easy way to tell whether you've been lulled into a false sense of security—or just gotten lazy.

Caution   Never carry gasoline cans in your vehicles, for the danger of a fiery crash is worse than running out of fuel.

- If you have young children, find out whether their schools have evacuation plans in place.

Local authorities have plans for the transportation of students, as well as children in day care, the hospitalized and nursing home residents, in an emergency. Speak with school officials or teachers about the plans affecting your children and ask what steps you as a parent should take in an emergency evacuation of local schools. Find out, in particular, if students will be taken to a predetermined mass-care facility and whether you should plan on going there, too, in an emergency.

- Be alert to government warnings.

The latest U.S. government terrorism warnings can be found at the Office of Homeland Security (www.whitehouse.gov/

homeland/), which also has links to state offices, the Centers for
Disease Control (www.cdc.gov), the Central Intelligence Agency
(www.cia.gov), Defense Department (www.defenselink.mil),
Federal Bureau of Investigation (www.fbi.gov), FirstGov
(www.firstgov.gov) and the State Department (www.state.gov),
which offers terror-related travel advisories.

Canadian information on terrorism can be found via the
government's central website at http://canada.gc.ca/. International
travel information is at www.voyage.gc.ca. The Royal
Canadian Mounted Police site is www.rcmp-grc.gc.ca. For the
United Kingdom, see the government's clearinghouse site U.K.
Resilience (www.ukresilience.info), plus the Foreign & Commonwealth
Office (www.fco.gov.uk), which offers global travel
information, and the Home Office (www.homeoffice.gov.uk).
The Prime Minister's Office is at www.pm.gov.uk. If you're
concerned about the Asia-Pacific region, you might visit the
Web sites of Australia's embassy in Washington, D.C.
(www.austemb.org), Federal Government (www.fed.gov.au) Department
of Foreign Affairs and Trade (www.dfat.gov.au) and
Prime Minister's Office (www.pm.gov.au).

Tip   Buy an all-hazards alert radio, which automatically
provides not only warnings of weather hazards like hurricanes
and tornadoes but also emergency messages from state and
local authorities.

• Treat official reassurances circumspectly.

In attempting to calm the public's nerves and cover their own
backsides, many government officials at times of crisis have
offered unreliable reassurances about public health and safety.
Look at how the anthrax outbreak was so mishandled at the
start. Why, for instance, were congressional office buildings
closed for decontamination but not the U.S. Postal Service
facilities that sorted and routed the tainted mail to Capitol Hill?
Clearly, some public-health officials were out of their depth.
They offered advice that may have cost people their lives. So,
take any reassurances made by government officials with a grain

of salt. Be circumspect. If you find their reassurances hard to believe, don't believe them.

- Stay informed, but don't rely solely on television for the latest news on terrorism.

Besides television news, make it a habit to read your local newspaper and regularly look at such major newspapers as *Los Angeles Times* (www.latimes.com), *The New York Times* (www.nytimes.com), *USA Today* (www.usatoday.com), *The Wall Street Journal* (www. wsj.com), *Washington Post* (www.washingtonpost.com) and *Washington Times* (www.-washtimes.com). Don't forget the major wire services, Associated Press (http://wire.ap.org/) and Reuters (www.reuters.com), plus the British Broadcasting Corp. (www.bbc.co.uk). (For additional online news sources, both domestic and foreign, see the section at the end of this book on where to get help and information.)

- Don't become complacent, and don't let your guard down.

Immediately following the attacks of Sept. 11 and the discovery of anthrax in the mail, everyone everywhere became anxious about their personal safety and the safety of their loved ones. As time went on and memories faded, people started getting "back to normal" in terms of commuting to work, shopping, traveling and handling mail. It was important that people did this, because it showed that they wouldn't be cowed by terrorism. There's a downside to "normal," however, and that is that people can become complacent. The danger of terrorism is very real, and that's something people all over the world mustn't forget. The defeat of Al Qaeda and the Taliban in Afghanistan hasn't made the threat go away. Sixty or more countries have terror organizations and cells with global reach. This means, of course, that people shouldn't let their guard down, lest they become the next victims.

Concentric Rings of Antiterrorism Defense

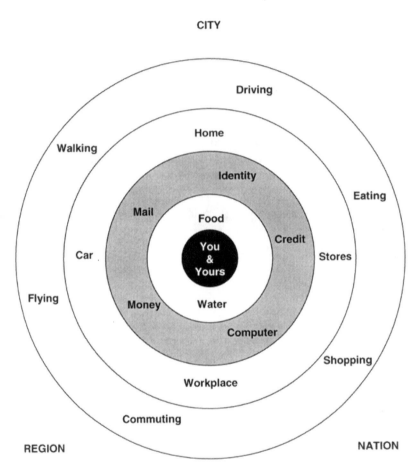

3.03. Basic Safety Precautions

To build, in effect, a perimeter defense around your home, family, money and possessions, think in terms of concentric rings—an outer ring encompassing a smaller ring, then another smaller ring, and so on.

- Safeguarding your home against terrorism and crime begins with locks and lighting.

The same security procedures will help to protect you and your home from both terrorists and criminals. The most important of these are sound locks and good lighting. Install tumblers that can't be picked (at least not easily), and reinforce door frames so doors cannot be forced or pried open. Install peepholes in windowless, exterior doors. On basement and lower-floor windows, be sure the locks are in working order and install jimmy-proof devices. However, if you install window gates or locks, nail the key for each one on the wall near the window—far enough away so a burglar couldn't reach it from the outside but near enough so you could find it quickly in an emergency. Use horizontal "charley bars" on sliding doors. People often use wooden sticks to secure sliding doors; burglars lift those out using coat hangers. Upgrade you garage-door locks. Criminals in passing cars using various electronic devices can open many garage doors. Have an accredited professional fit a tamper-proof lock. Install outdoor lighting connected to motion detectors, and keep hedges and bushes trimmed. Have some lamps hooked up to timers to go on and off when you're away overnight. Consider subscribing to a professional security service that will call the police or fire department in the event of a trespassing or fire emergency. And if you're so inclined, install a video security system of mini-cameras on your property to watch and record all comings and goings.

Tip   Be sure the address of your home is visible from the street. It makes it easier for emergency services to find you, especially at night.

Caution   Never leave spare keys hidden outside the house; instead, add a house key to your ring of car ignition and door keys. Remember, though, when giving a parking attendant your car key, give him only the one to the ignition.

- Be attuned to anything out of the ordinary in your neighborhood.

There's a fine line between being a conscientious neighbor and being nosy. Still, in this day and age, it pays to be aware of your surroundings. Try to develop a rapport with your neighbors so you may jointly work to safeguard the neighborhood. If you hear or spot something unusual, wait to see if anything develops. If you suspect a crime is being committed, inform law enforcement. Your actions could save a life.

Tip   Familiarize yourself with the locations of police and fire stations, hospitals, public telephones, and 24-hour stores and eateries near where you live and work. That knowledge could come in handy in an emergency.

- Install effective smoke and carbon-monoxide alarms.

Make sure you have an adequate number of smoke alarms in your home (at least one on each floor), including ones that can detect any carbon monoxide that might escape from your furnace or garage. Test the smoke detectors routinely, and replace their batteries regularly. It's said that smoke detectors more than double the chance of fire survival.

Tip   To ensure your smoke-alarm batteries are fresh, change them in the spring or fall when you reset your clocks, or on an annual national or religious holiday.

Caution   Smoke alarms only have a useful life of 10 years, after which they should be replaced even if they still appear to work.

- Have fire extinguishers around the house.

Have fire extinguishers handy and known how to use them; your local fire department likely offers training courses. Recognize that there are different types of extinguishers to combat different types of fires. A-type extinguishers are used to fight common combustible fires involving wood, paper and cloth. The B-type is used to extinguish flammable liquids, such as gasoline, grease and oil. And the C-type combats electrical fires in, say, heaters, computers, toasters and other household appliances. You can buy these different types in various combinations, such as BC or ABC fire extinguishers.

Tip   Consider buying collapsible ladders for upper-floor escapes, especially from bedrooms.

Caution   Fire extinguishers require regular inspections to ensure they still function properly.

- If you live or work in a high-rise building, practice your means of escape.

Don't just know where the emergency exits are in your building, walk to them every once in a while until it becomes second nature. That way, you won't waste precious time in an emergency. You'll know exactly what to do and where to head. Your expertise could, in fact, prove invaluable to your co-workers and family in the event of an explosion or other emergency.

Tip   Should you need to crawl to an exit, make some mental notes beforehand. Develop maps of your workplace and home in your mind, using furniture, equipment, doors and hallways as landmarks to help guide your way.

- Assemble an emergency-supplies kit.

Assemble a kit of emergency supplies and store it near your vehicles in case of a mass evacuation. Your kit should include the following: water (three gallons per person), non-perishable food (enough for three days), warm clothing, sturdy footwear, blankets (or sleeping bags), first-aid kit, flares, flashlights, battery-powered radio, cell phone, extra batteries, sanitation supplies (e.g., toilet paper) repair tools, shovel, ax, broom, rope, wire, disposable plastic bags, waterproof tarp (or tent), waterproof matches and cooking source (e.g., camp stove or Sterno). Add pet food if you have animals. Include litter if you have cats. Bring an extra set of car keys, too. You don't want to get locked out of your car miles from home. Pack a can opener, paper towels, premoistened towelettes, insect pray, sun block, water purification tablets, and disposal plates, cups and utensils. Also, carry credit and debit cards with you. You'll need road maps and a compass, too.

Tip   Be sure spare tires are in proper working condition.

Caution   Stored water and food should be changed every three to six months. Don't store plastic containers on concrete floors, because chemicals can leach through and spoil the contents.

- Exercise caution when drinking from streams, rivers, lakes and springs.

Many natural sources of water in the countryside are contaminated with diarrhea-producing germs, notably *Giardia* and *Cryptosporidium*. Although they aren't usually life-threatening, the illnesses that these germs produce aren't very pleasant and ought to be avoided. Moreover, experts caution, the diseases can be spread person to person via cysts that shed from the body or infected eating utensils. It's important, therefore, to wash your hands regularly when living outdoors, and wash all plates and utensils only with decontaminated water. Any water taken from streams, rivers, lakes and springs and intended for consumption should be boiled for at least one minute. Portable water filtration systems also are available at most camping stores. Iodine-based water treatment tablets also are available; however, although they work against *Giardia*, they aren't effective against *Cryptosporidium*.

- Have a properly outfitted first-aid kit.

Both the American College of Emergency Physicians (www.acep.org) and the American Red Cross (www. redcross.org) have compiled lists of items they believe should be in every first-aid kit. The kit should be kept together in one place, and every mature member of the household should know where it is and how to use each item in it. To carry the kit around, a small tote bag is recommended. Take the same precautions with your first-aid kit that you would with any medicine. Store it out of the reach of children, and only use products with child-safety caps. The items below will provide you with the necessary tools to handle many medical emergencies. All of the items are available at local pharmacies.

Recommended First-Aid Kit Contents:

- Acetaminophen, Ibuprofen, and aspirin tablets for headaches, pain, fever, and simple sprains or strains. (Aspirin should not be used for relief of flu symptoms or given to children.)
- Ipecac syrup and activated charcoal for treatment after ingestion of certain poisons. Use only on advice of a poison control center or the emergency department.
- Elastic wraps for wrapping wrist, ankle, knee, and elbow injuries.
- Triangular bandages for wrapping injuries and making an arm sling.
- Scissors with rounded tips.
- Adhesive tape and 2" gauze for dressing wounds.
- Disposable, instant ice bags for icing injuries and treating high fevers.
- Bandages of assorted sizes for covering minor cuts and scrapes.
- Antibiotic ointment for minor burns, cuts, and scrapes.
- Gauze in rolls and in 2" and 4" pads for dressing wounds
- Bandage closures: 1/4" and 1" for taping cut edges together.
- Tweezers to remove small splinters and ticks.
- Safety pins to fasten bandages.
- Tongue depressors to inspect the throat and mouth.
- Thermometer to take temperatures.
- Rubber gloves to protect yourself and reduce the risk of infection when treating open wounds.
- First-aid manual.
- Flashlight and spare batteries.
- List of emergency telephone numbers.

Other items might include eye drops, antibiotic ointments, diarrhea medication, cough medicine, antihistamines, ear and nose drops, cotton safety swabs, insect repellant, skin disinfectant, sun block, hydrogen peroxide and premoistened towelettes. A spray bottle containing a solution of 10 percent laundry bleach and 90 percent water can be used to disinfect objects.

Tip   For help in a case of poisoning, call the American Association of Poison Control Centers (www.aapcc.org) at 800-222-1222. If the victim has collapsed or isn't breathing, dial 911.

Caution   If a poison is ingested, seek the advice of a poison-control center, doctor or emergency room before taking any medications or inducing vomiting. A caustic chemical, for example, could destroy additional sensitive tissue if regurgitated.

- Don't forget to pack any prescribed medications and extra eyewear.

In an evacuation, remember to bring your prescription medications (and that includes any medications your pets may be taking), along with spare eyeglasses or contact lens and their associated cleansing materials. Having copies of drug prescriptions also may come in handy.

- Check out online first-aid advice regarding terrorist-type attacks.

First-aid manuals can be found at most bookstores, but free first-aid information on the Internet is hard to come by. One of the more interesting cost-free manuals available online is the U.S. Army's *First Aid for Soldiers* at www.vnh.org/FirstAidForSoldiers/fm2111.html. The University of Iowa and the U.S. Navy Bureau of Medicine and Surgery also have a Virtual Naval Hospital™ online (www.vnh.org) with invaluable information for patients and health providers on what to do in the event of a biological, chemical or nuclear attack.

Tip   Contact your local Red Cross chapter (www.redcross.org) to obtain a first-aid manual or get training in first aid and cardiopulmonary resuscitation (CPR).

• Know how to prevent or control shock.

Severely injured persons often go into shock. Knowing hot to prevent or control this can be helpful. However, a few important words of caution are in order first. If you suspect the victim has a broken neck or back, don't move him at all. Similarly, don't move him if he has head or abdominal wounds or a broken leg. Simply cover him with a blanket or piece of clothing to help keep him warm. Otherwise, lay the person on his back, unless a sitting position makes his breathing easier. Elevate his feet so they're higher than his heart; this increases blood flow to the brain and other vital organs. Prop up his feet with an object that would easily fall over. Loosen any binding clothing around his neck and waist. Cover him with something to keep him warm. Speak with the victim in a calm and reassuring manner to lessen his anxiety level and blood pressure. Tell him he'll be all right, that he's being cared for and that help is on the way.

Caution   It's recommended that if a chemical, biological or radiological device has been used, that you not touch victims so as to avoid becoming contaminated yourself.

• Be prepared to isolate yourself and your family in the event of a communicable-disease outbreak.

In the event of a terrorist-inspired outbreak of smallpox or other communicable disease, the best step to take to avoid exposure would be to limit contact with others until the authorities give an "all-clear." Businesses should shut down, and travel of any kind should be eschewed. To be on the safe side, it would be smart to take a few minutes to make a list of all the persons with whom you had been in immediate, personal contact within the previous week or so. If it turns out that you have contracted smallpox, say, that list of names could prove invaluable in saving lives.

• Have the necessary supplies to create a safe-haven room.

Inhalation of deadly or incapacitating germs, chemicals or radiological agents is the greatest danger to civilians in the even

Terrorism in the United States,
Activity by Target, 1980-1999

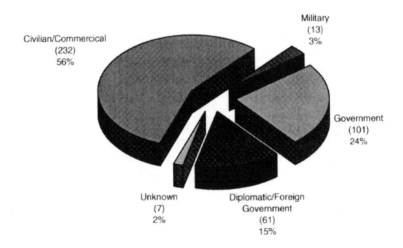

Civilian/Commercical
(232)
56%

Military
(13)
3%

Government
(101)
24%

Unknown
(7)
2%

Diplomatic/Foreign
Government
(61)
15%

Source: Federal Bureau of Investigation

of a terrorist attack with a weapon of mass destruction. Be able, therefore, to turn a room in your house, or even an entire small apartment, into a safe haven. Select a large, inner room on an upper floor, preferably with access to a bathroom and a telephone. Don't pick a room that has an air conditioner built into the wall or window. Store plastic/duct tape and sheets of heavy-duty plastic (6 mil at least) in or near the room so you can tightly seal all doors and windows in an emergency. Also have cloth and cotton wool to plug any large gaps, including keyholes. If an emergency arises, bring your survival kit of food, water, first-aid kit, portable radio, flashlights and other necessities into the safe-haven room and seal yourself off until the all-clear is given. The Oak Ridge National Laboratory has conducted several studies of the efficacy of safe rooms, and its findings are worth noting. The lab says that duct tape and plastic sheeting can "effectively reduce infiltration" of airborne agents. "Taping is essential to reduce air infiltration. Plastic sheeting is not a critical element for reducing air infiltration, but it makes sealing off large windows easier. Shrink-wrap window insulation kits [normally used to keep out wintertime drafts] may offer a good alternative for plastic sheeting," it explains. "The critical part of the problem is sealing off all routes of air infiltration. The weakest link is the edges of the seals and not the materials used. Inadequate taping and sealing will reduce the effectiveness of expedient sheltering. Overall, the choice of the room, the baseline tightness of the room, and human variability [i.e., care and physical ability] in implementing expedient protection will be the major factors in determining the effectiveness of expedient shelter. The latter factor raises issues for the elderly, mobility impaired or handicapped persons, who may lack the physical ability or resources to tape and seal." (See "Will Duct Tape and Plastic Really Work? Issues Related To Expedient Shelter-In-Place" at http://emc.ornl.gov/emc/PublicationsMenu.html.) In another study (available on the same Web page), the lab cautions against using wet towels as a vapor barrier at the bottom of a door, because the "wetted towel provides no vapor filtration and its effectiveness in infiltration reduction is unknown."

Tip   If there's a danger of a nuclear explosion, go to the basement of your house or building to avoid the blast, thermal radiation and radioactive fallout.

Caution   Don't pick a room that faces any nearby city that might be the site of an attack with a weapon of mass destruction, and don't pick a room that faces into the prevailing winds in your area.

- Don't be caught short in a run on food, water and other staples.

In the event of the poisoning of a water system or food supplies—or following a terrorist attack with chemical, biological or radiation weapons, or a breakdown in critical infrastructure—there doubtlessly would be runs on bottled water, packaged food and other staples. To avoid being caught short, stockpile a prudent supply of essentials. There's no need to warehouse a year's worth of supplies. In time, the authorities will most certainly arrive with potable water and emergency food rations. Still, you ought to stow away enough food and water to carry you and your family for a week at least. You might even want to squirrel away a little extra to hand out to a needy relative or neighbor. Be sure to have flashlights, candles, matches, a portable radio and extra batteries in case electricity is cut off. In addition, you should have an alternative means of heating food or boiling water, such as a camp stove, barbecue or canned cooking fuel (e.g., Sterno). Be sure, too, that you have enough fuel to last you a week. If the water or electrical systems are shut off, personal hygiene could become a problem, so store extra water so you can bathe, brush your teeth and flush toilets. Disposable cups, plates and utensils also could prove useful. And don't forget other staples that could run short in an emergency, such as toilet paper and hand soap. Periodically check the expiration dates on such perishables as batteries and bottled water. But don't just toss your old water away; expired water can be used for bathing or in toilets.

Tip　　Again, make sure you always keep adequate supplies of any prescription drugs (enough to last one to two weeks).

Caution　　Store-bought bottled water isn't meant to be kept for long periods; the plastic containers tend to fail or leak after about six months. It's thus best to purchase special containers intended for long-term storage or five-gallon water bottles from a private distributor. Never store plastic water bottles directly on top of a concrete floor, because the concrete will leech chemicals into the bottled water and degrade the plastic containers.

- Squirrel away a modest amount of cash in case ATMs go down.

Power outages caused by terrorist attacks on the nation's infrastructure or cyberterrorism against banking institutions could make cash difficult to come by. Automated teller machines

(ATMs) likely would be out of service. Credit and debit cards mightn't work at your local stores, and electric-powered cash registers could be frozen shut. Cash would be at a premium until the authorities sorted affairs out. So hide away a few dollars for an emergency.

3.04. Educating Children

Terrorism survival requires advanced planning. For a family, this means developing a game plan—one that addresses not only terrorism but also other common dangers, including house fires, crime and neighborhood disasters.

- Teach your children to dial 911.

There have been instances, much publicized in the news media, where a young child has dialed 911 and saved a life. Less publicized are the times when a child has called 911 and the police end up scolding the parents for letting the youngster play with the phone. What's a parent to do? We suggest you try role-playing. Have adults and children interchangeably act the parts of victim and rescuer, using an unplugged phone to dial 911. And add a third person to serve as the 911 operator. If you have enough people, you could add as many emergency personnel as you wish. The whole purpose of the exercise is to teach children not just how to use the telephone in an emergency, but also how to tell when there is an emergency and not to be afraid to seek help. In this way, the seriousness of the call will come across, and the chances are low that your child will ever call 911 on a lark.

Tip Make sure younger children know their last name and home address.

- Post a list of emergency names and numbers.

In a convenient spot, low enough for any member of your household to read, tack up a list of important names and phone numbers. These might be relatives, friends or next-door neighbors who could be contacted in an emergency. Also include your work numbers. When traveling, add the phone numbers at which you can be reached.

Caution   Children should never let an unfamiliar caller at the door or on the phone know they are home alone, so teach them to say something like: "Mom can't come to the phone (or door) right now." Remind children never to speak with strangers on the street, accept gifts from strangers, or go near a vehicle if the driver or passenger asks them a question.

• Practice home evacuation drills with your children.

Seconds can make the difference between life and death in a fire or explosion, so it's wise to have a home evacuation plan laid out in advance. With your children, go over all the different ways they could safely escape in an emergency. Make sure that each room has at least two ways out. Ensure that all windows, screens and doors open properly and that no obstructions, such as iron gates or heavy pieces of furniture, would block a speedy exit. Tell you children to stay low to the ground to avoid the toxic smoke and gases that collect near the ceiling in a fire. Have them cover the mouths and noses with handkerchiefs or cloth.

Tip   To help young children understand how to escape in an emergency, draw a floor plan of you home and have your kids trace various exit routes. Quiz your children regularly on fire safety and disaster planning.

• Educate your kids in fire detection.

Teach your children how to tell if fire is on the other side of a closed door by using the palm of their hand to feel for heat on the door, the doorknob and the crack around the door. Conduct fire drills at least twice a year—holding one in the daytime and the other at night—and explain the symptoms of carbon-monoxide poisoning (e.g., light-headedness, headaches, dizziness, nausea, vomiting and fainting).

Tip   Give each of your children a flashlight and a bell or whistle to keep at their bedside for use in an emergency.

- Instruct children never to enter or re-enter a burning building.

Make sure your children understand that they are never to enter or go back into a burning building—not to retrieve a pet, a toy or even you. Explain to them that even if you were trapped inside, you'd want them to remain safely outside, and tell them not to worry, because firefighters will rescue you.

- Practice rolling on the floor or ground to put out flames.

This is one exercise kids love. Teach them to drop to the ground and roll if their clothes are on fire. Explain to them that running only fans the flames.

Tip   For more information on escape planning and fire education for kids go to the Federal Emergency Management Agency website at www.fema.gov and the U.S. Fire Administration's website at www.usfa.fema.gov.

- Pick places to gather in an emergency, and ask people to serve as phone contacts.

One of life's worst experiences is not knowing if a loved one is okay following a calamity. To preclude this, pick two places— one near your home and another outside your neighborhood— to meet in an emergency. Also, ask a few friends and relatives to serve as emergency contacts if the members of your family become separated. Be sure you and your children carry those numbers with you. And give your older children mobile phones.

Tip   Choose at least one telephone contact from out of state in case the emergency disrupts local phone service or necessitates a large-scale evacuation.

- Don't neglect family pets in your emergency planning.

Plan to take your pets in an emergency evacuation. Know, though, that for health and space reasons, some emergency shelters may not accept animals. So have pet carriers that are large enough for your pets to stand up in and turn around. Train your pets to become accustomed to the carriers. If you must leave your pets behind, put them in safe locations, such as bathrooms, with access to flowing water. Don't put them in rooms where hazardous chemicals are stored. Leave them with plenty of dry food that won't spoil, and leave the water running in a sink or bathtub. (For more information on pet care in emergencies, see the recommended online readings listed at the end of this chapter.)

Tip   Contact your veterinarian to see if he plans to accept animals in an emergency.

Caution   Experts recommend separating dogs and cats, because the anxiety of emergency could cause them to act hostilely. Also, separate small pets from large ones.

- In a local emergency, consider helping a disabled or elderly neighbor.

If have to evacuate the neighborhood, besides rounding up the kids, dogs and cats, you might consider helping a disabled or elderly neighbor. Talk it over with your family first and then contact the person. It'll do your heart good. At the very least, inform any neighbor who is hearing- or sight-impaired of the local emergency. Inform the police or fire department of the person's location. Do the same for any neighbor who is mentally handicapped, paralyzed or unable to walk without assistance.

3.05. Computer and Internet Security

Don't think that cyberterrorism can't affect you. If your computer is hocked up to the Internet or if you download material from floppy disks or CDs and you don't take the proper precautions, you could someday find your system plagued by viruses or your stored information deleted or mangled.

U.S. Poll: Internet and Computer Security, December 2001

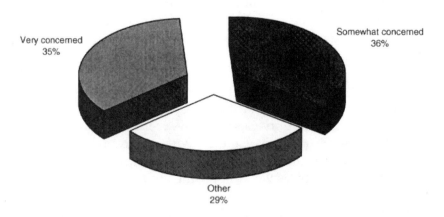

Very concerned
35%

Somewhat concerned
36%

Other
29%

Source: Information Technology Association of America

- Protect your personal computers and handheld devices with antivirus software and firewalls.

As advanced economies like the United States become increasingly information-dependent, cyberterrorism will become an ever-increasing danger. In early January 2002, experts discovered an especially vicious computer worm called "JS.Gigger.A@mm." Spread via e-mail, it tries to delete all your files and make it impossible for you to restart your computer. This is just one example of a growing Internet security problem. Malicious viruses, worms and Trojan horses are being sent around the world via infected e-mail, contaminated websites and pinging programs at such a fast rate that antivirus software providers now sometimes update their lists of known viruses on a daily (as opposed to weekly) basis. Some infected e-mail doesn't even have to be opened to activate; the "W32.Badtrans.B@mm" worm is an example of this. Hackers also have their computers programmed to scan all online

Internet users, looking for a vulnerable computer they can enter and exploit. "Backdoor.Palukka" is one. This backdoor Trojan horse gives a hacker access to your computer. Terrorists could employ Trojan horses, embedded in your computer and thousands of others, to execute denial-of-service attacks on any website in the world. They also could delete or retrieve your files, or disable your computer. It's imperative, therefore, that you install reputable antivirus software on all your computer equipment and erect firewalls as well. Then, you must discipline yourself to keep these updated continuously.

Tip   Good sources for the latest news on new viruses, worms, Trojan horses and hackers include: Carnegie Mellon University's CERT Coordination Center (www.cert.org), the National Infrastructure Protection Center (www.nipc.gov), Symantec Corp. (www.symantec.com) and the U.S. Department of Justice's Cybercrime website (www.cybercrime.gov).

- Make it a habit to update you computer software regularly.

Software manufacturers like Microsoft (www.microsoft.com) have automated facilities on their websites through which you can download updates, patches and fixes to correct security weaknesses in your computer's operating system and programs. It's amazing how often these security problems crop up. Unless you keep your software continually updated, sooner or later a malicious program will wreak havoc with your computer. Contact your computer's manufacture for assistance.

- Be protective of your online names and passwords, and don't pick ones that are easy to crack.

Too often people use the same name and password to access a variety of Internet sites. These sites might range from the registration-required site of *The New York Times* to an online bank or brokerage. The danger, of course, is that if someone gets your name and password, they could possibly trade on your accounts or even steal your money. Make it a point to use

Most Commonly Used Internet and PC Passwords in Britain, 2002

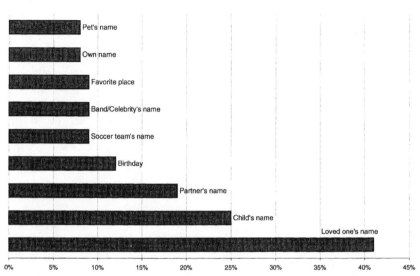

Source: Egg plc

different names and passwords for different sites. Don't use anything as simple as "bank1" or "IRA02," or nicknames like "Abby" or "Bill" that a hacker could deduce from your given name. Also, never use your birthday, your own name or Social Security number. An identity thief could use that information to establish fraudulent accounts or take out loans in your name. Interrupt any string of letters, as in a name, by interspersing a few numbers. Try using the first letters of a phrase or saying, such as TFTATFT or T42N24T as in "Tea for two and two for tea."

Tip   Mine the names of non-immediate family members (e.g., aunts, uncles, cousins, nieces, nephews, grandparents, etc.) or family friends for possible names and passwords that are easy for you to remember but hard for hackers to figure out.

• Have two different Internet Service Providers.

A terrorist attack on critical infrastructure could cause telephones to go dead. E-mail thus could become a vital communications link, as happened in New York City on Sept. 11 when the phone lines were jammed. However, if your home computer accesses the Internet via a telephone hookup, you'll be out of luck. Alternatively, there's no certainty that other Internet Service Providers (ISPs) won't be affected, too. To be on the safe side, subscribe to two different ISPs, if possible, and make sure that no more than one of them is linked via your home telephone.

3.06. The Safest Way to Handle Mail

Amazingly, long after the anthrax letter attacks of 2001, government authorities still couldn't agree on exactly how people should handle their mail. We've reviewed a number of sources of information, including the U.S. Postal Service (www.usps.com), the Centers for Disease Control (www.bt.cdc.gov), the Los Angeles County Department of Health Services (http://labt.org) and the British Government Co-ordination Centre (www.co-ordination.gov.uk). The recommendations below incorporate all of the suggestions made by these organizations and are augmented by our own understanding of the bioweapons threat. These suggested procedures offer the most thorough safeguards formulated to date. Let's go through the process step by step.

• Know how poisoned mail can harm you.

Biological agents (as discussed in the previous chapter on the nature of the threat) have to get into or onto your body somehow in order to do you harm. They usually do this in three ways: 1) Inhalation: You breathe in an airborne biological agent, and it enters your lungs. 2) Ingestion: You swallow the agent, and it gets into your digestive system. 3) Contact: You touch the agent or it comes in contact with your skin. There is another, less frequent way, and that's through an open wound or cut that permits the agent to enter the bloodstream. So to reduce the risk of biologically tainted mail infecting you, you want to avoid inhaling or ingesting the agent, or letting it linger on your skin or enter through broken skin. The following steps aim to accomplish that.

Caution   Don't eat, drink or smoke around mail.

- Begin by creating a regimented routine for handling your mail and stick to it.

Gone are the days when you can toss mail around willy-nilly. Treat your mail like you treat fresh meat, fish or poultry after bringing it home. Normally, you don't put it down just anywhere. No, you put it in the refrigerator until you're ready to cook it. Well, think of your mail in the same. Always put it in the same place until you're ready to open it. Select an isolated spot in your home (or office) that's away from food. Use the same location all the time. When you do sit down to open your mail, do it conscientiously. Always use a letter opener. Don't just tear your mail open with your fingers, because that could disturb any malicious contents, contaminate your skin and even cause a paper cut. Never ever blow into an envelope to open it. Don't shake letters or parcels. Don't pour out any powdery contents. Try to open your mail with a minimum amount of movement and disturbance to its contents. Keep your hands away from your nose, eyes and mouth while handling mail. (If you handle mail for a living or work near a mailroom or mailing machinery, see the chapter on business and building protection for more detailed recommendations to safeguard your health.)

Tip   In a multi-person household, it might be wise to designate one person as the primary mail opener. That's not to say that every member of your household shouldn't know the proper way of opening mail. But by designating a person to handle the chore, your family's anxiety level will be lowered and the chances of a mishap lessened.

Caution   Throw away your electric letter opener. Running letters through the machine increases the chances that a tainted letter's contents could become airborne.

- Make it a standard practice to wash with antibacterial soap immediately after touching mail.

Thoroughly washing your hands and wrists for at least 15 seconds with antibacterial soap can rid you of expose to such germs as anthrax. Make this a habit. Remember that terrorists use surprise as a means of spreading fear. When the next lethal-letter campaign begins, you won't be given advance warning.

`Caution`   Avoid hand contact with others until you wash up.

- Promptly discard all empty envelopes and parcels, and decontaminate the area.

Biological cross-contamination through the mails remains an ever-present danger—and one that foreign terrorists may decide to exploit in the future. All envelopes and emptied parcels thus should be discarded immediately after opening. Don't let the contents come in contact with the outside of envelopes or packaging after opening. Place all mail contents in a special, uncontaminated spot. Discard envelopes after opening by placing them in disposable plastic bags other than ones used for normal trash. Before reading your mail, decontaminate the surface area by moistening a paper towel with an antibacterial disinfectant and wiping the tabletop and any trays used to hold the mail. Don't spray the disinfectant onto the surfaces, because that could cause deadly microbes to fly into the air. Discard the used towels in the plastic bag, and seal it. When closing an envelope-filled bag, keep the opening away from your face, trying to avoid inhaling any emitted dust or getting any microscopic debris in your eyes.

`Tip`   Disinfect your letter opener and anything else you may have touched in the letter-opening process, such as a lamp or telephone.

`Caution`   If you have cuts on your hands or broken cuticles, wear latex or other protective gloves when handling mail or parcels, as biological agents can enter the bloodstream through broken skin.

• Wear protective gear if it gives you peace of mind.

There are no hard and fast rules about wearing protective gloves, masks and eyewear while opening mail. It would be safer if you did, but taking sensible precautions in determining whether a piece of mail is suspicious and following the instructions provided above should be sufficient, unless some new, major outbreak of a mail-borne illness occurs. Still, if it brings peace of mind, outfit yourself at a local medical supply store with disposal gloves, masks and eye protection. Some officials have pooh-poohed the wearing of masks, etc. for what appears to be political rather than health reasons. Treat whatever government authorities say on this matter with circumspection. Erring on the side of caution has never killed anyone. Anthrax-tainted letters have.

3.07. Detecting Lethal Letters and Parcels

International terrorist organizations haven't shown much interest in sending bombs through the mail (as of yet, that is), but domestic terrorists in the U.S. have. Today, there are around 200 known groups in the U.S. actively seeking forcible political change. The Los Angeles Police Department reports that its Bomb Squad responds to about 900 bomb-related calls a year, of which 35% actually involve explosive materials, including dangerous fireworks. Moreover, according to federal authorities, most U.S. bombers deliver the devices themselves.

"The probability of finding a bomb that looks like the stereotypical bomb is almost nonexistent," cautions the U.S. Bureau of Alcohol, Tobacco and Firearms. "Most bombs are homemade and are limited in their design only by the imagination of, and resources available to, the bomber." ("Bomb Threats and Physical Security Planning," Bureau of Alcohol, Tobacco and Firearms, U.S. Department of the Treasury, July 1987.) So, always be on guard.

Domestic vs. International Terrorism
in the U.S., 1980-1999

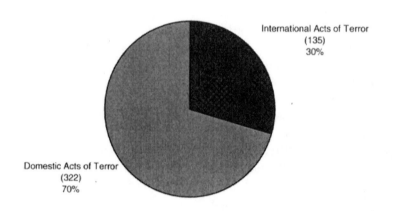

International Acts of Terror
(135)
30%

Domestic Acts of Terror
(322)
70%

Source: Federal Bureau of Investigation

- Carefully inspect your mail before opening, and know the telltale signs of suspicious letters and parcels.

Begin by scrutinizing your mail for any letters or parcels sent by an unfamiliar party. Take a careful look at items that seem suspect, paying close attention to postage, postmarks, labeling and appearance, including size, shape and weight. The signs below cover mail that could contain a biological agent, a toxic chemical or a bomb.

Postage: Look for excessive postage, no postage or non-cancelled postage.

Postmark: Crosscheck all labels against the stamped postmarks to see if they match. Be suspect of unexpected mail from a foreign country.

Labeling: Be wary of handwritten or poorly typed labels from unknown sources, as well as any mail addressed using purposely distorted handwriting or cut-and-paste lettering. Be cautious of mail that has no return address or that clearly has a fictitious return address. See if your name is misspelled, your job title is incorrect or your address is wrong. Be careful of mail addressed to you only by your job title and not your name, or mail addressed to someone no longer with your company. Finally, be suspect of any mail with odd restrictions or special handling instructions (e.g., "For Your Eyes Only," "RUSH," "Don't Delay," "Handle With Care," etc.) or a threatening message scrawled on it.

Appearance: Look for any crystals or powder on the surface, discoloration of the wrapping or envelope, oily spots or stains. If an item has an unusual odor, stay away from it. Visually inspect suspect items for protruding wires, aluminum foil, soft spots or ticking sounds. Get a general impression of a parcel by determining whether it has been sloppily wrapped, tied with an excessive amount of string or heavily taped. Look for packages that are lopsided, bulging, uneven or lumpy, oddly rigid or irregularly shaped.

Feel: Lift a suspect parcel to determine if it's excessively heavy for its size or lopsided with most of the weight on one side. This could indicate a bomb. Feel the item for any contents that may have settled to the bottom or corners. Powdery substances can often be felt through an envelope or package. Be careful, however, not to flex or bend a suspicious piece of mail.

Tip   Letter bombs or other lethal items needn't arrive via the postal system or even a private courier service. Often they're simply left in a mailbox or on a doorstep by the bomber.

Caution   Never shake a suspect piece of mail. If it's a bomb, it could explode. If it contains a hazardous agent, shaking could spread the contents into the air. And never stick your nose into a suspicious package or envelope to sniff its contents.

- Follow proper procedures if you encounter a suspicious letter or parcel.

If you're at home and discover suspicious mail, put the item down without shaking it or emptying its contents. Don't carry

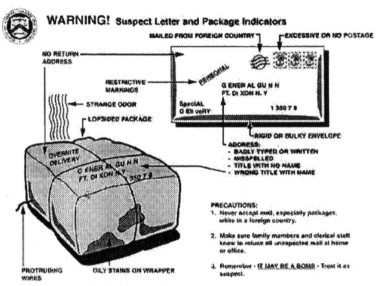

Source: Bureau of Alcohol, Tobacco and Firearms

the package or envelope to show to others or allow others to touch it. Promptly leave the room, closing doors behind you. Turn off all radios and cell phones in the vicinity, because they could trigger a bomb, and shut off the air-ventilation system. Vacate the premises, and call the police from a landline phone. Avoid touching anyone until you wash with soap and water if you suspect a biological agent.

If you're at work and you come across a suspicious piece of mail, put the envelope or package in a plastic bag or other container to prevent leakage of its contents. If a bag or container isn't available, cover the suspect item with anything that's at hand (e.g., clothing, newspaper, a trashcan, etc.). Leave the room, closing the door behind you, and tell workers in the area to vacate the building. Turn off radios and cellular phones. Call building security or the police using a landline phone. Request that the building's air-conditioning unit be switched off, and close any open windows in adjacent rooms. Seal off the area around the suspect mail, and keep others from entering until help arrives.

If you suspect a biological device, wash with soap and water, and get medical attention as soon as possible. If help takes long to arrive, disinfect yourself by washing your hands and arms with a mixture of one part household bleach to ten parts water, as this may reduce the possibility of absorbing an agent through your skin, but be very careful not get the solution in your eyes.

After washing up, make a list of all the people who were in the room or area when you spotted the suspect letter or package. Provide the list to law enforcement, public-health officials and your employer.

Caution   Never bring suspicious mail to a police station, fire department, post office or doctor's office. Leave it where it is, and let the experts handle it.

- Don't be deceived by a package's size.

Letter bombs can range from the size of a cigarette pack to a large parcel. The contents of letter bombs often are stiff or springy. Never bend a suspect item of mail because that could set a bomb off. Timers may or may not be used to detonate the device. Most often, the action of opening the parcel triggers the bomb. Again, listen for any ticking sounds and inspect for any exposed wires or aluminum foil. If you're the least bit concerned, call the police and leave the premises.

3.08. Lethal Mail Emergencies

No matter how careful people are, some mail bombs are bound to go off and the contents of some suspicious mail are certain to spill out. It's important, therefore, to know how to respond in these emergencies.

- Don't touch or disturb a suspected bomb, and don't use cellular telephones.

Letter and parcel bombs are individually constructed, so it's impossible to know in advance its precise triggering mechanism.

It could be timed to explode; it could have a tripwire, or it could be detonated by motion. It's imperative, therefore, to leave any suspected device alone. Don't touch or disturb it, and don't bring it to a police station or walk around with it, showing it to others. Evacuate the premises promptly, making sure that your family or co-workers are informed of the danger and get safely out of the house or building.

Notify police from a neighbor's house, pay phone or a nearby business using only a regular, landline telephone. Never use cellular telephones around a suspected bomb. Call law enforcement using only a regular telephone. This is crucial, because cell phone transmissions have the potential to detonate some bombs.

- If a suspicious powder spills from a letter or parcel, protect yourself and the others around you.

If case of a spill from suspect mail, don't try to clean up the powder or liquid. Cover your mouth and nose with a handkerchief or piece of cloth. Be careful not to touch you mouth, nose or eyes directly with your possibly contaminated hands. If you're at home, vacate the premises immediately and call the police. Close doors behind you as you leave, and be sure that everyone gets out of the house. Don't touch anyone until you've washed up.

Were the incident to occur at work, first protect your breathing, but avoid touching your eyes, nose or mouth directly with your hands. Gently cover the spill with a piece of clothing, newspaper or a trashcan; avoid creating a current that could cause the substance to become airborne. Leave the covering in place; don't remove it to inspect the spill. Evacuate the room, closing doors and windows; section off the area. Ask co-workers to leave the building and keep others from entering the site of contamination. Contact building security and the police. Have the air-conditioning system switched off. Wash with soap and water as soon as you can.

Wherever the spill takes place, remove your clothing and other personal items as soon as possible. Place the items in a plastic bag or seal-tight container. Give the bagged items to emergency responders. Ask that the bag be labeled with your name, telephone number and an inventory of the contents. Shower with lots of soap and water as soon as possible.

Compile a list of all the people who were in the room or area when the spill occurred, making special note of anyone who had actual contact with the powder or liquid. Provide the list to law enforcement, public-health officials and your supervisor. If it turns out that the suspect letter or package contained a toxic chemical or biological agent, seek medical assistance. If your home is contaminated, get professional help to make it habitable again. Don't re-enter the premises until the decontamination is completed.

Tip   If water isn't available, talcum powder or flour can be used to decontaminate for liquid agents. Sprinkle the powder over the affected skin area, wait 30 seconds, and wipe off with a rag or gauze pad. Note that the powder has absorbed the agent, so be careful not to inhale any dust. Cover your mouth and nose with a handkerchief, mask or piece of clothing. If possible, wear gloves while performing this procedure.

- If the suspicious powder becomes airborne, take special precautions.

A biological agent becomes airborne, protect your breathing. Leave the room, turning off any fans or air-conditioning systems and closing the door behind. Co-workers should evacuate and seal off the area, while you call the police and alter building security. The FBI, too, should be informed. Again, make a list of anyone who may have been exposed to the airborne agent and give it to the authorities. Follow the same decontamination procedures as above and seek medical help.

Tip   If antibiotics are prescribed, it may help to know that eating cultured yogurt can reintroduce healthy bacteria into the body and thus relieve some of the gastrointestinal distress often associated with antibiotic regimes.

- Evacuate immediately if a device explodes indoors.

Should a device containing a suspected biological or other warfare agent explode in your home or office, instruct everyone to leave the building immediately. Close all doors as you leave. If you're in a large office building, ask that the air-conditioning system be shut down. If possible, close open windows. Avoid touching your face, mouth, nose and eyes. Isolate all persons exposed to the explosion. Those who were exposed should avoid contact with others. Tell Good Samaritans to stay clear. Wait for treatment by emergency personnel. Later, compile a list of all persons believed to have been exposed to the detonation and provide it to authorities. Discard contaminated clothing in a plastic bag and then seal it.

- Close all windows and doors if an explosion occurs outside.

In the event a biological, chemical or radiological weapon should detonate outside your home or office, stay indoors. Close all windows and doors, and shut down any air-ventilation systems. Protect your breathing passages. Cover your mouth and nose with a handkerchief, piece of clothing or, if available, a mask. An improvised mask can be made by soaking a clean cloth in a solution of one tablespoon of baking soda mixed into one cup of water. Cover bare arms and legs. Bandage any cuts or abrasions. Don eyeglasses, sunglasses or goggles. Wash with soap and water. Avoid physical contact with others.

Caution   Many biochemical agents are heavier than air and tend to sink, so don't get on the floor. Remain standing until help arrives.

3.09. Biohazard Avoidance

Biological weapons are so stealthy that they could show up in many guises. These include food and perhaps even fragrance samples. No advance warning of such an attack will be given. It indeed could take days or weeks before anyone realizes what has happened. Therefore, you need to take prophylactic steps to avoid exposure to biohazards.

Weapons of Mass Destruction Incidents, Actual and Hoaxes, by Motive, 2000-2001

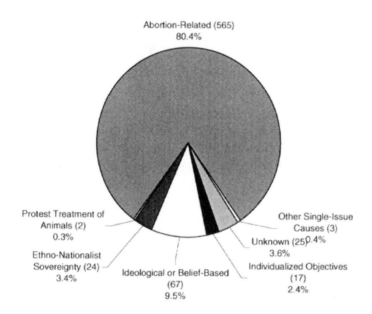

Source: Center for Nonproliferation Studies, Monterey Institute of International Studies

- Avoid seemingly accidental liquid spills or anyone using a spraying device.

Terrorists could spread toxic chemicals or communicable diseases via mists from handheld spray bottles, gas canisters or even overturned 50-gallen drums. Over large areas, a truck-mounted insect sprayer would be effective yet difficult to detect as being anything other than a routine activity. If you spot a team of suspicious-looking cleaners, say, hauling a large drum or spraying equipment in a crowded public building, move away and alert the police or building security.

Caution   Be wary of any spraying activity that takes place at night and hasn't been pre-announced by local officials.

• Throw away free samples of fragrances or food.

Terrorists are ruthless by nature. The usual rules of fair play don't apply as far as they're concerned. They can and will do anything that they think will kill, injure or otherwise frighten their targets. Chemical and perhaps biological warfare agents are in their arsenal of weapons (as well as the arsenals of some of the nation-states that support them). The big question for terrorists then becomes how to vector those agents to their targets.

A vector is simply the name given to the means by which a chemical or biological agent gets to its intended target. Conceivably, even a person who was wittingly or unwittingly exposed to an infectious disease could be used as a vector of biological terrorism. Poisoning samples of free food, say, delivered in the mail, would be one way. Another perhaps less obvious but more insidious way would be to disguise a biological agent as a perfume or a cologne sample. Take the scratch-and-sniff strips or the pull-open strips for fragrances commonly found in magazines or promotional mailings. If terrorists had a biological agent that, for example, activated only after it came in contact with oxygen, a fragrance strip would be a perfect vector. It wouldn't take much doing for terrorists to set up a dummy company, ostensibly selling food products or fragrances, and use it as a means of distributing poisons to the general public.

The best means of preventing such an attack would be to deny terrorists the potential vectors of food and fragrance samples by banning these items from the postal system, magazines and newspapers. You can only imagine the horror and carnage that would be caused if people throughout a city or county starting getting ill, collapsing and dying after smelling a perfume insert that had come in their Sunday newspaper. The risks are simply too great for the government (and governments globally) not to take preventative action against such a stealthy terrorist threat and for publishers voluntarily to do the same.

Until then, the old adage, "Let the buyer beware," takes on a new significance.

- Forego eating food from salad bars or restaurant smorgasbords.

Terrorist may decide to target eateries in large cities, financial districts or airports, or food establishments near government facilities and key businesses. A relatively easy way to poison food would be to lace open salad bars or unattended smorgasbords with biological (or chemical) agents. It's best, therefore, to avoid eating any food that has been within reach of the public.

- Exercise caution when buying food from street vendors or roadside stands.

Terrorists "sleepers," who be resident in a country for years and not show any signs of being anything other than hard-working immigrants, may have taken positions in the food industry as part of a plan to disseminate biological agents. That's not to say that every foreigner working around food is a potential terrorist. But it does mean that you should exercise caution in purchasing food from establishments where there is little or no supervision, such as sidewalk vendors and roadside stands.

- Be aware of common foodborne illnesses.

In 1984, a religious cult in Oregon contaminated restaurant salad bars and water glasses with salmonella bacteria, hoping to affect the results of a local election by incapacitating voters. No one died, but 751 persons fell ill with food poisoning. The U.S. government has since become so concerned that terrorists may contaminate the food supply that in early 2002 the Food and Drug Administration (FDA) urged the nation's food industry—from farmers and fishermen to food importers and restaurateurs—to beef up security. The recommendations included scrutinizing visitors more closely, performing background checks on potential employees and inspecting incoming and outgoing vehicles for suspicious activity.

Common foodborne illnesses are caused by *E. coli* and *Salmonella* bacteria, among others. Symptoms include acute intestinal distress with the sudden onset of headache, fever, abdominal pain, diarrhea, nausea and sometimes vomiting. In severe cases, the victims can die. Young children and the elderly are at particular risk. If you believe you've eaten tainted food, contact a physician or emergency room immediately. You also can call the U.S. Department of Agriculture's special meat and poultry hotline at 800-535-4555. For incidents involving food other than meat and poultry, call the FDA's 24-hour emergency number 301-443-1240.

- Examine store-bought food carefully for signs of tampering.

Food that has been tampered with often will change in appearance and texture. It may discolor or degrade quickly; it may become slimy to the touch and develop a foul smell. Cans containing contaminated food may bulge or buckle, and the metal tops of jars or bottles also may bulge. Beware of broken seals and punctured or undone plastic wrapping around fresh meat and poultry.

- Take precautionary steps in the kitchen.

Wash all fresh foods thoroughly, including meat, poultry and produce. Remove the outer layers of fresh vegetables and fruit. For those most concerned about bioterrorism, wash produce in soap and water or rinse in a highly diluted chlorine-bleach solution. Cook foods thoroughly.

- Wash your hands after returning from an outing, most especially if you used mass transit or a taxicab.

If a biological attack occurs and the symptoms take time to develop, the disease could spread fare and wide in a variety of ways. Exchanging handshakes can transfer germs. The common cold often gets transmitted from person to person via the hands. But there are other, less obvious routes of disease transmission. Philip M. Tierno, Jr., author of *The Secret Life of Germs: Observa-*

tions and Lessons from a Microbe Hunter, notes that "buses, trains, and taxis abound with surface, such handrails, that act as collecting areas and transfer points for germs." He advises that during and after traveling on mass transit or in taxis, you not touch your face, eyes, nose or mouth until you've had a chance to wash your hands. He even urges people to use tissues or paper towels when opening and closing doors in public buildings, especially washroom doors.

Tip   Tierno offers another interesting piece of health advice: Wear long pants or skirts when visiting public facilities, such as movie theaters, sports arenas or concert halls, because sitting down with bare legs could lead to the contraction of an infectious illness from germs on the seats.

- Stay away from persons who are purposely coming in close contact with strangers.

Given the fanatical and even suicidal nature of today's terrorists, nothing can be ruled out, including what only can be called walking bombs. This doesn't mean only suicide bombers with explosives strapped to their bodies. A terrorist could expose himself (or be exposed unwittingly) to a communicable disease, such as smallpox or plague, and then mingle with hordes of people to spread the disease. Beware of anyone in public who seems interested in getting close to strangers.

Tip   Be careful, too, whenever someone approaches you asking for information or if an argument or street scuffle breaks near you. Pickpockets often employ helpers to distract their targets.

- Stock up on inexpensive facemasks in case of a biochemical attack.

Experts at the Oak Ridge National Laboratory have found that commonly used N95 facemasks (costing under $2 apiece) are effective, as are HEPA (high-efficiency particulate air) masks, against the inhalation of chemical and some biological warfare agents, such as anthrax. N95 masks block 95 percent of particles that are three microns or more in diameter. Keep the masks at home and at work, as well as in your briefcases, purses and carry bags, and make sure that all members of your family have them.

- If you buy a gas mask, get the right one.

U.S. authorities and others tried to dissuade the public from buying gas masks following Sept. 11 and the subsequent anthrax outbreaks. On the other hand, most every Israeli has a gas mask (and knows how to use it), because of the continuous danger of an attack using chemical or biological weapons. Buy a gas mask if it makes you happy. It may not do you much good, however. First, you'd have to carry it with you at all times. Terrorists won't be giving advance warning of a biochemical attack. Second, even if you have one on hand, you could find that you'd donned it too late to prevent exposure to the toxic agent. Finally, protection against many types of biochemical weapons requires a complete outfit, covering the entire body from head to foot. What's more, any small gap or opening could let ambient air in and mean death or injury.

If you do buy a gas mark, get one that snugly fits around the contours of your face, neck and head. Otherwise, it's a waste of money. And don't buy old Army surplus; gas masks and filters are only good for so long. A lot of the equipment being sold since Sept. 11 is useless. Buy masks and filters only from reputable dealers; some offer masks made in Israel, which tend to be quite good. Note, too, that masks are made for children and infants, as well as adults. For a detailed discussion of protective gear, see "How Do I Know? A Guide to the Selection of Personal Protective Equipment for Use in Responding to a Release of Chemical Warfare Agents," published by the Oak Ridge National Laboratory and available at http://emc.ornl.gov/emc/PublicationsMenu.html.

- Weigh any decision to be vaccinated against a biological agent, such as anthrax, carefully.

Anthrax vaccine was made available to postal workers and others exposed to the contaminated letters that were sent anonymously in the U.S. mail in the fall of 2001. This followed a 60-day regime of treatment with antibiotics. It's as yet unclear how effective such vaccines are and what the side effects may be. Before making a decision, discuss the matter with your doctor.

Caution   Pregnant women have been advised not to take the anthrax vaccine, because it can apparently cause birth defects.

3.10. Spotting Suspicious Behavior

Historically, when eyewitnesses have been debriefed after a terror incident, they almost invariably agree on one thing: The perpetrator looked suspicious from the start. It takes a highly professional, extremely well-trained terrorist to have the poise needed to avoid detention completely. The pros are as cold as ice and rarely give themselves away. But not all terrorists are that well trained. Most are nervous and over-anxious. Others may be clumsy or dimwitted.

Be mindful, too, that many terrorists are engaged in activities other than in actual attacks. They may perform ancillary functions, such as reconnaissance, bomb making and weapons procurement. You need to be on guard, therefore, in case a terrorist surveillance team is targeting the building your work or live in for possible attack.

- Know how terrorist groups are organized and operate.

Most international terrorist groups have four primary organizational components, although individual cells may be subdivided in separate units (e.g., planning and execution):

Headquarters: This is where command and control is located. The head of a terrorist organization, with the help of his top lieutenants, will devise strategy, send out surveillance teams and make final decisions on which targets to strike and when the attacks are to occur.

Surveillance teams: They will travel on reconnaissance missions, looking for potential targets. Their chores include photographing, videotaping and mapping target sites, including the locations of doors, windows and lighting, appraising a site's level and means of security, and determining the best times for an attack. Members of the surveillance team may even know how develop their own photographs in makeshift darkrooms.

Logistics cell: This group will manufacture bombs, procure weapons, conduct ongoing surveillance and handle administrative chores, perhaps including the provision of money and fake identification for the attackers. Bomb-makers, besides acquiring and preparing the explosive materials (e.g., dynamite or plastic explosive), may create detonators from off-the-shelf items, such as radios, watches and encoders.

Attack team: These are the members of the terrorist group most highly trained in assault tactics, weapons handling, explosives, etc. They'll plan and prepare for the attack in minute detail, perhaps engaging in intelligence-gathering of their own. They'll then conduct the actual attack once they get the go-ahead from headquarters.

- Recognize the telltale signs of suspicious behavior.

Terrorists often will look out of sync with their surroundings. Their behavior will be inconsistent with that of the other people around them. Their focus may appear to be elsewhere. They won't act like everyone else, or share the same interest or concern (e.g., the bus is late, the line is moving too slowly, etc.). They will be nervous, perhaps jumpy, because they know what they're about to do. Something about them will seem strange or unusual. A group, for instance, may exit the same car or taxis but then act as if they don't know each other. That, you know, is odd. Or, a group may enter a facility together and then intentionally take seats far apart from one another. That, too, is strange. By now, you can probably tell something's going on. Your job, as a good citizen, is to alert law enforcement or building security.

Tip   On occasion, terrorists will give themselves away by the clothing they wear. They may have a winter coat in the

Terrorist Organization and Operations

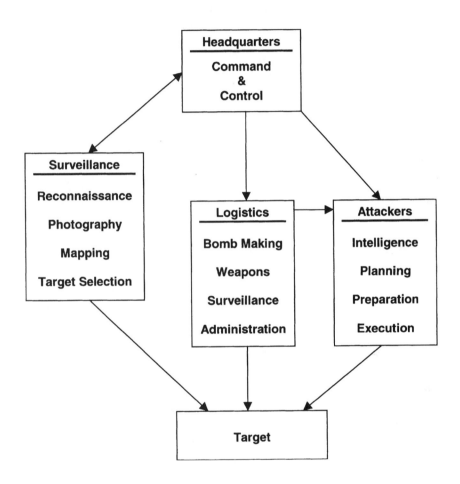

summertime or be overdressed at an event that calls for casual wear.

Tip Don't assume that a terrorist has to be a man. Women, too, participate in terror attacks, conduct pre-attack surveillance and carry out suicide bombings.

- Be aware of your surroundings at all times and alert to trouble.

Surprise is a hallmark of terrorism. However, the nature of their activities is such that they can't help but display some signs of what they intend. It may be the odd handling of a parcel or suitcase. They may be carrying guns or assault weapons that cannot be concealed completely. They may spill the beans in communicating too loudly with one another or talking on the phone. So stay alert and take in your surroundings with watchful eyes and open ears.

Tip   Wherever you are, scan the premises for the emergency exits and staircases, and think about potential escape routes. Make this a habit, especially when you're in a facility for the first time.

Caution   Take special care when you're near heavy objects that could fall on you or glass that could shatter in an explosion.

- Look to see whether or not the terrorist is wearing a facial disguise.

If a suspected terrorist has his face covered in a disguise, it signals that he wants to stay alive and plans to escape before, say, a bomb goes off. This means, of course, that you, too, will have time to escape, so exit the scene promptly and contact the authorities.

- Notice someone deviating from standard operating procedure.

We usually know, at least subconsciously, when someone is acting out of the ordinary. We get used to seeing certain routines performed in much the same way by various people functioning in the same capacity. We know, for instance, how janitors go about their chores, or repairmen or security personnel. If you spot a deviation from the norm, you may have spotted an imposter. Inform the authorities of your suspicions.

- Determine whether someone is paying too much attention to one particular thing.

A terrorist about to commit an act of violence knows his intended target. He'll, therefore, tend to fixate on it. Yes, he may avert his eyes every once and a while so as not to appear too obvious. Still, he can't help himself. His target is there, right before his eyes; he must look at it. He may have waited and trained for months or years for this moment. His level off concentration on his target will be immense. From the perspective of an outside observer, his fixation will seem odd and unusual. It will appear to be too much. So, again, contact the authorities to inform them of your suspicions.

Tip   A terrorist often will act oddly around police or security officers. He will pay a lot of attention to them from a distance, but when an officer draws near, he will put on an act, feigning ignorance and appearing oblivious to the fact that the officer is now in very close proximity.

- Take note of anyone trying to gain access to off-limits areas and security doors.

Pay attention to anyone attempting to enter a secure area or specially locked door without the proper uniform, visible credentials, or functioning keys or pushbutton codes. Raise an alarm if the person is having difficulty opening a security door, or if you see him leave and return to the same door and still be unable to open it.

- Be attentive to deliberate acts of concealment.

Carrying concealed weapons and bombs can be difficult, and terrorists sometimes give themselves away through an act of clumsiness or overt attempts at concealment. Watch for persons who may appear to be hiding something under their jacket or a coat hung over their arm. The bungle of a pistol strapped above an ankle, tucked into a waistband or held in a shoulder holster often can be seen, especially when the person moves. Also, be on the lookout for anyone who is overly protective of a seemingly innocuous package.

• Be alert to target reconnaissance.

Well before an attack, terrorists will conduct detailed surveillance of a target site. At first, it may be only to determine whether a site would make a good target. After a site has been chosen, additional reconnaissance will be carried out. Signs include photographing, videotaping and mapping the site, inquiries about security staffing and procedures. Terrorists also will be interested in locating a facility's entry and exit points, as well as gathering information on adjoining streets, major roadways and pedestrian traffic. They may even try to determine room sizes and heights, plus the thickness of walls. One of the attackers may conduct a personal walk-through of the facility, testing security and getting a firsthand impression of the target.

• Keep an eye out for unattended packages

Unattended parcels, boxes, briefcases or luggage left in public place should be assiduously avoided. Terrorists not wishing to blow themselves up in a suicide bombing use innocent-looking items to plant bombs containing timing fuses or remote-controlled detonators. Years ago, the head of a German bank was killed when his car passed next to a bomb-laden bicycle that had been left on the roadside. If you see an unattended item, particularly at an airport, mass-transit station or terminal, or a crowed street or store, alert the police immediately. Don't touch it or move it. It may turn out to be nothing. But these days, you can't assume anything is harmless. Even flashlights have been turned into bombs.

Tip Bombers tend to handle their deadly devices with care, so watch for anyone gingerly placing a package or other item in an unusual spot.

Caution   Alert security or the police if you see someone put a package at the back of a store shelf, in a planter, behind curtain or some other hiding place.

- Pay attention when a suspicious person drops an item into a curbside mailbox or garbage receptacle.

Terrorists have been know to drop package bombs into street containers, such as mailboxes and garbage cans, and then flee before the explosion. Pay attention if someone arouses your suspicions. If you see him drop something into a street container and hasten off, move away. Alert the people around you to flee, and contact law enforcement.

Caution   Be alert, too, to a passing vehicle that stops to deposit an item on the street or in a container and then speeds off.

- Know the warning signs of truck bombings in progress.

The FBI, though the National Infrastructure Protection Center (NIPC, www.nipc.gov) asked Americans in March 2002 to be alert for signs indicating plans to construct and detonate truck bombs. The agency had conducted an analysis of truck bombings to "determine whether any unique characteristics exist that might help identify, in advance, potential terrorist activity." It found that terrorist attempts might be pre-empted by remaining alert for a number of "indicators." outlined below. "While the presence of an indicator does not in and of itself suggest terrorism as a motive," it said, "the FBI's analysis reflects that further examination of the particular circumstances of each case might be in order when one or more of the following indicators is present." The FBI's truck-bombing indicators are:

- Theft or purchase of chemicals, blasting caps, and/or fuses for explosives
- Theft or purchase of respirators and chemical mixing devices

- Rental of storage space for chemicals, hydrogen bottles, etc
- Delivery of chemicals to storage facilities
- Theft or purchase of trucks or vans with a minimum 2,000-pound capacity
- Trucks or vans that have been modified to handle heavier loads
- Chemical fires, toxic odors, or brightly colored stains in apartments, hotel rooms, or self-storage units
- Small test explosions in rural or wooded areas
- Hospital reports of missing hands or fingers or of chemical burns on hands or arms
- Chemical burns or severed hands or fingers that have gone untreated
- Physical surveillance of potential targets (surveillance may include videotaping, particularly focusing on access points)
- "Dry Runs" of routes to identify any speed traps, road hazards, or bridges and overpasses with clearance levels too low to accommodate the truck
- Purchase of, or elicit access to, facility blueprints

The FBI encourages individuals to report information concerning criminal or terrorist activity to their local FBI office at www.fbi.gov/contact/fo/fo.htm or other appropriate authorities. Individuals may report incidents online at www.nipc.gov/incident/cirr.htm and can reach the NIPC Watch and Warning Unit at 202-323-3205, 888-585-9078 or nipc.watch@fbi.gov.

- Look to see if a stranger is lurking near your parked car.

A terrorist (or carjacker) may try to overtake you as you enter your vehicle. So as you approach your parked vehicle, look to see if anyone is anyone is lingering about or hiding behind a vehicle. If your instincts tell you something's unusual, walk away. Either return later, checking to see whether the person has left, or get help from law enforcement or building security. Be especially vigilant when returning to a vehicle left in a

U.S. Carjacking Locations, 1992-1996

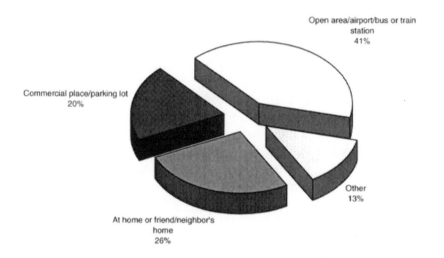

Open area/airport/bus or train station
41%

Commercial place/parking lot
20%

Other
13%

At home or friend/neighbor's home
26%

Source: Bureau of Justice Statistics, U.S. Department of Justice

parking lot at an airport, bus or rail station, or large shopping center.

Tip   If you use a remote-control device to unlock your vehicle's doors, set it so that it only opens the driver's door. Carjackers have been known to enter vehicles when the passenger doors are opened remotely.

• Keep in mind that a terrorist may be one of your customers.

The FBI issued a warning to law enforcement agencies in February 2002 about Valentine teddy bear bombs after receiving a tip that a man had purchased several stuffed bears, propone canisters and BB pellets at a retail store in California. The incident points out terrorists may buy many of their bomb-making materials (e.g., watches, timers, batteries, wiring, etc.) over the counter, so store clerks should be watchful for suspicious purchasers. Before launching an attack, moreover, terrorists will acquire information on their target, perhaps taking photographs and making detailed notes. It's very possible that a photo-processing store or computer repair shop might come across this information, in which case law enforcement should be informed. The same goes for dry-cleaners and the like who may come across revealing information left in an item of clothing. In addition, telephone repairmen, cable or satellite television installers, meter readers or deliverymen might see something suspicious in a home or apartment they visit.

Tip   Employees of restaurants, motels, hotels and bars should alert authorities if they overhear a discussion of a terror plot or if someone boasts of something "big" happening.

Caution   Be especially careful of anyone making requests that seemed aimed at acquiring information about security personnel and practices.

• Be wary of odd-acting neighbors.

Terrorists residing in a targeted country have to live somewhere until they execute their action. It may be house, apartment or hotel room. In any case, they are someone's neighbors. Moreover, they may have lived at the address for quite a long time, given that terrorist "sleeper" cells have been in place around the world for years awaiting their orders. Be particular suspicious of groups of relatively young foreign men who routinely gather at a neighboring house, apartment or hotel room and clearly are looking to see f they're being watched. Do they look behind them before closing the door? Do they peek through windows to see if anyone is outside observing their comings and goings? Is a neighbor overly secretive about his identity or what he does for a living? Does an apparently healthy, young man seem to have no visible means of support? Does he not regularly leave for work or school?

- Heed the FBI warning and police advice regarding apartment building tenants and rental applicants.

The FBI in 2002 published the following threat advisory: "There are indications that discussions were held about the possibility of terrorists renting apartment units in various areas of the United States and rigging them with explosives. The FBI has no information indicating that this subject advanced beyond the discussion stage." (Quoted in "Response Guidelines to the FBI Threat Advisory Concerning Apartment Buildings," Los Angeles Police Department.) Augmenting this warning, the Los Angeles Police Department (LAPD, www.lapd.org) compiled "Response Guidelines to the FBI Threat Advisory Concerning Apartment Buildings" and posted them on the Web "These guidelines are only advisory in nature," the LAPD says. "Apartment property owners and managers should refer to their own policies and legal advisors before taking any specific action. Questions concerning these guidelines can be directed to your local community police station commanding officer."

In following procedures for completing tenant applicant background checks, the LAPD advises apartment property owners and/or managers:

- Make sure prospective tenants have valid state identification.
- Verify that their vehicles are registered to the prospective tenant.
- Be cautious of prospective tenants using only rental vehicles.
- Take note of prospective tenants who have little or no previous rental history.
- Verify the prospective tenant is able to pay rent.
- Verify employment thoroughly.
- Be cautious of prospective tenant seeking month-to-month or week-to-week rentals.
- Pay attention to prospective or current tenants paying rent in cash or with money orders or third-party checks.

- Be cautious of prospective tenants seeking to rent only ground floor apartments, unless the request is related to a disability.
- Be cautious of prospective tenants who insist on renting only apartments that cannot be seen by other homes or apartments.
- Take note of prospective tenants who claim to operate non-zoned businesses—e.g., jewelry, industrial art, metal work, electric repair, chemistry, etc.

The LAPD further recommends:

- Observe new tenants when they move in to see if they are bringing in any unusual items—e.g., machinery; liquid containers, barrels, buckets or drums; sacks and bags; compressed air tanks; large batteries; electrical wire, or fireworks.
- Take note of any boxes carried with extreme caution, as well as any unusual or oddly sized packages being brought into units.
- Monitor apartment units for unusual odors, such as gasoline, diesel fuel, ammonia, sulfur, acids or fireworks.
- Watch for any unusual digging or trenching near ground floor apartment units.
- Be cautious of tenants who use an apartment in unusual ways—e.g., rarely occupy the unit and over-occupy the unit with more residents than allowed on the rental agreement.
- Look out for unusual guest traffic to a single apartment unit.
- Watch for tenants or guests using special knocks or signals devices, such as hanging towels, open or closed curtains, or a cushion or some other item positioned in a special way.
- Take note if a tenant changes door locks without approval.

Terrorists are most likely to seek housing in newer apartment complexes where tenants are less likely to know each other, high-rise apartment buildings with large numbers of units, or in densely developed areas, the LAPD says. It, therefore, suggests installing surveillance equipment and paying attention to activity in public areas.

- Trust in your instincts.

For all the importance placed on human intellect, the instincts we're born with also serve a vital function in helping to keep us safe. If someone or something doesn't seem right, pay attention to what your instincts are telling you. Remove yourself from the situation, and if you feel strongly enough about the potential for terrorism or other violence, tell a police officer or security staff of your concern.

- Don't hold back from contacting authorities; hesitation could cost lives.

Some people don't like to get involved in anything other than their personal business. Others are so afraid of as being thought of as silly that they'd never contact authorities about their suspicions. In this day and age, however, to be good citizens and responsible neighbors means setting aside any reluctance, second thoughts or hesitancy about contacting the authorities. Tips about suspicious persons and unusual activities will likely prove invaluable to catching terrorists—hopefully, before they've been able to carry out their dastardly deeds.

3.11. Are You Being Followed?

Terrorists normally put a targeted person under surveillance before they strike. Therefore, it's important to know how to detect surveillance and how to escape would-be attackers.

- Be on guard if you see the same strange person or unexplained car regularly.

While going about such daily routines as commuting to work, heading to school, cycling or jogging, take notice if you see the same unfamiliar person or vehicle again and again. This could be a sign that you're under surveillance. A person on foot may seem to be everywhere you go. Or you might see different cars occupied by the same person or persons waiting near your home or office. Alternatively, you may spot the same vehicle occupied by different people on different days. Be alert, too, to any illegally parked vehicles, parked vehicles containing occupants or parked vehicles in which activity seems to be taking place behind darkly shaded or louvered windows. Note also any vehicle that seems to be going out of its way to stay with you as you walk down the street. The vehicle might change speeds, go through red lights or stop at green lights to keep pace with you, or might wait ahead of intersections you've yet to cross. Anther sign of surveillance may be the use of flashing lights or horn taps to signal messages between moving vehicles.

Caution   Be especially wary about any rental van or commercial vehicle with unprofessionally painted identification marks that seems to be tailing you or that is inexplicably parked near your home or office.

• Double check by changing your routines.

If you notice the same person or vehicle popping up day after day, change your routines. Leave for work and go home at different times via different routes. Eat and shop at different establishments. Ask a friend to give you a lift. Drive a different car. Then, see if the same person or vehicle adapts to your altered schedule and habits.

• Use passive measures to spot surveillance when alone and on foot.

If you feel you someone is following you on the street, take passive steps to spot your would-be pursuer. One simply way is to turn around and retrace your course, watching to see if the suspicious person follows. Make an expected stop, say, to tie or fix your shoe and peer behind you to see what the other person does. Look in a window reflection or a handheld mirror to see if the person stops when you stop. Cross the street several times, and try to time it so you cross just before the traffic light changes. Finally, change you walking pace several times, slow-ing down and speeding up, and see how the person responds. If the person is still behind you, take active measures to get out of harm's way.

Tip Men could help assuage women's fear of being stalked if they were mindful of how their own innocent behavior might be misinterpreted. If you find yourself walking behind the same woman for a considerable time or distance, be aware that this may be worrying her, so cross the street or walk ahead of her.

- Elude your pursuer by taking active measures.

If you're being followed, the best thing to do is get help from a police officer, doorman or other form of security personnel. Otherwise, proceed to a safe location, such as a store, hotel, bank, restaurant or other public facility. Barring that, move toward a densely populated area. Get on a bus, if available, or hail a cab. But be careful that the taxi driver isn't in cahoots with your pursuer. Don't stop to wait for a cab and don't take the first one to come along. Instead, keep walking, look for a cab that's still well away in the distance and hail that taxi as it nears you. Other methods of eluding a pursuer are changing your appear-ance, say, by entering a building and removing you coat, sweater, tie, etc. You might also mess up your hair, or don a hat or scarf. If worse comes to worse, make a 90-degree turn and find a place to hide.

- While driving, implement passive measures to detect surveillance.

A variety of steps can be taken to confirm surveillance: circle the block, make a U-turn or change your speed and see if your pursuer stays with you. If you suspect you're being followed, drive to a safe haven or stop a passing police car or emergency vehicle.

Caution Don't pull your vehicle over to the side of the road unless it's to run inside a safe location. Stopping your vehicle may be just what your pursuer wants you to do, leading to a confrontation or worse.

- Take steps to elude a car that's following you.

Put other vehicles between you and your pursuer. Drive through traffic lights or stops signs, being careful not to get into an accident. Drive on the sidewalk, if necessary, again being careful not to hit anyone or anything. Avoid driving over grass, because it's slippery and your car could get stuck in mud or a ditch, and also avoid going the wrong way on a one-way street, because you risk a head-on collision or getting boxed in. Draw attention to yourself by keeping your hand on the horn of your vehicle. Turn on your flashers, so police can immediately spot your vehicle. If there's enough distance between you and your pursuers, stop your vehicle and immediately run into a safe-haven building.

- Never drive home if you're being pursued; go to a facility where you can get help.

If you drive home, you risk being overtaken by your attackers before you can get in the front door. Drive instead to a police or fire station, hospital emergency door or even an open gas station, and get assistance. Never get out of your vehicle unless you're certain you can get inside a building safely. If necessary, honk you horn until help arrives. Use a cell phone to call for help while en route to a safe haven.

Tip Try to get the license plate number of car that's following you, remembering that the plate number will read backwards in your rearview mirror.

- On mass transit, alert a bus driver or conductor, and don't get off at an isolated stop.

Your best bet if you feel you're being followed while riding a bus, train or subway is to inform the driver, engineer or conductor. Short of that, never get off at an isolated stop if you think someone's following you. Get off with other people at a location where a safe haven is nearby (e.g., a store, restaurant, hospital or, better yet, a police or fire station). If the person is still following your, ask for help and inform the police.

Tip   While waiting for the police, jot down a description of your pursuer.

- If attacked, scream—and scream, "Fire!"

Try to attract attention if you're assaulted or an attempt is make to abduct you. Screaming "Fire!" is a good way of getting people's attention.

For more on self-protection in public places, see the Chapter 4 on general travel safety.

Encyclopedia of Jihad

The Associated Press acquired an 11-volume Encyclopedia of Jihad, or holy war, reportedly stolen from the headquarters of bin Laden's fighters in Kandahar, also the home of Afghanistan's then-Taliban rulers. Here is an overview of the index to the encyclopedia, as published Oct. 1, 2001.

Book 1: Explosives

Eight chapters with diagrams and formulas to handle, manufacture and detonate explosives. How to disarm explosives; scientific theories; industrial terror; the use of liquid explosives.

Book 2: First Aid

Methods of first aid including the handling of psychological shock, the treatment of burns and electrical shocks. Describes the handling of several medical needs including delivering a child.

Book 3: Pistols, Revolvers

Illustrated guide to the care and use of pistols, revolvers and specialized hand-guns. Where to keep guns in the house and how to use silencers.

Book 4: Bombs, Mines

Illustrated manual on grenades, bombs, mines, mine fields and mine war. Recipes for mines made of raw materials; how to pass through a mine field.

Book 5: Security, Intelligence

How to spy; kinds of security; military intelligence; sabotage; communications; security within Jihad; secret observation; assassination; brainwashing; protection of leaders; laws of sabotage; arms use. Punishment of spies; Muslim and non-Muslim; interrogation; analyzing information; psychological war; poison use; opening locks; U.S. military training; assassination by riding a motorcycle.

Book 6: Tactics

Principles of war including battle organization, reconnaissance, infiltration, ambush; elaboration on incursion. Muslims are urged to follow the Jihad, established in Afghanistan against un-Islamic states and states where true Islam is not practiced.

Book 7: Weapons Making

The book consists mostly of diagrams of machinery for the manufacture of arms. On the manufacture of bullets and silencers; metal casting; the use of steel files.

Book 8: Tanks

The anatomy and history of tanks; their effectiveness and descriptions of diferent types. Cost of maintenance of tanks; how to drive a tank.

Book 9: Close Fighting

Physical fitness; ackedo and other forms of self-defense; how to overcome a rival. How to attack with knives, chairs; methods of releasing oneself from a grip.

Book 10: Topography Area Survey

Natural directions; using a compass; topography; following directions on maps; military area survey; area survey apparatus. This book looks at the estimation and measurement of distance, height and speed for military use.

Book 11: Armament

Use of small arms including antiaircraft arms, machine guns, rifles, antitank arms and artillery. Reviews mostly Russian weapons; offers practical details on the assembly, cleaning and use of weapons.

Source: Associated Press

3.12. Ambushes and Assassinations

Senior executives, like top government officials and celebrities, often have bodyguards, professional drivers trained in evasive maneuvers, and even bullet- and bomb-proof cars. Not everyone can afford such protection, however. Given that terrorists sometimes attack mid-level executives or government personnel, it's worthwhile knowing how to spot and avoid ambushes and preplanned assassinations. Of course, if you think your life is in danger, contact the police or FBI.

- Know the five primary means of assassination.

Terrorists typically murder their intended targets using bombs or gunfire in different ways. 1) A roadside bomb might be affixed to a utility pole, parked bicycle or car, construction barrier, detour sign or pushcart. 2) A car bomb might be planted in the victim's vehicle. 3) Gunfire may erupt from a stationary location like a fake construction site or parked car as the victim passes by, or the victim may be gunned down as he exits or enters his car, home or office. 4) Gunmen in a moving car or on a motorcycle may overtake a victim's car while he is driving. And 5) a terrorist may be working undercover as, say, a taxi driver and pick up his unwitting victim as a fare.

- Look out for terrorist surveillance and reconnaissance.

Prior to an attack, terrorists will conduct surveillance of an intended victim to assess his habits, patterns and routines, most especially his travel routes near his home and office. A reconnaissance team will then survey those routes, looking for choke points where a road narrows and vehicles are forced to move slowly. Be aware of any unusual activity that seems to be centered around you and the places you live and work.

- Conduct your own neighborhood reconnaissance.

To better spot an impending attack, you need to develop an instinctive sense of your surroundings, particularly near your home and office. Take drive to get an impression of what looks normal—so you can tell what isn't normal, should the occasion arise. Also, look for natural choke points that terrorists might exploit—narrow streets, blind spot in a road, roadside construction, etc.—and then avoid those areas.

- Recognize the curious signals of an impending on-the-road attack.

Here are a few of the ploys that terrorists sometimes use to abduct their target: striking your vehicle from behind with another car; cars (or even pedestrians) boxing you in at a light or stop sign; a fallen cyclist or pedestrian; a tree lying in the road; an overturned baby carriage or large barrier; phony flagmen, road construction and detours, and persons dressed in fake police or security uniforms.

- Get someone to watch your back if you think you're under surveillance.

If you feel the risk of attack or abduction is high, have someone watch your back to determine whether you're being tailed and targeted for an assault. Preferably, employ a professional to do this work. Otherwise, ask someone with enough brains and brawn to do the job without endangering himself to any substantial degree. With sufficient evidence of a plot against you, you should be able to get the assistance of law enforcement. Either way, if you are abducted while someone is watching your back, the police likely would have enough information to go on to track down your abductors and discover your whereabouts, hopefully, in relatively short order.

- On the road, don't stop to help strangers.

Terrorists (as well as carjackers) are known to use ploys like fake accidents and seemingly broken down vehicles to get at their prey. If you come across a road accident or stranded motorist, don't stop to help. Instead, call for assistance using your cell phone or the nearest public telephone.

- Take precautions by varying your everyday routines and routes.

Terrorists rely on a target's predictability and unvaried routines to carry off a successful ambush or assassination. You need, therefore, to mix up your transportation patterns and your daily schedule continually. Avoid taking the same routes every day, especially the streets and roads near your home and workplace. (The vast majority of terrorist ambushes and murders occur in very close proximity to the victim's home or office.) Also avoid narrow streets or places where construction is taking place and other choke points. Try to pick roads with multiple lanes and routes that allow for maximum speed. Don't drive near the curb; keep as close to the center of the road as possible. Vary your patterns when it comes to taking lunch-time strolls, picking up kids at school or day care, jogging, cycling or going to the gym. Leave for work and return home at different times. Enter and leave work using various doors. Shop at different stores, and eat at different restaurants. Steer clear of unlit areas and, whenever possible, avoid bridges and tunnels.

Tip   If there's a personal nameplate or "Executives Only" sign at your parking space at work, have it removed. Park in a different space everyday.

- Don't telegraph your exit from a building.

If you have a driver, don't let him idle at the door, waiting for you to leave a building. Have him pull up just as you ready to leave (or employ a decoy car). Both the failed assassination attempt on President Ronald Reagan in 1981 and the successful bid that killed Israeli Prime Minister Yitzhak Rabin in 1995 occurred as the men were about to enter limousines that had been waiting at the curbsides for so long that crowds had gathered. This gave their attackers plenty of time to get into place and prepare for the attacks. By blending into the crowds of onlookers, the assassins caught security off guard. If, however, the attackers hadn't been tipped off by the sight of the waiting cars, perhaps they might have been caught before a shot was fired.

- Know how to escape an ambush.

When driving, always leave enough room between you and the vehicle in front of you—most especially, whenever you come to a stop—to allow you room to maneuver. Give yourself enough room to turn your car around and head in the opposite direction if necessary. Otherwise, be willing to drive up on curbs, but try to avoid driving on slippery surfaces like grass.

Tip   To ensure you have sufficient room to turn around, never get so close to a vehicle in front of you that you can't see it's back tires touching the road.

- Counterattack if you're under fire and escape is impossible.

The best way to counterattack a moving vehicle that is firing on you is by forcing it off the road. Turn your vehicle into the terrorist's car and then accelerate as you push it off the road or into a stationary object like a parked car, tree or light stanchion. If your attacker is in a stationary car or behind, say, a construction barrier, ram it with your car, but only if escape is impossible. A motorcycle gunman (usually seated behind the motorcycle driver) racing by your vehicle would be seriously injured if not killed were you to open your car door as he passed. (Motorcycle assassinations became so rife in Italy and Colombia that both nations have banned second persons from riding on the backs of motorcycles and scooters.)

- Never take the first taxicab in line.

Terrorists have been known to take jobs as taxi drivers—both to give them cover as a sleeper in their target country and also to carry out assassinations and other assaults. It's wise, therefore, never to take the first cab in line when leaving a restaurant, hotel or office, especially if you think you may be have been targeted by a terrorist group. Hail a moving cab instead.

• Know how to inspect your vehicle for car bombs.

If you feel you may be targeted by a bomber, inspect your vehicle routinely. A proper inspection by one person normally takes 10 to 15 minutes. First, you need to become familiar with every part of your vehicle, including the engine compartment and undercarriage of your vehicle, so you'll notice anything that may be out of the ordinary. Get a sense of what looks normal. Use a flashlight and mirror to aid in the inspection process. Next, know what you're looking for in bomb detection. Telltale signs of bombs include strange wiring, cut wires, tape, lengths of fishing line, putty-like lumps (plastic explosive), boxes or other containers (concealing, perhaps, sticks of TNT), shunts from detonators, and unexplained smudge marks or grease.

Check the area around your parked vehicle, widening your search to a distance of 30 to 40 feet. Survey around and beneath the vehicle for discarded bits of tape, wire or wire insulation. Look for grease, scratches or scuff marks on the vehicle's exterior. Inspect for wires, foil or objects attached to the outside of your vehicle. Pay attention to the grill, hood release, bumpers, tires, hubcaps, wheel wells, gas cap, exhaust pipe, door seams and door locks. Check locks, windows and weather stripping for forced entry. Look under the car (preferably using a mirror), inspecting the chassis, exhaust pipes, drive train, gas tank, bumpers and areas beneath the trunk and seating compartment, especially for foreign objects.

Peer inside the car before opening the doors for any suspicious items or signs of intrusion. Note whether the angle or position of the seats has changed since you were last in the car. Look to see if anything is behind the rearview mirror or if the mirror's angle has changed. Check to see whether floor mats or items left on seats have been disturbed.

Carefully examine the seams around doors for wires before opening them. From outside the vehicle, check under the seats, headrests and dashboard (especially the ignition wiring). Check the glove compartment and ashtray; gingerly look behind the sun visors and in any door pockets. Pop the hood and inspect the engine compartment, paying close attention to the wiring and the firewall. Look for new wires, cut wires, tape, new-

U.S. Bombing Incidents by Target Type, 1977-1997

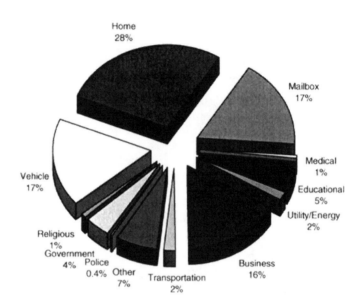

Source: Bureau of Alcohol, Tobacco and Firearms

looking objects (e.g., oil filter), foreign materials, and unexplained grease marks, scratches or smudges. Finally, inspect the seam around the trunk for wires; then, look inside.

Tip   It's wise to leave glove boxes and ashtrays open after parking your car. Also, leave the sun visors down. Keep an item on the front seat, such as a newspaper or tissues box, so you can see if it has been moved since you parked the vehicle. Install a lockable gas cap, car alarm and protective screen for your tailpipe. Whenever possible, keep your vehicle in a locked and alarmed garage.

Caution   Don't put pressure on seats with your hands or knees when inspecting underneath for an explosive device; some detonators are pressure-sensitive.

3.13. Gunfire, Grenades and Bombs

Most civilians don't know how to respond properly to the sounds of gunfire, hand grenades or bombs. Fight or flight is our instinctive choice. In cases of gunfire and explosives, however, neither of these responses may save your life. You have to discipline yourself, perhaps through role-playing or the use of your imagination, to think before reacting in such situations.

- Don't automatically run from the sounds of gunfire; think first of hitting the ground.

The best response in many situations involving gunfire (and explosives) is simply to drop to the ground, laying face down. Don't necessarily run, because that could expose you to stray bullets. Gunmen, moreover, tend to look for targets in their line of sight—and that includes fleeing pedestrians or building occupants. By hitting the deck, a gunman may overlook you or think you're already dead. Bombs, too, do the most damage to people nearby who are upright.

Tip Stay put until instructed by authorities to move. Otherwise, you risk being caught in crossfire or possibly being mistaken for a terrorist.

- Assume a tucked position to protect your body.

Protect your vital organs and major arteries by pulling your upper arms and elbows into your sides, thus guarding your heart and lungs, and cupping the palms of your hands over your ears, thereby covering the arteries in your neck and protecting your head and hearing.

- Drop to the ground, too, at the sight of a hand grenade or bomb.

Attempting to flee a hand grenade or bomb left on the street or carried by a suicide bomber could cost you your life, because grenade and bomb shrapnel flies outwards and upwards in a cone-shape. Hitting the ground immediately could save you from serious injury or death.

- Know the exceptions to the rules involving street terrorism.

There are exceptions to the general rule of diving to the ground in an act of street terrorism. If, for example, you're only a step or two away from a protective barrier, such as a vehicle, solid pillar, heavy planter, or the corner of a wall or building, you ought to get behind it as quickly as possible. If you have children with you, grab them and either drag them behind a barrier or drop on them, covering them with your body. Finally, if the terrorist is screaming demands or shouting slogans, this may give you time to flee before he acts.

As noted earlier, a facial disguise is tip-off to a terrorist's intention. Wearing a disguise usually means he plans to survive the attack and not blow himself up in a suicide bombing. What this tells you is that you probably have time to flee to safety.

- Learn the proper ways to crawl or roll to safety.

The way most people crawl would expose them to bodily harm in a terrorist street incident involving gunfire or explosives. Their backs and behinds likely would be up in the air, exposing their spines to potentially lethal or paralyzing injury. There are three recommended techniques, employed by most militaries, of staying low and getting to safety under fire.

Low or belly crawl: Keep your body flush to the ground, turning your head sideways. Begin by pushing both arms forward and bending your right leg, pulling it forward until the knee is as far as it will go. Then, move forward by pulling your body with your arms and pushing against the ground with your right leg. Continue this push-pull movement until you reach safety. This technique may be slow, but it greatly reduces your body's exposure to bullets and shrapnel.

High crawl: With your chest off the ground, rest your weight on your forearms and lower legs. Extend your knee well behind your buttocks, thus lowering the profile of you back and spine.

Crawl forward by alternately advancing your right elbow and left knee, then your left elbow and right knee. This technique saves time but exposes you to some danger. It, therefore, should be used only in incidents where gunfire isn't coming in your direction.

Roll: With your arms at your side or over your head, roll along the ground to safety. Obviously, this technique isn't intended for long distances, but it's valuable to know if you need to roll, say, under a nearby vehicle or piece of furniture.

Tip   Stay away from glass or heavy objects that could topple over in a blast.

- After an incident, beware of a possible second bomb in the area.

In Israel, Palestinian terrorists make it a practice to plant a second explosive device, usually in a parked car, in the vicinity of an initial attack. The aim is to kill or injure emergency personnel, as well as curious onlookers attracted to the initial explosion. Therefore, clear the area following a detonation. Don't let your curiosity get you killed.

- Get as much information as possible if you receive a bomb threat.

If you get a call from someone saying a bomb (or a chemical, biological or radiological device) is about to go off, stay calm and try to get as much information from the caller as possible. Keep the caller on the line as long as possible and get someone to call the police using a landline phone and not a cell phone. Indeed, have everyone turn off all cell phones and radios, which could trigger a bomb. Write down everything the caller says. Ask him where the device is located, what kind of device it is, what it looks like and when it's supposed to go off. Make notes of the caller's vocal characteristics and apparent emotional state (e.g., calm, giggling or distressed). Evacuate the premises. Don't touch any suspicious-looking packages. Inform the police that you took the call, because they'll want to debrief you. (See the chapter on business and building security for a detailed bomb-threat checklist.)

Tip   While evacuating, again, steer clear of heavy objects that could fall over and glass that could shatter.

3.14. Explosions, Fires and Collapses

The events of Sept. 11 show the importance of knowing how to escape from a building that has been attacked by terrorists or surviving if you've been pinned in a collapsed structure.

- In a building explosion, immediately get under cover.

Assuming you're not in close proximity to a bomb, your greatest dangers in a building explosion come from flying glass and falling objects. At the sound of an explosion, dive under the nearest desk, table or chair—or at least hit the floor—to avoid the shrapnel-like effects of the blast. Be especially careful if you're near a heavy object that could fall over and crush you. Once it's all over, leave the building and then proceed a good distance away for fear that a second explosion might occur outside. Cover you mouth and nose with a handkerchief or cloth, wetting it down if possible, to reduce the inhalation of dust, smoke and debris.

Tip   If you're in a wheelchair, it's advised that you stay in it in an explosion. Cover your head with your hands, and then ask someone for help in evacuating the premises.

- In a department store or other crowded public place, be careful not to get trampled.

Should an explosion occur in a crowded public place like a department store or transportation hub, you're biggest worry—apart from flying glass and falling objects—is stampede. Panic likely would follow an explosion (or, say, gunfire). This could result in many people being trampled or pinned against doors that won't open. Once the dust has settled, your best bet is to get out of the flow of traffic. Get behind a counter or next to a wall

U.S. Bombing Casualties by Target Type, 1977-1997

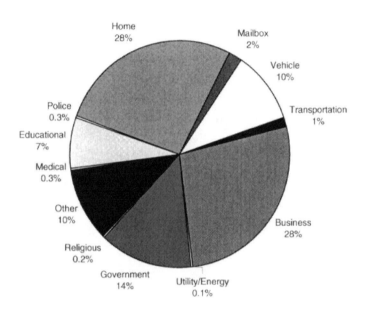

Source: Bureau of Alcohol, Tobacco and Firearms

or pillar. Scan the area for exits that aren't blocked. Pick the quickest route, and exit the building.

- Err on the side of caution in an emergency; it's better to be safe than sorry.

We've heard of one tragic case at the World Trade Center in which a young woman told her co-workers, "I'll be right with you," as they headed for the emergency stairs. The woman was never seen again. She said she wanted to make "one last call" to a client in London. That ill-fated decision cost the woman her life. Such a sad tale should serve as a reminder to everyone faced with an emergency to act and act quickly. Don't dally. Nothing, absolutely nothing, is as precious as life. When an emergency evacuation is called for, get out of the building as quickly and as safety as possible. Apologies can always be made later for a delayed phone call or a late e-mail. Whatever you leave behind at your desk will most likely be there when you get back. At worst, you'll have to buy a new briefcase, cell phone or laptop computer—but at least you'll be alive to go shopping.

- Don't follow instructions that don't instinctively sound right.

Numerous survivors of the Twin Towers attack reported hearing repeated announcements over the public-address system in one of the buildings, telling workers that the building was safe and to return to their offices. Some people followed that wrongheaded advice. One can only imagine their anguish (assuming they had time to reflect) once they realized the horrible mistake they'd made. Bad advice had sealed their fate. Others, many others, ignored the recommendation to return to their offices and instead continued down the staircases to safety below.

Although no one can be sure, odds are that most of the survivors simply decided to follow their instincts rather than the anonymous advice being blared over loudspeakers. It's a lesson worth remembering.

Each of us comes equipped with natural instincts that help to keep us alive and safe from harm. No one has to tell us, for instance, not to step off the edge of a cliff or into the path of a speeding car. We have an innate sense of what not to do. Only reason, or better, rationalization, can countermand our natural instinct for self-preservation. So, if it comes down to a split-second decision between following your head or your gut, go with your gut. Continue to do what you were doing in the first place. Do what your whole being is telling you to do. And don't second-guess yourself. Don't try to figure it all out. There isn't time. Just get out of harm's way—and think about it later.

- Survive a fire by staying low, protecting your breathing and moving quickly.

Try to evacuate the premises immediately in cases of fire. Shout to alert others to the danger. Don't waste time trying to save property; it could cost you your life. Fire can travel at lightning speed—up to 19 feet per second. Before opening a door in a fire emergency, feel it first for heat. Place the palm of you hand on the door, around the cracks and on the doorknob. If it's hot to the touch, don't open the door. Use another escape route. Close but don't lock doors behind you as you leave. Stay low to avoid any smoke. Smoke and poisonous gases first collect along the ceiling, so stay below the smoke level at all times. Knock on any doors you may pass to alert others to the fire. Leave by the nearest fire exit or stairway.

Tip Never use an elevator in a fire; the doors could open on a fire floor, incinerating you. And never go back into a burning building; the odds are you won't come out again alive.

• Protect yourself from smoke and flames if you're trapped.

If you're trapped in a burning building, use tape or moistened cloth to seal off the airflow from around and beneath the door, thereby reducing the amount of smoke that penetrates your room or office. Smoke inhalation kills more often than a fire's flames. Go to the window and signal for help. Be careful about opening windows fully, for the draft could suck smoke into the room. Instead open the windows just a few inches from the top or bottom to get fresh air. If a phone is available, call 911 and tell the operator your precise location in the building. Otherwise, dangle a sheet or piece of clothing from the window. Turn off the air conditioning if you can. If water is on hand, wet down the door nearest the fire. You also can moisten cushions or mattresses and then prop them up against the fire door, using furniture to hold them in place and repeatedly dousing them with water.

For additional fire survival and safety information, see the Internet pages of the U.S. Fire Administration (www.usfa.fema.gov), Los Angeles Fire Department (www.lafd.org) and New York City Fire Department (www.nyc.gov).

- If trapped in debris, conserve energy but still make your location known to rescuers.

Try to be calm if you're trapped in debris following a building collapse. Conserve your energy. Concentrate on your breathing to help calm your nerves and lower your blood pressure. Don't move around because that would accelerate and possibly impair your breathing. Use whatever means is at hand to signal your location to rescuers. Bells, flashlights, whistles or personal alarms are great if available. Otherwise, tap regularly on a wall or pipe. Try not to shout too much, for it will weaken you, cause you to lose your voice and inhale large amounts of dust. Yell only as a last resort, especially if you hear the sounds of rescuers nearby. Urination could help rescue dogs pick up your scent.

Caution It's advisable that untrained persons not attempt to rescue anyone trapped in a damaged building, for the chances of a secondary collapse are high. Leave the job to emergency personnel.

- Where there's time, there's hope.

Unless you are so unfortunate as to die instantly from a terrorist attack or other calamity, you normally have some amount of time, however small, to act. And that could make all the difference in terms of your personal survival. Never give up hope or the will to live.

3.15. Surviving as a Hostage

It may have been planned that way in advance or it may be the result of a botched attack, but too often innocent people find that they've suddenly become hostages to terror. If you find yourself in a hostage situation, it's important to remain calm. Don't do or say anything—especially in the first five minutes when an abductor is most on edge, but know that there are things you can do to improve your chances of survival.

- Never look your assailant in the eye.

Terrorists (and criminal kidnappers) are extremely nervous, especially in the early minutes of their action. Nerves sometimes give way to rash decisions. A terrorist is most likely to kill a hostage early on in an attack—usually is to make a point to the other hostages that he means business and to show authorities that he's willing to do anything. A human life is of little consequence to him. It's especially important, therefore, that you never look your abductor in the eye. Direct eye contact is often viewed as attempt by a hostage at intimidation or defiance. The defiant ones run a high risk of being killed.

- Don't do anything that would make you stand out from your fellow hostages.

Terrorists often feel a need to demonstrate their power and control over their hostages and send a message the authorities. This is another reason they may decide to make an example of one of their captives by murdering him in cold blood. The person may be picked at random. Alternatively, the person may have invited retaliation for having insulted his captors in some way. Or he may simply have said or done something that made him stand out in the terrorists' eyes. So, keep a low profile if you're taken hostage. Go along with whatever the terrorists may want you to do. Act passively and be cooperative.

Caution   Don't ever try to negotiate with terrorists or attempt to cut some kind of a deal.

- If your odds of surviving the hostage crisis seem low and you see a chance to escape, take it.

Most times it's wise just to stay put in a hostage situation. The authorities typically have the site surrounded. Eavesdropping devices probably are being used to listen and perhaps watch the terrorists, Sharpshooters may have the terrorists in their sights. However, there are incidences in which your chances of survival are low. That's especially true if the terrorists are bent on suicide, and the only reason they haven't already killed their hostages and themselves is that they are playing to

Terrorism in the U.S. by Group Class, 1980-1999

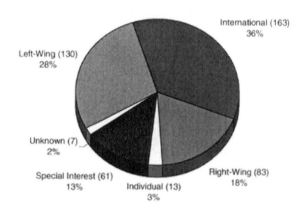

Source: Federal Bureau of Investigation

the media, airing their demands and hoping to stir up more fear and anxiety. In such a case, if you see an opportunity to flee, take it. It may be your only chance at survival. Think your escape route through, and time your move. Flee before the terrorists get a chance to tie you up or you become exhausted by a long ordeal. Wait for the hostage-takers to become distracted. Move quickly and silently. And don't look back. If you here a demand from the terrorists for you to stop, freeze. Don't move a muscle until you're told to. And don't say anything other than "Okay."

For more information on hostage and kidnapping survival, see the chapter on foreign travel, and for advice on dealing with a sexual assault, see the chapter on general travel safety.

3.16. Mass Attacks with Invisibles

In this day and age, it behooves everyone to be aware of the signs of an attack with a weapon of mass destruction and know how to survive it. The Interagency Intelligence Committee on Terrorism, led by Central Intelligence Agency, some years ago produced (and later declassified) a very useful handbook on chemical, biological and radiological incidents. It explains how to determine whether a weapon of mass destruction has been used and recommends steps to take for self-protection. The handbook was later revamped by the U.S. State Department for its diplomatic service. Both are available on the Internet. (The Web addresses are listed at the end of the chapter.) Here's a rundown.

"A chemical or biological attack or incident," says the State Department guide, "won't always be immediately apparent, given the fact that many agents are odorless and colorless and some cause no immediately noticeable effects or symptoms."

The CIA's "Chemical/Biological/Radiological Incident Handbook" further explains:

"Chemical, biological, and radiological material as well as industrial agents can be dispersed in the air we breath, the water we drink, or on surfaces we physically contact. Dispersion methods may be as simple as placing a container in a heavily used area, opening a container, using conventional (garden)/commercial spray devices, or as elaborate as detonating an improvised explosive device.

"Chemical incidents are characterized by the rapid onset of medical symptoms (minutes to hours) and easily observed signatures (colored residue, dead foliage, pungent odor, and dead insect and animal life). In the case of a biological incident, the onset of symptoms requires days to weeks and there typically will be no characteristic signatures. Because of the delayed onset of symptoms in a biological incident, the area affected may be greater due to the migration of infected individuals.

"In the case of a radiological incident, the onset of symptoms requires days to weeks and there typically will be no characteristic signatures. Radiological materials are not recognizable by the senses, and are colorless and odorless. Specialized equipment is required to determine the size of the effected area and if the level of radioactivity presents an immediate or long-term health hazard.

Because of the delayed onset of symptoms in a radiological incident, the affected area may be greater due to the migration of contaminated individuals."

• Learn the telltale signs of a chemical attack.

Indications that a chemical-weapons attack has taken place include:

Unusual oily droplets and films: Various surfaces might be covered in droplets or oily film; oily film might also coat water surfaces.

Unexplained odors: Smells may range from fruity and flowery to sharp and pungent. Some might be garlic- or horseradish-like. Others might resemble bitter almonds, peach kernels or new-mown hay. Whatever the odor, it would be completely out of character with the surroundings.

Low-lying clouds: Unusual low-level clouds or fog-like conditions unrelated to weather patterns might form.

Dead animals, birds and fish: There would be large numbers of dead and dying animals—wild and domestic, small and large—birds and fish, all in the same geographic area.

Lack of insect life: Normal insect activity on the ground, in the air and around water would be missing. Masses of dead insects might litter the ground, water surfaces and shorelines.

Foliage alteration: Trees, shrubs, bushes, lawns or crops might be dead, discolored or withered.

Odd physical complaints: Many people would exhibit water-like blisters, welts (similar to bee stings), rashes, pinpointed pupils, and choking and respiratory problems.

Mass casualties: Numerous individuals might suffer from nausea and disorientation; they could have difficulty breathing and might convulse to death.

Pattern of casualties: Casualties would be distributed in a distinct pattern associated with the way the chemical agent was disseminated. If a chemical agent were sprayed in an open area, there might be lower rates of illness for people who were indoors as opposed to outdoors. Alternatively, there would be more indoor casualties if the attack took place within a building.

Metal debris: Unexplained munitions-like materials might be found, and some could contain liquids.

Unusually dressed people: Groups of people oddly dressed, say, in long sleeves, or heavy clothing in the summertime or wearing protective garb might be seen, particularly near or in crowds.

Unauthorized spraying: Unexplained spray trucks, crop dusters or even handheld misters might be seen, particularly in densely populated areas.

• Note the signs of a biological mass attack.

A mass attack with a biological agent could result in the following:

Unusual numbers of sick or dying people or animals: Although symptoms would vary depending on the agent used, most biological weapons produce gastrointestinal illnesses and upper respiratory problems similar to colds or flu. Casualties may occur hours, days or weeks after an incident. The elapsed time depends on the agent used and the dose received.

Unscheduled and unauthorized spraying: It would be especially telling if spraying occurred outdoors during periods of darkness.

Abandoned spray devices: Unlike many chemical weapons, equipment used to disseminate a biowarfare agent would have no distinct smell.

• Determine whether a radiological attack has occurred.

A radiological attack, using perhaps a "dirty bomb," might produce:

Large numbers, of sick or dying people or animals: Casualties would begin to appear hours, days or weeks after an incident occurred. The timing depends on the radioactive material used and the dose received. Early symptoms include skin reddening and vomiting.

Metal debris: Unexplained bomb or munitions-like materials could be scattered about.

Radiation symbols: Discarded containers may display a radiation symbol.

Heat-emitting material: Various materials would seem to emit heat without any sign of an external heating source.

Glowing material and particles: If the material is strongly radioactive, it may emit a radio-luminescence and glow, particularly in the dark.

3.17. Did Terrorists Poison You?

Some chemical warfare agents are lethal, while others are survivable. Biological agents can cause symptoms resembling a cold or flu, although others trigger massive hemorrhaging or convulsions to death. Radiological weapons might only cause a "local" injury, say to the hands, but they also could have long-term (and perhaps deadly) effects.

What almost all of these agents have in common is their stealth. A terrorist attack using chemical, biological or radiological (CBR) agents might go sight unseen, and the public-health effects could take days, weeks or even months to show up.

The point is that self-diagnosis may prove important following a CBR attack, so know the signs and symptoms to look for. The Centers for Disease Control and Prevention (CDC), based in Atlanta, Georgia, has established a special bioterrorism Internet site (www.bt.cdc.gov) to provide information to the public on the symptomatic effects of various types of chemical and biological weapons agents. For healthcare professionals, it explains how to diagnose and treat victims. The Center for Civilian Biodefense Studies at Johns Hopkins University in Baltimore, Maryland (www.hopkins-biodefense.org) also provides similar public-health information.

• Recognize the symptomatic effects of chemical agents.

The following are brief summaries of the CDC information on chemical weapons, notably nerve agents, blistering agents, blood agents and pulmonary agents.

Nerve agents: Nerve agents interrupt the transmission of nerve impulses in the body and often cause death. Treatment consists of decontamination and drugs (e.g., atropine, pralidoxime chloride and diazepam), plus ventilation to support respiration and supportive care. Here are the main nerve agents:

Sarin: A colorless, odorless liquid that mixes readily in water, sarin can be ingested, inhaled or absorbed through the skin. Depending on the dose, the onset of clinical manifestations can vary from a few minutes to an hour. Signs and symptoms include visual disturbance, runny nose, chest tightness, nausea, vomiting, convulsions and death.

Soman: Another colorless and tasteless liquid that mixes readily with water, released soman evaporates rapidly, dissipates and eventually breaks down in the environment. Clinical manifestations include visual disturbance, runny nose, chest tightness, nausea, vomiting, convulsions and death.

Tabun: A colorless-to-brownish liquid, tabun can persist for one to two days under average weather conditions. It's primarily released as an aerosol or vapor. Clinical signs and symptoms include visual disturbance, runny nose, chest tightness, nausea, vomiting, convulsions and death.

VX: It's an amber-colored, oily liquid that will remain in the environment until it has been properly cleaned through decontamination methods. VX can enter the body through ingestion, inhalation, or through the eyes or skin. Health effects include constricted pupils, visual disturbance, runny nose, chest tightness, nausea, vomiting, convulsions and death.

Blistering Agents: Blister agents cause skin burns and blisters, and they may damage the eyes, airways, lungs and other internal organs.

Mustard: The health effects of mustard-gas exposure can be delayed up to 12 hours. Those exposed might notice the odor of mustard gas, which smells like onion or garlic. Hours after exposure, the skin may appear red. Upper respiratory problems such as difficulty breathing, coughing, painful sinuses or sore throat may occur. Over a period of hours, small blisters appear and gradually combine to form large blisters. There is no antidote for mustard exposure.

Lewisite: Its effects are immediate. Its vapor causes burning or pain in the eyes, nose and skin. Fresh air can increase the pain. Lewisite may produce visible tissue damage within several minutes of contact. Later, severe damage to the skin, eyes or airways may occur. Treatment consists of decontamination and use of the antidote British Anti-Lewisite.

Blood Agents: Some blood agents, such as hydrogen cyanide, can be more lethal than the phosgene gas used in World War I. Symptoms sometimes don't show up for hours after exposure. Because blood agents evaporate quickly, they're probably better suited for use in assassination than for mass terrorism.

Arsine: This is a highly flammable liquid or gas, which if it comes in contact with the skin or eyes is like liquid frostbite. It has a characteristic odor and is heavier than air; it may travel along the ground for some distance. Inhaled, it causes abdominal pain, confusion, dizziness, headache, nausea, shortness of breath, vomiting and weakness. Excessive exposure can affect the lungs, blood and kidney, and may result in death. Otherwise, treatment includes fresh air and the cleansing of contaminated areas.

Cyanogen Chloride: This non-combustible liquid, which has a pungent odor, also produces frostbite-like effects on skin and eyes. Symptoms also include confusion, drowsiness, nausea, sore throat, unconsciousness and vomiting. The onset of symptoms may be delayed by a few hours. Severe lung damage or death may result. Again, fresh air and the cleaning of affected skin or eyes are among the usual treatments.

Hydrogen Chloride: A non-combustible, colorless gas that's heavier than air, hydrogen chloride is extremely corrosive and has a pungent odor. The substance is corrosive to the eyes, skin and respiratory tract, causing a burning sensation, although the symptoms may be delayed by a few hours. Inhalation of high concentrations of the gas may cause severe lung damage. Fresh air, rest and bathing of wounds are among the treatments.

Hydrogen Cyanide: This gas or liquid, which has a characteristic odor, is extremely flammable. The substance irritates the eyes, skin and respiratory tract, causing pain and burning. It may affect the central nervous system, resulting in impaired respiratory and circulatory functions. Exposure may result in death. Fresh air and the irrigation of wounds are among the treatments.

Pulmonary Agents: If inhaled, these types of chemicals can result in varying degrees of pulmonary edema, usually after a symptom-free period that varies in duration with the amount inhaled.

Chlorine: This greenish-yellow gas has an irritating odor and is a potent eye- and skin-irritant. Chlorine also causes severe pulmonary irritation that may result in death. Chlorine exposure is difficult to diagnose. There is no specific antidote.

Cyanide: This colorless liquid prevents cells from using oxygen, resulting in death. Inhalation is the primary mode of exposure. Cyanide in moderate amounts may produce headache, nausea, dizziness, weakness or anxiety. A large amount of cyanide will produce loss of consciousness within seconds and death may occur within minutes. Successful treatment for acute cyanide poisoning depends on rapid treatment with oxygen and the use of antidotes.

Phosgene: This highly toxic substance, which smells like newly mowed hay, immediately irritates the eyes, nose and skin. It also produces tissue damage within several minutes of contact. Its signs and symptoms include eye and airway irritation, difficulty breathing, chest tightness and delayed pulmonary edema. There is no specific antidote for phosgene.

Tip   You can check on chemical-biological hoaxes and rumors at the CDC's Web page www.cdc.gov/hoax_rumors.htm.

- Know how to spot the symptoms caused by biological warfare agents.

Weapons of Mass Destruction Use, Possession, Attempted Acquisition, Plot and Threat with Possession, 2000-2001

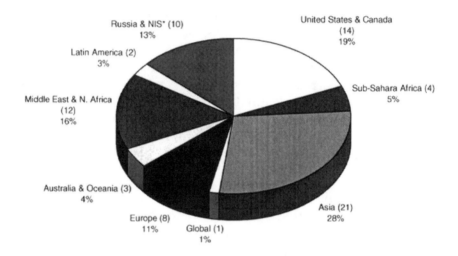

*Newly Independent States (NIS) of the former Soviet Union

Source: Center for Nonproliferation Studies, Monterey Institute of International Studies

Again, here are capsule summaries from the CDC and other advisories on biological weapons.

Anthrax: Symptoms vary depending on how the disease was contracted, but signs usually show up within a week. Flu-like symptoms can occur, including dry cough, chest discomfort, shortness of breath, fatigue, muscle aches and sore throat. Treatment may involve a multidrug regime, including ciprofloxacin or doxycycline, and the possible administration of an anthrax vaccine. There are three types of anthrax:

1) Cutaneous anthrax affects the skin. The incubation period ranges from one to twelve days. The skin infection begins as a small pimple, turns into a cyst or blister in one to two days and is followed by a necrotic ulcer as the flesh dies and decays. The lesion is usually painless, but victims may have

fever, malaise, headache and regional inflammation of lymph nodes. About 20 percent of untreated cases of cutaneous anthrax will result in death. Fatalities are rare if patients are given appropriate antimicrobial therapy.

2) Inhalation anthrax is the most lethal form of anthrax. Anthrax spores must be aerosolized in order to cause inhalation anthrax. The number of spores that cause human infection is unknown. The incubation period is unclear, but it's reported to range from one to seven days and possibly up to 60 days. Inhalation anthrax resembles a viral respiratory illness; initial symptoms include sore throat, mild fever, muscle aches and malaise. These symptoms may progress to respiratory failure and shock, with meningitis frequently developing.

3) Gastrointestinal anthrax has an incubation period of one to seven days. It is associated with severe abdominal distress followed by fever. The disease can take mouth-and-throat or abdominal form. Symptoms include lesions at the base of the tongue, sore throat, fever and regional swelling of lymph nodes. Lower bowel inflammation usually causes nausea, loss of appetite, vomiting and fever, followed by abdominal pain, vomiting blood, and bloody diarrhea.

Botulism: The symptoms of botulism set in within six hours to two weeks of exposure. They include double vision, blurred vision, drooping eyelids, slurred speech, difficulty swallowing and dry mouth. Muscle weakness descends through the body. First shoulders are affected, then the upper arms, lower arms, thighs, calves, etc. Paralysis of breathing muscles can cause a person to stop breathing and die unless mechanical ventilation is provided. Botulism isn't spread from one person to another. An antitoxin is effective in reducing the severity of symptoms if administered early in the course of the disease. Most patients eventually recover after weeks to months of supportive care.

Plague: Pneumonic plague occurs when *Y. pestis* infects the lungs. The first signs of illness in pneumonic plague are fever, headache, weakness and cough productive of bloody or watery sputum. The pneumonia progresses over two to four days and may cause septic shock and, without early treatment, death. Person-to-person transmission of pneumonic plague occurs through respiratory droplets, which can infect those who have face-to-face contact with the ill patient. Early treatment of pneumonic plague is essential. Several antibiotics are effective, but there is no vaccine against plague. Prophylactic antibiotic treatment for seven days will protect persons who have had face-to-face contact with infected victims.

Q fever: Only about one-half of all people infected with *Coxiella burnetii*, the bacteria that causes Q fever, show signs of illness. Most acute cases begin with the sudden onset high fevers, severe headache, general malaise, confusion, sore throat, chills, sweats, dry cough, nausea, vomiting, diarrhea, abdominal pain and/or chest pain. Fever usually lasts for one to two weeks. Weight loss can occur. About 30 to 50 percent of patients will develop pneumonia. Most patients recover within several months without any treatment. Only one to two percent of people with acute Q fever die of the disease. Doxycycline is the treatment of choice for acute Q fever. Antibiotic treatment is most effective when initiated within the first three days of illness.

Ricin: This poison is derived from castor-bean plants (used to make castor oil). As a biological weapon, it might be inhaled as an aerosol or ingested via poisoned food or water. Ricin poisoning can be fatal. If inhaled, ricin causes weakness, fever, chest tightness, cough and severe respiratory problems, including pulmonary edema. The poison kills by damaging the lungs. Ingested ricin produces intestinal bleeding and organ damage. Death from ricin poisoning can occur in a matter of days. No vaccine or antidote exists.

Smallpox: Smallpox, caused by variola virus, can spread from one person to another by infected saliva droplets that expose a susceptible person having face-to-face ill person. Persons with smallpox are most infectious during the first week of illness. The incubation period is about 12 days following exposure. Initial symptoms include high fever, fatigue, and head and back aches. A characteristic rash, most prominent on the face, arms and legs, follows in two to three days. The rash starts with flat red lesions that evolve at the same rate. Lesions become pus-filled and begin to crust early in the second week. Scabs develop and then separate and fall off after about three to four weeks. The majority of patients with smallpox recover, but death occurs in up to 30 percent of cases. Vaccination against smallpox isn't recommended to prevent the disease in the general public and therefore isn't available. In people exposed to smallpox, the vaccine can lessen the severity of or even prevent illness if given within four days after exposure. There is no proven treatment for smallpox.

Tularemia: This is one of the most infectious pathogenic bacteria known, requiring inoculation or inhalation of as few as ten organisms to cause disease. It isn't spread person to person, however. The Johns Hopkins University's Center for Civilian Biodefense Studies says that aerosol dissemination of *F. tularensis* in a populated area would result in the abrupt onset of large numbers of cases of acute fever beginning three to five days after exposure. Pneumonia, complicated by pleurisy, or an inflammation of the lungs, would develop in a significant number of cases over the ensuing days and weeks. Without antibiotic treatment, the clinical course could progress to respiratory failure, shock and death. Tularemia has been treated successfully with a variety of drugs.

Viral hemorrhagic fever: VHF refers to a group of illnesses that are caused by several distinct families of viruses. While some types of hemorrhagic fever viruses can cause relatively mild illnesses, many cause severe, life-threatening disease. Some VHF viruses can spread from one person to another; Ebola, Marburg, Lassa and Crimean-Congo hemorrhagic fever viruses are examples. Symptoms vary, but initial signs often include marked fever, fatigue, dizziness, muscle aches, loss of strength and exhaustion. Patients with severe cases of VHF often show signs of bleeding under the skin, in internal organs, or from body orifices like the mouth, eyes or ears. Although they may bleed from many sites around the body, patients rarely die because of blood loss. Severely ill patients may also show shock, nervous system malfunction, coma, delirium, and seizures. Some types of VHF are associated with renal (kidney) failure. There is no treatment or established cure for VHF.

Tip One way to know that your symptoms aren't the result of a flu is to get annual flu-vaccine shots.

3.18. Nuclear Reactor Emergencies

Radioactive materials would be life-endangering if terrorists successfully attacked a nuclear power plant or similarly struck a depot containing spent fuel rods or radioactive waste.

- Become familiar with the terminology used to describe the different types of nuclear reactor emergencies.

Commercial nuclear power plants have a system for notifying the public if a problem arises. There are four emergency classification levels:

1) *Notification of Unusual Event* is the least serious. It only means that emergency officials have been notified of an event at a nuclear power plant but the incident poses no threat to the public or plant employees. Therefore, no action on your part is necessary.
2) *Alert* indicates an incident has occurred that could reduce a nuclear plant's safety level but backup systems are still working. Emergency agencies are notified, but no action by the public is deemed necessary.
3) *Site Area Emergency* means that major problems with a plant's safety systems have progressed to the point that a release of some radioactivity into the air or water is possible. However, the release isn't expected to exceed federal Protective Action Guidelines beyond the site boundary. Thus, no action by the public is said to be necessary.
4) *General Emergency*, the most serious of the four classifications, means a nuclear plant's safety systems have failed and radiation could be released that would travel beyond the site boundary. State and local authorities would take

action to protect residents living near the plant. People in the affected areas might be advised to evacuate promptly or shelter in place. When the sirens are sounded, you should listen to your radio, television or tone-alert radios for information and instructions.

- If a warning sounds, don't panic.

An alert doesn't automatically mean evacuation. Tune to your local television and radio emergency stations for information and instructions. Note, for instance, that the sirens could be warning of a tornado, fire, flood, chemical spill or other local emergency. Authorities advise against dialing 911; other emergency numbers will be provided.

- Don't race to pick up your kids at school; call first, because they may have been evacuated already.

If an incident involving an actual or potential radiological release occurs, authorities plan to put the safety of school children first. If an emergency were declared, students within a 10-mile radius of the incident site would be relocated to designated mass-care facilities in a safe area. Usually, as a precautionary measure, school children are relocated prior to the evacuation of the general public.

- Follow your evacuation plan if instructed to leave the area.

If an evacuation is mandated, put your emergency-supplies kit of water, food and other provisions in your vehicle, also taking along your cell phone, credit cards, cash, prescription medicines, extra eyewear and games for your kids. Follow officially designated evacuation routes. If the roads are jammed, fall back on your alternative exit plan. Stay calm, and don't speed. Consider giving a neighbor a ride out of the area. Be especially mindful of any children who may be home alone, the elderly and disabled. If you don't have a car, public transportation is expected to be available, so go to your nearest bus stop or train station.

Tip   Before leaving home, lock all windows and doors; turn off the air conditioning, forced-air heating or cooling, fans and furnace, and close fireplace dampers and any outdoor vents. These steps will help to minimize radiation contamination.

Caution   Keep vehicle windows and air vents closed. Don't follow the vehicle in front of you too closely so as to avoid any contaminated dust that might be kicked up by its tires.

- Minimize your risk by putting time, distance and shielding between you and the site of a radiation incident.

"There are three factors that minimize radiation exposure to your body: time, distance, and shielding," advises the Federal Emergency Management Agency (FEMA). Here are its explanations and recommendations:

Time: Most radioactivity loses its strength fairly quickly. Limiting the time spent near the source of radiation reduces the amount of radiation exposure you will receive. Following an accident, local authorities will monitor any release of radiation and determine the level of protective actions and when the threat has passed.

Distance: The more distance between you and the source of the radiation, the less radiation you'll receive. In the most serious nuclear power plant accident, local officials will likely call for an evacuation, thereby increasing the distance between you and the radiation.

Shielding: Putting heavy, dense materials between you and the source of the radiation will provide shielding and reduce exposure. This is why local officials could advise you to remain indoors if an accident occurs. In some cases, the walls in your home or workplace would be sufficient shielding to protect you for a short period of time.

Tip   Travel upwind of the source of radiation. Also try to put hills, mountains, forests or groups of tall buildings between you and the incident site.

- If advised to stay indoors, take refuge in your safe-haven room or basement.

Begin the process by bringing children and pets inside. Anyone who has been outdoors should shower thoroughly, paying particular attention to hairy areas of the body. Remove all clothing and shoes worn outdoors and store them in sealed plastic bags; if contaminated, they will need to be destroyed. Pets that have been outdoors should be insolated in a room apart from people, with ample food and running water; remove any hazardous substances from the room. Consider if any neighbors may need assistance. Lock all windows and doors; turn off air conditioning, forced-air units, fans and furnace; close any outside vents, including fireplace dampers. Bring a phone, battery-powered radio, candles, matches and all other emergency supplies into your safe-haven room or basement. Seal windows and doors with tape and plastic sheeting.

Caution   Following a radiation incident, even one that occurred a good distance from your home, avoid eating food grown in your garden. Contamination can affect areas many miles from the accident or terrorist attack site.

- Make an informed decision on potassium iodide.

"The thyroid gland is vulnerable to the uptake of radioactive iodine," FEMA notes. "If a radiological release occurs at a nuclear power plant, States may decide to provide the public with a stable iodine, potassium iodide, which saturates the thyroid and protects it from the uptake of radioactive iodine. Such a protective action is at the option of state, and in some cases, local government."

Parents around the Indian Point power plant in Buchanan, New York, about 24 miles north of New York City, have become so concerned about a possible terrorist attack on the plant's two nuclear reactors that some have taken to stockpiling potassium iodide in the hopes preventing thyroid problems in their children. Certainly, parents living near other nuclear reactors are weighing the same decision.

Potassium iodide is a salt, similar to table salt. In fact, potassium iodide is used to iodize table salt. Its chemical symbol is KI. The U.S. Nuclear Regulatory Commission (NRC) requires states where people live within 10 miles of a nuclear power plant to consider stockpiling potassium iodide as "a protective measure for the general public in the unlikely event of a severe accident." The distribution of potassium iodide would supplement the usual protective measures of shelter and evacuation in a nuclear reactor emergency.

"Evacuation is the most effective protective measure in the event of a radiological emergency because it protects the whole body (including the thyroid gland and other organs) from all radionuclides and all exposure pathways. However, in situations when evacuation is not feasible and in-place sheltering is substituted as an effective protective action, administering potassium iodide is a reasonable, prudent, and inexpensive supplement to evacuation and sheltering," the NRC says. "Potassium iodide is a special kind of protective measure in that it offers very specialized protection. Potassium iodide protects the thyroid gland against internal uptake of radioiodines that may be released in the unlikely event of a nuclear reactor accident."

"When potassium iodide is ingested," the NRC explains, "it is taken up by the thyroid gland. In the proper dosage, and taken at the appropriate time, it will effectively saturate the thyroid gland in such a way that inhaled or ingested radioactive iodines will not be accumulated in the thyroid gland. Radioiodine uptakes from inhalation or ingestion, or both, could result in acute, chronic, and delayed effects. Acute effects from high doses include thyroiditis, while chronic and delayed effects include hypothyroidism, thyroid nodules, and thyroid cancer."

The U.S. Food and Drug Administration has approved potassium iodide as an over-the-counter medication, meaning it's considered relatively safe. Before stockpiling or taking potassium iodide, however, you should check with your doctor or pharmacist.

• Take note of the cancer risks from radiation exposure.

Radiation causes cancer. "Current evidence suggests that any exposure to radiation poses some risk," says the U.S. Environmental Protection Agency (EPA, www.epa.gov). "There is no level below which we can say an exposure poses no risk." The EPA suggests keeping three important considerations in mind:

1) The more radiation a person receives, the greater the chance of developing cancer.

2) It's the chance of cancer occurring, not the kind or severity of cancer, that increases as the radiation increases.

3) Most cancers don't appear until many years after the radiation is received—typically, 10 to 40 years.

3.19. Mass Destruction Attacks

From the perspective of survival, you needn't separate the four classes of mass-destruction weapon—i.e., chemical, biological, radiological and nuclear—into individual categories. Two will do. Although each of these four weapon types is unique, three of them kill and injure in very similar ways. Chemical, biological and radiological (CBR) weapons are similar in many respects when it comes to survival tactics. Nuclear bombs, however, are different. They emit energy in the form of blast, thermal radiation and nuclear radiation and thus require special survival techniques.

This observation is important for it means that you need differentiate between only two broad categories of terrorist weaponry in order to know how to respond in the event of a mass-destruction attack. This foreknowledge could save vital time. It means, for instance, that you needn't identify the exact agent used in order to know what actions to take. Clearly, the brilliant flash of light, violent wind and ominous sound of a nuclear blast aren't to be confused with a chemical, biological or radiological weapon (even one dispersed using a conventional explosive). We'll, therefore, deal with CBR weapons and nuclear bombs separately in instructing you on how to survive. Let's begin with CBR agents. (Take note that the survival techniques for a CBR attack also apply to a terrorist incident at, say, a hazardous chemicals facility that might hurl contaminants into the air and coat a neighboring area.)

- First and foremost, protect your breathing in a CBR attack.

CBR weapons kill and injure most often as result of the inhalation of the toxic agent, so the first and most important step to take is to protect your breathing. Cover your mouth and nose with either a mask or cloth (e.g., a handkerchief, towel or piece of clothing) as you evacuate the contaminated area.

- Cover up by donning layers of protective clothing.

Cover all exposed skin surfaces as much as possible by putting on layers of clothing, including a thick overcoat, sturdy boots, heavy gloves and a hat. But don't waste too much time gathering up clothes, especially if the incident occurred near your location.

- If you're outdoors and some distance from the attack site, head upwind.

Again, the aim is reduce your exposure to any toxic agent you might inhale, ingest or get on your skin. You, therefore, want to get out of the way of any airborne agent being disseminated by the wind. So, travel with the wind blowing in your face. Close your vehicle's windows, and seal air vents. Don't tailgate, because you don't want churned up dust getting into your vehicle.

Tip   If you can't tell which way the wind is blowing, do what golfers do: Drop something very light from you fingertips and watch which way it drifts. Don't, however, pull up blades of grass, as golfers are wont to do, for the grass could be contaminated. Instead, use a bit of paper or tissue that may be in your purse or pocket. Even lint or hair will do.

- If you're indoors and some distance for the attack site, stay put.

Since CBR agents can be taken by the wind, being outdoors following a mass attack always entails some level of risk. If you're a good distance for the attack site, say several miles away, you're best bet is to remain indoors. Roads will be chaotic and dangerous. Bring children and pets indoors, and follows the procedures laid out above for handling a nuclear-reactor emergency. Because CBR agents are heavier than air, move to the highest possible floor.

- If you're indoors and a lethal agent has contaminated the interior of your building, evacuate and travel upwind.

To get out of harm's way, you need to reduce your exposure as much as possible if a CBR agent has been released in your building. This could have occurred as a result of an explosion or the poisoning of the building's ventilation system. Evacuate the building, taking pains to avoid or minimize passage through the contaminated area. Close doors behind you as you leave, along with windows, if possible. Keep going until you find emergency assistance.

Caution   Assuming you may have been contaminated, don't touch anyone—or let others touch you—except for trained emergency personnel. Various CBR agents can be transmitted by personal contact.

- If you're outdoors and an outdoor CBR incident takes place in your immediate vicinity, seek refuge indoors.

Get clear of the source of the contamination as quickly as possible. If the air is saturated with a CBR agent, fleeing on foot along streets or driving down roads will only increase your exposure. Instead, seek refuge in a building, making sure it isn't at the epicenter of the incident. Move away from doors and windows. Go to the highest floor and find, if possible, a windowless inner room. Most CBR agents are heavier than air and sink over time, making higher floors safer than lower ones.

If you can only find rooms with windows, make sure none of the windows was open during or after the attack. Before entering the room—or before allowing anyone else in—discard any contaminated clothing. Strip to your underwear if you have to. Place your clothes in a bag or container and leave it outside the safe-haven room. Shut down any air-ventilation system, if possible. Tightly seal any windows and doors with plastic tape. Plug keyholes with cloth. Use cloth or paper also to fill gaps around and under doors. If heavy-duty plastic bags or sheets (preferably, six mil or more) are available, use them to cover the doors and windows.

Tip   If you spot a bottled-water cooler, bring it into the room. You may need it.

- Put barriers between you and the attack site.

It can be helpful to try to put physical barriers between you and the site of a CBR incident. These might be natural barriers, such as hills, mountains and dense forests, or manmade ones, such as tall or large buildings—or even vehicles if you're very near the epicenter of the attack. The barriers will act as a shield, potentially blocking your exposure to lethal agents.

- Wash as soon as possible if splattered with a CBR agent.

If no water is available and the agent was a liquid, use a powder like flour or talc to dry off the affected skin. Brush off the residue, being extremely careful not to inhale any of the dust. Be careful how you discard any towels or cloth you may use.

- As soon as possible, discard the clothes you've been wearing and shower.

Once clear of the contaminated area, remove all external apparel (i.e., clothes, shoes, gloves and hats) and leave them in a sealed bag outside. Proceed to a shower, thoroughly washing your body with soap and water. Showering needs to be accomplished as soon as possible after a CBR attack. But don't simply flush water over your body. Give yourself a really good scrubbing, preferably with antibacterial soap. Scrub your skin aggressively and irrigate your eyes with water.

- Follow the instructions of national emergency response teams.

A national emergency response plan, involving federal, state and local agencies, will be activated if a large quantity of biological/chemical agents or radiation is released, and the public will be advised to take basic protective measures. As a example what to expect, consider the following verbatim advice from the CDC on the steps to take in a radiological emergency:

- Seek shelter in a stable building and listen to local radio or television stations for national or local emergency-alert information.
- Follow the protective-action recommendations from state or local health departments. Reduce your potential exposure and adverse health consequences by getting away from the radiation source, increasing your distance from the source, or keeping behind a physical barrier such as the wall of a building.
- If an event involves a nuclear power plant, a national emergency response that has been planned and rehearsed by local, state, and federal agencies for more than 20 years will be initiated. If you live near a nuclear power plant and have not received information that describes the emergency plan for that facility, contact the plant and ask for a copy of that information. You and your family should study the plan and be prepared to follow instructions from local and state public health officials.

"Local authorities will issue public health and safety statements advising precautions to take to avoid potential exposure to radiation," the CDC adds. "Until the amount of contamination is determined, the following precautionary measures are recommended to minimize risk:

- Remain inside and avoid opening doors and windows.
- Keep children indoors.

- Turn off fans, air conditioners, and forced air heating units that bring in fresh air from the outside. Use them only to recirculate air already in the building.
- Go to the nearest building if you are outside. If you must go outside for critical or lifesaving activities, cover your nose and mouth and avoid stirring up and breathing any dust. Remember that your going outside could increase your exposure and possibly spread contamination to others.
- Be aware that trained monitoring teams will be moving through the area wearing special protective clothing and equipment to determine the extent of possible contamination. These teams will wear protective gear as a precaution and not as an indication of the risks to those indoors.
- Avoid eating fruits and vegetables grown in the area until their safety is determined.

("Nuclear Event Response," Centers for Disease Control and Prevention.)

3.20. Surviving a Nuclear Blast

Nuclear explosions are devastating, but they are survivable in many instances. People in the immediate vicinity probably won't know what hit them. However, the greater the distance you are from ground zero, the higher are your chances of survival. Much will depend on your knowledge of the safety steps you need to take within seconds of the detonation and then in the hours and days that follow.

- To survive a nuclear explosion, first know its physical effects.

Survival is a major problem if you're near a nuclear explosion. "A nuclear detonation creates a severe environment including blast, thermal pulse, neutrons, x- and gamma-rays, radiation, electromagnetic pulse (EMP), and ionization of the upper atmosphere," explains the Federation of American Scientists (FAS, www.fas.org). "Depending upon the environment in which the nuclear device is detonated, blast effects are manifest-

Physical Effects of a Moderate-Sized Nuclear Explosion
(3 to 10 kilotons)

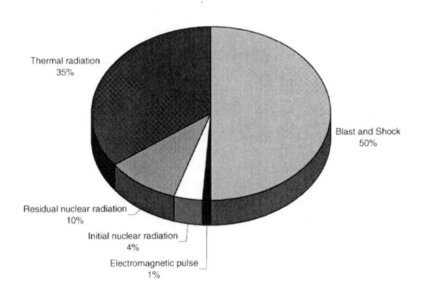

Thermal radiation
35%

Blast and Shock
50%

Residual nuclear radiation
10%

Initial nuclear radiation
4%

Electromagnetic pulse
1%

Source: U.S. Department of the Army

ed as ground shock, water shock, 'blueout,' cratering, and large amounts of dust and radioactive fallout. All pose problems for . . . survival."

Energy from nuclear explosion is transferred to the surrounding area in three forms: blast, thermal radiation and nuclear radiation. "The distribution of energy among these three forms will depend on the yield of the weapon, the location of the burst, and the characteristics of the environment," says the FAS. "For a low altitude atmospheric detonation of a moderate sized weapon in the kiloton range, the energy is distributed roughly as follows: 50% as blast; 35% as thermal radiation; made up of a wide range of the electromagnetic spectrum, including infrared, visible, and ultraviolet light and some soft x-ray emitted at the time of the explosion; and 15% as nuclear radiation; including 5% as initial ionizing radiation consisting chiefly of neutrons and gamma rays emitted within the first minute after detonation, and 10% as residual nuclear radiation. Residual nuclear radiation is the hazard in fallout."

In a surface nuclear blast, say from a nuclear device that might enter a seaport in a container shipped from overseas, the effects are less extensive those of an air burst but still pose serious dangers, especially in the immediate surrounding area. As the FAS explains, "A surface burst is an explosion in which a weapon is detonated on or slightly above the surface of the earth so that the fireball actually touches the land or water surface. Under these conditions, the area affected by blast, thermal radiation, and initial nuclear radiation will be less extensive than for an air burst of similar yield, except in the region of ground zero where destruction is concentrated. In contrast with air bursts, local fallout can be a hazard over a much larger downwind area than that which is affected by blast and thermal radiation."

- Know the different types of radiation released by a nuclear bomb.

Herewith are the U.S. Environmental Protection Agency's (EPA's) comments on the four types of radiation, or fallout, released by a nuclear bomb (or a radiological dispersal device):

Alpha particles can travel only a few inches in the air and lose their energy almost as soon as they collide with anything. They are easily shielded by a sheet of paper or the outer layer of a person's skin. Alpha particles are hazardous only when they are inhaled or swallowed.

Beta particles can travel in the air for a distance of a few feet. Beta particles can pass through a sheet of paper but can be stopped by a sheet of aluminum foil or glass. Beta particles can damage skin, but are most hazardous when swallowed or inhaled.

Gamma rays are waves of pure energy and are similar to x-rays. They travel at the speed of light through air or open spaces.

Concrete, lead, or steel must be used to block gamma rays. Gamma rays can present an extreme external hazard.

Neutrons are small particles that have no electrical charge. They can travel long distances in air and are released during nuclear fission. Water or concrete offers the best shielding against neutrons. Like gamma rays, neutrons can present an extreme external hazard.

- Understand a nuclear bomb's physiological effects on the body.

Blast, drag forces (produced by the winds created by a nuclear explosion), thermal radiation and ionizing radiation produce the physiological effects characteristic of nuclear explosions. Bodily injuries include flash blindness, ruptured eardrums and lungs, cuts and punctures from flying debris (particularly glass), burns and radiation poisoning.

A nuclear device used by terrorists probably would be relatively small, say less than 10 kilotons (KT). (A kiloton is equivalent to 1,000 tons of TNT). As a result, ionizing radiation would the primary source of casualties requiring medical care. For larger weapons of more than 10 KT, thermal radiation would be the primary cause of injury.

A U.S. Army manual, written in 1993 for healthcare providers, offers a telling glimpse at the effect on the human body of a nuclear explosion and resulting radiation. (See "Health Service Support In A Nuclear, Biological, And Chemical Environment" in the recommended readings at the end of the chapter.)

Blast waves: "The rapid compression and decompression of blast waves on the human body results in transmission of pressure waves through the tissues. Resulting damage is primarily at junctions between tissues of different densities (bone and muscle), or at the interface between tissue and airspace. Lung tissue and the gastrointestinal system (both contain air) are particularly susceptible to injury. The tissue disruptions can lead to severe hemorrhage or to air embolism; either can be rapidly fatal," the Army manual says. "Lung damage is a relatively serious injury, usually requiring hospitalization, even if not fatal; whereas eardrum rupture is a minor injury, often requiring no treatment at all."

Drag forces: "The drag forces (indirect blast) of the blast winds are proportional to the velocities and duration of the winds. The winds are relatively short in duration, but can reach velocities of several hundred kilometers (km) per hour. Injury can result either from missiles impacting on the body, or from the physical displacement of the body against objects and structures," the manual notes. "The drag forces of the blast winds produced by a nuclear detonation are so great that almost any form of vegetation or structure will be broken up or fragmented into missiles. Thus, multiple, varied missile injuries will be common." Of particular concern are small, sharp missiles, such as flying glass. Moreover, the Army warns, "the drag forces of the blast winds are strong enough to displace even large objects (such as vehicles), or to cause the collapse of large structures (such as buildings) resulting in serious crushing injuries. Man himself can become a missile."

Thermal radiation: "The thermal radiation emitted by a nuclear detonation causes burns in two ways—by direct absorption of the thermal energy through exposed surfaces (flash burns); or by the indirect action of fires in the environment (flame burns). Indirect flame burns can easily outnumber all other types of injury," explains the manual. "Thermal radiation travels outward from the fireball in a straight line; therefore, the amount of energy available to cause flash burns decreases rapidly with distance. Close to the fireball all objects will be incinerated."

Besides the burns caused by thermal radiation, the Army notes that the "initial thermal pulse can cause eye injuries in the forms of flash blindness and retinal scarring. Flash blindness is caused by the initial brilliant flash of light produced by the nuclear detonation. This flash swamps the retina, bleaching out the visual pigments and producing temporary blindness. During daylight hours, this temporary effect may last for about 2 minutes. At night, with the pupil dilated for dark adaptation, flash blindness will affect personnel at greater ranges and for greater durations. Partial recovery can be expected in 3 to 10 minutes, though it may require 15 to 35 minutes for full night adaptation recovery. Retinal scarring is the permanent damage from a retinal burn. It will occur only when the fireball is actually in the individual's field of view and should be a relatively uncommon injury."

Ionizing radiation: A nuclear burst results in four types of ionizing radiation: neutrons, gamma rays, beta and alpha radiation. "The initial burst is characterized by neutrons and gamma rays while the residual radiation is primarily alpha, beta, and gamma rays. The effect of radiation on a living organism varies greatly by the type of radiation the organism is exposed to," the manual says. "When radiation interacts with atoms, energy is deposited resulting in ionization (electron excitation). This ionization may involve certain critical molecules or structures in a cell, producing its characteristic damage.

"Two modes of action in the cell are direct and indirect action. The radiation may directly hit a particularly sensitive atom or molecule in the cell. The damage from this is irreparable; the cell either dies or is caused to malfunction. The radiation can also damage a cell indirectly by interacting with water molecules in the body. The energy deposited in the water leads to the creation of toxic molecules; the damage is transferred to and affects sensitive molecules through this toxicity. The two most radiosensitive organ systems in the body are the hematopoietic [i.e., blood cell-producing] and the gastrointestinal systems."

- Close your eyes and drop to the ground if you seen a flash of brilliant light.

Protect your eyesight by closing your eyes if you see the brilliant flash typical of a nuclear explosion. Then, take cover. A nuclear explosion's blast, winds and fireball rapidly extend from the epicenter, destroying most everything in their path. It's vital, therefore, to dive for cover immediately to avoid being killed outright or injured by flying debris or flames. Take refuge under a desk, table or vehicle. Stay as low to the ground as possible. Keep your legs together, pull your elbows into your sides and cover your ears with the palms of your hands. This protective

Blast Effect of 150-Kiloton Nuclear Explosion 16 Seconds After

Detonation at the Foot of the Empire State Building

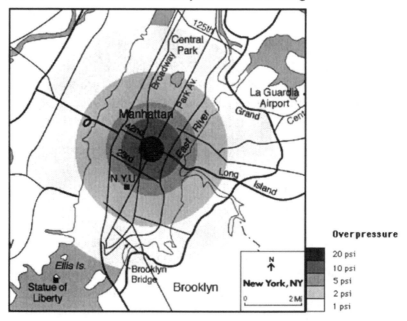

Source: AJ Software & Multimedia/Atomic Archive

posture will protect as many vital body organs as possible. Cover your mouth and nose with a cloth to protect your breathing. Stay down until the blast wave has passed and the winds have died down. Beware of falling objects, teetering structures or wrecked vehicles leaking fuel. Watch out, too, for gas that could be seeping from broken utility lines or live electricity wires lying on the ground.

• Don heavy clothing and protect your breathing.

As in any attack with a weapon of mass destruction, it's important to cover your skin, mouth and nose. This will reduce the chances of being contaminated via skin contact, inhalation or ingestion. Put on the heaviest garments you can find, including an overcoat, boots, gloves and a hat. Cover your mouth and nose with a mask, handkerchief or cloth. Once away from the scene of destruction, discard your contaminated clothing and wash thoroughly.

- Put time, distance and shielding between you and radiation.

Time, distance, and shielding will reduce your odds of contamination from radiation. The injurious effects of a nuclear explosion dissipate over time. Distance, of course, gets you further away from the source of contamination. And shielding, such as groups of large buildings, hills, mountains and forests, helps to block the spread of lethal radiation. Move upwind of the site. Close your vehicle's windows, and seal air vents. Stuff clean cloth into the vent holes in the passenger compartment. If your windows leak, cover the seams with plastic tape.

Some people, alas, will find themselves between a rock and a hard place. Take Long Island, New York. If a nuclear blast occurred in New York City and the winds were blowing due east, Long Island residents wouldn't have many safe options. The only bridges and tunnels off the island are at the western end, meaning that fleeing residents would have to head toward the attack site. Their best bet, therefore, would be to get off the island by boat or plane.

Caution   Don't drive too close to the vehicle in front of you; its tires will kick up radioactive dust than could get into your vehicle.

- Treat everything and everyone as if they were radiation-contaminated.

Touch only what you have to, for most exposed items will be contaminated with radiation. That includes foodstuffs and water—and people, too. Don't drink tap water or water from outdoor sources, such as streams or lakes. If you're not properly protected, touching someone else could expose you to radiation. Likewise, others could be exposed to your own radioactive contaminants. Seek supplies of food and water from emergency personnel as you get farther away from the epicenter of the blast. Otherwise, obtain food and bottled water that has been inside a store or home.

• Understand the effects of radiation poisoning.

Here's the EPA's verbatim explanation of the effects of radiation on humans:

> "Radiation effects fall into two broad categories: deterministic and stochastic. At the cellular level, high doses of ionizing radiation can result in the severe dysfunction—and death—of cells in the body. At the organ level, if a sufficient number of cells are affected, the function of the organ is impaired. Such effects are called 'deterministic.' Deterministic effects have definite threshold doses, which means that the effect is not seen until the absorbed dose is greater than a certain level. Once above that threshold level, the severity of the effect increases with dose. Also, deterministic effects are usually manifested soon after exposure. Examples of such effects include radiation skin burning, blood count effects, and cataracts.
>
> "In contrast, stochastic effects are caused by more subtle radiation-induced cellular changes (usually DNA mutations) that are random in nature and have no threshold dose. The probability of such effects increases with dose, but the severity does not. Cancer is the only observed clinical manifestation of radiation-induced stochastic effects. Not only is the severity independent of dose, but also, there is a substantial delay between the time of exposure and the appearance of the cancer, ranging from several years for leukemia to decades for solid tumors. Cancer can result from some DNA changes in the somatic cells of the body, but radiation can also damage the germ cells (ova and sperm) to produce hereditary effects. These are also classified as stochastic; however, clinical manifestations of such effects have not

been observed in humans at a statistically significant level.

"The nature and extent of damage caused by ionizing radiation depend on a number of factors, including the amount of exposure, the frequency of exposure, and the penetrating power of the radiation to which an individual is exposed. Rapid exposure to very large doses of ionizing radiation is rare but can cause death within a few days or months. The sensitivity of the exposed cells also influences the extent of damage. For example, rapidly growing tissues, such as developing embryos, are particularly vulnerable to harm from ionizing radiation."

- Get immediate medical attention; if none's available, wash thoroughly with warm water.

The following are verbatim excerpts from the medical emergency guidance provided to doctors and hospitals by the radiation exports at Oak Ridge Associated Universities (www.orau.gov). The information could prove invaluable if you can't immediately get medical assistance following a nuclear explosion.

"Contaminated patients can have radioactive materials deposited on skin surfaces, in wounds, or internally (ingested, inhaled, or absorbed). Reassessment of the contaminated patient's airway, breathing, and circulation are done in the decontamination room prior to attention to the patient's radiological status. Level of consciousness and vital signs are assessed promptly and the patient's condition is stabilized. After examining the entire patient and identifying all injuries, a complete radiological survey should be done. . . .

"Contaminated wounds are first draped, preferably with a waterproof material, to limit the spread of radioactivity. Wound decontamination is accomplished by gently irrigating with saline or water. More than one irrigation is usually necessary. . . . Embedded radioactive particles, if visible, can be removed with forceps or by using a water-pik. Puncture wounds containing radioactive particles, especially in the fingers, can be decontaminated by using an 'en bloc' full thickness skin biopsy using a punch biopsy instrument. After the wound has been decontaminated, it should be covered with a waterproof dressing. The area around the wound is decontaminated as thoroughly as possible before suturing or other treatment.

"Contaminated burns (chemical, thermal) are treated like any other burn. Contaminants will slough off with the burn eschar. However, dressings and bed linens can become contaminated and should be handled appropriately. Contaminated body orifices, such as the mouth, nose, eyes, and ears need special attention because absorption of radioactive material is likely to be much more rapid in these areas than through the skin.

"If radioactive material has entered the oral cavity, encourage brushing the teeth with toothpaste and frequent rinsing of the mouth. If the pharyngeal region is also contaminated, gargling with a 3-percent hydrogen peroxide solution might be helpful. Gastric lavage may also be used if radioactive materials were swallowed. Contaminated eyes should be rinsed by directing a stream of water from the inner canthus to the outer canthus of the eye while avoiding contamination of the nasolacrimal duct. Contaminated ears require external rinsing, and an ear syringe can be used to rinse the auditory canal, provided the tympanic membrane is intact.

"Decontamination of the intact skin is a relatively simple procedure. . . . The simplest procedure is to wash the contaminated area gently under a stream of water (do not splash) and scrub at the same time using a soft brush or surgical sponge. Warm, never hot, tap water is used.

Cold water tends to close the pores, trapping radioactive material within them. Hot water causes vasodilation with increased area blood flow, opens the pores, and enhances the chance of absorption of the radioactive material through the skin. Aggressive rubbing tends to cause abrasion and erythema and should be avoided. . . . The decontamination procedure stops when the radioactivity level cannot be reduced to a lower level."

- Check out the Nuclear Blast Mapper to see how you'd fare after a detonation.

Would you survive the fallout from a nuclear blast? There's an interesting (albeit not totally scientific) way to find out. The Public Broadcasting Service (PBS) has a fascinating online feature called the Nuclear Blast Mapper. It shows the pressure damage and radioactive fallout that would follow a nuclear blast in most cities and major countries of the world. You pick the city in which the nuclear device would detonate and the mapper shows you the most likely path of destruction.

The nearby map shows the radioactive fallout a week after a one-megaton nuclear surface explosion in New York City with a due east wind. According to PBS, at a distance of up to 30 miles, residents would receive "much more than a lethal dose of radiation," with death occurring within hours of exposure. About ten years would need to pass before levels of radioactivity in this area dropped low enough to be considered safe by U.S. peacetime standards. Ninety miles out from the epicenter, the radiation dose would still be lethal, killing people in 2 to 14 days.

At 160 miles distance from New York, calculates PBS, the fallout would causes "extensive internal damage, including harm to nerve cells and the cells that line the digestive tract." This would result in a loss of white blood cells and temporary hair loss. Finally, at a distance of 250 miles, there would be no immediate harmful effects, but the fallout would result in a temporary decrease in white blood cells. Two to three years will need to pass before radioactivity levels in this area drop low enough to be considered safe by U.S. peacetime standards, notes PBS. The fallout from New York City could extend Bridgeport,

Radioactive Fallout from a One-Megaton Nuclear Surface Blast

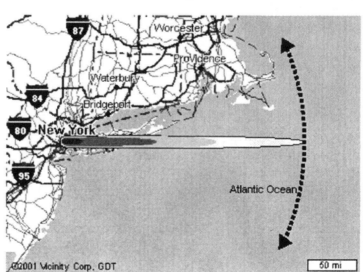

Source: Public Broadcasting Service

Connecticut, Providence, Rhode Island, or Cape Cod, Massachusetts if the winds blew toward the east-northeast.

The PBS mapper draws its information mainly from "The
Effects of Nuclear War," produced by Congress's Office of
Technology Assessment in 1979 (see the recommended readings
at the end of the chapter). The zones of destruction mapped out,
says PBS, are "broad generalizations and do not take into
account factors such as weather and geography." The mapper
can be found at www.pbs.org/wgbh/amex/bomb/sfeature/ma-
pablast.html.

3.21. Tips for the Elderly and Disabled

In the wake of Sept. 11, many people have become more
neighborly and willing to extend a helping hand. Don't hesitate,
therefore, to contact friends, relatives and even neighbors you
don't know about providing you with assistance in the event of a
terrorist incident or other emergency. If some people reject your

appeal for assistance, don't let it upset you. They'll eventually get their reward for their selfishness.

- Fill out an emergency health information card and keep copies around the house.

Communication with emergency personnel could be difficult following a terrorist attack or other crisis. No one can count on being conscious or coherent following a terror incident. If you are elderly or disabled and require special care, this could prove to be a serious problem.

The American Red Cross suggests that the disabled and elderly should fill out an emergency health information card. The card tells rescuers what they need to know about you if they find you unconscious or incoherent, or if they need to help evacuate you in a hurry. The card should list the medications you take and the healthcare equipment you use, as well as any allergies or sensitivities you may have. Also list the names of people who should be contacted in an emergency. Make multiple copies of the card to keep in your purse or wallet, near the doors to your home, in your car and if appropriate, in your wheelchair pack.

Tip Keep a working flashlight handy in case you have to signal emergency personnel.

- If you're disabled or elderly, you should augment your emergency supplies.

Make sure your have enough prescription medicines and other necessary medical supplies (e.g., medication syringes, colostomy, respiratory, catheter, padding, distilled water, etc.) to last one to two weeks in the event of an emergency. If you have a respiratory, cardiac or multiple chemical-sensitivities condition, store towels, masks, industrial respirators or other supplies you can use to filter your air supply. Be sure, too, that you have a non-electric can opener and a battery-power radio (and extra batteries) in case the electricity goes out. If you use a hearing aid, keep spare batteries on hand. And stay in contact by phone with your friends and relatives.

Follow the instruction of emergency personnel if you're asked to leave your home. Leave your valuables in a safe place at home rather than taking them with you. The chances are higher that you'd lose them as opposed to having their stolen from your unoccupied home. See that your pets are taken care of by a friend or neighbor, brought with you or left at home with plenty of food and running water.

Tip The American Red Cross says that if you are unable to afford extra supplies, you should consider contacting one of the many disability-specific organizations, such as the Multiple Sclerosis Society, Arthritis Foundation and United Cerebral Palsy Association. These organizations may be able to assist you in gathering extra low-cost or no-cost emergency supplies or medications.

• Establish and maintain a personal support network.

You may already have a personal assistant, but an emergency could make transportation impossible, preventing your helper from reaching you. As a backup, establish a personal support network of friends and neighbors who could lend a hand in an emergency. If you don't know many people in your neighborhood, contact a local church, synagogue or mosque and ask if they could provide names of people living nearby who'd be willing to lend you a hand in a crisis. But don't just file those numbers away. Dial them every once in a while, saying hello and telling your network that you're practicing just in case an emergency should happen.

Tip Ask in advance if any of your contacts would be willing to take care of your pets in the event of an evacuation.

• Discuss things over in advance with the members of your support network.

The American Red Cross recommends the following seven important items you should discuss with and give to the members of your personal support network:

1) Make arrangements, prior to an emergency, for your support network to immediately check on you after a disaster and, if needed, offer assistance.
2) Exchange important keys.
3) Show where you keep emergency supplies.
4) Share copies of your relevant emergency documents, evacuation plans and emergency health information card.
5) Agree on and practice a communications system, but don't count on the telephones working.
6) You and your personal support network should always notify each other when you are going out of town and when you will return.
7) The relationship should be mutual. Learn about each other's needs and how to help each other in an emergency. You could be responsible for food supplies and preparation, organizing neighborhood watch meetings, interpreting, etc.
• Ask your helpers to read some literature on how to assist you in an emergency.

The Internet sites of the American Red Cross (www.redcross.org) and the Federal Emergency Management Agency (www.fema.gov), among others, have considerable amounts of literature on how to assist the elderly, the immobile and the disabled in emergencies, including ones related to terrorism. Ask the members of your support group to familiarize themselves with the available literature so they can better prepare for an emergency and know instinctively what to do should a crisis strike.

Tip If you use a wheelchair or other special equipment, show them how it operates. If you have difficulty speaking, ask someone to record a message you can use over the phone in an emergency; the message should include your name, address and the nature of your disability.

• Get your local police to conduct a home security check.

Police departments are well aware of the special needs of the elderly and disabled, and they're also aware that criminals often see the elderly and disabled as easy marks. Therefore, contact your local police department and ask an officer to conduct a security check of your home. This would have the added benefit informing the police of your location and needs in the event of a local emergency.

3.22. Dealing with Stress

Americans, indeed the world, went through a lot on Sept. 11. Witnesses to those events won't soon forget the ghastly, surreal sights or the pain and sadness of seeing so many innocent lives lost in a few short hours. Then, too, there was the fear about opening the mail that developed with news of the lethal anthrax letters sent to members of the media and Congress. New worries are cropping up almost daily—concerns about attacks on nuclear power plants or cyberterrorism disrupting vital infrastructure. It's, therefore, worth taking note of the stress that most us have felt since that September morning and to discuss a few healthy coping mechanisms.

• Don't be afraid to talk about your feelings and thoughts about terrorism.

In the many interviews with the recovery teams, police, firefighters and construction crews working at ground zero in New York, most everyone has the same message: To cope, we talk. Keeping emotions bottled up inside isn't healthy. So speak with friends, relatives, co-workers or professional counselors about your worries about terrorism. You'll probably be surprised to learn that you aren't alone in your feelings and thinking. And that knowledge alone can be a great relief.

Tip Staying physically healthy is important to your emotional well-being, so eat right and exercise regularly.

U.S. Poll: Government's Ability to Prevent
Cyberterrorism, December 2001

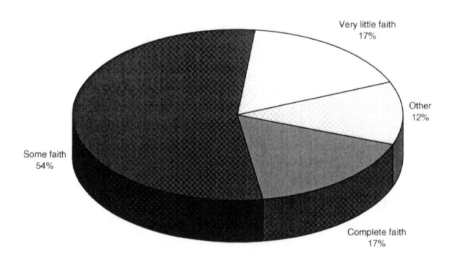

Source: Information Technology Association of America

- Getting out of yourself by giving of yourself is a great stress-buster.

Stress develops as we internalize our feelings, sometimes so much so that we become totally egocentric. The more we focus on our problems and our worries, the worse they may become. Indeed, our difficulties could spiral out of control, resulting in severe depression, aggression or substance abuse. A surefire way of defeating stress is to get out of yourself. That means focusing on others. So lend a helping hand somewhere. Give of yourself. Volunteer to help with a charitable cause, pay more attention to your family and relatives, and do the occasional good deed.

- Try yoga-type breathing exercises to relax.

While we don't profess to be expert in yoga, we do know one simple exercise that provides considerable relief from stress. What's particularly nice about it is that it doesn't require you to contort yourself into knots. It involves only breathing. Begin by closing your eyes and mouth and breathe in through your nose but only fill your lungs by amount one-quarter capacity. Count slowly to ten and then exhale slowly through your mouth. But don't exhale any old way. Blow the air out. And blow it out slowly, very slowly, as if you were trying to keep a feather afloat. Next, fill you lungs up a bit more, hold the breath, and then blow out the air. Again, take in more air, hold it and blow. Soon you'll feel as if your lungs are filled from your belly to your shoulders. After 10 to 20 minutes of this, you should feel much more calm and relaxed.

Caution   Novices may hyperventilate. If you feel dizzy, remain seated and breathe in and out of a paper bag or moderate-sized container, recirculating the same air over and over until you feel better. This will return the level of carbon dioxide in your blood back to normal and relieve your wooziness. And, please, don't perform this breathing exercise while driving.

- Get out and enjoy life; socialize and keep your intellect in charge.

The world can be too much for us. Take time to smell the roses, explore the world, meet new people, and perhaps do some of the things you always meant to do but never seemed to find the time. You only live once, as they say. Take time for a bit of self-reappraisal. Write down a few things you'd like to do before you turn old. Then do them. Make good use of your weekends and vacations. Get away from the television and read a good book or listen to music. Take a stroll. Life wasn't intended to be all work. Socialize with others, and don't be ruled by your emotions. Keep your intellect in charge.

- Reinforce your sense of security by taking proactive antiterrorism measures.

"Nothing in life can prepare you for the horror of an act of terrorism that robs you of your sense of security and, in some instances, a loved one," notes "Coping After Terrorism: A Guide to Healing and Recovery," published by the U.S. Department of Justice's Office for Victims of Crime. "Recovering from a traumatic event will take a long time and will not be easy." It's vital, therefore, to reinforce your sense of personal safety and security. The reading of this book is a start. Gain strength from the knowledge that you are being proactive in implementing antiterrorism measures. Appreciate your own self-reliance, and rest assured that whatever can be done you have done.

3.23. Helping Children Cope

Children can take the news of a terrorist attack (or any disaster) particularly hard. In some cases, a child's reaction can become so severe as to result in post-traumatic stress disorder (PTSD). Several articles are listed at the end of this chapter to provide parents with an in-depth understanding of the potential problems and remedies. Here's a brief overview.

- Understand that reactions to traumatic events vary with the age of the child.

Children may react to a horrific event almost immediately or long afterwards. They may lose trust in their parents or all adults, fear a reoccurrence of the event and show signs of emotional disturbance. A lot depends on the age of the child. Children five years of age and younger, says the National Institute of Mental Health (NIMH), may fear being separated from their parents; cry, whimper or scream; become immobile or aimless; tremble; express fright in their faces, and cling. These young children also may show signs of regressive behavior, acting like babies again (e.g., thumb-sucking, bedwetting and fearing the dark).

Youngsters six to 11 can become withdrawn, disruptive and irritable. They may refuse to go back to school, display outbursts of anger and cause fights. They might not be able to pay attention or they may have nightmares. These youngsters also may complain of stomachaches or other imaginary illnesses. They, too, could show regressive behavior, or become depressed, anxious, and guilty or even emotionally numb. Adolescents 12 to 17, says the NIMH, may response in ways similar to adults, suffering flashbacks, nightmares or emotional numbness. Depression could lead to substance abuse. They may display antisocial behavior and decline academically. They also could have difficulty sleeping, complain of phantom illnesses, and feel guilty, angry and even suicidal.

- Talking with your children is a big help.

Children affected by trauma need reassurance, and experts recommend that talking with your children can help a great deal in the healing and recovery process. Honest answers to questions are the best, though child psychologists emphasize that you should tailor your answers to the age of the child. In general, children want to be assured that they're safe and that their parents are safe. Be open and supportive. Tell them that actions are being taken to catch the people who were responsible for the attack and that the government is trying to make sure it never happens again. Don't, however, promise that it will never happen again. And limit the amount of television exposure your children have to the scenes of violence or disaster.

- Listen to your children with love and understanding.

Children should be encouraged to talk following a national trauma. Help them find ways to express themselves, because they need to vent their thoughts and fears, experts say. So be attentive and listen to them with understanding and provide them with reassurance. Assuage their fears, rid them of any extreme worries, and let them know they're loved and being cared for. Recognize, too, that children tend to personalize a traumatic event, expressing concerns about the well-being of relatives and friends. Let them speak or meet with grandparents and other relatives to reassure them that everyone in the family is all right. At the same time, don't dismiss your child's feelings out of hand. Acknowledge their thoughts and appreciate their reasoning. Don't make them feel stupid or think they're wrong to feel as they do. But then explain to them why they needn't feel or think they way they do.

- Try to make your children's lives more predictable and stable.

Child psychologists say that parents have to do their part in helping their children overcome the emotional disturbance caused by acts of terror or other disasters and violence. Reintroduce routines into the home to make your children's lives once again predictable and stable. Make it a point to gather together as a family. Play games, engage in sports, read to your children, plan outings, and visit relatives and friends. Also, set a good example. Children often mimic their parents, and if they see you return to life as normal, so may they. Your youngsters will pay close attention to how you're responding to events. That means you must deal with any emotional issues you may have following a terrorist incident. You might share your feelings with your children and then them how you coped.

- If problems persist, seek professional help for your child.

The danger of a traumatic event leading to severe emotional and academic difficulties is very real. Problems such as post-traumatic stress disorder (PTSD) or substance abuse could follow. If a child remains unable to cope with a traumatic event long after its occurrence, seek professional help. Consult with your child's doctor or school for recommendations, or contact the National Center for PTSD at www.ncptsd.org or 802-296-6300.

3.24. Recommended Online Reading

"Animals and Emergencies," Federal Emergency Management Agency (FEMA), www.fema.gov/fema/anemer.htm.
"Backgrounder: Radiation–Sources And Potential Hazards," FEMA, *www.fema.gov/library/radback.htm*.
"Biological/Chemical Threats by Post," U.K. Government Co-ordination Centre, www.co-ordination.gov.uk.

"Biological Diseases/Agents Listing," Centers for Disease Control, *www.bt.cdc.gov/Agent/Agentlist.asp.*

"Bioterrorism," U.S. Food and Drug Administration, *www.fda.gov.*

"Bomb Threats and Physical Security Planning," Bureau of Alcohol, Tobacco and Firearms, U.S. Department of the Treasury, *www.atf.treas.gov.*

"Chemical Agents Listing and Information," Centers for Disease Control, *www.bt.cdc.gov/Agent/AgentlistChem.asp.*

"Chemical/Biological/Radiological Incident Handbook," Interagency Intelligence Committee on Terrorism, Central Intelligence Agency, *www.odci.gov/cia/publications/cbr_handbook/cbrbook.htm.*

"Coping After Terrorism: A Guide to Healing and Recovery," Office for Victims of Crime, U.S. Department of Justice, *www.ojp.usdoj.gov/ovc/.*

"Coping with A National Tragedy," American Psychiatric Association, www.psych.org.

"Crime Prevention Advice," British Home Office, *www.homeoffice.gov.uk/crimprev/cp_index.htm.*

"Crime Prevention Tips," Los Angeles Police Department, *www.lapd.org/bldg_safer_comms/prevention_main.htm.*

"Crime Prevention Tips for People with Physical Disabilities," Los Angeles Police Department, *www.lapd.org/bldg_safer_comms/prevention/phys_dis.htm.*

"Disaster Preparedness for People with Disabilities." American Red Cross, *www.redcross.org/pubs/dspubs/terrormat.html.*

"The Effects of Nuclear War," Office of Technology Assessment, Congress of the United States, May 1979, *www.fas.org/nuke/intro/nuke/7906/index.html.*

"Emergency Food and Water Supplies," FEMA, *www.fema.gov/library/emfdwtr.htm.*

"Expedient Respiratory and Physical Protection: Does a Wet Towel Work to Prevent Chemical Warfare Vapor Infiltration?" Sorensen, J., and Vogt, B., Oak Ridge National Laboratory, ORNL/TM-2001/153, 2001, *http://emc.ornl.gov/emc/PublicationsMenu.html.*

"Fire Safety Factsheets," U.S. Fire Administration, *www.usfa.fema.gov*.

"Foodborne Diseases," National Institute of Allergy and Infectious Diseases, National Institutes of Health, www.niaid.nih.gov/publications/foodborne.htm.

"Guidance for Radiation Accident Management," Oak Ridge Associated Universities, *www.orau.gov/reacts/guidance.htm*.

"Hazardous Materials Accidents," FEMA, www.fema.gov/library/hazmatf.htm.

"Health Service Support In A Nuclear, Biological, And Chemical Environment," U.S. Department Of The Army, April 1993, *www.adtdl.army.mil/cgi-bin/atdl.dll/fm/8-10-7/toc.htm*.

"Helping Children and Adolescents After a Disaster," American Academy of Child and Adolescent Psychiatry, *www.aacap.org*.

"Helping Children and Adolescents Cope with Violence and Disasters," National Institute of Mental Health, *www.nimh.nih.gov/publicat/violence.cfm*.

"Helping Children Cope with A National Tragedy," American Psychiatric Association, www.psych.org/disaster/childrentragedy91201.cfm.

"House And Building Fires," FEMA, *www.fema.gov/library/housef.htm*.

"How Do I Deal With My Feelings?" American Red Cross, *www.redcross.org/pubs/dspubs/terrormat.html*.

"How Do I Know? A Guide to the Selection of Personal Protective Equipment for Use in Responding to a Release of Chemical Warfare Agents," Foust, C., Oak Ridge National Laboratory, ORNL/TM-13343, 1999, *http://emc.ornl.gov/emc/PublicationsMenu.html*.

"How to Recognize and Handle a Suspicious Package or Envelope," Centers for Disease Control, *www.bt.cdc.gov*.

"Letter and Package Bomb Detection Techniques," Bureau of Alcohol, Tobacco and Firearms, U.S. Department of Treasury, *www.atf.treas.gov/pub/index.htm*.

"Mail Handling Guidelines," Los Angeles County Department of Health Services, *http://labt.org*.

"A Nation Online: How Americans Are Expanding Their Use of the Internet," Economics and Statistics Administration, U.S.

Department of Commerce, *www.esa.doc.gov/508/esa/nationon-line.htm*.

"New York Example: 150-Kilton Nuclear Explosion at the Empire State Building," Atomic Archive, AJ Software & Multimedia, *www.atomicarchive.com/Example/ExampleStart.shtml*.

"Nuclear Power Plant Emergency," FEMA, www.fema.gov/library/radiolo.htm.

"Nuclear Power Plant Locations," International Nuclear Safety Center, Argonne National Laboratory, *www.insc.anl.gov*.

"Nuclear Power Plants Around the World," Virtual Nuclear Tourist," *www.nucleartourist.com*.

"Nuclear Power Plants in the U.S.," U.S. Energy Information Administration, *www.eia.doe.gov/fuelnuclear.html*.

"Nuclear Weapon Effects," Federation of American Scientists, *http://fas.org/nuke/intro/nuke/effects.htm*.

"Pets and Disasters," FEMA, *www.fema.gov/fema/petsf.htm*.

"Potassium Iodide and Emergency Preparedness," U.S. Nuclear Regulatory Commission, *www.nrc.gov/what-we-do/radiation.html*.

"Radfacts: Some Basic Information for Reporters on Radiation and Radiological Emergencies," U.S. Environmental Protection Agency, *www.epa.gov/radiation/rert/*.

"Radiation Emergencies," Centers for Disease Control and Prevention, *www.bt.cdc.gov*.

"Response Guidelines to the FBI Threat Advisory Concerning Apartment Buildings," Los Angeles Police Department, *www.lapd.org*.

"Responding to A Chemical-Biological Threat: A Practical Guide," Bureau of Diplomatic Security, U.S. Department of State, *http://ds.state.gov/publications/keepingsafe.htm*.

"Safe Water Practices in the Back Country: Avoiding Giardiasis and Cryptosporidiosis," Oregon State University, *http://eesc.orst.edu/agcomwebfile/edmat/html/ec/ec1431/ec1431.html*.

"Security of the Mail," U.S. Postal Service, *www.usps.com*.

"Special Collections: Terrorism," U.S. General Accounting Office, *www.gao.gov/terrorism.html*.

"Talking to Children about War and Terrorism: 20 Tips for Parents," by David Fassler, M.D., American Psychiatric Association, *www.psych.org/disaster/20tipsparents11801.cfm.*

"Terrorism: Preparing for the Unexpected," American Red Cross, *www.redcross.org/pubs/dspubs/terrormat.html.*

"Tips for Overseas Travel: Actions If Attacked," U.S. Army Corps of Engineers, *www.swf.usace.army.mil/ppmd/Security/ SLE_Tips.htm.*

"Tips for People with Special Needs & Concerns," American Red Cross, *www.redcross.org/pubs/dspubs/terrormat.html.*

"Your Family Disaster Plan," FEMA, *www.fema.gov/library/fam-plan.htm.*

"Your Family Disaster Supplies Kit," FEMA, www.fema.gov/ library/diskit.htm.

"What is Radiation?" U.S. Environmental Protection Agency, *www.epa.gov/radiation/rrpage/rrpage2.html.*

"Will Duct Tape and Plastic Really Work? Issues Related To Expedient Shelter-In-Place," Sorensen, J., and Vogt, B., Oak Ridge National Laboratory, ORNL/TM-2001/154, 2001, http:// emc.ornl.gov/emc/PublicationsMenu.html.

Chapter 4

How to Travel Safely in General

Our feelings about traveling since Sept. 11 have leaned toward extremes: complacency ("There's nothing I can do about terrorism."), fatalism ("If I'm going to go, I'm going to go.") or trepidation ("I'm not flying anywhere. Period."). And that's precisely how terrorists want you to react to their horrific deeds. If you're too complacent or fatalistic, you lose and the terrorists win. You lose because you may neglect to take steps that could save your life, and they win because they have another easy target. If you're too apprehensive, the terrorists win and you lose. They win because fear of terrorism rules your life, and you lose because you've given up part of your freedom. In all three cases, it's win-win for terrorists and lose-lose for you.

It doesn't have to be this way. You can strike a balance that reduces your fear or complacency about traveling and increases your chances of returning home from a trip safe and sound. The question is, how?

This chapter provides the answer—and provides it in a most interesting way. You might call it osmosis. In science, this occurs when a solvent passes from one side of a membrane to the other. It takes place all the time in the human body, as substances pass through cell walls and are absorbed. In the realms of the mind and emotions, osmosis occurs when we absorb new ideas, feelings or attitudes, seemingly without effort. These new concepts needn't be drilled into us. Instead, they become part of us, changing us, by our mere exposure to them.

After reading this chapter, you should discover something rather remarkable. You'll find that you'll already feel better about the prospect of traveling. You'll be neither complacent nor afraid. Instead, you will have a newfound confidence. Your outlook will be different. You'll feel sure that you can go about your business and take your vacations in a normal fashion. But "normal" won't mean the same thing it used to. The procedures set out here will give you a new understanding of what it means to travel safely. If you heed this advice and follow the recommended steps, you'll develop an entirely new travel routine and mindset. And those two elements—routine and mindset—will help to protect you from harm when traveling either domestically or overseas.

By way of analogy, consider the qualities that make for a good or bad driver. A good driver follows a practiced routine and drives defensively. A bad driver doesn't. The differences between the two are their routines and their mindsets. (And you know which one you'd rather be in a car with.) The same applies to travel of any kind, be it for business or pleasure, at home or abroad. If you follow a strict, studied routine and adopt the proper, proactive mindset, you'll have a much better chance of skirting hazards and getting home alive and unharmed.

Travelers of all types should review the suggestions in this chapter as they pertain to travel safety in general. More specific advice for those planning overseas trips is provided in the next chapter, "How to Travel Safely Abroad." Before going any further, though, consider this suggestion:

• Be willing to change and receptive to new ideas.

Appreciate first that you can't simply will yourself to be safe. Travel security requires an investment of time and effort. Reading this chapter is a start—but only a start. Next, be willing to change. Your old travel habits are not appropriate in this new day and age of terrorism. Finally, be receptive to new ideas and new ways of doing things. Approach travel security with an open mind, and jettison your old notions about safety. Don't reject suggestions out of hand or let preconceptions get in the way, because most assumptions about travel safety formed over years of experience are no longer valid.

4.01. Everyday Commuting

Many Americans think they're really only vulnerable to terrorism when they're traveling by air on a long-distance trip for business or pleasure. Fact is, though, terrorists—notably in the Middle East but in Europe and Asia as well—often target

U.S. Carjackings, Distance from Home, 1992-1996

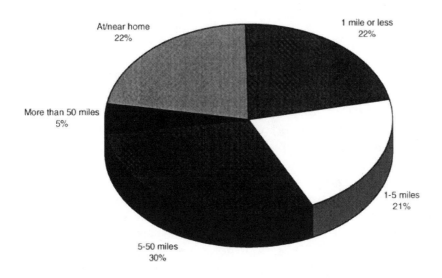

Source: Bureau of Justice Statistics, U.S. Department of Justice

commuters on buses and trains. What's more, bridges and tunnels used by commuters are also on the list of potential terrorist targets.

- Keep an eye out for unattended items when using mass transit.

Because terrorists seek to kill and injure as many people as possible, mass transit offers a perfect target. That's why it's so important to notify authorities immediately of any unattended package, box, briefcase, luggage or canister you may come across while commuting via train, subway or bus. Unattended items could pose a serious threat and shouldn't be dismissed lightly. Similar caution should be taken in any public place where large numbers of people gather. Twelve Japanese commuters died and another 5,700 were injured when deadly Sarin nerve gas was released into the air at a crowded Tokyo subway station in March 1995. A similar attack occurred almost simultaneously in the Yokohama subway system. Five members of the Aum Shinrikyu cult carried out the attacks, which involved placing containers of gas in subway stations and cars. Japanese courts have since sentenced several of the terrorists to death.

- Learn how to spot suspicious behavior on streets, buses and trains and at transportation stations.

To recap our more lengthy discussion of suspicious behavior in the preceding chapter, terrorists are often nervous and almost always look out of place in their surroundings. They don't behave like the others around and may be so preoccupied that they appear strange and unusual—as if something is pressing on their minds. They may even be jumpy. A group of men and even women, who at first seem to know each, may suddenly act like strangers. Their actions may deviate from normal behavior, as if they were acting or imitating the everyday procedures followed by, say, janitors. They may be on the lookout for the police and also may pay far too much attention to something. Most often, the object of their attention is their intended target.

Note, too, that terrorists conduct reconnaissance missions prior to any attack, so you might see them photographing, videotaping or mapping a location, testing out security doors or attempting to gain entry to areas that are off limits to the general public. Spanish police in July 2002, for instance, arrested three Syrians suspected of being Al Qaeda members, and one of them had five videotapes containing images of New York's World Trade Center, Statue of Liberty and Brooklyn Bridge, San Francisco's Golden Gate Bridge, Chicago's Sears Tower, and California's Disneyland and Universal Studios, as well as an unidentified New York airport.

- Scout out the emergency exits at transportation stations you regularly use.

Time is precious in an emergency. You could do yourself a big favor in the event of a terrorist incident at a commuter station if you know in advance all of the available exit ways from the train, bus or subway stations that you regularly use. Take some time and look around for the exits. Think about how you would get out of a specific location in a hurry. And don't consider just the most obvious routes of egress, because they could become jammed in an emergency. Scout out some of the less obvious exits, as well as places where you could take cover if, for example, gunfire were to break out.

Tip If you routinely use a major commuter hub that's a tempting target for terrorists (e.g., Boston's South Station or New York's Pennsylvania Station), consider changing your daily routine and taking an alternative route to and from work. You might, for instance, be able to catch your normal train but at a different station.

Caution Falling objects and flying glass cause many deaths and injuries in terrorist explosions. While waiting for your bus or train, therefore, make it a point not to stand under or near anything that could harm you in a blast.

- Avoid rush hour by changing your commuting times, especially if you use major bridges or tunnels.

The crush of commuters at rush hour presents a tempting target for terrorists. That's because the types of devices they most commonly use (e.g., bombs) have their greatest effect in crowded places. Terrorists, therefore, look for venues where people are forced to be concentrated in large numbers or congregate voluntarily in mass gatherings. Crowded rush-hour train and bus stations are two such examples, but there are others. Terrorists, for instance, have set their sights on major bridges (as noted above) and tunnels. It's impossible to say in advance how well tunnels would hold up if a massive truck bomb exploded. It would depend on the age and construction of the tunnel and the size and location of the bomb. Most bridges would hold up rather well after the detonation of a car or truck bomb, with one exception. Bridges with two decks pose a special risk. The containment created between the upper and lower levels would magnify the force of a blast on the lower deck and could, under the right conditions, result in wholesale devastation and perhaps cataclysmic collapse.

Save for security checkpoints that might detect a bomb-laden vehicle, a commuter's only protection is to avoid the times at which terrorists would be most likely to attack. And those times are, of course, when bridges and tunnels are most heavily used—namely, rush hours. If possible, therefore, it might be wise to adjust your commuting schedule (or even your work hours) so as to avoid rush-hour traffic. The same rule holds for commuters using mass-transit trains, subways and buses that cross bridges or go through tunnels.

Tip Talk with your company about telecommuting. You may be able to do work at home and reduce the number of days you have to commute to the office.

- Never park in underground garages.

Terrorists already know that one way to cause mass destruction and maybe even bring a building down is to plant a car or truck bomb in an underground parking garage. So find another place to park that's outdoors. And when you do park, leave the front of your car pointing out so you can exit as quickly as possible in case a suspicious persons is lurking about, and always check the interior of you car before getting in to see if an attacker is hiding in, say, the back seat. Also, park as close to an exit as possible. Consider asking for an escort to your car, especially when traveling at night.

4.02. Getting Informed

Information is knowledge, and knowledge is power. The better informed you are about the nature of the terrorist threat as it pertains to your travel plans, the safer you will be. Don't look at the task of acquiring travel-related information as a burden; think of it as an investment.

- Familiarize yourself with your travel destination by reading the local newspapers and listing to local radio news online.

Don't create an artificial separation between terrorism and crime. Either one can be lethal. So make it a point to know what's happening at your travel destination. But don't rely on your hometown newspaper to give that information. Instead, go online and read the local papers and listen to local radio news in your travel city—especially one you're visiting for the first time.

We recommend three directories of local newspapers links: Kidon Media Links (www.kidon.com/media-link/index.shtml), even though based in the Netherlands, has links for virtually every newspaper in the U.S. (as well as the world). You can also find newspaper links at NewsLink (http://newslink.org) and NewsDirectory.com (www.newsdirectory.com). For the most complete list of radio stations with online feeds, go to Radio-Locator (www.radio-locator.com). (For travelers heading overseas, see our discussion in the next chapter on how to keep abreast of foreign news—and even get online English translations of foreign-language news.)

Caution   Be sure to keep your computer's antivirus software updated, and we strongly recommend that you invest in a firewall if you don't already have one.

- Ask friends and colleagues for insights about your travel destination.

Reading a newspaper or listening to radio news can only tell you so much about potential risks of crime or terrorism at your travel city. Get as much information as you can from people who live there or have been there recently, such as co-workers, employees of your company based at your destination, clients you plan to meet, friends or relatives.

Tip   Strike up a conversation with passengers next to you on your outbound flight. If they live or work at your travel

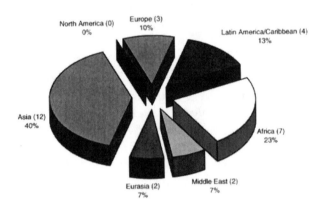

Source: Federal Aviation Administration

destination, they, too, might offer some invaluable insights, especially about the parts of town to avoid.

- Avoid long waits at U.S. border crossings.

Given the potential for injury at U.S. border crossings were, say, a car bomb to go off or a gunfight to break out between terrorists and border guards, the less time spent waiting in line, the better off you'll be. For border-crossing wait times, see the U.S. Customs Service's website www.customs.gov. Click "Travel Information" or go directly to www.customs.gov/travel/travel.htm.

4.03. Flying Smart

Airports and jetliners are two primary terrorist targets, yet air travel is today an integral part of our lives—especially, our business lives. This has presented most of us with a dilemma: How to balance the need to travel by air against the risk of a terrorizing attack? Well, there are smart and not-so-smart ways to fly. By following some basic procedures, you can cut your risk of becoming involved in a terrorist incident and increase your chances of survival if you do become an unfortunate victim.

- Check ahead for the latest news of any terrorist threat or other security problem.

For special advisories concerning terrorist and other security threats at your travel destination, call the U.S. Department of Transportation's Travel Advisory Line at 800-221-0673. This recorded announcement provides the latest U.S. and overseas travel warnings. (Travelers headed overseas also should call the U.S. State Department's hotline at 202-647-5225.) The Federal Aviation Administration's Air Traffic Control System Command Center at www.fly.faa.gov provides up-to-the-minute information on arrival and departure delays at airports throughout the country. For flight-specific information, you must contact your airline.

- Dress sensibly when you fly, giving special thought to your shoes.

Wearing a formal business suit or a stylish dress could prove a hindrance if a quick evacuation of an airplane or airport is required. Causal dress is much more appropriate for air travel these days. Roomy clothing that doesn't restrict motion is advisable. Also, wear clothes made of natural fabrics, such as cotton, wool, denim or leather. In a fire, synthetics tend to melt. If you aren't carrying luggage in which you can store your business attire, at the very least wear sensible shoes. Carry your dress shoes or high heels in your briefcase or handbag and change into them later.

Tip   Dress to cover as much of your skin as possible. This will help to protect you from cuts, abrasions and skin-burn if you have to slide down a plane's emergency chute.

Caution   Avoid sandals, because they could pose a problem if speed and surefootedness are called for. Women should be aware that nylon stockings can melt, causing injury when sliding down a plane's emergency chute.

- Choose paper tickets over paperless ones.

If you have an option, ask for a traditional paper ticket. It will get you through security check-in quicker than an electronic, paperless one. A paper ticket also comes in handy if you need to change airlines because of a flight delay or cancellation. Airlines usually are reluctant to accept paperless tickets issued by another carrier.

Tip   Avoid aisle seats, as the chances of injury or death in a hijacking are greater for those passengers seated along the aisle.

- Don't brush off the importance of keeping an eye on your bags and knowing whether someone else handled them.

All of us know the drill: We're asked at check-in whether we packed our own bags and whether we left them unattended at any time. Most of us are so bored hearing the questions that we reply with automatic, unthinking answers. Fact is, we're being all too indifferent to the seriousness of the problem and dangerously blasé in answering security questions. Terrorists and criminals have successfully used unwitting passengers to carry bombs or other dangerous items on board aircraft—either by tricking them into carrying packages aboard or by slipping objects into unwatched bags. So think twice before you answer those routine luggage questions the next time you're at a check-in counter. If you have any doubts, be honest and say so. A little white lie in this case could cost you your life.

Tip   Don't bring wrapped gifts with you. You may be forced to unwrap them at the security checkpoint, causing you unnecessary delay. Also, before getting to security checkpoints, place in your carry-in luggage any cell phones, pagers, keys, lighters or other items that will trigger the metal detectors.

- Spend as little time at the airport as possible.

Airports, in and of themselves, are high-risk locales because they are prime terrorist targets. On December 14, 1999, an alert U.S. border guard decided to check the contents of a vehicle being driven by Ahmed Ressam, an Algerian national, who was trying to cross from Canada into the State of Washington. The officer found a huge stash of high explosives. Upon further investigation, it was determined that Ressam intended to bomb Los Angeles International Airport on the eve of the 2000 millennium celebration. After his conviction, Ressam testified that he had received money and training at terrorist camps run by Osama bin Laden in Afghanistan. ("Trial of a Terrorist: Inside Ressam's Millennium Plot," transcript, Public Broadcasting Service, WNET, New York, 2001.)

Airports appeal to terrorists as sites to attack for a variety of reasons: 1) Airports have high concentrations of people, meaning that any terrorist attack with explosives, gunfire, or biochemical weapons is sure to result in many casualties. 2) Airports are mainstays of modern economies in which business often requires long-distance travel; airport attacks, therefore, have ripple effects throughout an economy in that they make people hesitant to fly. 3) Airports are high-profile targets in that an airport attack anywhere is sure to garner worldwide publicity—publicity that terrorists crave. It therefore behooves travelers to spend as little time in airports as possible. And one of the easiest ways is to avoid checking in luggage.

Caution Stay away from heavily glassed areas in airports in case a bomb goes off; don't stay in areas outside the security zone, and if you see a disturbance, move away because it could be an unfolding terrorist incident or a ruse staged for thieves to snatch your luggage or wallet.

- Whenever possible, don't check any luggage; carry all of your belongings on board.

Being able to carry all your belongings aboard a flight means you will spend less time at the check-in counter and you won't have go to baggage claim upon arrival at your destination. You should have luggage that will fit either under a plane seat or in the overhead bins. The maximum size carry-on bag for most airlines is 45 linear inches (i.e., the total of the height, width, and depth of the bag). The Federal Aviation Administration has a hotline, 800-322-7873, open weekdays during normal working

**Incidents Against Aviation and Airports
by Global Region, 1996-2000**

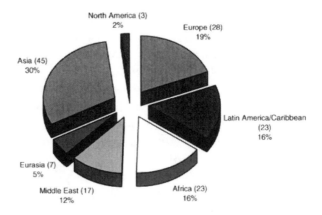

North America (3)
2%

Europe (28)
19%

Asia (45)
30%

Latin America/Caribbean
(23)
16%

Eurasia (7)
5%

Middle East (17)
12%

Africa (23)
16%

Source: Federal Aviation Administration

hours, designed to answer consumer questions about carry-on baggage, as well as such other issues such as child restraints and turbulence problems. Also, check with your airline to see how many items they allow on board. Carriers normally permit only one carry-on item of luggage and one personal item, like a briefcase or handbag. Next, pack light. The quicker you're in and out of an airport, the safer you'll be.

Tip   If you do check baggage, include sufficient clothing in your carry-on items to get you through the next day. You never know when your checked bags will be lost or delayed.

Caution   Don't exchange items between bags while waiting in line at check-in, security screening or customs, as this could raise suspicions.

• Never make yourself a slave to your luggage.

Pack light so you can get in and out of travel hubs quickly, without need of assistance. Having to find a porter is not only a costly and time-consuming nuisance, it also impairs your ability to avoid trouble at air or rail terminals. The last thing you want to do these days is to linger at known venues of terrorist attack or criminal activity. Make sure that any suitcase too large or heavy to carry comes with wheels. And also make sure that your luggage is of light construction. By that, we don't mean luggage that's going to fall apart, but suitcases that are constructed of light yet durable materials.

Traveling light usually requires packing well in advance—especially if traveling for several days or weeks. Only by packing well ahead of time can you determine whether or not you'll be able to manage without help. Traveling light also means packing only necessities. That's often easier said than done, however. The difference between a necessity and a non-necessity isn't always clear. But there is a surefire way to tell. Upon returning from your next trip, make it a point to itemize the contents of your luggage. Look at the clothes your wore and items you used—and then look at all the rest. You'll likely find plenty of clothing and paraphernalia that served no purpose and only weighed you down. This post-return sorting process will help you separate necessities from non-essentials. Make a list of your travel necessities—and stick to it the next time you pack for a trip.

Tip   Another way to travel light, especially on long trips, is to buy clothes at your destination. Prior to your return, you can mail or ship home items that are too much to carry. Besides, clothes bought abroad or in a fashion city might make nice additions to your wardrobe. Be aware, however, that you may be charged duty on items sent back to the U.S. from overseas, including clothing bought in the U.S. or that you have long owned. For more information, see "Mailing Goods to the United States" at www.customs.gov/travel/travel.htm.

- Always try to keep one hand free when carrying your luggage.

Anyone overloaded with baggage is a target for criminals and terrorists. If it takes all you can do merely to keep hold of your belongings, you won't be able to react quickly in a threatening situation. Make it a rule always to keep one hand free at times when traveling with luggage. That means either packing light or using a luggage rack on wheels.

Tip Have your hotel launder and dry-clean your clothes. That way, you won't have to carry as much. Be sure to check ahead to ensure that your hotel has laundry and dry-cleaning services and find out how long it normally takes to get clothes back.

- Carry only product samples that you can handle without assistance.

When the nature of your business requires you to show samples, you want to make traveling with them as easy as possible. The last thing you want to do is dally at an airport or a rail station waiting for a porter. So ensure that you can carry both your samples and your personal belongings without assistance. If your sample item is very large or heavy, don't bring it with you when you travel. Have it shipped to your destination in advance. You have several options here: 1) ship the samples to your company's office in that city; 2) send them to your hotel; 3) ship them to your customer's office, or 4) have the shipper hold them until your arrival.

Tip Travel in pairs. You and a co-worker could handle samples, as well as your luggage, without additional help.

- Make any checked luggage easy to spot.

There's nothing worse when waiting for luggage at an airport baggage carousel than to find that someone else is traveling with bags that are identical your own. You face the prospect that another traveler will mistakenly walk away with your luggage (or vice versa). Moreover, if your luggage is hard to distinguish from everyone else's, you may end up standing at the carousel longer than necessary as your bags make repeated passes before your unseeing eyes.

Adding a distinguishing mark to your luggage solves the problem. Adhere a few decals or masking tape to your bags, or tie something distinctive around the handles. That way you can spot your bags immediately and be out of the airport while your fellow passengers are still straining to find their luggage. But make sure that you can see the marking from a distance. The reason for making your bags distinct to your eyes is, after all, to get you out of the terminal as quickly as possible. In our age of terrorism, loitering at airports isn't wise.

- At an airport baggage carousel, position yourself near the luggage chute.

We don't know if Einstein was the first to postulate this or not, but time takes longer when you're waiting for your luggage. Besides the boredom of waiting, however, the baggage-claim area of an airport isn't a place you want to be these days. Terrorists are always on the lookout for spots where people congregate. At airports, there are two high-density locations: the check-in counters and baggage claim. The fastest way to get out of harm's way is to retrieve your bags as soon as possible (assuming you need to check any luggage at all). And the easiest method of getting your bags quickly is to stand near the chute from which luggage emerges and slides onto the carousel. This will ensure that you won't have to wait for your luggage to make a slow journey around the carousel to your outstretched hands.

- Don't advertise your corporate affiliation on your luggage or ID tags.

Be sure nothing visible on your luggage identifies your company or your job title. Corporate logos or titles like "Chairman and CEO" will tip off would-be kidnappers and extortionists. Don't use business cards as luggage tags, and always use ID tags that cover your name and address. Provide your name, along with the street address and phone number of your company. Avoid using your home address and number just in case you're abducted and ransom is demanded. In most instances, it's better that your abductors contact your employer as opposed to your family.

Tip   You can increase your chances of retrieving lost luggage if you include identification *inside* as well as outside your bags. Before getting rid off lost luggage, airlines typically look inside to see if they can identify the owner.

- Beware of anything you find on a plane, however innocuous it might appear, that could contain a bomb.

If you find what appears to be forgotten luggage in an overhead bin or a piece of electronic equipment, such as a CD or cassette player, left on the floor or wedged in or under your seat, report it immediately to a flight attendant. It could well be a bomb planted by terrorists.

- If seated next to an emergency door, take your responsibility seriously.

Emergency evacuations are serious business, and seats next to emergency doors carry a heavy responsibility. Moments can mean the difference between life and death in a crashed and burning plane. In the event of a hijacking, furthermore, aircraft emergency exits could be your route to freedom. So take the time to read the instructions on how to open an emergency door and unfurl the slide. Lives could depend on it. If you aren't physically or emotionally up to the task, ask for another seat.

- Don't race down aircraft aisles or make any move toward the cockpit.

With air marshals now aboard flights, especially ones bound for such high-security destinations as Washington, D.C. and New York City, any unusual moves around the cabin could get you attention you neither need nor want. Who wants to be tackled and handcuffed when all you intended to do was to beat a hasty path to the lavatory? Think about you movements when aboard an aircraft (and at airports). Don't do anything that might raise suspicions, like deciding to stroll up to the cockpit door.

Caution   Never joke about having a bomb, carrying a weapon or being a terrorist. You could easily find yourself in handcuffs.

4.04. Air Travel Security Rules

Following the tragedy of Sept. 11, Congress enacted and President Bush signed new aviation security legislation, which, among other things, established the Transportation Security Administration (TSA). The agency's mission is to protect the U.S. transportation network—most especially, airlines and airports. The TSA, for example, is the organization responsible for the new list of items that air travelers are barred from bringing into aircraft cabins. These new rules, as well as other TSA advisories, are worth reviewing.

- Avoid airport hassles by leaving barred carry-on items at home or put them in your check-in luggage.

On its website www.tsa.gov, the TSA provides a list of items that will not be allowed through airport security checkpoints. The list, however, isn't all-inclusive, the TSA notes, and "other items that may be deemed to present a potential threat may also be prohibited." Here are the items barred from aircraft cabins, as of mid-2002:

Items Prohibited in Aircraft Cabins in the U.S.

Ammunition	Brass knuckles	Dynamite
Automatic weapons	Bull whips	Fire extinguishers
Axes	Cattle prods	Flare pistols
Baseball bats	Compressed air	Golf clubs
BB guns	guns	Gun lighters
Billy clubs	Corkscrews	Gunpowder
Blackjacks	Cricket bats	Hammers
Blasting caps	Crow bars	Hand grenades
Bows and arrows	Disabling chemicals	Hatchets
Box cutters	or gases	Hockey sticks

Hunting knives
Ice axe/Ice pick
Knives (any length)
Kubatons
Large, heavy tools
(e.g., wrenches,
pliers)
Mace
Martial arts devices
Meat cleavers
Metal scissors with
pointed tips
Numchucks/
nunchaku
Pellet guns
Pen knives

Pepper spray
Pistols
Plastic explosives
Pool cues
Portable power
drills
Portable power saws
Razor blades (not in
a cartridge)
Religious knives
Replica weapons
Revolvers
Rifles
Road flares
SCUBA knives
Sabers

Screwdrivers
Shot guns
Ski poles
Spear guns
Starter pistols
Straight razors
Stun guns or shock-
ing devices
Swords
Tear gas
Throwing stars
Toy transformer ro-
bots (forms a
toy gun)
Toy weapons

Source: Transportation Security Administration

The TSA further says: "Passengers should be aware that there are no provisions for returning banned items to them when they are left at the security checkpoint. In addition, those who attempt to bring banned items through the checkpoints are subject to civil penalties of up to $1,100 per violation in addition to criminal penalties."

Tip The items most commonly left at the checkpoints, says the TSA, are scissors of all types, pocketknives, corkscrews and mace. Leave these items at home or put them in your check-in luggage. Also, check the TSA website or call your air carrier for updated lists.

- Know the special provisions for some check-in items, including items completely barred from aircraft.

The TSA has a number of special provisions regarding items stowed in your check-in luggage. Firearms and starter pistols may be transported in checked baggage so long as they are unloaded and declared to the airline at the ticket counter before you go to the screening checkpoint. Small arms ammunition for personal use may be carried in checked baggage but only if securely packed in fiber, wood or metal boxes, or other packaging specifically designed to carry small amounts of ammunition. One self-defense spray (e.g., pepper spray or mace) not exceeding 4 fluid ounces may be carried in a checked bag if it has a positive means to prevent accidental discharge. Compressed-air guns, fire extinguishers, flare pistols and gun lighters are regulated as hazardous materials and may only be transported as cargo on passenger planes under strict limitations in quantity and packaging.

Items entirely forbidden in air transportation include disabling chemicals or gases, dynamite, gunpowder, hand grenades, plastic explosives, road flares and tear gas.

Caution   Note that many other items, not referred to here, are restricted or forbidden aboard aircraft because they're deemed hazardous materials. Call the Hazardous Materials Information Center at 800-467-4922 for information. Violations of hazardous materials rules, the TSA warns, may result in fines of up to $27,500 per violation, as well as criminal fines and/or jail.

- Review the TSA's guidelines for boarding flights.

Besides allowing yourself extra time for airport check-in— approximately one to two hours—review beforehand the following TSA guidelines for boarding flights in the U.S.

Check-in:

- A government-issued ID (federal, state, or local) will be requested. Each traveler should be prepared to show ID at the ticket counter and subsequent points, such as at the boarding gate, along with an airline-issued boarding pass.
- Curbside check-in is available on an airline-by-airline basis. Travelers should contact their airline to see if it is available at their airport.
- E-ticket travelers should check with their airline to make sure they have proper documentation. Written confirmation, such as a letter from the airline ac-

knowledging the reservation, may be required to pass through a security checkpoint.

Screener checkpoints:

- Only ticketed passengers are allowed beyond the security checkpoints. (Arrangements can be made with the airlines for non-travelers accompanying children, and travelers needing special assistance to get to the gate.)
- Don't discuss terrorism, weapons, explosives, or other threats while going through the security checkpoint. Don't joke about having a bomb or firearm. The mere mention of words such as "gun," "bomb," etc., can compel security personnel to detain and question you. They are trained to consider these comments as real threats.
- Each traveler will be limited to one carry-on bag and one personal item (such as purse or briefcase). Travelers and their bags may be subject to additional screening at the gate.
- All electronic items (such as laptops and cell phones) are subject to additional screening. Be prepared to remove your laptop from its travel case so that each can be X-rayed separately.
- Limit metal objects worn on your person or clothing.
- Remove metal objects (such as keys, cell phones, change, etc.) prior to passing through the metal detectors to facilitate the screening process. (Putting metal objects in your carry-on bag will expedite the process of going through the metal detector.)

At all times:

- Control all bags and personal items.
- Do not accept any items to carry onboard a flight from anyone unknown to you.

**Aircraft Hijackings and Commandeerings
by Global Region, 1996-2000**

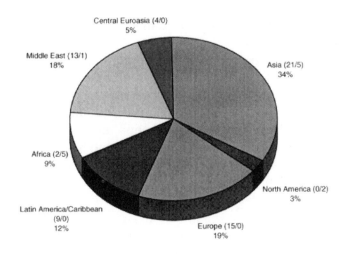

Source: Federal Aviation Administration

- Report any unattended items in the airport or on an aircraft to the nearest airport, airline or security personnel.

The TSA further says that if you have photo identification for your children have those with you and also bring a printout of your E-ticket itinerary. For further information, contact: Transportation Security Administration, 400 Seventh St. SW, Washington, DC 20590, 866-289-9673, www.tsa.gov. Consumers with concerns or complaints about airline or airport safety or security should call the Federal Aviation Administration at 800-255-1111 or go to www.faa.gov.

4.05 Young or Disabled Air Travelers

Recognizing that the new airport security procedures can make travel with young children or travel by persons with disabilities or special needs more difficult, the aviation authorities, among others, have issued some special guidance.

- Build children's confidence by putting security procedures in a positive light.

Pessimists view a glass as half-empty; optimists see it as half-full. Attitude, in other words, can have a large bearing on how young travelers respond to heightened security at airports and elsewhere. Parents, therefore, should talk with their children about the new security procedures before getting to the airport, putting an accent on the positive and eschewing the negative. Point out how security keeps us safe and helps us to get where we're going. Don't speak of dangers or threats, and don't discuss Sept. 11 unless *they* bring it up and then explain that that won't happen to them or to you. You might reassure them that the bad men who did that are dead.

Tip   The Centers for Disease Control and Prevention offers special advice for keeping children healthy while traveling at www.cdc.gov/travel/child_travel.htm.

- Heed the TSA's advice when traveling with children.

"Before entering the line for the passenger checkpoints," the TSA recommends, "parents should discuss the entire process with their children so they will not be frightened or surprised. Parents should advise children that their bags will be put in the X-ray machine but it will come out at the other end and that someone may ask to see mom's shoes but they will return them, etc."

The following is addition TSA advice for parents and guardians, reprinted here verbatim:

General Travel Tips for Traveling with Children:

- Every person regardless if they are adults, children, or babies must undergo screening to proceed beyond the security checkpoint.

- ALL child-related equipment must go through the X-ray machine if it fits (i.e., strollers, umbrella strollers, infant carriers, car and booster seats, backpacks, baby slings, etc.).
- When child-related equipment does not fit through the X-ray machine, the equipment will be visually and physically inspected.
- Parents should talk to their children before coming to the airport and let them know that it's against the law to make threats such as "I have a bomb in my bag". Threats made jokingly (even by a child) can result in Law Enforcement being summoned to the security checkpoint, the entire family being delayed, and could eventually result in being fined, or arrested.
- Ask screeners for assistance to help reunite you with your bags and child-related equipment, if needed.
- Follow the security rules regarding toys, notably toy guns.

Traveling with Infants or Toddlers:

X-Ray Machines:

- All carry-on baggage including children's bags must go through the x-ray machine. This means all child seats, baby carriers, diaper bags, blankets, toys, etc., anything that is carried onto the plane.
- Babies and children must be removed from their strollers/infant carriers so that they can undergo visual and physical inspection. Babies should NEVER be left in an infant carrier while the equipment goes through the X-ray machine.
- Ensure all bags hanging on and carried under child-related equipment are removed from the equipment and put through the X-ray machine.
- To expedite the screening process, passengers should collapse/fold child-related equipment when they arrive at the checkpoint and place the equipment on the X-ray belt.

Metal Detectors:

- If walking through the metal detector sets off the alarm, each alarm must be resolved on each person (including children) going through the metal detector.
- If a person is carrying a child through the metal detector and it alarms, the alarm will be resolved for both the adult and child.
- The person cannot pass the child to another person behind or in front of them during this process.
- Do not pass your child to the screener to hold. The screener cannot hold or attend to your child.
- Ideally, if a child can walk, it would best that the child walk through the metal detector independently.

For further information, contact: Transportation Security Administration, 400 Seventh St. SW, Washington, DC 20590, 866-289-9673, www.tsa.gov.

- Passengers with disabilities or special needs should seek assistance at airports.

In light of stepped-up airport security, special provisions are being made for passengers with disabilities or special needs, particularly during the screening process. Herewith, verbatim, is the TSA's "Security Screening Advice for Passengers with Disabilities:"

General:

- Remember, you can always ask for and receive a private screening.
- Make sure medications are properly labeled (professionally printed label identifying the medication or a manufacturer's name or pharmaceutical label).
- It is recommended that you notify your airline in advance if you have special needs or need assistance at the airport.

- It is recommended that you notify your airline if you need an airline representative to accompany/help you to your gate.
- It is recommended that you check with your airline on the procedure for getting a pass/authorization for your companion/assistant to accompany you through the security checkpoint and to your gate.
- The limit of one carry-on bag and one personal item (e.g. purse or briefcase) for each traveler does not apply to passengers with disabilities medical supplies, equipment, mobility aids, or assistive devices.
- Mobility aids and assistive devices permitted through the security checkpoints include: canes, walkers, crutches, prosthetic devices, body braces, wheelchairs, scooters, augmentation devices, Braille note takers, slate and stylus, service animals, and diabetes related equipment/supplies as specified below.

Mobility Disability:

- As you proceed through the security checkpoint, don't hesitate to ask screeners for assistance with your mobility aid and carry-on items.
- It will expedite the screening process if you let the screener know your level of ability (e.g. whether you can walk, stand, or perform an arm lift).
- Inform screeners of any special equipment or devices that you are using and where this equipment is located on your body. This will help the screener to be careful of that equipment if a physical search is necessary.
- Let screeners know if you cannot remove your shoes when additional screening is necessary.
- If you can remove your shoes, ask screeners for assistance if needed.
- To expedite the process, ensure all bags and satchels hanging from, carried under or on your equipment are put on the x-ray belt for inspection.

- Ask the screener to reunite you with your carry-on items and assistive device once x-ray inspection is completed.

Hearing Disability:

- If the screening process is unclear to you, ask the screener to write the information down, or look directly at you and repeat the information slowly.

Visual Disability:

- Ask the screener to
  - Explain the security procedures
  - Describe what will happen next
  - Let you know where the metal detector is located
  - When you will be going through the metal detector
  - Let you know when there are obstacles you need to avoid
- Let the screener know when you need someone to escort you through the screening process.
- Notify screener if x-ray inspection (i.e., Braille note takers) will harm the equipment you may be using. Ask for your device to be visually and physically inspected instead of x-ray inspection.
- Ask the screener to reunite you with your carry-on items and assistive device once x-ray or physical inspection is completed.
- Ask the screener to reunite you with your computer or electronic items that required additional screening.
- Ask the screener to verbally direct you toward your gate once the screening process has been completed.

Service Animals & Guide Dogs:

- There is no documentation required to take your service animal through the security-screening check-point.

- The service animal/guide dog and its belongings will require a physical inspection (i.e., whether they walk through the metal detector together or the animal walks in front or behind the user with the user continually maintaining control of the animal with the leash, harness/halter, etc.).
- Advise the screener on how to best screen your service animal or guide dog.
- This inspection includes: the animal and its belongings (collar, harness, leash, backpack, vest, etc.).
- Ask the screener to not take off the animals' belongings during this inspection since this is a sign to the animal that they are off work.
- Service animals/guide dogs should not be separated from their owner.

Hidden Disability:

- Passengers with a hidden disability can, if they chose, advise screeners that they have a hidden disability and may need some assistance or need to move a little slower than others.
- Family members or traveling companions can also advise screeners when they're traveling with someone who has a hidden disability, which may cause that person to move a little slower, become agitated easily, and/or need additional attention.
- Notify screeners if you have special equipment that cannot go through the x-ray machine. Request a physical/visual inspection of your equipment instead of x-ray inspection.
- Notify screeners if you need to sit down before the screening process is completed.

Persons With Diabetes:

- Notify the screener that you have diabetes and are carrying your supplies with you.

- Make sure insulin (vials or outer box of individual doses), jet injectors, pens, infusers, and preloaded syringes are marked properly (professionally printed label identifying the medication or manufacturer's name or pharmaceutical label)
- There is no limitation on the number of empty syringes that you will be allowed to carry through the security checkpoint; however you must have insulin with you in order to carry empty syringes through the checkpoint.
- Lancets, blood glucose meters, blood glucose test strips can be carried through the security checkpoint.
- Notify screeners if you're wearing an insulin pump and ask if they will visually inspect the pump since it cannot be removed from your person.
- Insulin pumps and supplies must be accompanied by insulin with professionally printed labels described above.
- If possible, advise screeners when/if you are experiencing low blood sugar and are in need of medical assistance.

Persons With Pacemakers:

- It is recommended that individuals with a pacemaker carry a Pacemaker Identification Card (ID) when going through airport security.
- A Pacemaker ID card is typically issued by your doctor or hospital where you received your implant.
- This ID card may be helpful when you are trying to clear airport security.
- Advise the screener that you have an implanted pacemaker, show the screener your pacemaker ID, if you have one, and ask the screener to conduct a pat-down inspection of you rather than

you walking through the metal detector or being hand-wanded.

Assistive Devices:

- Notify screener if x-ray inspection will harm your equipment. Ask for your device to be visually and physically inspected instead of x-ray inspection.
- You can ask for a private screening for the visual and physical inspection of your prosthetic device and/or body braces.
- Crutches, canes, and walkers will need to go through the x-ray machine.
- If equipment cannot fit through the x-ray, then the screener will perform a visual and physical inspection of your equipment.
- Collapse canes whenever possible before they are put on the x-ray belt.
- Ask for assistance with your device(s) if needed.
- You should not be asked to remove your prosthetic device or body brace for it to undergo x-ray inspection. Prosthetic devices and body braces should be visually and physically inspected once you have walked through the metal detector.
- Screeners will need to see and touch prosthetic devices and body braces as part of the physical and visual inspection.

For further information, contact the Transportation Security Administration, 400 Seventh St. SW, Washington, DC 20590, 866-289-9673 or www.tsa.gov. If you experience a problem or have a complaint, contact the U.S. Department of Transportation's Aviation Consumer Protection Division, which has a 24-hour complaint line, 202-366-2220 (TTY 202-366-0511), or go to www.dot.gov/airconsumer/.

- Find out about accessibility at your travel destinations.

Civilian Casualties and Terror Attacks Worldwide, 1991-2001

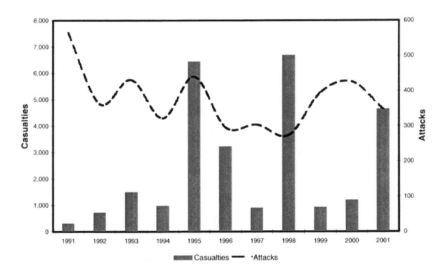

Source: U.S. Department of State

The U.S. Architectural and Transportation Barriers Compliance Board (a.k.a. Access Board), a federal agency, offers a variety of free publications for travelers with disabilities. Contact the board at Suite 1000, 1331 F Street NW, Washington, D.C. 20004-1111, 800-872-2253 or 202-272-0080 (TTY 800-993-2822 or 202-272-0082), www.access-board.gov.

4.06 Selecting a Hotel

Hotel selection requires more than merely considering cost, convenience and comfort. Safety and security must also become part of the selection process.

- Make safety, not price, your prime consideration when selecting a hotel.

"That's easy for you to say. You don't know my company." If that was your immediate reaction to the above recommendation, you're working for the wrong company. Any firm willing to endanger you so it can save money may not deserve your loyalty.

Caution Check with the front desk to find out whether any of your hotel's entrances are locked at night; you don't want to be wandering about in the dark, searching for an open door.

- Don't just book the hotel nearest to your meetings or branch office.

Make the quality of the neighborhood in which your hotel is located a top consideration. It's tempting to pick the hotel nearest to your planned meetings or your company's branch office. And, indeed, these locations might be great in the daytime. But what about at night? Do they the roll up the sidewalks? Do the streets become deserted? In most cases, it's best to find the safest area nearest to your points of call or your local office and then select your hotel accordingly. (We make an exception to this rule when it comes to foreign travel; our specific recommendations appear in the next chapter.) Find out, too, about the neighborhoods you plan to visit or pass through. Crime usually concentrates in different parts of a city like pools of water after a storm. Don't think that just because your hotel is in a safe area, that the districts a few blocks away are equally tranquil.

Tip Always carry your room key with you; don't leave it with the front desk, because thieves and kidnappers look in hotel mailboxes to see which guests aren't in their rooms.

- Avoid hotels that have underground garages.

Terrorists love underground garages. On February 26, 1993, Arab terrorists planted a massive truck bomb in the parking garage beneath the World Trade Center in New York City. The blast killed six persons and injured more than a thousand. Even though hotels have tightened garage security, there's little to stop a determined suicide bomber from driving through barricades and setting off an underground explosion that would likely cause the building above it to collapse. It's simply not worth the risk of staying on top of an underground garage. Find another hotel.

- Make sure your hotel isn't a firetrap.

There's a fast and easy way to find out whether a hotel or motel in the U.S.—or even on Guam, the Northern Mariana Islands, Palau, Puerto Rico or the Virgin Islands—meets federal standards for fire and life safety. The U.S. Fire Administration (which is part of the Federal Emergency Management Agency) has an online database at www.usfa.fema.gov/hotel/search.cfm that you can search. If a hotel or motel makes the grade, you'll see a yellow "go" sign.

The database is an outgrowth of the Hotel and Motel Fire Safety Act of 1990, which attempted to save lives by promoting fire and life safety in hotels, motels and other places of public accommodation. The law mandates that federal employees on official travel must stay in public accommodations that adhere to these life and safety standards. In fact, federally funded meetings and conferences cannot even be held at locations that don't meet these requirements. The federal standards require hardwired, single-station smoke detectors in each guestroom and automatic sprinkler systems, with a sprinkler head in each guestroom. Hotels or motels with fewer than four floors are exempt from the sprinkler requirement.

Tip   If you simply enter the name of the city, state or island you intend to visit, the database will produce a list of all approved accommodations.

- Don't hesitate to switch hotels if your needs aren't met or you sense something's wrong.

Hoteliers want your business and therefore most are willing to accommodate any reasonable request. However, if you find yourself in a hotel that's unwilling to meet your needs, don't hesitate to switch to another one. Indeed, if for any reason you feel uncomfortable at the hotel in which you've been booked, move on. Your instincts are probably right. Whatever it is that you're feeling, odds are there is something wrong with your accommodations. You may not be able to put your finger on it or put it into words, but when your sixth sense tells you that you're not safe, you probably aren't. Don't waste time trying to figure it out. It's not worth it. Call another hotel, pack up and leave.

4.07 Extra Security Precautions

Personal safety in this day and age requires self-assertiveness. Travelers must become more demanding about their accommodations, for example, than they had in the past. Not only will this help to better ensure your safety, but it also will raise awareness among hotel management that they need to pay more attention to counterterrorism measures.

- Be particular about your hotel room and try to pick the floor you stay on.

Several considerations have to be weighed before accepting a hotel room. Assess the potential risks you face in that city. Is it a city afflicted with considerable crime? Is it known for terrorist incidents? When traveling overseas, weigh these additional concerns: Is there much public dissention with the government? Is there a history of arson or bombings of public buildings or attacks on foreigners? Then think about the room location that would best negate the more likely risks.

If kidnapping and burglary are common, don't accept a room that has a balcony or is low to the ground (e.g., on the first or second floor). Look out the windows of your room to see they can be accessed easily via the top of a wall or fence or from a fire escape. In high-crime cities, don't stay in a room looking out on dimly lit areas. If the chances are high that a terrorist bomb could explode in front of the hotel, don't accept a room that faces the street. If arson is a worry, don't stay above the fifth floor, because most fire ladders don't extend much higher. And make sure all doors and windows lock properly.

Tip   Hotel rooms on the third to fifth floors are to be preferred for maximum safety and ease of fire rescue or emergency escape.

Caution   Don't mention your room number when in places where you might be overheard, such as in elevators or restaurants.

- Reject hotel rooms with sliding doors.

Rooms with sliding doors can make for great views or nice strolls outside. But, frankly, have often do you really use them? Once, maybe. Sliding doors are open invitations to criminals, kidnappers and terrorists. Put your safety first, and get another room.

Tip   If you have no choice but to stay in a room with a sliding door, not only lock it and use the security bar but also use an empty dresser drawer for added safety. Place the drawer lengthwise on top of the door track and push it squarely into the corner of the doorframe. That way, if someone forces the door open from the outside, he won't be able to get it open completely; the dresser drawer will be in the way. Don't use broom handles or small pieces of wood to block sliding doors. An expert burglar will lift those out with a coat hanger.

- After getting your key, always be escorted to your room by a hotel employee.

Once you've checked in and gotten your key, insist on getting someone to escort you to your room and ask him to wait while your do a bit of reconnaissance. Check everyplace a criminal or terrorist might be lurking in wait. Look in the bathroom, closets, behind drapes and under the bed. If there are connecting doors to adjoining rooms, make sure they're locked. Only then dismiss the bellhop (with a tip). It would be prudent to follow the same procedure each time you return to your room, keeping the door ajar until you're satisfied no one else is there.

• Make your very first outing a walk to the nearest fire exit.

On the back of most hotel doors is a floor diagram showing your room location and all emergency exits. Grab your key and take a stroll to the nearest emergency exits, being sure to count the number of doors you pass along the way. Keep a mental note of the route. And, if there is a fire and the halls fill with smoke, crawl along the floor, counting the doors, until you reach the exit. Never use an elevator in a fire, because the doors could open on the fire floor and you'll be burned to a crisp.

• Know what to do in a fire.

In a hotel fire, it's vital to remember to do one thing first: Press your hand against the top of the door, the doorknob and the crack around the door to feel for heat. If the door is hot to the touch, DON'T open it. There's most likely a ball of fire on the outside that could consume you in an instant. Fire can travel at upwards of 18 feet per second. If the door is hot to the touch, call the desk for help. Wet some towels or pillowcases and stuff them into door cracks to keep smoke out of your room. Swinging a wet towel around the room can catch smoke particles.

Look out the window to see if any rescuers have arrived. But don't open your window all the way unless the smoke becomes unbearable; an open window can create a natural draft that could suck smoke into your room. Open a window from the top to let out heat and smoke and at the bottom for fresh air to breathe. Cover your mouth and nose with a moist cloth and wait for help to arrive. Signal emergency personnel from your window to show them your location. Wave a sheet out the window. Use the hotel phone or your cell phone to help firefighters find you; you could flash a mirror or a lamp to signal your whereabouts to rescuers. If you have a whistle, use it. For more information on fire safety, go to the U.S. Fire Administration's website at www.usfa.fema.gov.

Tip If you must exit through smoke, clean air will be several inches off the floor. Get down on your hands and knees, and crawl to the nearest safe exit.

`Caution`   Don't go back into a fire for anything! Your life is your most valuable possession.

- Stow your shoes, robe, wallet and passport next to your bed.

In the event of an emergency, you may have to dash out of your room in hurry. The less time that takes, the better. So keep everything you *really* need near to hand. Keep your wallet and keys (and passport, when overseas) on the nightstand next to your bed. Put your shoes and a robe within easy reach. You may also want to keep your briefcase and laptop similarly nearby. But whatever you do, don't try to take all your belongings with you in an emergency evacuation. Things always can be replaced. You can't be.

`Tip`   Store your wallet and other important items in your room safe while bathing. If you're abroad and want to conceal your U.S. citizenship from causal observers, buy a plain cover (available at most stationary stores) for your passport.

- Keep your belongings tidy so you can leave a hotel at a moment's notice.

You never know when you may be called away suddenly or need to leave your hotel in a hurry. When time is of the essence, you don't want to be scurrying about your room, gathering up scattered clothing, papers and toiletries. So keep things neat. And, if you've left clothes to be cleaned, don't worry about them; they can always be shipped to you later. Depending on the situation and reason for your early departure, you may or may not want to leave a forwarding number and address with the front desk. If you suspect that the information could fall into the wrong hands, simply tell the desk to email you or call your office should the need arise.

`Caution`   Be sure to inform your family, your company and the people you plan to meet (as well as the local U.S. embassy or consulate, if you're overseas) of your move. You don't want them worrying if they call the hotel and find you're no longer there.

- Inspect the contents of your luggage before checking out of your hotel.

One way terrorists could plant a bomb aboard a plane would be to tamper with an unsuspecting traveler's luggage while it was still in his hotel room. So inspect the contents of your luggage before checking out of your hotel. If you find anything suspicious, leave the room immediately and then call the police.

- Be suspicious of unexpected mail.

If you receive unexpected mail at your hotel or branch office, treat it with suspicion. Follow the mail-handling procedures laid out in the earlier chapter on personal safety. Recognize, too, that mail from an unknown source means that someone knows you're in town. This could pose a risk of abduction or worse, especially when you're overseas. If you're worried, contact the police or the local U.S. embassy or consulate, and consider changing hotels—and don't leave a forwarding address or phone number other than your home office.

Caution   Be wary, too, of any packages left outside your hotel room and envelopes stuck under your door or left on your car windshield.

- Be careful about hanging signs on your hotel door.

Normally, signs like "Do Not Disturb" or "Make Up the Room" are placed on hotel room doors to provide instructions the staff. But in this day and age, they also provide valuable information to would-be thieves and attackers. Forego placing any signs on your hotel room door. Call to request service; that goes for meals as well. Don't leave a breakfast list out; call instead.

- When answering your hotel room door, always keep the door chained or blocked with a doorstop.

You may have ordered room service or be expecting a guest, but how can you be sure that a criminal doesn't lurk on the outside of your hotel door? A look through the peephole may be little help if you can't see the person on the other side or if you don't know what the person is supposed to look like. So the best thing to do is to keep the door between you and a visitor for as much time as needed to determine that he don't intend you any harm. There are two easy ways to do this: One is to always keep your hotel room door chained. To greet a waiter or a guest, open the door first with the chain on to ascertain that the person is, in fact, who you expect him to be—and not a criminal expecting to push his way into your room. A second way is to carry a rubber doorstopper with you. Although most hotels have chains on their doors, you may want added protection. By prepositioning a doorstop within inches of your door, any attempt at forcible entry will be stymied long enough for you to cry out for help and get to the phone to call hotel security. Rubber doorstoppers are cheap and, light, and can found in most hardware stores. Don't hesitate to buy one and make it part of your travel kit. Alternatively, portal travel locks can be used to secure hotel doors.

Caution   When leaving or returning to your hotel room, check the corridor for any suspicious persons. If you sense danger, go back into your room or get back on the elevator and inform hotel security.

- Be especially alert on stairs and in elevators in unfamiliar buildings.

While on a trip, you'll probably enter many buildings for the first time. This means that your knowledge of building security will be extremely limited. You won't necessarily know, for instance, if a building has a history of robberies or muggings. So be on guard when moving about unfamiliar buildings—and that includes your hotel. Of all the places you might be attacked, a building's stairs and elevators are the most likely spots. Before taking the stairs, look up and down the staircase and listen for any unusual noises. If you suddenly hear footsteps moving in a hurry, exit at the nearest floor and wait until the commotion stops. If you spot someone lurking below, again exit and wait until the coast is clear. And never use a staircase where the doors automatically lock behind you. When an elevator's doors open, don't get on if you see someone or something that doesn't look right; wait for the next car. If you're already in an elevator and a person enters whose look disturbs you, get off immediately.

Tip When you're in an elevator, especially in an unfamiliar building or in a high-risk city, always position yourself within reach of the emergency alarm.

- Never walk down dark alleys or empty streets.

Dark passageways and deserted streets are notorious for abductions, robberies, muggings and sexual assaults. The criminals know the territory and position themselves to take a captive, rob a passerby or rape a woman. Their tactic is to use surprise to gain the advantage. So do your homework. Study quality maps showing the main thoroughfares near your hotel or branch office. Always walk down well-lighted streets, and if possible, use routes where there a lot of other pedestrians or plenty of cars passing by. Kidnappers tend to avoid well-lighted, heavily traveled streets, knowing there are better spots in town to victimize the unwary. Ask at your hotel or branch office about the parts of town you should avoid. You don't want to get off a subway, say, and suddenly find yourself in the midst of thieves.

Tip Carry adequate travel insurance, covering theft, lost luggage and the like; comprehensive annual policies are the most cost-effective for frequent travelers.

- Ask at your hotel for the names and numbers of at least two car services.

It's easy to find yourself in a place in a strange city where there simply aren't any taxis. It may be that the hour's late or you may have strayed off the beaten track. So make it a point

International Terrorist Attacks by Global Region, 1991-2001

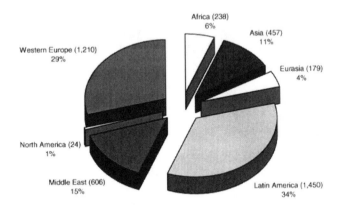

Africa (238)
6%

Asia (457)
11%

Western Europe (1,210)
29%

Eurasia (179)
4%

North America (24)
1%

Middle East (606)
15%

Latin America (1,450)
34%

Source: U.S. Department of State

before leaving your hotel to ask the desk for the names and telephone numbers of at least reliable car services. Besides convenience, those numbers could prove to be lifesavers if you end up in a crime-ridden part of town, particularly late at night.

Tip   Keep the address and phone number of your hotel with you at all times. This is particularly important overseas, where getting a phone number from directory assistance can be a challenge if you don't speak the language.

4.08. Dealing with Violence

Most people aren't prepared to deal with random acts of violence—be they criminal or terrorist in nature. Thinking the problem through and knowing how to respond beforehand can greatly lessen your chances of serious injury or death in a violent confrontation.

• Never make eye contact with an assailant.

Whatever you do, don't ever make direct eye contact with an assailant or anyone who you suspect might do you harm. Eye contact raises an attacker's stakes in a confrontation, and he's likely to become more aggressive as a result. Not only is eye contact intimidating to an attacker because it represents a personal challenge, it also reminds him that he could be identified if he's later caught by the police. He's thus likely to become more violent.

- Choose flight over fight.

An assailant represents an unknown entity. You have no idea what his true intentions are, how powerful he is or how determined he is to do you harm. Our natural instinct when attacked is either to flee or fight; the prudent course is to flee. The problem is that our pride can sometimes cloud our judgment. Unless you're properly trained in the art of self-defense, it isn't sensible to try to fight off your attacker if fleeing him would be just as easy. Flight, of course, isn't always an option. You may find yourself locked in a confined space, such as an elevator, or you might be surrounded by a group of thugs. Still, if there's any chance of escape, take it.

- Scream, if someone tries to mug you or abduct you.

If you're attacked, it's better to attract attention than to be bundled off quietly. Sometimes, people hesitate to yell because they think it will upset their attacker. Well, that's precisely what you want to do! You want to throw him off stride. You want to give him something to think about. Your attacker, more than likely, has rehearsed the attack in his mind. He thinks he has everything figured out. He knows precisely what he intends to do. But, then, you disrupt his plans by screaming. For a moment, he's not sure how to respond. And at that very moment you have the advantage and a chance of escape. Your screams have thrown your attacker for a loop. So, by all means, scream. And get over the any idea that screaming may upset your attacker; he is planning to harm you.

• Scream, "Fire!" You'll get more attention that way.

The best way to get help when you're being attacked is to gain the attention of people nearby. It's a funny thing about human nature, though. If you cry out for someone to call the police, people most often pull back, crab-like, into their shells. They give your cry for help a second thought. "Does she really need help?" they wonder. "Is this just a girlfriend-boyfriend tiff? A wife-husband dispute? Do I really want to get involved?" Odds are they won't do anything, leaving it for someone else to call the police. So don't yell, "Help! Police! Police. Somebody, call the police!" Instead, scream, "Fire! Fire! Help! There's a fire! Fire!" Such a request elicits a totally different response from people within the sound of your voice. They will most likely call the fire department—as opposed to the police—and then they'll rush to see what's the matter.

Why do people do this? Why do they respond more positively to screams of "Fire!" than to pleas for police help? It's boils down to self-interest. An attack on you isn't a direct threat to the others around you. And when you ask them to call the police, it means that you're asking them to get involved in something in which they aren't an immediate party. But when fire is involved, the whole situation changes. Fire is a threat to *them*, a threat to the people living and working in the surrounding neighborhood. That makes their response to your screams different. They *will* call the fire department, because they care about *themselves*. By screaming "Fire!" you turn their self-interest to your personal advantage. It's not your welfare they care about so much; it's their own safety and property that they're worried about. They don't want to see their homes and businesses go up in flames; they don't want to be trapped in a burning building. So they'll call their local emergency number to protect not you but themselves.

A scream of "Fire!" does one other thing. It's likely to catch your attacker completely off guard. As many times as he may have rehearsed his crime in his mind, as often as he has attacked people before, a scream of "Fire!" is totally new and unexpected. It's something out of the blue, out of the ordinary. Indeed, if your scream is really effective, your attacker may even stop to look around to see where the fire is. Now, that's just what you want. You want that split second to flee your attacker—and have a good laugh to boot.

- Consider taking a self-defense course to boost your confidence.

Some travelers find that taking a self-defense course reduces their anxiety and boosts their confidence. While we don't necessarily recommend that you try to overpower an attacker (unless you are especially gifted in martial arts), just the knowledge that you can defend yourself can be a significant morale-booster. More important, if you expect to make trips to parts of the world known for their high crime rates, some basic training in self-defense is a must. Never forget, however, that a defensive action on your part will elicit a response from your attacker. Usually, his reaction will fall into two categories: fight or flight. If an attacker himself comes under assault, he must decide whether to fight back or run away. It's impossible to predict which choice he'll make with any certainty. On the one hand, if he has a violent temperament, an aggressive action on your part might only make the situation worse and put you further at risk of serious bodily harm. On the other hand, if your attacker is a scared kid, he may opt to run away if you display any talent in self-defense. Amateur assailants are often highly nervous and frightened; hardened criminals usually aren't.

Don't get us wrong. By all means, resist an attacker if he means to do your physical harm or attempts to abduct you. Put up a struggle. And yell for help. But getting into a fight with an attacker might not be the best choice in every circumstance. It all depends on the nature of the attack, the capabilities of your attacker and how good you are at self-defense.

4.09 Tips for Women

At our executive-security firm, Interfor Inc., we're constantly asked to provide advice for women travelers. That's not surprising. Women represent a growing percentage of business travelers. Furthermore, many of today's business assignments take women to unfamiliar and sometimes dangerous parts of the world. Then, too, when traveling on vacation, more and more women are opting to make unescorted sojourns.

What concerns female travelers most is the sense that criminals view them as easy prey. This is indeed a serious problem. If you feel you're likely to become a victim of crime, you aren't going to function well as a business traveler—particularly when it comes to traveling abroad—and you're going to be reluctant to travel alone (even within your own country). The best way women can overcome any fear or trepidation about traveling—whether it's for business or pleasure, at home or abroad—is to take the proper precautions. The suggestions listed below are the best techniques we know of for women to stay safe when traveling—especially, for women traveling alone.

Our recommendations serve a dual purpose: Not only are they practical tips that can help to protect you against crime, but they'll also serve to boost your self-confidence. Simply knowing that you've taken every possible precaution lowers travel anxiety. And a person who is self-confident is less likely to become a mark for a criminal. Criminals are good at spotting people, particularly out-of-towners or foreign visitors, who show signs of fear, confusion, over-anxiety or bewilderment. They see any of these signs in a traveler's demeanor—particularly, a female traveler's demeanor—as increasing their chances of getting away with a crime. In a sense, fear of becoming a crime victim may actually increase the likelihood that you will become a victim. So the best thing you can do for yourself is to lessen your own level of uncertainty and anxiety, especially about traveling to places that you've never been to before or to parts of the globe known to be high-risk destinations.

The following steps aim to help you lower your anxiety and boost your confidence by teaching you how to stay safe when away from home. The techniques are tested and are known to defeat criminals. Making them a habit will lower the chances that you will fall prey to a criminal and also will give you more peace of mind about traveling on business or for pleasure. We further recommend *Safety and Security for Women Who Travel* by

Sheila Swan and Peter Laufer, which discusses the things you should do before you leave and en route to foreign destinations, as well as how to cope with difficulties after you've arrived at your destination. The paperback, published in 1998 by Traveler's Tales, doesn't address post-Sept. 11 issues. However, it remains a useful guide for women travelers. Excerpts from the book are available online at the Traveler's Tales website (www.travelerstales.com).

- Use only your last name and first initial when booking a hotel room, and don't let the world know your room number.

Criminals are always on the lookout for women traveling alone. One way to reduce your exposure is to book your hotel using only your last name and first initial. Also, don't make any other reference to your gender, such as Ms., Miss or Mrs. When you're handed you room key, if the desk clerk announces your room number loudly enough for an eavesdropper to hear, ask for a different room and tell him not to make the same mistake twice.

- If crime is very bad at your destination, conduct business meetings at your hotel—and book a suite!

In some cities and foreign countries, it simply doesn't pay to travel around much. Crime can be so rampant that no matter what precautions you take, you're likely to become a crime victim sooner or later. In such cases, the wisest tack is to turn you hotel space into a quasi office and conduct your business affairs there. That way, you'll have the security of the hotel to protect you. But book a suite. You don't want guests getting the wrong idea when you invite them to your room, and keep the bedroom door closed to reinforce the point. Most important, only let guests into your room that you absolutely trust; if you have any doubts, conduct your meeting elsewhere in the hotel. You might find a quiet place in the hotel lobby to discuss business, or you could invite your guest to a business meal at the hotel restaurant. Be mindful of local customs and attitudes, however. In some places around the world, inviting a man to dinner is tantamount to a proposal of marriage—and sometimes marriage without the ring.

Tip We recommend that you stay at a U.S. hotel chain when overseas. An American hotel is likely to have better security (and perhaps better rooms) than the average hotel overseas.

- Avoid walking the streets alone after dark and always stride with confidence—and a whistle.

Nighttime is not the right time to be out and about, unescorted, particularly in a foreign city where the threat of crime or terrorism is significant. If you must be out in the dark, take taxis or call a car service. But no matter the time of day, whenever you're on the streets, always walk with sense of purpose, displaying self-assuredness and resolve. Your body language will make you appear less vulnerable, and a would-be assailant may well let you pass and wait for easier prey.

It helps, too, to know where you're going. So make a daily itinerary, map out your routes beforehand and remain confident along you route. If you start to feel anxious about your surroundings, walk close to other people. That doesn't mean you have to strike up a conversation. Merely stick close enough to make it appear that you are part of a larger group. And, if you do need to ask a question of a stranger, approach a woman. She's more likely to be sympathetic—and protective—than a man might be.

You also should consider carrying a whistle with you. Attackers hate noise and may well flee if you sound an alarm. Be sure, however, to keep your whistle someplace handy. It defeats the purpose if you have to fish for it in the bottom of your handbag. Pepper spray is another option, but not one that we recommend. Your aim is to get away from any assailant, not engage him in combat. Also, when overseas, there may be laws banning such devices.

Tip Onboard the plane, ask a female flight attendant about any safety tips she may have concerning your travel destination.

- Never keep important documents or large amounts of money in your purse.

Purses are the first things that thieves go for. Many thieves don't even need to use force or the threat of violence to separate you from your handbag. They'll simply snip your purse strap and walk away with your bag. Many are so good at purse-snatching that you won't notice what's happened until it's too late. Still, it helps to have a bag with a strap that's long enough for you to wear across your neck and chest. While you may not be able to prevent a skilled thief from absconding with your purse, you can at least limit the damage by not keeping important documents (including your passport), large sums of cash and all of your credit cards in your purse. Vital documents might be kept in a briefcase or any travel bag that you have to hold in your hand. It's much harder for a thief to wrestle away something that you have a grip on. Also, try to wear a piece of clothing that has pockets (preferably on the inside), or buy a money belt or waist pack to hold your passport, extra cash and at least some of your credit cards. Money belts can be found in stores that cater to travelers and also can be bought online at such sites as Amazon.com.

Tip When walking down streets, keep your handbag on the side of your body that's away from the road to avoid someone in a passing car snatching it; on escalators, keep your bag away from the escalator that's moving in the opposite direction.

- Wear sunglasses to avoid unwanted attention.

One of the more interesting tips for women travelers that we've heard is to wear sunglasses so as to avoid unwanted advances. Sunglasses, of course, give an air of self-confidence. They are a way of appearing above the fray. More important, sunglasses hide your eyes. Anyone seeking to get your attention needs to make eye contact. Without that, you can simply walk away and the chances are the interloper won't follow.

- Think twice before taking orders from a policeman, particularly in a foreign country.

In their book, *Safety and Security for Women Who Travel*, Swan and Laufer urge women to take a moment to assess any order from a policeman or other authority figure. "Remember," they say, "some will be using their badge of office to try to take advantage of you and will consider you especially vulnerable because you are a foreigner and a woman." In developing nations, they add, "rogue policemen may offer to drop serious charges against you for sexual favors." Refuse the offer, "politely but firmly," and take your chances with the criminal justice system, Swan and Laufer advise—and we concur.

We would add that you should not allow yourself to be bullied by a badge. Be courteous and respectful, but not pliant or afraid in your dealings with police. If you're overseas and the situation warrants, tell the officer you intend to call the U.S. embassy and point to your cellular phone. But NEVER grab for the phone before telling the officer what you intend to do. He might think you're reaching for a gun.

Tip   If at night police signal for you to pull your car over, turn on your directionals and drive slowly to a well-lighted area before stopping.

- Dress and act appropriately when overseas to avoid encounters with police.

Women travelers abroad should act and dress "conservatively," Swan and Laufer say, because "your appearance can instigate unnecessary interactions with authorities." In Muslim countries, for instance, loose-fitting clothes that cover your arms and legs would be appropriate. The authors further note that women are not welcome everywhere overseas; some places, notably religious shrines, specifically enjoin women from entering. So follow local customs if you want to avoid frivolous encounters with the police. Swan and Laufer also offer another helpful tip: Spend a little time at a local café and observe how

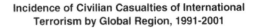

Incidence of Civilian Casualties of International
Terrorism by Global Region, 1991-2001

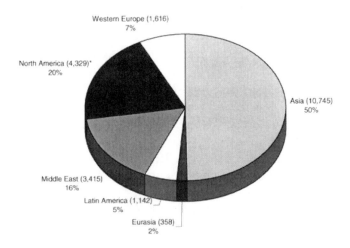

*The North America data for 2001 include an estimated 3,000 dead at the World Trade Center but no estimate of the number injured.

Source: U.S. Department of State

the local women dress and behave, particularly with men. That is an excellent way to gain insight into a culture.

4.10   Sexual Assault

Sexual assault is a fact of life, and no amount of wishing will make it go away. Worse, rape and other sexual assaults are particularly common in many parts of the world, raising the risks of overseas travel for women. Still, there are things you can do to lessen your chances of becoming a victim of a sexual assault and to hasten your recovery if the unfortunate happens. The following advice includes suggestions from the National Crime Prevention Council (www.ncpc.org), the U.S. State Department's Bureau of Diplomatic Security (http://ds.state.gov) and the British Foreign & Commonwealth Office (www.fco.gov.uk). You may wish to consult these or other sources of information on sexual-assault and rape prevention.

- Take precautions to reduce your risk of sexual assault or rape.

Mindset: Protecting yourself begins with keen awareness. Always be alert wherever you go, and use your head. Walk with confidence and a sense of purpose. Let no one get the impression that you're wandering around aimlessly and alone. Maintain a constant awareness of your surroundings. Look around to see who's near you and what's going on in your vicinity. Go with your instincts. If a situation or location makes you uncomfortable or uneasy, don't think twice. Leave! Rationalization can get you in trouble.

Don't let alcohol or drugs cloud your judgment. If you are at a bar or reception, always keep your drink in your hand. If you step away and return to your table or seat, ask for a new glass of whatever it was you were drinking. Reserve your trust for only a very few people. You never know who may have slipped something into your drink while you were away. And that goes for people who work at your company, as well as clients and strangers.

Hotel Room: Upon arriving in your room for the first time and then every time you return, keep the door open until you've checked the premises for anyone who may be hiding in wait. You can prop the door open with a piece of luggage, always left nearby, or a doorstop. Avoid using your handbag or briefcase for this purpose, as someone might snatch it from behind your back. Also, when you first arrive in your hotel room, make sure that the locks work on all widows and any doors to your room, and whenever you return, check to see if the locks are still in the same position as when you left.

After you're satisfied you're alone, chain the door behind you and bring a rubber doorstop along as backup. When answering the door, keep the chain on until you know for sure who's on the other side. Never open your door to strangers. When in doubt, don't be embarrassed to phone the front desk for verification. Don't walk about the hotel corridors looking for a soft-drink machine or ice dispenser; call room service. Keep a light on in your hotel room at night—even when you're sleeping. Don't say, "I can't sleep with the light on." Practice the technique at home; you'll get used to it.

Walking: Avoid walking or jogging alone, especially at night. Stay in well-traveled, well-lighted areas. Wear clothes and shoes that give you freedom of movement. Be careful if a stranger asks for directions. Keep your distance from the person or the car he's in. Walk down the middle of sidewalks, staying clear of hedges, doorways and alleyways—and passing cars. And walk facing traffic. That makes it impossible for someone to follow right next to you in a car. It also makes it harder for someone to pull you into a vehicle. If you think you're being followed, change direction and head for an open store, restaurant or even a lighted house. If you see a police officer, tell him of your concern. You could also hop aboard a bus or hail a cab. Otherwise, approach someone, preferably a woman (or a couple), and say that you feel a bit uncomfortable walking alone and ask if she'd mind some company. It's probably not wise to say that someone's following you, because she, too, may become afraid and avoid you like the plague.

Driving: If you've rented a car, have your key ready before you reach the car. Look around the car as you approach. Before getting in, check the back seat for anyone who might be lurking there. In fact, before you even leave your car, move up the front seat, so you can see more easily into back-seat area when you return. Also, check to see if the front seat has been returned to its original position. If it has, leave immediately and get help.

If your car is in an underground garage, ask the front desk for an escort. Keep your car facing outward in parking lots to make getaways faster and easier, and park as close to an exit as possible. Always park in well-lighted areas, and keep car doors locked at all times. On the road, never roll down any window other than your own, and even then, never roll down your window all the way. Don't allow for enough room for someone on the outside to get their arm in the car. Never pick up hitchhikers. And, of course, don't hitchhike yourself. If your car breaks down, call the rental company for assistance. Be wary of offers of help from strangers. Don't stay in you car if you don't have to; go to a nearby shop or café—and tell the rental company where you'll be. If assistance is unlikely to arrive quickly, get a cab or car service to take you back to your hotel. If you've broken down on a highway or a deserted road, call for assistance and stay put until help arrives, keeping your doors locked. If you don't have a cell phone or if you can't reach the rental company, lift up the hood, get back in the car, lock the doors and turn on your flashers. If an emergency call box is nearby, use it.

Tip   If you need to get someone other than your rental company to fix the car, rental firms will often reimburse your expenses, so ask for a receipt from the repairman.

- Know what to do if someone tries to rape or sexually assault you.

How should you handle a rape attempt? A lot depends on your physical and emotional state, the particular situation and location, and the attacker's personality. In other words, there are no hard and fast rules—except one: Never forget that survival is your uppermost goal. Weigh anything else against that. First, try to escape. Scream. Be rude. Make noise to discourage your attacker from following you. And, as we suggested earlier, pull out your whistle and blow. If that doesn't work, talk and stall for time, so you can assess your options. You might be able to discourage your attacker by vomiting or even picking you nose. If you decide to fight back, be quick, determined and effective. Target the eyes or groin. If the attacker has a weapon, you may have no choice but to submit. Do whatever it takes to survive.

- Take care of yourself following a sexual assault or rape.

Even if you haven't decided to report an attack to the local police, at least call the local U.S. embassy or consulate if you're overseas. Preferably, do report the rape or sexual assault to the police or a rape crisis center. The sooner you inform authorities of an attack, the greater the chances the assailant will be caught.

Measures Taken by U.S. Carjacking Victims, 1992-1996

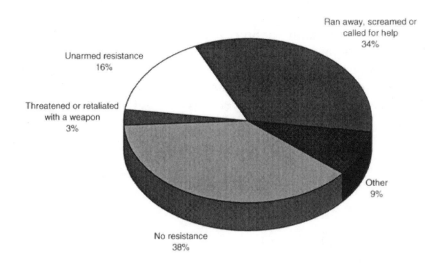

Ran away, screamed or
called for help
34%

Unarmed resistance
16%

Threatened or retaliated
with a weapon
3%

Other
9%

No resistance
38%

Source: Bureau of Justice Statistics, U.S. Department of Justice

Preserve all physical evidence. Don't shower, bathe, change clothes, douche or throw any clothing away until the police or rape counselors tell you it's okay to do so. Go to a hospital emergency room or a doctor for medical care immediately. Try not to go alone. Do not drink any alcohol to cope with post-assault stress and emotions, as this could affect your memory and your ability to report the crime accurately.

Finally, if you have been raped or sexually assault, never feel guilty. Rape is not your fault. A rapist means to exert power over someone, often a stranger. You just happen to be the person he picked. You likely were in the wrong place at the wrong time. So never blame yourself for being an innocent victim. Get counseling to help deal with the feelings of anger, helplessness, fear or shame that often follow rape. It always helps to talk to someone about a rape, whether it occurred last night, last week or last year.

4.11. Carjacking Survival

Every year, there are at least 49,000 attempted or successful carjackings in the U.S., according to the latest U.S. Department of Justice data. Carjackers manage to steal the vehicles about half of the time, and weapons are used in 83% of all reported cases. Victims are injured in 23% of the successful thefts and 10% of the unsuccessful ones. The Justice Department says that although data on fatal carjackings aren't available, about 27 homicides by strangers each year involve automobile theft, and some of these may be carjackings. Carjacking is even a more serious problem overseas, particularly in developing nations. Four-wheel drives and sport utility vehicles are especially prized. These are the countries that the U.S. State Department says have the highest rates of carjacking:

Latin American:
   Brazil;
   El Salvador;
   Mexico;
   Peru;
   Venezuela.

Africa:
   Algeria;
   Cameroon;
   Central African Republic;
   Cote d'Ivoire;
   Gabon;,
   Namibia;
   Nigeria.

South Africa:
   Yemen;
   Zimbabwe.
Europe:
   Albania;
   Northern Ireland;
   Yugoslavia.

For country-specific information on carjacking, consult the U.S. State Department's travel advisories online at http://travel.state.gov/travel_warnings.html.

- Spot a carjacking before it happens.

In terms of carjacking, your times of greatest vulnerability are when you're slowing down or stopped, say, at a light. It's imperative, therefore, that you keep all car doors locked and all windows rolled up in high-risk cities and foreign countries. Carjackers often will put up an artificial roadblock. It could be debris in the road, a felled tree or a car blocking passage. If you encounter any of these, don't get out of your car to inspect the problem and always leave enough room in front of you— preferably, two car lengths'—so you can turn your car around. If there's a car ahead of you, an easy way to gauge the correct distance is to stop far enough behind so you can still see where the car's back tires meet the road. Carjackers many times will have an accomplice pin you in from behind to prevent you from backing out of the ambush, so again leave as much leeway in front of you as possible.

Be on the alert for strangers lurking about a cash machine. Carjackers stake out automatic teller machines (ATMs), particularly those located in dark, isolated areas. If you need cash at night, find an ATM in a well-lighted area, preferably near an open business establishment. Other venues for carjackings are public garages, mass-transit parking lots, shopping malls, 24-hour grocery stores, self-serve gas stations and car washes, and highway exit and entrance ramps.

Tip   If you spot suspicious activity at the intersection ahead, slow down and try to time the light, so you can drive straight through without stopping.

Caution   Beware of bump-and-run carjackers. These bandits bump you from behind and when you go to inspect the damage, an accomplice gets in your car and drives off.

Carjackings in the United States, 1992-1996

Annual Average	Total	Completed	Attempted
Incidents	48,787	24,520	24,267
Victims	53,452	27,710	25,742
Rate per 10,00 persons	2.5	1.3	1.2
Percentages			
No Weapon	17%	8%	25%
With Weapons	83	92	75
Firearm	47	72	22
Knife/other	36	20	52
With Injury	16	23	10
Reported to police	79	100	57

Source: Bureau of Justice Statistics, U.S. Department of Justice

- Frustrate a carjacker's plan by throwing your car keys away.

If you have left your car doors open and a carjacker gets in, immediately turn off the ignition and throw the keys as far as you can, either through an open window or by opening the door. By throwing the keys away, you'll have defeated the carjacker's plan and knocked him off balance. Now he can't force you to chauffeur him (which was probably his plan). Without keys to the car, most likely he'll abandon the effort and flee.

Caution   Don't be the first to run out of the car, because the carjacker may shoot you in the back. Wait until he starts to get out of the car, then you do the same. Run away from the car and seek help. There's no shame in running away. It's the smart thing to do for your own protection.

- If faced with a weapon, comply with the carjacker's demands.

In a life-or-death situation, accede to the carjacker's demands. Don't argue. Preferably, you'll have had time to get the keys out of the ignition. In which case, hand them over and ask if you can leave. If you simply try to run away without first asking permission, the carjacker might shoot you. If the he doesn't respond to your request, try to win his sympathy by telling him you have a family.

Tip If you're driving and the carjacker fires a gun at police, intentionally crash your car. You're more likely to survive the impact of an elective crash than an exchange of gunfire.

Caution Never make any promises to your attacker. Don't say, "I promise I won't tell the police what you look like," because that will make him more nervous and fearful and he might kill you to eliminate you as a witness.

L. Hijacking Survival

The four plane hijackings of Sept. 11 were unusual in two respects: 1) The hijackers took over the planes using box-cutters and other small knives, although bombs also were mentioned. Hijackers more typically use guns. 2) The hijackers never intended to land the planes. Most hijackings are used as means of gaining prisoner releases and on occasion ransom money. With the concerted effort to increase air-travel security since the carnage of Sept. 11, it's impossible to say what tactics hijackers will employ in the future. But don't expect terrorists simply to abandon this favored meaning of inflicting damage and striking fear into their enemies.

- Know what to expect in a plane hijacking and what to do during a commando rescue operation.

Familiarize yourself with what happens in a typical airplane hijacking so you won't be taken by complete surprise should you ever become a victim. You can expect to hear a lot of noise, commotion and movement around the plane, even though you may not be in a position to see any of the activity. There could be shooting. You may hear the hijackers yelling at passengers, telling them to stay seated, not to move and to be quiet. You might even hear an announcement over the plane's public-address system, given by a hijacker or crewmember, informing you of the hijacking, making bogus claims about being diverted or simply saying nothing is wrong.

Hijackers often will force passengers to take new seats in order to pack everyone together. There have been instances in which hijackers have separated passengers by religion, race, sex or citizenship. Your passport and wallet may be taken from you. Overhead luggage bins may be ransacked, and seats scoured for cell phones, computers, briefcases and purses.

If the plane lands, passengers and crew may be used as bargaining chips. Some may be released in exchange for food and water. Others might be executed. Appreciate that hijackers aren't viewed as criminals in every country in the world. The hijackers and the government of the country in which you land may share the same political ideology. Local officials may have more sympathy for the terrorists than for you and the other passengers. So don't automatically expect rescue efforts to be made. But don't become visibly angry because the hijackers may single you out and make an example of you to your fellow passengers.

If you land in a country that opposes terrorism, don't expect your plane to take off again. Authorities will do everything to keep your aircraft on the ground, including blocking runways, denying aviation fuel and even shooting out the tires. You can expect a rescue attempt to be made—and it's likely to be violent. The plane's doors could be blown open; deafening stun grenades, emitting thick smoke, might go off, and gunfire could erupt. So stay down, placing your head low to the floor. Follow any instruction rescue commandos give you. You might be told, for instance, to stay down or to crawl to the emergency exits. If instructed to exit the plane, you may want to raise your hands in the air as if surrendering; whether this is necessary depends on the specific situation. Should a fire break out, quickly head for the nearest exit.

It's vital that you say and do nothing if you notice a rescue effort being mounted—for example, if you see commando forces, perhaps dressed all in black, climbing onto the wings, running beneath the plane or propping ladders up against the fuselage. Don't give a hint of what you see to anyone, even the passengers seated next to you. The element of surprise is essential to a successful rescue, and you don't want to do anything that might tip off the hijackers.

Don't be surprised or insulted if your rescuers treat you at first as if you're one of the hijackers. It's procedure. Security forces need quickly to determine whether any hijackers are attempting to disguise themselves as passengers. Finally, if a hijacking ends overseas, U.S. officials will help you get home. Expect to be debriefed by law enforcement and perhaps U.S. intelligence agents.

Tip   If a hijacker grabs the passenger next to you to use as a shield during a commando raid, try to pull her back. A woman's life was saved that way in March 1991 when commandos of the Singapore Armed Forces retook a hijacked Singapore Airlines plane.

Caution   Don't attempt to conceal your passport, money or valuables, as this could attract the attention of a hijacker, who may hurt or kill you as a warning to the other passengers.

- Never look your abductor in the eye.

The number one rule in a hijacking, or any type of abduction, is: Never look your abductor (or abductors) in the eye. Direct eye contact intimidates a hostage-taker and creates in him a fierce animosity toward you. He'll single you out as a troublemaker and may make an example of you to the other passengers.

All Air Hijacking Incidents Annually, 1975-2000

	U.S.-Registered Aircraft	Foreign-Registered Aircraft	Total	U.S. as Percentage of Total
1975	6	13	19	32%
1976	2	14	16	13%
1977	5	26	31	16%
1978	7	17	24	29%
1979	11	13	24	46%
1980	21	18	39	54%
1981	7	23	30	23%
1982	9	22	31	29%
1983	17	15	32	53%
1984	5	21	26	19%
1985	4	22	26	15%
1986	2	5	7	29%
1987	3	5	8	38%
1988	1	10	11	9%
1989	1	14	15	7%
1990	1	39	40	3%
1991	1	23	24	4%
1992	0	12	12	0%
1993	0	31	31	0%
1994	0	23	23	0%
1995	0	9	9	0%
1996	0	14	14	0%
1997	0	10	10	0%
1998	0	9	9	0%
1999	0	11	11	0%
2000	0	20	20	0%
Total	103	439	542	19%

Source: Federal Aviation Administration, Office of Civil Aviation Security

- Don't try to be a hero in the first five crucial minutes of a hijacking.

Your behavior during the first five minutes of a hijacking (or kidnapping) largely will determine how you'll come out of it in the end. In those initial minutes, a terrorist is very nervous and perhaps scared. Even though he planned his action in advance, the reality of it means he's facing a lot of unknowns as events unfold. This makes him uptight and trigger-happy. Anything that adds to his fears could lead to disaster. In the first few minutes of a hijacking, therefore, do everything your abductor tells you to do you. This isn't the time to react to the hostage-taking, unless you're trained for it.

Security professionals, such as sky marshals, know that the first few minutes of a terrorist incident are preciously the time for them to counterattack, because the perpetrator isn't set yet, he's still nervous and he's uncertain. Trained personnel will use this window of opportunity to take over the situation. They don't want to wait until the terrorist becomes set and relaxed, because then he's in control and security personnel may no longer be in a position to respond. The abductor may tie up his victims or corral them. Advantage, abductor. Most victims of hijackings, of course, aren't trained security personnel. They're average people traveling on business or vacation. So don't try to be a hero in the first five minutes of a hostage crisis. Keep uppermost in your mind the fact that yours isn't the only life at stake. You're likely one of a number of hostages. A foolhardy action on your part—particularly during those first crucial minutes of an attack—could endanger the lives of everyone on board. So sit tight, be quiet and don't make a move. Say a prayer if that's agreeable to you.

A hijacker begins to let his guard down after the first five minutes of the attack. Why? Because he's physically and emotionally spent. The adrenaline rush that came with the initial assault has worn off, and he has become physically and mentally exhausted. He's now less alert and slower to respond. After the first few minutes, be on the lookout for ways to overtake or flee your hijacker. A group of physically fit passengers could well take him down. You might start with a barrage of shoes, thrown at the hijacker by everyone in close proximity, as others passengers rush him. To frighten and distract him, everyone should yell. However, you must be very careful and weigh the consequences. People could be shot and killed. If the hijacker actually has a bomb, the entire jetliner could be destroyed. At high altitude, a bullet through a window or the fuselage could lead to rapid depressurization of the plane. And, if your hijacker is a well-trained, professional terrorist, your odds of success are very low. Still, there are situations in which passengers can defeat a hijacking. Keep that in mind. But, again, never do anything during the first five minutes of a hijacking.

Tip Try to fly on wide-body jets; hijackers often avoid these planes because of the large numbers of passengers usually on board.

• Appear fully cooperative and observe your attacker.

Look passive and cooperate fully as the hijacking unfolds. Put your head down. Don't ask questions. Don't yell or shout. Don't do anything. Be controlled and reserved. Tell yourself to be calm. If a terrorist addresses you, answer in a normal tone of voice. Observe, out of the corners of your eyes or with quick glances, the hijacker's actions and reactions. Watch to see exactly what he's doing, without making eye contact.

• Don't speak unless spoken to.

Don't address your captors unless you're spoken to first, and then keep your answers brief. Never volunteer information to the hijackers, and try not to tell them anything that could help them.

Caution Avoid being seen talking with fellow passengers, and don't overtly signal or shout to relatives, friends or colleagues seated elsewhere on the plane.

• Don't try to negotiate or reason with your abductors.

You may be a hostage, but that doesn't all of a sudden make you a professional negotiator. That's not your job. Don't try to reason or negotiate with your abductor. For one thing, the incident has just happened. Your hijacker (or kidnapper) has just carried out his planned assault; he's not going to let you go. He can't, no matter what you say. Neither is he in a frame of mind conducive to fruitful discussion, most especially not with the people he has just taken captive. Your abductor needs time to calm down and get his head straight.

Caution If you or a fellow passenger requires help, get the attention of a crewmember. Don't speak to a hijacker unless spoken to or if he has already rendered similar assistance to other passengers. And never volunteer information to an abductor.

- Develop a mental picture of the hijacker.

Try to get a good description of your abductor (or abductors). It will assist authorities later. But it also may help you to escape. Gauge his size, height and age; note his other physical characteristics (e.g., hair color), and look for any scars or tattoos. Try to determine his nationality, paying particular attention to any use of foreign words. If he addresses a compatriot by name, remember it. To determine whether you have a chance of escape, sense if he's an amateur or a professional terrorist. An amateur hijacker will usually wave his weapon around, yell and scream, and perhaps propagandize. He'll be highly nervous, and he also may act erratically. A professional, by contrast, will be low key, calm, relaxed and in control of himself. He'll speak logically, often in a normal tone of voice. He'll appear to have either done this before or rehearsed it many times. You may have a chance of escape if the hijacker is an amateur, but it's highly unlikely that you'll be able to flee from a trained professional.

- If the opportunity to escape unharmed presents itself, take it.

Passengers on hijacked aircraft have been able to open emergency doors and flee when their abductors' guards were down. If the aircraft is large and the number of hijackers few,

Incidents Against Aviation and Airports
Worldwide by Category, 1996-2000

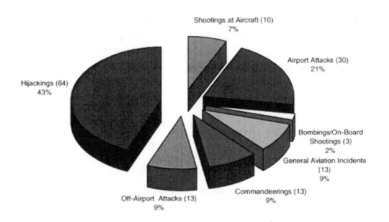

Shootings at Aircraft (10)
7%

Airport Attacks (30)
21%

Hijackings (64)
43%

Bombings/On-Board
Shootings (3)
2%

General Aviation Incidents
(13)
9%

Commandeerings (13)
9%

Off-Airport Attacks (13)
9%

Source: Federal Aviation Administration

you might be able slowly to head back to the rear doors while
the plane is on the ground. If you know how to open the door
and unfurl the slide, you could get away before the terrorists
notice. But be very careful. You're putting your life and the lives
of the other passengers at risk. Still, hijackers aren't perfect.
They make mistakes. They can't be in all places at all times. So
be on the lookout for opportunities to escape.

Tip   A good time to escape is at night, when the hijackers
likely are suffering from sleep-deprivation and their senses are
dulled.

4.13. Airplane Evacuation

Most travelers have never had to evacuate an aircraft—and
probably never will. Still, an understanding of the procedures

and knowledge of the precautions you ought to take in the event of a crash landing can significantly improve your odds of survival.

- Jump feet first onto the emergency chute if you have to evacuate a plane.

Our immediate thought about how to get onto a slide is to sit down, then slide. It likely goes back to our childhood playground days. But in an emergency airplane evacuation, that's the wrong thing to do, because sitting down wastes precious time and could lessen the chances that all of the passengers behind you will have enough time to escape. The Federal Aviation Administration recommends that you place your arms across your chest, elbows in, and put your legs and feet together. Then, jump feet first. Don't worry about breaking the chute; they're built to withstand the abuse. Clear the slide immediately, but be careful not to run into any oncoming emergency vehicles. And never return to a burning plane. Also, leave all your possessions behind if you have to evacuate an aircraft. If there's smoke, stay low and follow the floor lighting to the nearest exit.

Tip It's a good idea on any flight to take note of the nearest exits prior to takeoff.

Caution Women should remove their high-heeled shoes and nylon stockings before getting on an emergency slide. A heel could catch on the way down, causing injury such as a twisted ankle or a broken leg. The friction of the slide will melt nylon, possibly causing burns.

- Learn a few safety steps that could save your life in the event of a plane crash.

Hardly anyone ever reads the information cards stuffed into seat-back pouches on airplanes, and reading the following tips is no substitute. However, we've come across a number of crash survival tips we'd like share:

- Count the number of rows between you and the nearest exit. Look both in front of you and behind you. You may not be able to see in a smoke-filled cabin.
- Fasten your seatbelt snugly around your pelvic area, not your stomach.
- Pay attention to the flight attendant's safety briefings and instructions.
- Know how to open regular and emergency doors and windows.
- When over water, know where the life jackets and life rafts are stowed, and how to release them.
- Remove all sharp objects, such as pens, from your pockets.
- Get into the "brace" position early. Don't wait until trouble happens. Bend over with your head down, and grab hold of your knees or ankles.
- In an emergency evacuation, leave your personal effects. Just go.
- Crawl on the floor if the smoke is dense.
- Jump over seat tops if you have to.
- Before evacuating into deep water, take your shoes off first. They can waterlog and drag you under.
- Consider buying a smoke hood and carrying it with you on all your trips.

Three in four fire fatalities are caused by smoke inhalation. It would be wise, therefore, to consider buying your own smoke hood. These aren't yet standard safety equipment on airlines, but more and more people are making the investment for their own safety. Here are two smoke hoods we've come across: Air Security International's Quick4™ is a respiratory protective escape device designed to reduce the health risks and mortality rates associated with inhalation of toxic fumes. It costs $159.00. To order, call (713) 430-7300 or go to www.airsecurity.com. Brookdale International Systems, a DuPont Canada company, offers EVAC-U8™ Emergency Escape Smoke Hood, which combines a DuPont Kapton™ hood and air filter to protect against deadly toxic smoke while evacuating from fire, chemical or other emergencies in aircraft, as well as in homes, offices, factories, hospitals, hotels and marine vessels. It costs $74.95. To order, call 800-459-3822 or 604-324-3822. Or go to either www.evac-u8.com or www.smokehood.com.

4.14. Corporate Travel Procedures

Besides implementing the recommendations above, companies of all sizes should establish new safety and security procedures to ensure that their executives and employees are safe while traveling on business and provide a ready means of communications in emergencies.

- Require business travelers to submit detailed itineraries.

Businesses should know where their traveling employees are at all times. Companies of all sizes, therefore, should require employees to submit detailed travel itineraries prior to departure, primarily to help to ensure the traveler's safety and to assist law enforcement if the employee goes missing. Requisite information should include flight schedules, hotels, rental cars, and the names, addresses, phone numbers, times and dates of all scheduled meetings. Travelers should update this information, via phone or email, as circumstances warrant.

Tip Self-employed business travelers and vacationers should establish a similar routine, leaving an itinerary and contact information with a relative or friend.

- Every firm should have a dedicated travel manager.

Large corporations, of course, have whole departments that handle business travel, but many small firms don't. Given the uncertainties and risks associated with terrorism, every company should have a dedicated travel manager—even if the task is assigned to someone on a part-time basis as an adjunct duty. A travel manager serves a multi-functional role. In some cases, he'll book flights and make hotel and rental car reservations. But his most important responsibilities should be to stay abreast of the latest terrorist threats in the U.S. and around the world, to provide updates to traveling employees on a periodic basis, to know where traveling employees are at all times and to serve as *the* contact person in emergencies.

- Create 24-hour hotlines and recorded threat updates.

Business travelers on the road need to feel connected to their home offices in this day and age. There are three good means of accomplishing this: 1) Create a 24-hour hotline that employees can use to reach someone at the company. Establish a backup telephone number as well in case the local telephone system should fail. 2) Provide prerecorded voice messages on the latest terrorist threats, both in the U.S. and overseas, which traveling employees can call into. The State Department, Federal Aviation Administration, FBI, newspapers, television and newswires should serve the sources of the information. 3) Offer the same hotline and information services via the Internet, using email and password-protected Web pages.

- Rethink security procedures involving your corporate aircraft.

Many executives are avoiding commercial aviation in favor of corporate aircraft to forego the delays associated with post-Sept. 11 airline travel. These same executives, however, may be unwittingly exposing themselves to other dangers, such a tampering with parked corporate jets, hijacking or abduction for ransom. Corporations with their own aircraft need to rethink security. All luggage and parcels should be identified before being put on a plane. Especially when overseas, never rely on airport security to guard your parked jet. Hire your own security force to stand watch. And make sure that your caterer is reliable. In a foreign country, it may be best for a member of the crew to pick up food and beverages at your hotel for consumption in-flight.

- Take out ransom insurance and have security-service firms on call.

The danger of kidnapping for ransom, particularly in countries at high risk of terrorism or violent crime, means that most every firm should have ransom insurance. In addition, companies should maintain a list of professional security firms in the U.S. and overseas that could supply bodyguards or otherwise assist a traveling employee who's in danger or distress.

4.15. Recommended Online Reading

Safety and Security for Women Who Travel by Sheila Swan and Peter Laufer, excerpts at the Traveler's Tales website www.travelerstales.com.

"Security Tips for Air Travelers," Federal Aviation Administration, www.faa.gov.

"Self, Home and Family," National Crime Prevention Council, www.ncpc.org.

"Sexual Assault: Reducing the Risk and Coping with an Attack," Bureau of Diplomatic Security, U.S. Department of State, http://ds.state.gov/about/publications/keepingsafe/.

"Travel Briefing: FAA's Fly Smart Guide," Federal Aviation Administration, www.faa.gov/apa/traveler.htm or www.faa.gov.

"Travel Safety and Security Tips," Corporate Travel Safety, www.corporatetravelsafety.com.

"Travelers and Consumers: Security Guidelines," Transportation Security Administration. www.tsa.gov.

5

How to Travel Safely Abroad

Given the current U.S.-led war on terrorism, Americans are potential targets of attack wherever they may be. This poses a special problem for U.S. citizens traveling abroad. Terrorists may well find it easier to continue their assault on the United States not by infiltrating its borders but by attacking its citizens overseas. Thus, you, as an American traveler abroad, may come to feel the wrath of terrorists seeking to wound the United States as a nation. This isn't to say that you should simply put away your bags and stay home. Rather, it's intended as a warning.

It's important to put the risk of foreign travel into perspective. Statistically, you're far more likely to become a victim of crime overseas than a victim of terrorism. In that sense, the dangers of traveling abroad today aren't all that much greater than they used to be—at least when it comes the chances that any one individual traveler will fall victim to violence. Still, the threat of terrorism cannot be ignored. Americans will be targeted. So what's required is a redoubling of our efforts to stay safe. The recommendations below attempt to do just that. But don't forget to review the travel safety precautions laid out in the preceding chapter, "How to Travel Safely in General." For travelers planning trips overseas, the two chapters are inseparable.

Civilian Casualties of International Terrorism Yearly by Global Region, 1991-2001

	Africa	Asia	Eurasia	Latin America	Middle East	North America*	Western Europe	Grand Totals
1991	3	150	7	68	33	0	56	317
1992	28	25	0	374	236	1	65	729
1993	7	135	1	66	178	1,006	117	1,510
1994	55	71	151	329	256	0	126	988
1995	8	5,639	29	46	445	0	287	6,454
1996	80	1,507	20	18	1,097	0	503	3,225
1997	28	344	27	11	480	7	17	914
1998	5,379	635	12	195	68	0	405	6,694
1999	185	690	8	9	31	0	16	939
2000	102	898	103	20	78	0	4	1,205
2001	150	651	0	6	513	3,315	20	4,655
Totals	6,025	10,745	358	1,142	3,415	4,329	1,616	27,630

*The North America data for 2001 include an estimated 3,000 dead at the World Trade Center but no estimate of the number injured.

Source: U.S. Department of State

5.01. Out of Harm's Way

Avoiding trouble spots around the world is the surest means of surviving terrorism. So get in the habit of checking the latest official travel warnings.

- Before leaving for a foreign country, check the U.S. State Department's latest travel warnings.

You can hear the latest travel warnings and other recorded information about foreign destinations by calling the U.S. Department of State in Washington, D.C. at 202-647-5225. You also can get that information via automated telefax by dialing 202-647-3000 from your fax machine. Or you can go to the State Department's website at www.state.gov. In addition to warnings about travel to individual countries, the State Department also issues regional and worldwide cautions. On July 1, 2002, for instance, it advised:

"The U.S. Government continues to receive credible indications that extremist individuals are planning additional terrorist actions against U.S. interests. Such actions may be imminent and include suicide operations. We have no further information on specific targets, timing or method of attack. We remind American citizens to remain vigilant with regard to their personal security and to exercise caution. Terrorist groups do not distinguish between official and civilian targets. Recent attacks on worshippers at a church and synagogue underline the growing possibility that as security is increased at official U.S. facilities, terrorists and their sympathizers will seek softer targets. These may include facilities where Americans are generally known to congregate or visit, such as clubs, restaurants, and places of worship, schools or outdoor recreation events. Americans should increase their security awareness when they are at such locations, avoid them, or switch to other locations where Americans in large numbers generally do not congregate. American citizens may be targeted for kidnapping."

Tip   The State Department's 202-647-5225 number also can be used by friends and families at home to get help in emergencies involving U.S. citizens overseas.

• Get on the U.S. State Department's email list for the latest terrorism advisories.

The U.S. State Department now offers a free email distribution service on terrorist-related news and information. It's a real boon for anyone planning a trip abroad or travelers already in a foreign country. The bulletins cover a wealth of subjects from new travel warnings and updated passport information to speeches by government officials and daily State Department press briefings. You can pick from the various categories to get just the emails you'd like. The list includes a special, nearly-all-encompassing category called "America Responds: Building a Global Coalition Against Terrorism," which provides all of the State Department's announcements on the post-Sept. 11 global antiterrorism effort. If you subscribe to that particular list, be aware that you can expect a substantial number of emails. The subscription process is as simple as can be. Go to www.state.gov/www/listservs_cms.html, make your selections and type in your email address. That's it. You're done. And if the email traffic becomes too much or you no longer need the information, you can cancel your subscription to any or all of the lists by completing an online signoff form.

- Consult the international travel warnings issued by the British and Canadian governments.

Besides the U.S. State Department, the British Foreign and Commonwealth Office and the Canadian Department of Foreign Affairs and International Trade also issue timely, country-by-country travel warnings and other announcements. What makes these reports so interesting (and so valuable) is that they don't always agree with the U.S. State Department's assessment. Sometimes Britain or Canada (or both) will conclude that conditions in a foreign land are worse than the State Department is letting on, or they will provide more detailed information about the form and specific location of the threat. At other times, the British and Canadians may be more sanguine than the U.S. State Department. The British website is at www.fco.gov.uk, and the Canadian site is at www.voyage.gc.ca/destinations/menu_e.htm.

- Don't be lulled into a false sense of security simply because you're on vacation.

Vacations are, of course, times to relax. That's why we take them after all. But the desire for rest and relaxation mustn't result in letting down your guard. Stay as alert on vacation as you are when traveling on business.

- Monitor the news for your foreign travel destination.

When in Rome, they say, do as the Romans do. Well, today we ought not be so concerned about local customs as local news. Take full advantage of the Internet and bring yourself up to

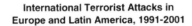

International Terrorist Attacks in Europe and Latin America, 1991-2001

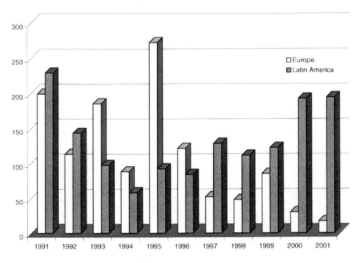

Source: U.S. Department of State

speed on what's happening at your foreign travel destination. You don't want to be surprised by a local problem or a foreign crisis if you can help it.

As good as official travel advisories may be, you owe it to yourself—and your family—to do more. No one should depend solely on the government for information on possible terrorist threats or other developments, such as political disturbances, riots, an economic meltdown, a local crime wave or a public-health crisis, that could endanger your health and safety overseas. You should, therefore, get into the habit of following the local news for the countries you intend to visit—and don't wait until the last minute. Prepare in advance, perhaps weeks in advance, by making a review of foreign news part of your daily routine. Keeping abreast of foreign news means more than watching the nightly news on television or reading foreign dispatches in your daily newspaper. It requires digging. Thankfully, the Internet makes it possible to follow the news virtually anywhere in the world in real time.

Our contact information in the back of this book contains a slew of websites you can go to for foreign news. But here, let's discuss a few important news sources that ought to become part of your regular reading if you travel overseas frequently:

Agence France-Presse (www.afp.com), headquartered in Paris, is the world's oldest news agency, founded in 1835 by Charles-Louis Havas, said by some to be the father of global journalism. Its worldwide network takes in 165 countries, of which 110 are home to AFP bureaus, with the remaining 50 covered by non-AFP local correspondents. Besides its French-language service, AFP also carries news in English, as well as in Arabic, German, Portuguese and Spanish.

Associated Press (http://wire.ap.org), based in New York, has won 47 Pulitzer Prizes since its founding in 1848. Today, it has 242 bureaus worldwide, with some 3,700 staff members, and serves about 1,700 newspapers and approximately 5,000 radio and television stations. It, too, supplies news in several languages, including English, German, Dutch, French and Spanish.

British Broadcasting Corp. (www.bbc.co.uk) is probably better known by its initials, BBC. Founded in 1922, the BBC is far and away the most well-rounded news organization in the world. Of particular note are its online news dispatches from nearly every spot on the globe and its online radio news feeds. It even has weather reports for most anyplace in the world. Based in London, the BBC is financed by what are called "licensing fees," collected annually by the British government from television-set owners throughout the U.K.

Reuters (www.reuters.com), also headquartered in London, was founded in 1851 by Paul Julius Reuter and quickly established a reputation as a prime source of fast, accurate and unbiased foreign news. Today, Reuters is widely considered to be the world's leading news and financial information organization, with 204 offices worldwide and more than 18,000 employees.

Yahoo! is also useful. While Yahoo! is Internet portal and not a news service per se, it's still a terrific catchall resource for keeping on top of the news (http://dailynews.yahoo.com). It offers news from a wide variety of sources, including many of the wire services listed above. Most useful of all, perhaps, is its search facility, which lets you to look up news concerning a specific country or city. You can use "Advanced Search" (http://search.news.yahoo.com/search/news/options) to find news items going back 30 days. After entering your keywords (e.g., "terrorism tokyo" or "crime paris"), you can save the resulting URL as a "favorite," which means you can retrieve news fitting your search parameters at anytime without having to reenter your search terms. (URL stands for "universal resource locator" and refers to the http://www address you see at the top of your browser.)

Among foreign weekly news magazines, *The Economist* (www.economist.com), based in London, and the *Far Eastern Economic Review* (www.feer.com), a Dow Jones & Co. publication based in Hong Kong, offer the best perspectives on social, political and economic conditions around the world. Two other news organizations also deserve mention, especially for business readers. *The Wall Street Journal* (www.wsj.com) and Britain's *Financial Times* (www.ft.com) are the leading business and financial newspapers in the world. Both provide news online, although only paid subscribers can access the complete edition of *The Wall Street Journal.*

Finally, to show you just how far the Internet has come in providing access to international news, even the English edition of Russia's Pravda news agency (http://english.pravda.ru/) is available online. There's also Middle East News Online (www.middleeastwire.com), which carries dispatches from various news agencies in the region and gives you a sense of how the West's antiterrorism campaign is viewed by the Arab press.

Tip Monitor the radio broadcasts of the Voice of America and the BBC World Service.

Caution Be sure to keep your computer's antivirus software updated, and we strongly recommend that you invest in a firewall if you don't already have one.

- Take advantage of the Internet's free translation services to read the foreign-language press.

While the Internet has plenty of news sources in English, you may find it necessary to read news that appears only in a foreign language. Finding foreign-language newspapers, wire service and magazines on the Internet isn't a problem. This trouble comes when you don't know the language. Well, now there's a solution.

Foreign languages are no longer the barriers to information they used to be, thanks to automated, online translation services. You can as easily read a newspaper written in, say, French or German as in English. What's more, some of these online translation services are free! Our favorite free online translator is AltaVista's Babel Fish (http://world.altavista.com). It will translate into English bits of text or even entire Web pages from Chinese, French, German, Italian, Japanese, Korean, Spanish, Portuguese and Russian. While the quality of the translations wouldn't get you an "A" in school, the results are reasonably accurate and certainly sufficient to give you the gist of a story. Directions for the translator are simple and straightforward. And, again, once you have the resulting URL, you can save it as a "favorite" and go back to it at any time.

- Know where to find links to the foreign-language press.

There are several places to find the Web addresses for foreign-language newspapers. The very best place to go, in our opinion, is Kidon Media Links (www.kidon.com/media-link/index.shtml) of the Netherlands, which has links for virtually every newspaper and wire service in the world. We do not mean hundreds of links . . . or even thousands. We mean tens of thousands of media links, including magazines and TV and radio stations. Kidon also tells you the language of a publication and how often it's published. Another worthwhile site is NewsDirectory.com (www.newsdirectory.com). You also may want to check out Radio-Locator (www.radio-locator.com), which has links to more than 10,000 radio stations around the world. Unfortunately, Sorry, there are no free online translators for the spoken word.

- Consider a country's economic condition when assessing the risk of going there.

In assessing the potential risk of violent street demonstrations or individual acts of violent crime, you must take into account a country's economic circumstance. A major currency devaluation, a huge rise in inflation and unemployment, a dramatic downturn in an economy—any of these could spark rioting, particularly in an already-poor country. Street riots, for example, followed the recent money crisis in Argentina and the devaluation of the Turkish lira. Worse, Mexico's peso crisis of 1994-95 so damaged the economy that many out-of-work Mexicans turned to crime. Conditions in Mexico City indeed became so bad that car drivers refused to stop for red lights or stop signs, flew over speed bumps and never rolled down their windows for fear of carjacking, abduction and murder. Thus, it probably wouldn't be wrong to say that the worse off a country is economically, the greater the likelihood of violent crime. As a foreigner traveling in an impoverished country, destitute locals might perceive you as a rich foreigner, someone who is likely to be carrying a lot of money and valuables. You might also be viewed as an important foreign business executive who would command a king's ransom if kidnapped.

5.02. Staying Connected

Because new terrorist threats or incidents could affect Americans overseas, and conditions in a foreign country can change in an instant, you must keep on top of the latest news while traveling outside the U.S. Here are some suggestions:

- Bring a laptop and stay only in hotels that provide for Internet hookups in your room.

Keeping abreast of breaking news about terrorism or crime that could directly affect you becomes most important when you're actually overseas. So bring a laptop computer or other Internet-capable device with you on your trip, and stay only in hotels where you can make a direct connection to the Internet from your room. Also, make sure you can retrieve your emails

International Terrorist Attacks in Africa and Middle East, 1991-2001

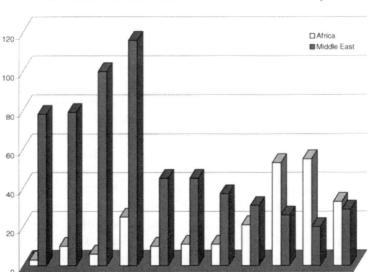

Source: U.S. Department of State

while traveling. And store your laptop not in its original carrying case but in a common, nondescript bag or satchel that won't attract a thief. Avoid public spaces in hotels that permit guests to use computers to access the Internet and get email. Terrorists know that foreigners congregate in these areas, and thus these spaces are potential targets of terrorist attack. Criminals, too, could enter the hotel's computers later to try and retrieve sensitive information or data concerning your financial accounts. Therefore, do all you computer-related work in the privacy of your room or at the local branch office of your company. And never leave your computer in your room when you go out. Not only is your computer valuable to a thief, but the data stored within could be used to perpetrate a financial fraud or identity theft. Either take your computer everywhere you go, or put it in the hotel safe—but not your room safe. Room safes aren't very safe at all.

Tip Be advised that telephone jacks in many parts of the world are incompatible with U.S. phone cords, so you'll need to buy a plug adapter. Also, U.S. Customs may claim that you bought your laptop overseas; if you want to avoid paying duty, carry a copy of your receipt.

Caution If you bring a laptop computer to Russia, you could be forced to leave it there. Russia's State Customs Committee has stated that there are no restrictions on bringing laptop computers into the Russian Federation for personal use. The software, however, can be inspected upon departure. Worse, some computer equipment and software brought into Russia by foreign visitors have been confiscated because of the data they contain or the software's encryption technology. (Encryption, of course, is standard in many programs.) In addition, the importation and use of Global Positioning Systems (GPS) and other radio electronic devices are subject to special rules and regulations in Russia. For more information on rules concerning computers and GPS devices, see the State Department's advisory at http://travel.state.gov/gps.html. You can also contact the State Customs Committee of the Russian Federation, Russia 107842 Moscow, 1A Komsomolskaya Place. Its main telephone is 7-095-975-4070. Or you can call 7-095-975-4095 to get clearance to use personal items.

- Rent or buy a cellular telephone with international roaming that will function at your foreign destination.

Cellular telephone networks around the world are incompatible with U.S. wireless technology and radio frequencies, meaning most cell phones used in the U.S. probably won't work overseas. Most foreign countries use a digital platform called Global System for Mobile (GSM) communications. More than 500 million cell-phone owners in 162 countries, representing 70% of the world's wireless subscribers, use the GSM standard.

You can buy GSM phones in the U.S. from such makers as Ericsson and Nokia, including international service, but be careful because some phones won't work in Japan, Korea and Latin America. Remember, too, that you need to be signed up with an international roaming service for a GSM phone to work. It's best, therefore, to contact your wireless service provider first and ask questions. You may already have international-roaming access. VoiceStream (www.voicestream.com) sells and rents world phones with international roaming. Cingular Wireless (www.cingular.com) also provides this service. To rent a world phone with international roaming, consult the list of cell-phone rental companies listed in the back of this book. But *caveat emptor.* Let the buyer beware.

The good news is that most of the world's modern economies have cellular phone systems that are more advanced than those in the United States. In parts of Asia, for example, you can use a cell to get a soft drink from a machine dispenser or pay for your dry-cleaning. This may come as a surprise to many of us who think of the U.S. as the world's technology leader. While that's true in many instances, it's not the case with cell phones. And there's a reason for it. State-run telephone systems have long dominated much of the world's telecommunications, especially in Europe. These state enterprises had been so horribly run and so unaccountable that businesses typically had to wait months or even years to get new telephone lines installed; private residences needing a new phone line could expect only a slightly shorter wait.

It's no wonder, then, that when cellular-phone services emerged, consumers and businesses outside the U.S. beat a path to their door. With so much pent up demand for telephone service around the world, the cell-phone industry began growing by leap and bounds, offering the very latest in new gadgetry, technology and service. Moreover, in developing economies, such as China, where the landmass involved can be huge, the installation of cellular technology made a lot more sense than stringing thousands of miles of telephone lines.

Tip   Be sure to pack spare cell-phone batteries.

Caution   In Russia, you have to obtain permission to bring in a cellular telephone. An agreement for service from a local cellular provider in Russia is required, according to the U.S. State

Department. That agreement and a letter of guarantee to pay for the cellular service must be sent to Glavgossvyaznadzor (the State Inspectorate for Communications), along with a request for permission to import the telephone. Based on these documents, a certificate is issued. This procedure is reported to take two weeks. Without a certificate, no cellular telephone can be brought into the country, whether or not it is meant for use in Russia. Glavgossvyaznadzor can be reached at Russia 117909 Moscow, Second Spasnailovkovsky 6; telephone 7-095-238-6331 or fax 7-095-238-5102. For more information, see the State Department's advisory at http://travel.state.gov/gps.html. You can also send an inquiry by mail or via facsimile to Consular Section, American Embassy, 19/23 Novinskiy Bulvar, 123242 Moscow, Russia; fax (011-7)(095) 728-5358. Inquiries from the United States can be sent to Consular Section, AM/EM–PSC–77, APO AE 09721.

- Beware of wiretapped phones and intelligence debriefings.

Foreign intelligence agencies are known to tap the phones of important foreign visitors, especially business executives. They also may debrief the people you meet with to discuss business— and even local hires working at your branch office. So be careful with trade secrets and other proprietary information.

5.03. Foreign Airline Safety

The safety records of many foreign airlines, especially in the Third World, are abysmal. It frankly isn't safe to fly on most of the world's airlines. Of the 210 or so countries and other domains that occupy the globe, only 77 are known to meet minimum air safety requirements. That's roughly one in three. It's not a ratio that inspires confidence. Therefore, unless you use a knowledgeable travel agent to book your flights, you need to do some research to ensure your safety when using carriers other than U.S.-based airlines while traveling overseas.

- Verify that any foreign airline you use meets U.S. safety standards.

International Terrorist Attacks in Asia and Eurasia, 1991-2001

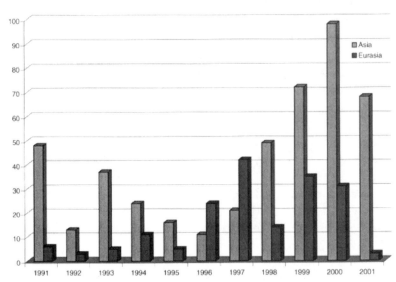

Source: U.S. Department of State

Air travel is the safest in those countries that have had their air systems reviewed and approved by the U.S. Federal Aviation Administration. The FAA, in effect, rates airline service around the world as either safe or unsafe. The FAA doesn't say this in so many words, however. It doesn't, for instance, tell you whether a particular foreign airline is okay to fly. But you can deduce that from information that the FAA supplies under something called the International Aviation Safety Assessment Program (IASA). Under the program, begun in 1992, the FAA assesses the civil aviation authority of each country with service to the United States. These civil aviation authorities are the FAA's equivalents abroad. The FAA's assessments determine whether or not a civil aviation authority overseeing airline operations to and from the United States meets the safety standards set by a United Nations' body known as the International Civil Aviation Organization (ICAO).

The FAA has two ratings for the status of a foreign civil aviation authority: 1) It complies with ICAO standards, or 2) it doesn't comply with the standards. To be in compliance means a civil aviation authority has been assessed by FAA inspectors and has been found to license and oversee air carriers in accordance with ICAO aviation safety standards. When a country isn't in compliance, it means the FAA has assessed the civil aviation authority and determined that it doesn't provide safety over-sight of its air-carrier operators in accordance with the mini-mum safety oversight standards.

The latest FAA safety ratings for some 100 countries can be found online at www.faa.gov/apa/iasa.htm or by calling the FAA's weekday, working-hours number at 800-322-7873. The FAA also has 24-hour safety hotline at 800-255-1111, which is primarily used to report safety violations, although you can speak with an FAA representative to discuss a time-critical safety issue. There's a big problem with the FAA's list, however; it doesn't cover every country in the world. Excluded are those nations that haven't sought an FAA safety rating. To make up for this shortcoming, we've gone the extra mile and listed below not only the countries known to be in non-compliance with mini-mum safety standards but also many of those that haven't been assessed at all by the FAA for air worthiness.

To be fair, however, we must note that the lack of an FAA safety review doesn't automatically mean that a country's airlines are unfit to fly. The FAA only rates those countries that either already have airline service to the U.S. or have applied for such service. This means, of course, that the FAA has never rated many small countries or island nations that have no need for their own airline routes to the U.S. Still, the names of these countries are worth knowing. The reason: You may have a choice to fly to the same destination on an airline based in a country that is FAA-approved and one that isn't. Take Kenya, for example. Both Kenya Airways and British Airways have flights to and from London. But Kenya doesn't have an FAA safety rating; Britain does.

FAA safety-approved countries: Argentina, Aruba, Australia, Austria, Bahamas, Belgium, Bermuda, Brazil, Britain, Brunei Darussalam, Bulgaria, Canada, Cayman Islands, Chile, China, Columbia, Costa Rica, Czech Republic, Denmark, Egypt, Ethiopia, Finland, France, Fiji, Germany, Ghana, Guyana, Hong Kong, Hungary, Iceland, Ireland, India, Indonesia, Israel, Italy, Jamaica, Japan, Jordan, Kuwait, Luxembourg, Marshall Islands, Malta, Malaysia, Mexico, Morocco, Netherlands, Netherlands Antilles (Curacau, St. Martin, Bonaire, Saba and St. Eustatius), New Zealand, Norway, Oman, Panama, Peru, Philippines, Poland, Portugal, Romania, Russia, Saudi Arabia, Singapore, South Africa, South Korea, Spain, Sweden, Switzerland, Taiwan, Thailand, Trinidad and Tobago, Turkey, Ukraine, United Kingdom, Uzbekistan, Western Samoa and Yugoslavia (Serbia and Montenegro).

Countries cited by the FAA as not meeting minimum air safety standards: Bangladesh, Belize, Bolivia, Cote d'Ivoire, Democratic Republic of the Congo (formerly Zaire), Dominican Republic, Ecuador, El Salvador, Gambia, Guatemala, Haiti, Honduras, Kiribati, Nauru, Nicaragua, Organization of Eastern Caribbean States (including Anguilla, Antiqua and Barbuda, Dominica, Grenada, Montserrat, St. Lucia, St. Vincent and the Grenadines, St. Kitts and Nevis), Pakistan, Paraguay, Suriname, Swaziland, Turks and Caicos, Uruguay, Venezuela and Zimbabwe.

Among the 100 or so countries and domains that haven't been reviewed, for one or another reason, by the FAA, here are some names to keep in mind: Armenia, Azerbaijan, Belarus, Benin, Bhutan, Botswana, Burkina Faso, Burundi, Cambodia, Cameroon, Cape Verde, Central African Republic, Chad, Comoros, the Congo, Croatia, Cyprus, Djibouti, Eritrea, Estonia, Gabon, Georgia, Kazakhstan, Kenya, Kyrgyz Republic, Laos, Latvia, Lesotho, Lithuania, Macedonia, Madagascar, Malawi, Maldives, Mali, Martinique, Mauritania, Mauritius, Micronesia, Moldova, Monaco, Mongolia, Mozambique, Namibia, Nepal, Niger, Nigeria, Papua New Guinea, Qatar, Rwanda, Senegal, Seychelles, Sierra Leone, Slovak Republic, Slovenia, Somalia, Sri Lanka, Sudan, Syria, Tajikistan, Tanzania, Togo, Tonga, Tunisia, Turkmenistan, Tuvalu, Uganda, United Arab Emirates, Vanuatu, Vietnam, and Zambia.

Now, you may be saying to yourself, "Wait a minute. Some of the countries not in compliance with FAA's standards have

Air Hijacking Incidents Worldwide by Carrier Registry, 1975-2000

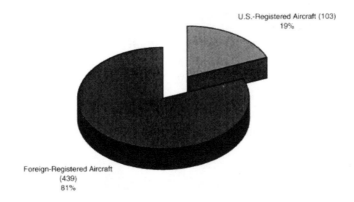

U.S.-Registered Aircraft (103)
19%

Foreign-Registered Aircraft
(439)
81%

Source: Federal Aviation Administration

flights in and out of the U.S." Well, that's right. The FAA doesn't necessarily ban air carriers based in those countries from providing service to and from the United States, but it does keep them under surveillance. Here's how the FAA explains it: "In general, carriers from countries in Category 2 [non-compliance] status with existing flights to the United States at the time of the assessment will be allowed to continue operations at current levels under heightened FAA surveillance. Expansion or changes in services to the United States by such carriers are not permitted." Meanwhile, countries whose airlines don't already fly to the U.S. aren't permitted to commence U.S. service so long as they remain in non-compliance with minimum safety standards.

Tip   Again, try to fly wide-body planes, because terrorists often avoid hijacking them.

- Factor in the risk of terrorist retaliation against the airlines of countries at war with terrorism.

In the aftermath of Sept. 11, the U.S. formed a rather loosely-knit global coalition to fight terrorism. Some countries have taken this commitment more seriously than others. Britain, for example, launched missile strikes against Afghanistan to coincide with the U.S. assault in the fall of 2001; later, British and Canadian troops fought alongside U.S. troops in the region. Other countries, such as Belgium, France, Germany, Israel, Pakistan, Singapore and Spain, have rounded up terrorist suspects, and still others have cut off the terrorists' money supply.

Terrorists may decide to retaliate against members of the global antiterrorism coalition—perhaps by hijacking or bombing their airliners—but it's impossible to say which countries would be at the most risk. Nonetheless, when considering flying on an airline based in a foreign country, the prominence that country has had in the war against terrorism is worth noting.

Tip Use the U.S. State Department's website www.state.gov to stay informed about the activities of the global coalition against terrorism.

5.04. Avoiding Danger

With terrorists and criminals on the watch for foreigners, notably Americans, you need to take a precautionary approach to almost everything you do when traveling abroad. Here are suggestions on how to avoid some common mistakes:

- Don't exchange currency at the airport.

Criminals often target foreign visitors exchanging large sums of currency at airport banks and foreign exchange kiosks. If you need foreign currency for a taxi ride from the airport to your hotel, call the banks in your hometown before you leave to find one that will sell you the foreign currency you need. Otherwise, only exchange money at the hotel or a reputable bank.

Tip   You could avoid the cost of a taxi ride by taking the hotel limousine from the airport.

- Don't deal in the "black market" when exchanging currency.

Currency controls are still in force in some countries. This usually means that the "official" exchange rate, established by the national government, is a lot lower than the rate offered on the "black market." U.S. dollars are highly prized around the world, especially in countries that have experienced ruinous currency devaluations. In those countries, the black-market trade in U.S. dollars is brisk. Indeed, don't be surprised if you're approached on the street by someone willing to exchange the local currency for dollars at a much better rate than the official one. Resist the temptation. First, you might be lured into a trap and robbed of all your valuables. Second, you might be given counterfeit money. Third, you might end up with a handful of old notes that have been taken out of circulation and are essentially worthless. Finally, you could land in jail. Buying and selling currency on the black market is illegal in many countries. For information on currency laws, see the U.S. State Department's individual country warnings and announcements at http://travel.state.gov/travel_warnings.html.

- Hide maps and guidebooks when driving overseas.

When driving overseas, don't display signs of your foreignness by having English-language maps and travel guides in plain view in your car, especially when getting fuel or picking up food. Bury those items under a piece of clothing. The same goes for English-language newspapers, such as the *International Herald Tribune* or *The Wall Street Journal.*

- Try to avoid large, self-park garages.

Parking garages are haunts for attackers, especially overseas. Therefore, use valet parking whenever you can, such as at restaurants and hotels, and try to avoid multilevel self-parking garages. Whenever possible, park your car in the open and in a well-lighted area visible to passersby.

- Arrange your itinerary so as to drive in the daytime.

Don't start a long drive so late in the day that it will keep you on the road into the night. Try to drive only in the daytime when on a lengthy excursion. If you're going to encounter trouble while driving overseas, it's most likely to occur at night.

Caution   Don't rely on the auto coverage offered by your credit card company; it usually doesn't cover such items as overseas medical expenses or personal liability.

- In general, stay at U.S. hotel chains when abroad.

"Isn't it asking for trouble to stay at an American hotel?" you may be asking yourself. "Aren't American hotels the most likely targets of terrorism?" Well, yes, in some countries that may be true. In places where the risk that Americans will be singled out as terrorist targets is very high, staying at a U.S. hotel chain may not be the most sensible thing to do. However, if the risk is that high, it's probably not wise to travel to the country at all until the threat subsides.

In reality, the greatest risks you'll face when traveling abroad will concern violent crime and food and health dangers. Security at U.S. chains tends to be much better than average. This lessens the chance that you could fall victim to burglary, assault, abduction or murder while at your hotel. U.S.-owned hotel also conduct more sophisticated employee background checks and have better door locks and fire-safety regimes. The personnel background checks are especially important. Unless you can trust the hotel staff, you could be vulnerable to theft or worse. Indeed, rogue hotel employees have been known to provide information about guests to kidnappers and extortionists.

Less dramatic but no less risky is the danger of food poisoning. Sanitary procedures in the kitchens of U.S. hotel chains are a cut above average. In addition, U.S.-owned hotels tend to have qualified local doctors on call in case of health emergencies and also know which hospitals will provide you with the best care. Further, U.S. hotel chains typically have more modern communications facilities, making it easier to make calls, receive faxes, get on the Internet and retrieve your email. For Americans traveling overseas, U.S.-owned hotels also afford a natural affinity, meaning you'll probably be treated better and your safety and health will be a higher priority than at a foreign-owned hotel. Also, U.S. hotel chains are less likely to have secret surveillance cameras and listening devices in your room, planted by a state intelligence agency. But be aware that most hotels, pool areas and bars tend be hangouts for pickpockets and other unsavory characters.

Finally, for Americans overseas, U.S.-based chains are more likely to agree to your special requests. You may, for instance, want the hotel to keep copies of vital information in case of an emergency or contact the U.S. embassy if something goes tragically wrong. Managers of these hotels, while they may not be Americans themselves, must eventually answer for their conduct to their superiors in the United States. And the last thing a U.S. hotel chain wants is bad publicity. So odds are you'll receive the best treatment at hotels overseas that are part of U.S.-based chains.

Tip   Check with the regional security officer at the local U.S. embassy for a list of hotels used by U.S. officials visiting the area.

Caution   If you're arriving after 6 p.m., be sure your hotel reservation is guaranteed; you don't want to be wandering around a strange city late at night looking for a room.

- Think of the front desk at your hotel as "command central."

Take advantage of the security that your hotel itself offers. For example, make copies of your passport, visa, driver's license, health insurance cards, credit and bank cards, and prescriptions for drugs, eyeglasses or contact lenses and place them in a securely sealed envelope. Then ask the front desk to put the package in the hotel safe. Having spare copies of your important documents and credit cards will make it a lot easier to get replacements if the originals are lost or stolen.

To help keep these private papers out of the wrong hands, affix a piece of strong tape or melt a bit of wax over the envelope's seal before handing the package over to the front desk for safekeeping. That way, you'll be able to tell afterwards whether anyone has pried open your personal papers. Tell the hotel what you'd like them to do in case of an emergency and provide the names and telephone numbers, as well as email addresses, of people they should call. If you have a serious medical condition or a life-threatening allergy—to penicillin or shell fish, for example—make the hotel aware of these, so they may inform a hospital or emergency medical technicians should the need arise.

In other words, think of your hotel's front desk as military command central, with you as a five-star general. Determine how the hotel can serve you, don't be shy about asking the front desk to do things for you and give instructions on how you want them to handle certain situations. Also, leave a copy of your daily itinerary with the front desk, including scheduled meeting times, names, addresses and phone numbers. Should you go missing, this information could prove invaluable to the police and even save your life.

Caution   We strongly recommend that you not hold these kinds of discussions in the open where an eavesdropper could hear you. Ask to be taken to a private office to discuss matters with the hotel manager. Also, try to develop a personal rapport with at least one senior staff member, who you could rely on in a pinch.

- Inform the local U.S. embassy of your presence and store vital documents there.

No matter how brief your stay in a foreign country—most especially one in which the risk of terrorism or other violence is high or if you are an executive with an internationally known company that could be a terrorist target—be sure to call the local

U.S. embassy or consulate to inform them that you're in the country. See the last chapter in this book for the phone numbers of U.S. embassies and consulates around the world. You can also get this information online from the U.S. State Department at http://usembassy.state.gov. The names of key U.S. diplomatic personnel around the world can be found at www.foia.state.gov/mms/KOH/keyofficers.asp.

Next, if you plan to stay more than a day or two make copies of your passport, visa, driver's license, and health-insurance, bank and credit cards and leave them with the embassy. And don't forget to retrieve these materials prior to departure. Inform the embassy, too, of any health conditions or serious allergies and provide a list of people to contact in an emergency.

Tip Ask about the embassy's hours and where to go in an emergency.

- Resist taking your spouse or children along at times of crisis or to high-risk destinations.

These aren't normal times, and many of the pleasures of international travel in the past no longer pertain. Traveling with your spouse or children is one of them. Be loving but be firm. Tell your family that it's neither the time nor place for them to accompany you overseas. Make it up to them by taking them on a trip to a safer locale after you get back.

5.05. Streetwise Advice

When in a foreign country, you're most vulnerable to attack when you're on the street. One reason is that terrorists and criminals usually canvass the streets, particularly near hotels and offices of foreign businesses, looking for targets of opportunity to kidnap or rob. Another reason is that foreigners tend to stick out on the street, especially if they make ostentatious displays of wealth.

- Never take the first taxi in line.

**Americans Killed or Wounded in International
Terrorist Attacks Worldwide, 1994-2000**

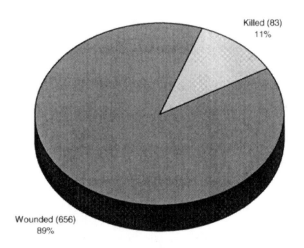

Killed (83)
11%

Wounded (656)
89%

Source: U.S. Department of State

If a group is out to kidnap you, one of the easiest ways is to gain your unwitting cooperation. Taxis are an especially useful method of deceiving an intended victim. A taxi might wait outside your hotel for your departure, or a compatriot might signal to the cabdriver that you're about to leave. To better ensure your safety, take the second or third taxi in line, but never the first one. Also, beware of unmarked cabs. Ask at the hotel desk for the names and phone numbers of reputable taxi, car or limousine services.

Caution   Never let anyone direct you to a specific taxi.

• Vary your daily routines and routes.

Don't get into the habit of taking the same route at the same time every day from your hotel to, say, your branch office. Kidnappers and terrorists look for patterns. Vary your route and daily routine by asking the driver to take you by a specified site (e.g., a famous park, monument, or museum) before going on to your final destination. Also, leave and return to your hotel at different times of day. Furthermore, don't always eat at the same restaurant or go to the same tavern. Alternate any stores you might otherwise visit daily during your stay. If you're driving a rental car, park in different spaces, with the front of the car always pointing out, and keep the gas tank at least half full to avoid being stranded or left searching for gasoline late at night.

Caution   If you rent a car abroad, purchase the liability insurance; otherwise you could face a major and costly headache in the event of an accident.

- Carry enough local coins to make a phone call.

International travelers commonly think of foreign coins as a nuisance. They generally can't be redeemed after you leave a country, so you're usually stuck with whatever you have in your pockets. However, don't eschew all foreign coins. You may need to make a local phone call in a hurry and your cell phone, for whatever reason, may not be working. If you're out of coins, you're out of luck. So make it a point to carry at least enough pocket change to call your hotel.

Tip   Many international airports have charity boxes in which you can donate your leftover foreign coins. If you frequently travel to one foreign country, put your extra change in a marked envelope and store it next to your passport to use on your next trip.

- Move away from public disturbances.

A loud disturbance on a public street is the kind of trouble you want to avoid. Don't be nosey. It could be a political protest about to turn violent or a terrorist-inspired incident. It could even be a distraction, used by pickpockets and purse-snatchers to lift the wallets and purses of onlookers. Don't get involved in any street disturbance, and move away as quickly as possible in the opposite direction.

• Don't advertise your nationality or foreignness.

Opportunistic criminals and terrorists look for foreigners. A good way to protect yourself abroad, therefore, is to look inconspicuous. You do that by appearing to blend in with the local population as much as possible. Of course, in certain areas of the world, that may be impossible. If you stand 7' 1" like Los Angeles Laker center Shaquille O'Neal, you're going to stand out on the streets of Tokyo no matter what you do. Still, there are ways to avoid sticking out like a sore thumb in a foreign land. First, never wear anything that gives your nationality away. You may be proud to be an American, for instance, but displaying an American flag pin on your lapel when traveling in, say, the Middle East might not be the smartest thing to do. Second, try not to wear clothing that automatically identifies you as a foreigner. That's not to say that you should take up wearing a turban when in India. That would only make you look foolish (and criminals eat fools for lunch). Instead, consider the cut and color of your clothing, and pick suits and outfits that most closely match those worn by the indigenous population. Finally, eschew wearing T-shirts, sweatshirts or caps that identify you as an American.

Caution   Backpackers should resist the temptation to sew USA emblems and American flags on their packs.

Keep your voice down on the streets of high-risk cities.
If you're in a high-risk foreign country or city, speak as little as possible on city streets. Your native tongue or just the sound of your voice could resonant a mile away. If you must carry on a conversation, speak softly so as not to let strangers hear. Remember that eavesdropping is a tool used by criminals and terrorists to select victims.

- Learn a few common phrases to get around a foreign city.

Not everyone has a gift for languages. Still, if you can learn enough common foreign phrases to get you where you're going, you'll give the appearance of being familiar with the territory. You may not pass for a native, but at least you won't broadcast the fact that you're a complete neophyte. There's plenty of software available to help you learn foreign words and phrases, without incurring the time and expense of in-person lessons. Of course, nothing is as good as being taught a foreign language by a native speaker or an experienced teacher. However, for travelers who make only the occasional trip to a particular country, using a CD to learn a few helpful phrases may be just enough to get by.

Caution   Be suspicious of anyone who approaches you wanting to "practice English" or talk about the United States or politics of any kind; it's impossible to say these days if such an unsolicited approach is innocent or a ploy by a terrorist or kidnapper.

- Always look like you know where you're going, even when you're lost.

Give the impression of self-assurance wherever you go. The process should begin the moment you arrive overseas. Know precisely where your hotel is located, giving the taxi driver the name and street. But say it in a way that makes it sound as if you've been there before, even if you haven't. Mention the nearest cross street, perhaps. Follow the same procedure when asking a taxi to take you to a business meeting or restaurant. If you get lost, try not to show it. Never panic. Rather, go into a shop or café and ask for assistance. Otherwise, hail a cab or find the nearest phone and call a car service. Always book your hotel accommodations in advance. Never wander the streets looking for a place to stay. Do the same thing when dining out. Make reservations and know how to get to the restaurant before you leave your hotel. Sadly, much of the spontaneity traditionally associated with foreign travel died on Sept. 11.

• Don't telegraph the fact that you're a stranger in town.

To lower your vulnerability in a foreign country, avoid doing the things that most first-time visitors do. For example, don't open up street maps or guidebooks in public. Try to memorize your route. Barring that, make a copy of the section of the map or guidebook you'll need that day. Glancing at what appears to be just a piece of paper is much less conspicuous than unfolding a huge map. If worse comes to worst, take a seat at a café, order a refreshment and ask someone to point the way on your map. If you're a tourist rather than a business traveler, there may be other things to keep in mind. More than likely, you'll want to see the sights—e.g., museums, art galleries, historic sites, etc. There's no need, however, to advertise that you're a foreign tourist. For example, if you want to go a famous museum by taxi, don't tell the driver, "Take us to the National Museum." Instead, give the driver nearby street coordinates and walk the rest of the way to the museum's entrance. Finally, if traveling to a high-risk area of the world, don't take your camera along. Standing on the street snapping pictures instantly tells a criminal or terrorist that you're from out of town. Buy photographs instead.

Caution   Avoid pointing to things in public. You can always tell the tourists outside the Empire State Building; they're the ones with their fingers in the air.

• Avoid public displays of wealth.

Displays of affluence make a criminal's heart grow fonder. You're only asking for trouble if you flaunt your wealth, especially in impoverished countries. Don't wear expensive jewelry or watches. And never take any family heirlooms abroad. Your rule of thumb should be: If you can't bear the thought of parting with a keepsake, leave it at home. Also, in some poor countries, displays of wealth can trigger hostility and resentment. As a foreigner, you could be subjected to some especially harsh treatment by the locals.

• Keep any consumption of alcohol to a minimum.

It's vital to keep your wits about you these days, particularly overseas, so strictly limit any consumption of alcohol when traveling. And never drink and drive.

- Don't keep all your credit cards and ID in one place.

Pickpockets are highly expert in many cities in the world. They are often far better trained, more experienced and much more sly than anything experienced on, say, the streets of the United States. Pickpockets abroad are usually small in size and young. But don't let age, or even gender, fool you. Pickpockets come in all ages, sizes and genders. But what they all share in common is the desire to get at your money, your valuables and, most especially, your credit cards. You can, of course, call your credit card companies to report a theft. But what do you do after that, particularly if you're overseas? The loss of your credit cards all at once could turn into a real nightmare. The smartest thing to do, therefore, is make it next to impossible to have every one of your cards stolen at the same time. Simply keep your credit cards in different places, so if your wallet is lifted, for instance, you'll still have a card in your pocket or briefcase to fall back on.

Tip Be especially cautious when getting off a train, bus or escalator, as those are prime locations for pickpockets and purse-snatchers.

- Be on guard against identity and passport theft.

Next to killing or injuring you, a terrorist would like nothing better than to steal your identity. Phony passports and identification cards are an essential part of a terrorist's toolkit. Buy special clothing or a body pack in which you can hide your identity papers.

- Immediately report the theft or lose of your passport or credit cards to the proper authorities.

If your passport is lost or stolen, immediately inform the local U.S. embassy or consulate. You'll need to speak to the American Citizens Services unit of the Consular Section, where you'll be directed on how to obtain new passport photos. If you're about to leave the foreign country, provide the Consular Section with details of your departure schedule. Further information on lost or stolen passports is available at http://travel.state.gov/lost_passports_abroad.html. If your credit cards have been stolen, you'll need to contact your card providers and the U.S. Federal Trade Commission. The FTC serves as the federal clearinghouse for complaints by victims of identity theft. The FTC enters identity theft and fraud-related complaints into its "Consumer Sentinel," a secure, online database available to hundreds of civil and criminal law enforcement agencies worldwide. The FTC can be reached at 877-FTC-HELP (877-382-4357) or online at www.ftc.gov. Its website contains an online form that you can use to report the theft of your identity. (For a more in-depth discussion of how to avoid identity theft and how to restore your credit should a theft occur, see Chapter 6 on protecting your money and go to the FTC's website.)

5.06. Staying Healthy

Even though the goal of this book is to help you survive terrorism and other violence, we'd be remiss if we didn't share what we know about protecting your health overseas. Of all the dangers that international travelers face, health threats are by far the biggest. You are, in fact, more likely to die from a disease contracted in a foreign country than from a terrorist or criminal attack. Here, then, are the most significant health issues you need to consider before going abroad.

- Be aware of any infectious diseases at your travel destination.

The Centers of Disease Control and Prevention (CDC) provide up-to-date information on international health problems that could pose serious hazards to travelers. Countries infected with quarantinable diseases are listed in the CDC's "Blue Sheet," which is updated every two weeks. The CDC's Travel website www.cdc.gov/travel/index.htm also has tips on how to prevent insect bites and how to protect yourself against food- and water-borne illnesses (e.g., avoid ice because it could be made from contaminated water). You might also visit Travel Health Online at www.tripprep.com for additional information.

Tip Inspections scores for cruise ships are found in the CDC's "Green Sheet," which is also available at the above Web address.

- Get immunized before going abroad.

You can get vaccinated against many travel-related diseases at most state and local health departments. To find the location of the office nearest you, see "Public Health Resources: State Health Departments" at www.cdc.gov/mmwr/international/relres.html. For information on private travel clinics in the U.S. and overseas that offer immunizations, contact the International Society of Travel Medicine at P.O. Box 871089, Stone Mountain, GA, 30087-0028, 770-736-7060, www.istm.org or the American Society of Tropical Medicine and Hygiene at 60 Revere Drive, Suite 500, Northbrook, IL 60062, 847-480-9592, *www.astmh.org*.

Tip The CDC provides information on traveling globally and returning to the U.S. with pets and animals at www.cdc.gov/ncidod/dq/animal.htm.

- Know who the good doctors are and which hospitals and clinics are safe.

It's wrong to assume that you can get the same quality of medical treatment overseas as you can in the U.S. Getting proper medical attention can be especially difficult in developing nations, but even in many of the world's industrialized nations, healthcare can be hit or miss. The problem of inferior medical care around the world therefore requires you to become proactive. You need to look out for yourself by ensuring that you're seen by a qualified physician and, if necessary, admitted to a safe, well-run hospital or clinic.

The U.S. State Department provides the names of qualified doctors and hospitals around the world at http://travel.state.gov/

acs.html. The local U.S. Embassy in a foreign country will do the same. (See our contact list in the back of the book for embassy telephone numbers.) Another terrific resource that we recommend is the International Association for Medical Assistance to Travellers (www.iamat.org). IAMAT, a non-profit group founded in 1960, informs travelers of worldwide health risks, protective immunization and where to turn when a medical problem arises. Membership is free. Its online directory of physicians directs members to participating physicians, specialists, clinics and hospitals in 125 countries. IAMAT continuously inspects clinics, hospitals and physicians' offices around the world and reviews professional qualifications. Its telephone number in Canada is 519-836-0102, and its U.S. number is 716-754-4883.

- Recognize that blood supplies overseas aren't always safe.

Although governments are loathe to admit it, blood supplies are tainted with disease in more foreign countries than you probably imagine. Until recently, for instance, AIDS was a serious problem affecting blood supplies in several West European countries. In regions such as Asia and Africa, AIDS remains a major problem. Blood can also be tainted with hepatitis and other life-threatening disease. Take nothing for granted if you're admitted to a hospital overseas.

- Bring copies of drug prescriptions and an extra set of glasses or contact lenses.

Running out of a prescribed medicine while abroad can be a nightmare. Pharmacists won't refill the medication simply based upon the information on the label made out by your local pharmacy. You'll be forced to see a doctor, and that can prove to be a difficult, time-consuming chore. Make it a point, therefore, to bring copies of all your prescriptions with you. Follow the same procedure in terms of eye care. If you wear glasses or contact lens, bring along spares. It's also a good idea to pack any over-the-counter medications that you use regularly (e.g., Tylenol or antacid). Women should further take note when packing that many brands of feminine-hygiene products frequently aren't available overseas and that the products that are on the shelves are often of inferior quality compared with those found in the U.S.

Tip   If worse comes to worst, have you personal physician back in the States send you a new prescription via overseas courier.

Caution   When returning from overseas, U.S. residents can import up to 50 dosage units of a controlled medication without a valid prescription. But the medications must be declared at Customs upon arrival, must be for your own personal use and have to be in their original container. Travelers should be aware that drug products not approved by the U.S. Food and Drug Administration (FDA) cannot be brought into the country. Also, the FDA warns that such drugs are often of unknown quality and generally discourages buying drugs sold in foreign countries. For more information, go to the websites for the U.S. Customs Service at www.customs.gov and the FDA at www.fda.gov.

- Carry adequate medical insurance, and sign up with an air-ambulance service.

Have adequate heath insurance, and be sure the plan covers you when you're overseas. Carry both your insurance policy identity card as proof of insurance and a claim form. Remember, too, that Social Security Medicare doesn't cover medical or hospital expenses incurred outside the U.S. Senior citizens, prior to departure, might contact the American Association of Retired Persons (www.aarp.org) for information about foreign medical care coverage with Medicare supplement plans. Another good idea is to sign up with an air-ambulance service, which can whisk out of a foreign backwater, or indeed any country, and get you to a proper hospital for emergency treatment. A list of air-ambulance services appears at the back of this book, You can find a similar list online at the U.S. State Department http://travel.state.gov/medical.html. Seniors, in particular, should be aware that some air-ambulance services will provide you with escorts who will fly home with you via a commercial airliner if you're not so desperately ill as to require an air ambulance but do need the assistance of a private helper.

Tip   Your life could be taken at any moment in an accident or act of violence, so carry sufficient life insurance to meet the needs of your family. Also, leave a power of attorney with a family member or friend before you head overseas.

Caution   Air ambulances are expensive. A flight could easily run you $10,000. So get special insurance or join a program to cover the expense. Most regular health insurance plans don't cover the cost of air ambulances.

5.07. If All Goes Wrong

The State Department offers a fair amount of information and help to U.S. citizens (and their relatives) who find themselves in the midst of a crisis while traveling abroad. Be sure to take advantage of it.

- Heed official U.S. warnings to defer travel to or to leave a foreign country.

It doesn't happen often, but the U.S. State Department does on occasion instruct America citizens to avoid travelling to or staying in a country that is in violent turmoil or on the brink of war or where the lives of Americans are directly threatened. In June 2002, for example, as tensions between India and Pakistan escalated, the State Department issued travel warnings for Americans to "defer all but essential travel" to those countries and authorized all non-essential U.S. personnel and their families to leave. And after a June 14 car bombing in Karachi, State further said that it "strongly urges" American citizens in Pakistan to depart. Prudence dictates following such official advice. The State Department's travel warnings are posted at http://travel.state.gov/travel_warnings.html.

- Map at least two emergency escape routes out of a foreign country.

In this day and age, you can never tell when a country may erupt in violence or become the target of a concerted terrorist campaign. You may, therefore, need to leave a foreign country in a hurry. Plan an exit strategy, based on at least two different routes of escape. Designate where you'd go and how you'd get there in case of an emergency. If the situation is extreme, you may want to eschew commercial air travel, for fear airports and air travel will be dangerous. If rioting breaks out and if Americans are singled out, airports will be not only chaotic but also prime targets for attack. You're best bet may be to travel by road to a neighboring country and hop on a plane from there. This will require some preplanning. If you have a rental car, get a map and determine a route to the safest neighboring country. If not, think of someone who might drive you (e.g., a company employing residing in-country, a client, car service or off-duty hotel employee). And prepare a small survival kit filled with essentials (e.g., medicines, extra glasses, food and water) that you can grab in a hurry. Contact the local U.S. embassy or consulate for advice; you might also ask if you could get a ride out of the county with a member of the diplomatic staff. Also, see the State Department's advice on evacuations at *http://travel.state.gov/crisismg.html*.

Tip   If you have no other choice but to fly out commercially, pick a destination other than the U.S. Select a safe-haven country, like Switzerland. Note, though, that some of these countries require visas. So check in advance about any entry requirements or restrictions.

- Get help from the State Department if you're stranded overseas and need financial assistance.

If you're a U.S. citizen and run out of money while overseas, the State Department will lend you a helping hand. Destitute or stranded Americans should contact the Overseas Citizens Services of the Office of American Citizen Services and Crisis Management at (202) 647-5225 or through the local U.S. embassy or consulate. More information is available at http://travel.state.gov/finance_assist.html.

- Contact the State Department if a relative becomes embroiled in a foreign crisis.

Families whose U.S. citizen relatives are directly affected by a foreign crisis should contact the Department of State through its Office of American Citizens Services and Crisis Management at 202-647-5225. If a 24-hour task force or working group is established in the Department of State Operations Center to manage the crisis, you'll be directed to the Task Force at 202-647-0900. For more information, see "Crisis Awareness and Preparedness" at http://travel.state.gov/crisismg.html.

- Should a death occur overseas, be prepared for a complicated and costly process to get the remains returned to the U.S.

The State Department's Office of American Citizen Services and Crisis Management (ACS) says that approximately 6,000 Americans die outside of the U.S. each year and that the majority of these are long-term residents of a foreign country. ACS assists with the return of remains for about 2,000 Americans annually. (Call 202-647-5225.) When an American dies abroad, a consular officer notifies the next of kin about options and costs for the disposition of the remains. Costs for preparing and returning a body to the U.S. are high and are the responsibility of the family. Often local laws and procedures make returning a body to the U.S. for burial a lengthy process.

- Don't expect too much official help if you get arrested abroad.

If you're arrested in a foreign country, you're pretty much on your own. The ACS says that more than 2,500 Americans are arrested abroad annually. More than 30% of these arrests are drug related, and over 70% of drug-related arrests involve marijuana or cocaine. The rights an American enjoys in the U.S. "do not travel abroad," notes the ACS. "Each country is sovereign and its laws apply to everyone who enters regardless of nationality. The U.S. government cannot get Americans released from foreign jails." ("When You Need Help," The Office of Overseas Citizens Services, Department of State Publication 10252, revised May 10, 2002.) A U.S. consul will insist on prompt access to an arrested American, provide a list of attorneys and information on the host country's legal system, offer to contact the arrested person's family or friends, visit on a regular basis, protest mistreatment, monitor jail conditions, provide dietary supplements, if needed, and keep the State Department informed.

ACS also is the point of contact in the U.S. for family members and others who are concerned about a U.S. citizen arrested abroad. A toll-free hotline at 888-407-4747 is available from 8:00 a.m. to 8:00 p.m. Eastern time, Monday-Friday, except U.S. federal holidays. Callers who are unable to use toll-free numbers, such as those calling from overseas, may obtain information and assistance during these hours by calling 317-472-2328. For after-hours emergencies, Sundays and holidays, call 202-647-4000 and request the Overseas Citizens Services (OCS) duty officer.

Tip Relatives, friends or colleagues can use the same phone numbers to try to track down a U.S. citizen who has gone missing overseas. The ACS fields about 12,000 such requests each year.

5.08. Kidnapping Survival

Kidnapping is much more common abroad than in the U.S. In recent years, Colombia, in particular, has become notorious for kidnappings for ransom. In Russia, too, several American business travelers have been kidnapped and even murdered in recent years.

Here, according to the U.S. State Department, are the countries in which kidnappings occur most frequently: In Africa, Angola, Democratic Republic of the Congo, Ethiopia, Kenya, Nigeria, Rwanda, Somalia, Uganda and Yemen; in Asia, Indonesia and the Philippines; in Europe, Georgia and Russia, and in Latin America, Colombia, Ecuador, El Salvador, Honduras, Mexico, Nicaragua and Venezuela. For country-specific informa-

Total Anti-U.S. Attacks by International Terrorists by Global Region, 2001

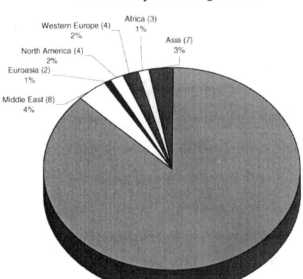

Source: U.S. Department of State

tion on kidnapping, consult the U.S. State Department's travel advisories online at http://travel.state.gov/travel_warnings.html.

• Know when you're being targeted for abduction.

You may be able to spot telltale signs indicating that you're being targeted for abduction. These include: people who are clearly taking too great an interest in you; repeated sightings of the same people observing you, say, while entering and leaving your hotel or branch office; strangers who have asked others about you; an accidental encounter with a stranger who then tries to strike up a conversation, asking who you are, where you come from, what you do for a living and how much money you make, and any sign that you are being followed on foot or trailed by a car. Immediately inform the U.S. embassy, police, your company and your hotel of your suspicions. You might consider cutting you trip short and returning at a later date to complete your business. And remember, too, that a kidnapping can take place anywhere—in your hotel room, on the street and even in a taxi.

Tip Don't invite extortion by engaging in activities that are illegal or compromising.

• Try to attract attention if you're being kidnapped.

You may get only one chance to prevent a kidnapping, so try to attract as much attention as possible if the attack takes place in public. If you're in your hotel, yell. And yell, "Fire!" Other guests are more likely to respond to a scream of "Fire!" than to a cry of "Help!" However, if faced with a gun or knife and the risk of injury or death is great, go quietly.

• Conserve your strength and look for landmarks if you're bundled off.

Know that if the kidnapper succeeds, you may be blindfolded, knocked unconscious or drugged. You might even be forced into the trunk of car. If you're conscious, don't struggle; conserve your strength, for it's likely your meals in captivity will be few and far between. If you're in a vehicle, see if you can spot any landmarks along the way to help authorities later.

• Don't look your kidnapper in the eye.

Never look your kidnaper in the eye. That's the first rule to follow in a kidnapping or any hostage situation. Direct eye contact intimidates an abductor and creates in him a fierce animosity toward you. He may decide to treat you particularly harshly or violently. He could bind you painfully tight and threaten you with death. Instead, be cooperative. Don't ask questions. Don't get angry. Don't be antagonistic. Rather, be controlled and reserved. Tell yourself to be calm and that everything will work out all right. Pray, if you're so inclined.

- Be humble and try to gain the sympathy of your kidnappers.

If kidnappers are holding you for ransom, be humble and appear helpless. Don't do anything to make your captors nervous or afraid. Don't act like you're James Bond. Don't threaten them with retaliation and revenge, because they may decide to kill you. Tell your abductors, "I'm not a hero, and I'm not trying to be hero." Never demean or insult them, and never invent stories about being wealthy and important or offer to pay them off. Don't put on airs and say things like: "I'm very rich. I have jewelry at the hotel. Take me there and I'll give it to you." If you make yourself out to be rich, your abductors will never believe you if you admit to them later that you really are poor. Abductors do make mistakes and occasionally kidnap someone who has little or no money to meet their ransom demands. If you find yourself in such a situation, first let things play out a little. Your kidnappers will need time to relax before you can attempt to reason with them. Then, tell them the truth: "I want you to know, contrary to what you think, I'm not rich. I've got a wife and kids like you. I'm just here trying to make a living."

Tip   Try to maintain a sense of humor. It will help personalize you to your abductors and could help to gain their sympathy.

- Assess your chances of escape.

Time and again in abduction situations, a kidnapper will let down his guard down as the ordeal wears on. This could present you with a chance to escape or overpower him. If you mean to flee, see if your abductor is preoccupied and not looking in your direction. Determine whether you can release yourself if you're tied up. Look for a ready avenue of escape. Be certain, however, that you're physically and mentally attuned to the task. If you have doubts, it's better to do nothing. In general, we don't recommend attempting to overpower an assailant, unless you are clearly up to it. It's vital that you be physically fit and trained, preferably in the martial arts, if you intend to take down your captor.

If you mean to escape, be certain that you're in a good position to carry it off. You must time an escape well to have any chance of success. Begin by gaining the kidnapper's trust. Choose your best route of egress, say a window or door, and move nearer and nearer to it on successive occasions over a period of days or even weeks. The kidnapper will grow used to your behavior. Then, when the time's right—say when he's far away from you and distracted—go for it. Be very careful, however. A mistake on your part could cost you your life. You have to assess the situation thoroughly and determine whether you can be effective in your action, be it trying to overpower your captor or running away. If you've determined that your attacker is a professional, don't do anything. Just sit there. A professional is prepared for attempts by his captives to retaliate or escape. Even long into an abduction, his attention span, emotional balance and physical strength haven't been sapped. A well-trained terrorist or professional kidnapper simply isn't going to make the kinds of mistakes that would give you an opening to either disarm him or escape.

- If you manage to escape, don't try to hide.

It's natural to hide from danger. But that would be a mistake if you just escaped a kidnapper. If you run and hide, say in the woods, the first person likely to find you is your abductor. So rather than hide, you must do the precise opposite: Run toward people, houses, populated areas or business districts. Stay out in the open where people can see you. If you're in a remote, wooded area, look for roads, listen for the sound of traffic or trains, and scan the horizon for buildings or spires.

- While a hostage, try to stay mentally and physically fit.

Your mental and physical health is bound to suffer in captivity. You'll probably be held in a small, confined space and may be tied up or chained for long stretches. You'll be fed infrequently, the quality of the food will be inferior and the portions will be small. Kidnappers do this for a reason: To weaken you. It's imperative, therefore, that you try to stay as fit as possible, both mentally and physically. Exercise if you can, and use your mind. Don't dwell on your plight. And remain hopeful.

- If you receive a ransom demand, don't use the same phone to call the police.

Kidnappers making ransom demands check to see if the police are being called. They do this by waiting a few minutes after making their initial call and then calling the same telephone number back. If the phone line is busy, they assume you're talking with the police. Should you receive a ransom demand, call for help from another phone—a cell phone or a neighbor's phone. But do call the police and the FBI. Never try to handle a demand for ransom on your own.

Tip   Contact the employer of the person who's being held for ransom. Many companies have ransom insurance. Interestingly, many ransom insurance policies require policyholders never to announce that they have such insurance or to say which employees are covered by the plan. It could turn out that the person being held hostage is covered by ransom insurance but doesn't know it.

- Take out ransom insurance if your employees travel overseas often.

It makes no sense to be penny wise and pound foolish in this age of terrorism and kidnapping for ransom. Consider the plight of Thomas Hargrove, a Texas science writer. He was working in Colombia when he was kidnapped in September 1994 by the Revolutionary Armed Forces of Colombia. He was held hostage for 11 months until his family reportedly came up with a $500,000 ransom payment. Ransom insurance is widely available. (The names of several insurers are listed in the final chapter of this book.) Companies that frequently send employees overseas or have foreign subsidiaries are the ones most in need of ransom insurance.

• Know when to hire professional bodyguards.

In November 1986, the president of France's Renault auto-mobile company, Georges Besse, was shot to death in Paris by the French Marxist-Leninist group Action Directe. Three years later, Deutsche Bank Chairman Alfred Herrhausen was assassi-nated in Frankfurt, Germany by terrorists with the revolutionary Red Army Faction. The point is, if you're a target and you don't know it, the terrorists have got you. So you have to know when to get professional help. The risk of being attacked is greatest for executives of companies viewed as symbols of the United States or any country that's an integral part of the global coalition against terrorism. Terrorists are publicity-seekers. The bigger the name of your company, the higher your position in that company and the better known you are, the greater risk you face. It may be that you only require advice on how to protect yourself and what to avoid overseas. Others may need fulltime bodyguards

5.09. Recommended Online Reading

"Countering Terrorism: Security Suggestions for U.S. Business
    Representatives Abroad," Bureau of Diplomatic Security,
    U.S. Department of State, http://ds.state.gov/about/publica-
    tions/terrorism/.
"Evacuation," U.S. Department of State, http://travel.state.gov/
    crisismg.html.
"Personal Security Guidelines for the American Business Trav-
    eler Overseas," Overseas Security Advisory Council, U.S.
    Department of State, www.ds-osac.org/publications/de-
    fault.cfm.
"A Safe Trip Abroad," U.S. Department of State, http://trav-
    el.state.gov/asafetripabroad.html.
Safety and Security for Women Who Travel by Sheila Swan and Peter
    Laufer, excerpts at the Traveler's Tales website
    www.travelerstales.com.
"Security Tips for Air Travelers," Federal Aviation Administra-
    tion, www.faa.gov.

"Sexual Assault: Reducing the Risk and Coping with an Attack," Bureau of Diplomatic Security, U.S. Department of State, http://ds.state.gov/about/publications/keepingsafe/.

"Travel and Living Abroad," U.S. Department of State, www.state.gov.

"Travel Briefing: FAA's Fly Smart Guide," Federal Aviation Administration, www.faa.gov/apa/traveler.htm or www.faa.gov.

"Traveler's Health," Centers for Disease Control and Prevention, www.cdc.gov/travel/.

Chapter 6

How to Safeguard Your Money and Identity

For every action, there is an equal and opposite reaction, Sir Isaac Newton informs us. Well, that's as true of terrorism as it is of the laws of motion. Terrorists aren't going to accept the international clampdown on their finances. It's entirely likely that terrorist groups and smaller terrorist cells scattered around the world will turn to larceny as a means of supporting themselves. So expect to see an increase in financial fraud and identity theft in coming years as terrorists look for new sources of financing.

"There are a number of vulnerabilities or high-risk areas in the financial services sector that can be exploited by terrorist and other criminal organizations," Dennis M. Lormel, chief of the FBI's Financial Crimes Section, told a House committee in October 2001. "Terrorist cells often resort to traditional fraud schemes to fund their terrorist activities. Prevalent among these are credit card fraud, identity theft, insurance fraud and credit card bust-out schemes, The ease with which these individuals can obtain false identification or assume the identity of someone else, and then open bank accounts and obtain credit cards, make these attractive ways to generate funds. The growing use of the Internet and the relative anonymity it provides make it even easier to open bank accounts and obtain credit cards on-line using an alias." ("Cutting off the Financial Lifeblood of the Terrorists." Dennis M. Lormel, Financial Crimes Section, Federal Bureau of Investigation, Statement for the Record, House Committee on Financial Services, October 3, 2001.)

Identity theft, which only really took off as a major problem in the 1990s, might well prove to be the most profitable for terrorists, simply because identity theft is so difficult to detect. It's also much more lucrative than merely getting a handful cash or purchasing a carload of goods with stolen credit cards. If you lost your credit card, for instance, it probably wouldn't take you long to notice and report the problem to your card issuer. In cases of identity theft, however, more than a year usually elapses before a victim realizes his identity has been stolen. And by that time, the thief likely has gotten away with huge sums of money and fraudulently purchased goods and services. Some identity thieves, matter of fact, have been known to take out loans to buy cars under other people's names.

Easy access to personal data contained in public records, some of which are available online, is a major concern. In some states and locales, you don't have to be the person of record in order to gain access to sensitive information, such as a date and place of birth. Consider, too, that at least one of the terrorists who conducted the attacks of Sept. 11 reportedly created a fake identity using a deceased person's Social Security number.

Then again, we also face the nightmarish prospect of cyberterrorism. This could result in a whole raft of financial problems for all of us. It would be akin to the worst-case scenarios envisioned for Y2K, when the changeover from 1999 to 2000 was expected to cause computers to crash on a grand scale and for voluminous amounts of vital data to be lost. Well, even though Y2K wasn't nearly as bad as had been expected, the potential for financial disruption wasn't lost on terrorists, who now know the damage that could be inflicted on a country's economy—even the global economy—if they managed to cause massive computer and communications chaos.

Why, you may ask, haven't terrorists done this already? The answer is, they haven't come to trust it yet. For terrorists to make the transition to cyberterrorism, they'll first have to believe in its effectiveness. "Normally, terrorists only make that trust or that leap if they've built [the weapon] themselves, [if] they've experimented with it, and they know for a fact it will work. Then they're willing try their one-time shot at using this type of weapon," says William Church, a former U.S. Army Intelligence officer and cyberterrorism expert. "The other transition point is mentality, or mental mindset, you might say. They must know it, they must trust it, but more importantly, it has to feel right to them. If you look at the Irish Republican Army [IRA], which was probably the closest [to developing cyber weaponry] before they made peace, they were on the verge of it." He notes that the IRA had "computer-oriented" terrorist cells and already had attacked British infrastructure by placing "real or phony bombs in electric plants to see if they could turn off the lights in London." (Quoted in "Analyzing the Threat Of Cyberterrorism," by John Borland, *TechWeb News*, Sept. 25, 1998.) The next step, of course, would be to use computer-generated cyberterrorism to attack communications systems and financial institutions. Appreciate that this wouldn't wreak havoc in just the business world. It could as easily affect our personal finances.

And lest we forget, terrorists aren't the only ones after your money. "The Internet provides criminals with a tremendous way to locate numerous victims at minimal costs," Thomas T. Kubic, deputy assistant director of the FBI's Criminal Investigative Division, told a congressional panel in May 2001. "The victims of Internet fraud never see or speak to the subjects, and often don't know where the subjects are actually located. Crimes committed using computers as a communication or storage device have different personnel and resource implications than similar offenses committed without these tools. Electronic data is perishable—easily deleted, manipulated and modified with little effort. The very nature of the Internet and the rapid pace of technological change in our society result in otherwise traditional fraud schemes becoming magnified when these tools are utilized as part of the scheme." ("Internet Fraud Crime Problems," Federal Bureau of Investigation, Statement for the Record, Subcommittee on Commerce, Trade and Consumer Protection, House Committee on the Energy and Commerce, May 23, 2001.)

All of this means, of course, that each of us will have to become increasingly vigilant, looking out especially for signs of financial fraud and identity theft. Here, then, is some helpful information on what to look for and how to handle problems should they arise:

Methods of Identity Theft Reported to the FTC, 1999-2001

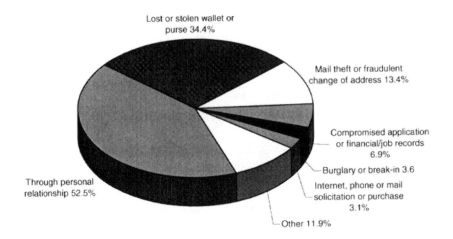

Source: Federal Trade Commission (Note: Percentages add to more than 100 percent because some victims reported that multiple methods were used to steal their identities.)

6.01. Fraud and Identity Theft

One in three U.S. households have become victims of white-collar crime, including fraud and identity theft, according the National White Collar Crime Center. Between November 1999 and June 2001, nearly 70,000 Americans reported that their identities had been stolen. The top five states for identity theft are California (17%), New York (9%), Texas (7%), Florida (7%) and Illinois (4%). Traffic in stolen credit cards, meanwhile, is so rife that auction houses, of sorts, have sprung up on the Internet, dealing in long lists of thousands of stolen card numbers.

- Be aware of the telltale signs of credit fraud and identity theft.

The trouble with many financial frauds and most identity thefts is the time lag. Victims usually don't discover that they have a problem until long after the criminal activity has occurred. You might, for instance, get a call from law enforcement or be turned down for a loan. Your bank or credit card company may inform you of a problem with your account. Or you may simply discover one day that the money in your checking account is gone.

Here are some of the typical indications that you've become a victim of fraud or identity:

- You get a call or letter stating that you have been approved or denied for a credit card for which you never applied.
- You receive credit card, utility or telephone bills with your name and address, but you never requested any of the services.
- You no longer receive your credit card or bank statements.
- You no longer get mail that you normally expect.
- Your credit card statement includes unauthorized purchases.
- Your bank or credit card company says it has received an application for credit with your name and Social Security number, but you didn't apply.
- You're told by a collection agency that it's collecting for a defaulted account established with your identity, but you never opened the account.

On average, according to the Equifax credit bureau, 14 months go by between the time a person's identity is stolen and the time the victim is made aware of the theft. ("Equifax Credit Watch™ Provides Early Warning Of Identity Theft To Consumers," press release, Equifax, Inc., April 10, 2001.)

Under the law, the financial institutions involved must bear the brunt of any loss. But the victim is still saddled with damaged credit and must spend months, if not years, regaining his credit worthiness. In the meantime, he may find it difficult to obtain loans, get a job or an apartment, or just write checks.

- Before skimping on precautions, appreciate the full cost of
  identity theft.

Losing your credit, your identity and even your money isn't
the end of the world, of course. Life does go on. But we must
warn you of the difficulties you'll face in straightening out your
financial affairs, including credit restoration, if your identity is
purloined. The task can last years—and cost thousands of
dollars—before everything's ironed out.

In 1998, Congress passed the Identity Theft and Assumption
Deterrence Act (18 U.S.C. § 1028(a)(7)), which prohibits "know-
ingly transfer[ring] or us[ing], without lawful authority, a means
of identification of another person with the intent to commit, or
to aid or abet, any unlawful activity that constitutes a violation of
Federal law, or that constitutes a felony under any applicable
State or local law." The offense, in most circumstances, carries a
maximum term of 15 years' imprisonment, a fine and criminal
forfeiture of any personal property used or intended to be used
to commit the offense.

The decision to make identity theft a federal offense was
prompted in large measure by one notorious case. The perpetrator, a convicted felon, stole a man's identity and then incurred
more than $100,000 of credit card debt, obtained a federal home
loan, and bought homes, motorcycles and handguns—all in the
victim's name. He even called his victim to taunt him, saying
that he could continue to impersonate the man for as long as he
wished because identity theft wasn't a federal crime. The
imposter then filed for bankruptcy, again using the victim's
name. The victim and his wife spent more than four years and
$15,000 to restore their credit and reputations. The criminal,
however, only served a brief stint in jail for making a false
statement (to procure a firearm); he made no restitution to his
victim for any of the harm done. (Cited in "What Are Identity
Theft and Identity Fraud?" Fraud Section, Criminal Division,
U.S. Department of Justice, June 5, 2000.)

- Make sense of your wallet and carry only essential money
  cards and ID with you.

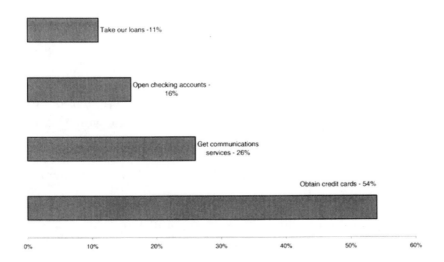

What Identity Thieves in the U.S. Do in Other People's Names

Take our loans -11%

Open checking accounts - 16%

Get communications services - 26%

Obtain credit cards - 54%

Source: Federal Trade Commission

Odds are, if you opened your wallet right now, you'd be surprised at all of the goodies a purse-snatcher or pickpocket would inherit. More than likely, your wallet's contents include at least one major credit card, a bankcard and your driver's license. But it's also likely that you've been carrying around charge cards for stores you haven't been to in ages, other credit cards you don't use anymore because they've expired, a PIN (personal identification number) written down somewhere and perhaps your Social Security card. In fact, you may have put your Social Security card in your wallet so long ago that you can't remember why you needed it in the first place.

A stash like that is a thief's dream. He can now go about stealing your identity without much trouble, because he has your name, address, date of birth and Social Security number.

Isn't it time you straightened out your wallet? Remove all non-essential credit cards and pieces of identification, most especially your Social Security card, as well as anything with your PIN number on it. Make it a rule to carry only essential ID and the bank and credit bank cards that you use regularly. It should go without saying that your birth certificate doesn't belong in your wallet, purse or briefcase. If you need to bring it somewhere, be sure to return it promptly to the safety of your home and store it (along with other vital documents) in a secure, fireproof container or safe.

Tip   If you are required, for instance, by a check-cashing firm to show your Social Security card, ask whether they'll accept an alternative piece of identification. If not, take your business elsewhere.

   • Protect you credit and ATM cards and card numbers from misuse or theft.

Always know where your credit and bank cards are. Use commonsense and never leave them lying around. Don't leave your wallet or purse unattended at work or in restaurants, health clubs or shopping carts. And don't leave a wallet, purse or handbag in open view in your car, even when the doors are locked. And don't forget to get your card back after you've made a transaction. If you hand your card over to a cashier, watch carefully to see that it's only swiped through one scanning machine. Dishonest storeowners and crooked employees have been known to install a computerized second reader that can record a card's coded information, which later can be used to engage in fraud and identity theft. If you see your card swiped in more than one device, report it to law enforcement, the district attorney's office and the Better Business Bureau.

Tip   An easy rule to follow when making credit card transactions is to keep your wallet in you hand until your card's returned; that way, it's unlikely you'll leave a store or restaurant without your card.

   • Be careful when using ATMs, especially at night.

Before using an ATM, especially at night, take a look around for any suspicious persons or activity. If you have any worries, go to another ATM location—preferably one that is in a well-lighted area and where you can be seen. Have your card ready; don't fumble through your wallet or purse in front of the machine. Let no one see you enter your PIN (personal ID number), using your body to block the view of the keypad. Count your money later, and always take any receipts of your transaction with you. Finally, double-check that you have your ATM or credit card before leaving the machine.

Tip Check your ATM receipts to see if your bank account number is printed out; if it is, ask your bank to remove it.

- Commit your PIN to memory.

Safeguard any PINs (personal identification numbers) by never writing them down on anything you keep in your wallet or purse. And don't, as some people do, write your PIN on the back of your bankcard. Memorize the number.

- Review your list of passwords and select better ones if necessary.

People tend to fall into patterns—patterns that criminals and terrorists can easily exploit—when selecting computer or Internet passwords. So don't use a PIN that a thief could crack easily, such as a birthday, the name of a loved one or the name of your hometown. Intersperse letters and numbers randomly when creating your PIN, and avoid using the same PIN for all your cards and online accounts. Consider these "Password Tips" from the Chicago Federal Reserve Bank:

DO

- Use alphanumeric characters (letters and numbers)
- Change your passwords regularly
- Close on-line profiles and accounts when no longer used
- Log off unattended computers and invoke password screen savers

- Use different passwords for each Internet access and e-mail account
- Use first letters of a phrase to create passwords you can remember (e.g., I want a new blue SUV in August = iwanbs08)

DON'T

- Share your passwords
- Use actual words from a dictionary
- Leave your passwords out where they can be seen
- Use the same password for more than one web profile/account
- Use previously used passwords
- Use easy to guess passwords, such as birthdays, anniversaries, nicknames, social security numbers or website names

For more information, see the Chicago Fed's "Money $mart" guide to "Safekeeping Web Profiles and Passwords" at www.chicagofed.org.

- Beware of postal theft of your credit card information.

Fraud can occur even before your credit card arrives. Postal theft is one of the leading ways that thieves make off with valuable credit cards. Therefore, if the arrival of a new card or your monthly statement is more than two weeks late, the American Bankers Association recommends the following: 1) Contact the U.S. Postal Service to see if anyone has forwarded your mail to a different address. 2) Check with your bank or credit card company to ask if your statement or card has been mailed. And 3) contact the stores and businesses that normally send you monthly bills to check for any changes in your accounts. If you suspect postal theft, contact the Postal Inspector at 800-372-8347 or 800-ASK-USPS, www.usps.com/postalinspectors or through your local Post Office.

Tip Sign any new card you receive immediately, and keep track of the date on which you expect a new or renewed card to arrive. If it's late, call the card issuer.

Caution If requested to return a card in the mail, say, after closing an account, cut it into pieces before putting it in the envelope.

- Never give your account number out over the phone

Unless you've initiated a call, don't give your credit card or bank account number out over the phone—and even then only provide it if you're certain of the integrity of the person or company you're dealing with. It's a virtual certainty that if you receive an unsolicited call and the caller eventually requests your credit or bank card number, it's a scam. Con artists have even been known to call and say they represent your bank and need your PIN number.

Tip When using a credit card online, make sure the website is secure. You can tell if a site's secure by the small key or lock symbol that appears at the bottom of your browser window.

- Know how to handle credit card receipts to avoid fraud.

When signing a credit card receipt, draw a line through the blank space above the total so the amount can't be changed later. Never sign a blank receipt. Tear up any carbons before handing the slip back. And save all your receipts to check against your monthly statements. Moreover, never put your address, telephone number or driver's license number on a credit card slip; such a request should be treated with suspicion.

- Inspect your bank accounts for tampering.

Reconcile any ATM or online financial transactions with your monthly bank statement, and call your bank immediately if you discover a discrepancy. It's also wise to keep your checkbook balance up to date and call your bank's automated service line regularly to check on your latest transactions and confirm your balance. Write down the date of these calls in your checkbook. Report any irregularities to your bank. Also, store your canceled checks and bank statements in a safe place.

Tip   Similarly check your telephone bills for any unusual charges or irregularities.

- Be very protective of your Social Security number.

Among the vital statistics needed to pull off identity theft, your Social Security number (SSN) is probably one of the more difficult to acquire. That's for a couple of reasons: 1) Most people don't carry their Social Security cards around with them, and 2) most people are naturally wary about giving their Social Security number out. Think before you give out your SSN and ask yourself: Does this person really need my number? Why do they want it? Have I ever given it out before to a company like this one or in this kind of transaction? Your best bet is simply never to give your SSN to anyone over the telephone, unless you know for certain that they're on the up and up. Usually, companies can wait to get that information, so tell them that you'll send it to them in the mail. That will buy you time to verify the authenticity of the request and the company's credentials.

Caution   Never select the option, offered at some state motor vehicle department, of using your Social Security number as your driver's license number. If you've already chosen that option, change it and get a new driver's license.

- Inform law enforcement and government attorneys of financial scams.

If someone tries to scam you or fails in a bid to steal your identity, report the incident to local law enforcement, your district attorney, state attorney general and local Better Business Bureau. You never can tell. Your report might be the one that finally nails this person or group. In this new age of terrorism, volunteering information about attempted and realized financial fraud is something of a patriotic duty. Who knows what heinous plot you might foil with one simple phone call. Telephone numbers of state and district attorneys general can be obtained from directory assistance or the National Association of Attorneys General at 202-326-6000 or *www.naag.org*. And don't feel embarrassed. The National Fraud Information Center (NFIC) reports that telemarketers alone defrauded nearly 39,000 people out of a total of $5.7 million in 2000, with an average loss of $1,462. The most popular phone scams involved prizes, magazine and credit card sales, work-at-home offers and "advance-fee loans." Internet fraud, including online-auction and general-merchandise scams, took nearly 7,000 people for $4.4 million in phony sales in the first 10 months of 2001. The average loss per person was $636, up from $427 in 2000. ("Telemarketing Fraud Statistics 2000," National Fraud Information Center, National Consumers League.) You can report fraud to the NFIC by calling 800-876-7060 or online at www.fraud.org.

- Contact the FTC for the very best information on card fraud and identity theft.

For more information or assistance regarding card fraud or identity theft, the place to go is the Federal Trade Commission. Its website, www.ftc.gov, is chockfull of information, or you can call the FTC hotline, 877-FTC-HELP (877-382-4357).

6.02. Prophylactic Measures

Because it often takes a considerable length of time for a victim to become aware of a financial fraud or identity theft, it's best to takes prophylactic steps in advance to protect yourself.

- Order copies of your credit report.

At least once a year, order copies of your credit reports from the three major credit-reporting agencies—Equifax (www.equifax.com), Experian (www.experian.com) and Trans-Union (www.transunion.com). Upon receipt of the reports, check for any unauthorized activity. If you discover information in your credit file that doesn't pertain to you (e.g., credit card or

U.S. Identity Theft Victims by Age Group, 1999-2001

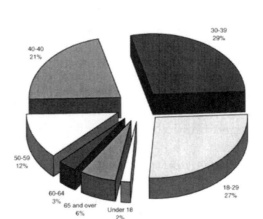

Source: Federal Trade Commission

bank accounts you never had, delinquent payment notices, applications for credit, etc.) inform the relevant creditors that you suspect attempted fraud and/or identity theft.

• Consider subscribing to an identity-protection service.

Several useful services will monitor your credit files on a daily basis for possible fraud and identity theft. They normally inform you within 24 hours of any suspicious activity involving credit associated with your name. The cost of these services range from $50 to $90 a year, but at the same time they do save you the trouble and expense of having to contact credit agencies annually. Most important, having your credit files constantly monitored means that you're likely to spot fraud or identity theft quickly, thus limiting any damage an imposter might do to your credit standing. Identity Guard (www.identityguard.com) is one monitoring service, offered by TransUnion and Intersections Inc. Another is Equifax Credit Watch (www.equifax.com), and a third, called Credit Manager, is offered by Credit Expert (www.creditexpert.com) in conjunction with Experian

- Give out your mother's maiden name sparingly.

We were shocked some time ago when a renowned newspaper, which should have known better, asked us to provide our mother's maiden name over an unsecured Internet connection as part of an online subscription. Of all your means of self-identification (e.g., birth certificate, Social Security number or driver's license), you're mother's maiden name is your most valuable and thus should be the one that you guard most dearly. Your mother's maiden name serves as sort of a universal password to verify that you are who you say you are.

Absolutely never give at her maiden name before first thinking through the reason for the request to determine whether it's legitimate. In the main, there are only two reasons you should provide your mother's maiden name to anyone: 1) to open a new financial account, attend a school or get hired for a job, and 2) to respond to a request from an institution with which you have an account, educational tie or job that needs to check your identity. Consider any other request for your mother's maiden name, especially one made over the telephone during an unsolicited call, as an attempt to steal your identity.

- Maintain only a minimum number of credit cards.

Carrying around a multitude of credit cards is dangerous, so first rid your wallet or purse of unneeded cards. Then rethink the number of credit card accounts you maintain. View each of your credit cards as opening for a thief, and minimize your risk by reducing the number of your credit accounts. Begin by canceling all unused cards.

- Destroy unsolicited, pre-approved credit cards.

Pre-approved credit card applications are an easy way for someone to steal your identity. They merely apply for the cards and then request a change of address. Worse, once they have the card, they can wheel it to apply for others—depending on what *your* income is. This can turn into a torrent of fraudulent credit requests, ranging from auto loans to cellular phone services. You can have your name removed from credit card prescreening programs, which are operated by the nation's three credit reporting bureaus, by calling 888-5OPTOUT (or 888-567-8688). One call will notify all three credit bureaus and should eliminate this source of junk mail. Otherwise, contact them individually: Equifax, 800-525-6285, www.equifax.com; Experian, 888-397-3742; www.experian.com, and TransUnion, 800-680-7289, www.transunion.com.

- Reduce the personal information about you that's in circulation.

Beyond eliminating unsolicited credit card offers, various law-enforcement authorities also recommend that you reduce the amount personal information about you that's in circulation by taking the following steps: Sign up with the Direct Marketing Association's Mail Preference Service and Telephone Preference Service (www.the-dma.org or Box 643, Carmel, NY 10512) to get your name deleted from junk-mail, email and telemarketing lists. And remove your name and address from telephone books and reverse directories; begin by contacting your telephone company.

- Personal checks should carry only your name.

Most people provide far too much information on their personal checks. Your checks should carry only your name. Leave your address and telephone number off the next batch of checks you order. That information is immensely valuable to a thief and can be too easily acquired by simply getting hold of one of your checks for a moment or two.

- Before doing business with an Internet bank, make sure it has a legitimate bank charter.

Depositing money in a phony bank is one way of being swindled. It's the sort of fraud that can really occur only via the Internet. It's hard to imagine a bank in your neighborhood being there one day and gone the next, but the Internet makes such bold schemes possible. Every legitimate bank has a banking charter and is federally insured through the Federal Deposit Insurance Corp. Check with the FDIC (www.fdic.gov) or the Federal Reserve (www.federalreserve.gov) before opening an online bank account.

- Be careful what you throw in the trash, both at home and in public.

If you close a checking account, don't just toss the unused checks away. Carefully destroy them before discarding, paying particular attention to the account number; be sure that the number is at least torn in half and deposit the halves in different garbage bags. Then, don't set these out all at once for trash pickup. Distribute the scraps of paper over different pickup days. Do the same for old bills, cancelled checks, credit card receipts, bank statement, mutual fund records and any financial document that contains vital information about you, such as your birth date and Social Security number.

At restaurants, always take your credit card receipts with you, and never throw them into a trash container on the street. Also, once you've signed your credit card receipt, rip out and tear up any attached slips of carbon. After using an ATM, wait for the receipt and take it with you. Never leave it behind, and don't simply throw it in the trash. Bring it home and keep it with your other financial receipts.

Tip If cyberterrorism were to disrupt the banking system, your receipts could prove more valuable than you think.

- Buy a paper shredder for your home.

Take precautions against "dumpster diving." That's when thieves go through garbage looking for valuable information. Buy a paper shredder, especially if you do a lot of financial paperwork at home—or have a home office—or discard a lot of job-related materials at home. Even if you tear important documents up into pieces, a determined thief who's after your identity won't be deterred. It may take him time, but eventually he be able to put enough material together to be able to impersonate you, open up accounts in your name and then vanish before you even aware of what has happened.

Tip   Use paper shredders to destroy unwanted credit card solicitations that come in the mail.

Caution   Only shred the unwanted contents of your mail. Never shred envelopes or package coverings, because they could become contaminated with a biological agent should an outbreak like the anthrax-letter campaign of 2001 reoccur. Discard envelopes by following the mail-handling safety steps laid out in the chapter on personal and family protection.

• Use regular U.S. Postal Service boxes to mail checks.

An erect red flag on your mailbox is an invitation to a thief, who'd like nothing better than to get his hands on one of your personal checks. So when mailing payments by mail, use the Postal Service's regular mailboxes and not the one at the end of your driveway.

• Print out copies of all online financial transactions.

Whether you trade stocks or pay bills online, get into the habit of printing out hard copies of all the financial transactions you conduct via the Internet and then store them in a safe place. The reason is simple: Should cyberterrorists attack financial institutions and their databases, records of online transactions could be compromised. Printouts attesting to stock trades, bill payments and the like would serve as backup verification.

6.03. Lost or Stolen Cards

Identity assumption in check fraud occurs, says the U.S. Comptroller of the Currency, when criminals learn information about a bank customer (e.g., name, address, bank account number, account balance, Social Security number, employer, and home and work phone numbers) and use the information to

U.S. Credit and Debit Card Fraud by Type, 1999

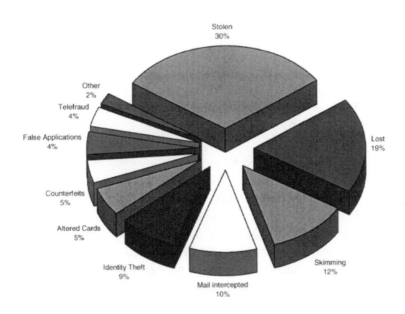

Source: The Nilson Report/epaynews.com

misrepresent themselves as the real bank customer. The thieves may then alter account information, create fictitious transactions or draw money out.

• Report the loss or theft of credit or bank ATM cards as quickly as possible.

Report the loss or theft of a credit card or bank ATM card to the card issuer as quickly as you can because the timing of your report will affect your financial liability. Many companies have toll-free numbers with 24-hour service to handle emergencies. Then follow up with a letter, giving them your account number, the approximate time and date you first noticed your card was missing and the date on which you called to report the loss.

- Keep a list of all your account and card number in a secure
  location

It helps to have a list (kept in a safe place) of all your account
and card numbers, including card expiration dates and the
telephone numbers of the card issuers. That'll speed up the
process of reporting any lost or purloined cards. Take this
information with you when traveling, but never keep the list in
your wallet. It won't do you much good if the list gets stolen
along with everything else in your wallet.

- Subscribe to a credit card registration if you hold multiple
  cards.

For a $10 to $35 annual fee, you can subscribe to a card
registration service that will notify the issuers of a theft or loss of
your credit cards and bankcards. You need make only one
phone call to report all lost or stolen cards, instead of having to
contact each card issuer individually. Most service companies
will request replacement cards at the same time. Purchasing a
card registration service may be convenient, but it isn't required
to limit your exposure to liability. Federal law gives you the right
to contact your card issuers directly in the event of a loss or
suspected unauthorized use. If you decide to sign up for a
registration service, compare offers. Carefully read the contract
to determine the company's obligations and your liability. For
example, be sure the company will reimburse you if it fails to
notify card issuers promptly.

- Know how to limit your loss from stolen or lost credit and
  ATM cards.

The Fair Credit Billing Act (FCBA) and the Electronic Fund
Transfer Act (EFTA) offer procedures for you to use if your cards
are lost or stolen. You also may want to check your homeowner's
insurance policy to see if it covers your liability for card thefts. If
it doesn't, some insurance companies will allow you to change
your policy to include this protection.

The following procedures are recommended by the U.S. Federal Trade Commission (FTC) to deal with financial losses resulting from lost or stolen credit and ATM cards:

Credit Card Loss: If you report the loss *before* the cards are used, the FCBA says the card issuer cannot hold you responsible for any unauthorized charges. If a thief uses your cards before you report them missing, the most you will owe for unauthorized charges is $50 per card. This is true even if a thief uses your credit card at an ATM machine to get cash. However, it's not enough simply to report your credit card loss. After the loss, review your billing statements carefully. If they show any unauthorized charges, send a letter to the card issuer describing each questionable charge. Again, tell the card issuer the date your card was lost or stolen and when you first reported it to them. Be sure to send the letter to the address provided for billing errors. Don't send it along with a credit card payment or to the address you normally use to make payments, unless you are directed to do so.

ATM Card Loss: If you report an ATM card missing *before* it's used without your permission, the EFTA says the card issuer cannot hold you responsible for any unauthorized withdrawals. If unauthorized use occurs before you report it, the amount you can be held liable for depends upon how quickly you report the loss. For example, if you report the loss within two business days after you realize your card is missing, you will not be responsible for more than $50 for unauthorized use. However, if you don't report the loss within two business days after you discover the loss, you could lose up to $500 from unauthorized withdrawals. You risk *unlimited* loss if you fail to report an unauthorized transfer or withdrawal within 60 days after your bank statement is mailed to you. This means you could lose all the money in your bank account and the unused portion of your line of credit established for overdrafts.

If unauthorized transactions show up on your bank statement, report them to the card issuer as quickly as possible. Once you've reported the loss of your ATM card, you cannot be held liable for additional amounts, even if more unauthorized transactions are made. This means, of course, that you must make it a point to open your monthly statements promptly upon receipt, and then check the charges against the receipts you've accumulated over the past month. Alternatively, you could make a habit of checking you bank balance more than once a month either online at your bank's website or via your bank's 24-hour computerized telephone accounts service. Call the "billing inquiries" phone number on your statement to resolve any discrepancies. Card issuers are required to investigate billing errors reported to them within 60 days of the date your statement was mailed to you, so keep the envelope if it is postmarked.

- Report an act of fraud to law enforcement and credit bureaus to begin the fraud-resolution process.

If you become a fraud victim, the first thing to do is call your local police or sheriff's office. But don't use the emergency number. Instead, call the office's regular phone number, which can be found in your phonebook or obtained from directory assistance. The authorities frown on frivolous 911 calls. Informing law enforcement of credit fraud isn't something you can avoid, because you'll need a complaint number from police to provide to credit reporting agencies and your creditors.

Next, report all stolen cards—both credit cards and ATM cards—to the card issuers and request new cards. Follow the call with a written notification, and cite the date and time of your initial call to the company. You'll probably have to fill out affidavits of forgery to establish your innocence with banks and card issuers. Appreciate that you aren't the only victim; these institutions may suffer a financial loss. If you suspect mail theft was involved, contact the postal inspector. Mail theft, by the way, is a felony. Also, contact the Federal Trade Commission to report the incident.

Get in touch with all three of the credit bureaus listed below, so you can prevent any further damage to your credit standing and begin the process of credit restoration. Each creditor may have a different process for handling a fraud claim. Make sure you understand exactly what is expected of you, and then ask what you can expect from the creditor. Take notes of all phone calls, asking for names, department and phone extensions; record the times and dates of your calls. At the conclusion of a fraud investigation, ask all involved creditors for a document stating you aren't responsible for the debt.

Credit Bureau Fraud Departments:

Equifax, Consumer Fraud Division, P.O. Box 740256, Atlanta, GA 30374; Ph.: 800-525-6285 or 404-885-8000; Fax: 770-375-2821; www.equifax.com.

Experian, National Consumer Assistance Center, P.O. Box 2002, Allen, TX 75013; Ph.: 888-397-3742; www.experian.com.

TransUnion, Fraud Victim Assistance Department, P.O. Box 6790, Fullerton, CA 92834; Ph.: 800-680-7289; Fax: 714-447-6034; www.transunion.com.

Government Agencies:

Federal Trade Commission, 877-438-4338, www.ftc.gov.

U.S. Postal Inspection Service, 800-372-8347, www.usps.com/ postalinspectors.

Social Security Administration, 800-269-0271, www.ssa.gov.

- Identity theft is a federal crime, so report it to Washington.

Identity theft is no laughing matter. It's a federal felony, punishable under the Identity Theft and Assumption Deterrence Act of 1998 (18 U.S.C. § 1028(a)(7)), as well as a crime in roughly half the states, so treat it accordingly. Report any case of identity theft promptly to the Federal Trade Commission, which has a special ID theft hotline, 877-438-4334, or use the form on its website, www.ftc.gov.

- Seek professional assistance if you've been defrauded.

If you believe you've been defrauded and have questions, contact TransUnion's Fraud Victim Assistance Department (FVAD), which was established in 1992 to detect, prevent and rectify credit fraud and assist fraud victims. It's staffed by employees trained in detecting and resolving all credit fraud-related situations; they also can explain the many applicable laws, regulations and consumer-relations policies. You can email the FVAD at fvad@transunion.com. It will respond to your email as soon as possible. Should you require an immediate answer, however, you may wish to call its toll-free number, 800-680-7289, Mondays through Fridays, 5:30 a.m. to 4:30 p.m. Pacific Standard Time.

6.04. SSN and Check Theft

To get a sense of how a stolen Social Security number (SSN) can lead to more egregious crimes, consider the first federal prosecution under the Identity Theft Act of 1998. The Milwaukee office of the Social Security Administration (SSA) opened an investigation into a Wisconsin man who was receiving Supplemental Security Income (SSI) payments. During the course of the investigation, it was discovered that he had acquired the Social Security number of another individual and then used this number to secure employment as a cleaning-crew supervisor. As a result, he gained access to the offices of the Wisconsin Supreme Court and stole over $80,000 in computer equipment. Meanwhile, he lied to SSA officials in a statement for determining continuing eligibility for SSI, claiming that he was unemployed and continued to receive full SSI payments. The man used the stolen SSN to secure a State of Wisconsin identity card, to open bank accounts and file fraudulent tax forms under the victim's name and SSN. He was indicted in April 1999 for identity theft, SSN misuse and making false statements and later arrested after authorities tracked him down in Chicago. He pled guilty to using the identity of another person to obtain employment and then using that employment to commit burglary. The man was sentenced to 21 months in prison and ordered to pay over $62,000 in restitution to the Wisconsin Supreme Court.

- Contact SSA if you suspect someone else is using your identity.

Defrauding Social Security has already become big business. In fiscal year ended Sept. 30, 2000, the SSA's Office of Inspector General received nearly 47,000 allegations of misuse of Social Security numbers. These included charges of identity theft, in which stolen numbers were used to collect Social Security

**Alleged Means of ID Theft Reported to
Social Security Administration, 2001**

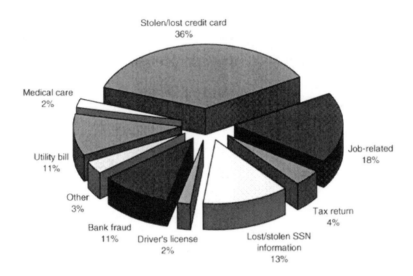

Source: Social Security Administration/General Accounting Office

benefits or gain employment under another person's name. So immediately contact the SSA if you suspect someone else is using your identity by calling 800-269-0271 or 800-772-1213 or going to www.ssa.gov.

- Report stolen check and check fraud to your bank and check verification companies.

If you discover your checks have been stolen or find that checks have been cashed that you didn't write, contact your bank immediately and stop payment. It's further recommended that you close the account immediately and open another one with a new account number. Similarly, if your ATM card has been lost, stolen or otherwise compromised, cancel the card as soon as you can and get another with a new PIN.

If your checks have been stolen or misused, contact the major check verification companies to request that they notify retailers not to accept these checks. You can ask your bank to notify the check verification service with which it does business. The major check service companies are: National Check Fraud Service, 843-571-2143; SCAN, 800-262-7771, TeleCheck, 800-710-9898 or 800-927-0188; CrossCheck, 707-586-0551; Equifax Check Systems, 800-437-5120; National Processing Company, 800-255-1157, and International Check Services, 800-526-5380. You'll probably have to fill out affidavits of forgery to establish your innocence with your bank and any recipients of stolen checks. These institutions are joint victims with you and could face financial loss. Also, contact the U.S. Postal Inspection Service at 800-ASK-USPS or www.usps.com/postalinspectors/welcome.htm.

Tip   To safeguard delivery of your checks, especially if your mailbox doesn't lock or if you live in a high-crime area, tell your bank you don't want your checks sent to you in the mail and that you would prefer to pick them up at your bank branch.

- Get a new driver's license number if yours has been misused.

If someone has been using your driver's license number to cash bad checks or to engage in other financial fraud, insist that your state motor vehicle department issue you a new license number. You may be asked to prove that you've been damaged by the theft of your driver's license and/or the misuse of you identity. Be persistent if the bureaucrats give you a hard time.

6.05. Restoring Your Credit

Patience will be required in getting your credit restored. The paperwork can be mind numbing. But don't be discourteous. Remember that you can get more with honey than with vinegar.

- Know how to get your credit restored if you fall victim to fraud.

The moment you're identity is stolen your credit is damaged. Using your name and credit information, the imposter will ring up purchases, withdraw cash and maybe get a telephone number in your name. This may not last long, but the amounts involved can be huge. And creditors can't help but think you're the person who owes them all that money. It's then left up to you to reclaim your identity and restore your credit. You need to straighten things out with creditors, remove inaccurate information from your credit report and take steps to prevent any further fraud.

Here are the procedures that TransUnion, one of the nation's leading credit bureaus, recommends you follow:

Review Your Credit Reports: Get copies of your credit reports from all three credit bureaus—Equifax, Experian and TransUnion—and review them for any unauthorized account and inquiry information. Should any of the information on your credit file not pertain to you, please contact the credit grantor directly and ask about the account or inquiry.

Contact Creditors: Explain your situation to the credit grantor and ask for an explanation of the procedures for fraudulent accounts or charges. You may be required to complete an "Affidavit of Fraud" and/or send additional documents. These may include a police report, copy of driver's license and documents from other credit card companies confirming the accounts as fraudulent. Once each creditor acknowledges fraud, ask the creditor to send you and all major credit reporting agencies a letter of confirmation. TransUnion suggests you keep a log of all phone conversations when dealing with each credit card company and financial institution. Log dates, names and notes about what you discussed with each company. Follow up with each company and ask about the progress of the investigation. The inquiries shown on your report can remain there for two years. However, inquiries determined to be fraudulent are removed upon that determination.

Contact Credit Reporting Agencies: Contact the major credit reporting companies and request that a protective statement be added to your credit file. Be sure to ask how long the statement will remain on your report. Ask each company if any recent activity appears on your credit file. If so, ask for each name, address and telephone number of any unauthorized account or inquiry. In addition, ask to receive a copy of your credit file for you to review. Review the reports for any unauthorized activity and also contact those creditors to ask about the account or inquiry. Keep in mind that each of the major credit reporting bureaus has different procedures. It is best that you contact each company and ask about the procedures.

Contact Financial Institutions: Notify your financial institution. Cancel your checking account and request a new account number. If you are unsure about any outstanding checks, stop payment. If you have experienced fraudulent use of your checks, contact one of the companies that collect, report and investigate returned checks. (See above for the names and phone names of these companies.)

Contact the Social Security Administration: If your Social Security number was fraudulently used, contact the Social Security Administration (SSA) at 800-772-1213 or www.ssa.gov. Social Security numbers may only be changed when proper documentation is submitted to the SSA. TransUnion doesn't recommend that you change your Social Security number, as this may cause future complications.

Complete a Dispute Form: You may also complete and return a dispute form and attach any documentation from all credit card companies that were victimized, although the form is not required to submit a dispute. Once your dispute form and/or documents are received in our office, we contact each creditor involved and verify the account information you are disputing. Our investigation may take up to 30 days, at which time we send you an updated copy of your credit file reflecting the results of our investigation.

Order Your Credit Report: Once a year, order reports from all of the major credit reporting companies. Check for any unauthorized activity. Should any information on your credit file not pertain to you, contact the creditors and question the account and/or inquiry.

6.06. Cyberterrorism Precautions

Look at the prospect of cyberterrorism disrupting your personal finances much as you did the Y2K problem, taking steps to minimize the impact a major disruption in communications and financial institutions would have on your life and personal finances.

- Keep important paper records of your personal accounts and finances.

Keep paper records so you can compare your bank and financial statements against your personal records in the event of a cyberterrorism meltdown. Here's a list of many of the documents to hang on to: all bank and savings account statements; paycheck stubs and records of other income, including deposit slips; brokerage account statements and confirmation receipts that show when transactions took place; credit card statements, canceled checks and receipts that show when payments and charges were made; records of all loan balances and payments, and records of all regular charges such as utility bills and insurance premiums.

- Store important or irreplaceable documents at two different locations.

For whatever reason, you could face the nettlesome problem of having to replace vital documents, some of which might be irreplaceable. So you're best off making duplicates of important papers and storing either them or the originals in a secure place like a safety deposit box, a fireproof container at a relative's house or your lawyer's office.

Important Documents Storage		
	Location of Original	Location of Duplicate
Birth certificates	————	————
Adoption papers	————	————

Marriage certificate	_____	_____
Divorce papers	_____	_____
Citizenship papers	_____	_____
Bank accounts	_____	_____
Investment accounts	_____	_____
IRAs & 401(k)s	_____	_____
Deeds & titles	_____	_____
Mortgages & loans	_____	_____
Car titles	_____	_____
Insurance policies	_____	_____
Insured assets data	_____	_____
Wills	_____	_____
Special instructions	_____	_____
Passports	_____	_____
Tax records	_____	_____
Medical records	_____	_____
Fingerprints, etc.	_____	_____
Diplomas	_____	_____

- Be able to verify any direct deposits or payments.

If you have your paychecks or other income directly deposited in your bank account or have bills paid automatically, retain all paycheck receipts and billing information so you can contest any mistakes. If you travel abroad or rely on international financial transactions, make sure you have all records needed to resolve potential financial glitches. And if you use a computer software program, print out statements from time to time to use as backup.

Tip   Keep enough cash on hand to cover any shortfalls, or hold multiple bank accounts, providing redundancy in the event cyberterrorist activity is directed at individual financial institutions.

- Get a printed history from your lenders.

Ask your lenders for printed histories of the payments on your mortgage, car loans and other debts. Verify the principal and interest paid. Be sure to request this information at least once a year, and know that some institutions charge a fee for these records.

• Check that your funds are adequately insured.

Should an act of cyberterrorism bring a U.S. bank or thrift institution crashing down, don't worry; you're probably insured against any loss. The Federal Deposit Insurance Corp. (FDIC), founded in 1933, guarantees your checking, savings and money market deposit accounts, as well as certificates of deposit, held in FDIC-insured depository institutions, such as banks and thrifts. The basic FDIC insurance limit is $100,000 per institution. A new FDIC online service at www2.fdic.gov/edie/allows you to check to see if your accounts at any single institution exceed the insurance limit. Individual Retirement Accounts (IRAs) held in FDIC-insured banks are separately insured up to $100,000. However, investment products that aren't insured include mutual funds, annuities, life insurance policies, stocks and bonds. For more information, call the FDIC at 877-275-3342 or 202-942-3147.

6.07. Terror-Related Internet Scams

The dust of the Sept. 11 attacks had barely settled before illicit charities sprang into action, attempting to bilk people out of their money by claiming that donations would go to help victims and their families. Then, hard on the heels of the 2001 anthrax outbreaks, numerous websites and senders of unsolicited email began to offer Ciprofloxacin—or Cipro, as it's commonly called—and other antibiotics to a nervous American public. The offers turned out to be fraudulent for the most part, prompting a consumer warning from the FTC. The agency also told dozens of website operators to stop making unproved claims about bioterrorism protection, including phony protective clothing, and to halt sales of imported gas masks with expired filters.

The consumer alerts on Cipro and similar scams, written by the FTC in conjunction with the Centers for Disease Control and

Prevention and the U.S. Food and Drug Administration (FDA), bear repeating:

- Talk to your healthcare professional before you use any medications.

Unless you are specifically notified or instructed by public health officials, the FTC says, there is no need to obtain or take antibiotics to prevent anthrax. Confirming an infection requires a doctor's examination and diagnosis. This is particularly important for anthrax. The FTC notes that a general questionnaire doesn't provide enough information—or the right kind of information—for a healthcare professional to determine the answers to several important questions: Will a particular drug will work for you? Is it safe to use? Would another treatment be more appropriate? Will there be adverse reactions with another medication you're taking? And do you have an underlying medical condition, such as an allergy, that could make the drug harmful?

- Be aware that some Internet sites sell ineffective drugs.

Some websites may claim to sell FDA-approved drugs, like Cipro, made to meet U.S. standards. But they may be selling a similar drug made elsewhere, where there may be no guarantee of appropriate manufacturing standards, warns the FTC. There also may be no way for you to tell whether a drug is an ineffective "knock-off" just by looking at the pills. In fact, the drugs could be counterfeit or even adulterated with dangerous contaminants.

- Only buy prescription drugs from reputable vendors.

"Would you buy a prescription drug from a sidewalk vendor?" asks the FTC rhetorically. Online, anyone can pretend to be anyone. Because it is easy to fake email addresses, be mindful of who you're buying a product from. You may send the website your money and not get the real thing, or anything, in return. To ensure that the site is reputable and licensed to sell drugs in the United States, the FDA recommends that you check with the National Association of Boards of Pharmacy (www.nabp.net or 847-698-6227) to determine whether a website is a licensed pharmacy in good standing.

The FTC and FDA also issued these additional cautions to consumers:

- Don't buy prescription drugs from sites that offer to: 1) prescribe them for the first time without a physical exam, 2) sell a prescription drug without a prescription, or 3) sell drugs not approved by the FDA. According to the American Medical Association, prescribing medication without a doctor's examination is considered substandard medical care.
- Don't do business with websites that do not provide you with access to a registered pharmacist to answer questions.
- Avoid sites that don't provide their name, physical business address, and phone number. Otherwise, you will never know whom you're dealing with and how to reach them if there is a problem.
- Don't purchase from foreign websites at this time. It is generally illegal to import the drugs bought from these sites; the risks are greater, and there is very little the U.S. government can do if you get ripped off.
- If you buy drugs online, pay by credit or charge card. If you pay for online purchases by credit or charge card, the Fair Credit Billing Act will protect your transaction. Under this law, you have the right to dispute charges under certain circumstances and withhold payment while the creditor is investigating those charges. In the case of unauthorized use of a consumer's credit or charge card, consumers generally are held liable only for the first $50 in charges. Some cards may provide additional warranties or purchase protection benefits.

For more information on consumer fraud and anthrax treatments, go to the FTC's homepage, www.ftc.gov, or the federal government's consumer-advice website, www.consumer.gov. Information on how anthrax is properly treated can be found on the FDA's site, www.fda.gov, and the Centers for Disease Control's site, www.cdc.gov.

- Buy gas masks and the like only from reputable dealers.

Other post-Sept. 11 Internet scams included sales of gas masks with expired filters and false claims that certain clothing would protect against chemical, biological and nuclear attack. Treat almost every antiterrorism website advertising goods for sale with skepticism. Buy products only from reputable dealers offering guarantees, including the return of your money if you're not satisfied.

- Follow the FTC's "charity checklist" before making donations.

The FTC has composed the following "charity checklist" to ensure that your donations actually benefit the people and organizations you intend to help.

- *Ask for written information, including the charity's name, address and telephone number.* A legitimate charity or fund-raiser will give you materials outlining the charity's mission, how your donation will be used, and proof that your contribution is tax deductible.
- *Ask for identification.* Many states require paid fund-raisers to identify themselves as such and to name the charity for which they're soliciting. If the solicitor refuses, hang up and report it to local law enforcement officials.
- *Call the charity.* Find out if the organization is aware of the solicitation and has authorized the use of its name. If not, you may be dealing with a fraudulent solicitor.
- *Watch out for similar sounding names.* Some phony charities use names that closely resemble those of respected, legitimate organizations.

- *Know the difference between "tax exempt" and "tax deductible."* Tax exempt means the organization doesn't have to pay taxes. Tax deductible means you can deduct your contribution on your federal income tax return. Even though an organization is tax exempt, your contribution may not be tax deductible. If deductibility is important to you, ask for a receipt showing the amount of your contribution and stating that it is tax deductible.
- *Beware of organizations that use meaningless terms to suggest they are tax exempt charities.* For example, the fact that an organization has a "tax I.D. number" doesn't mean it is a charity: all nonprofit and for profit organizations must have tax I.D. numbers. And an invoice that tells you to "keep this receipt for your records" doesn't mean your donation is tax deductible or the organization is tax exempt.
- *Be skeptical if someone thanks you for a pledge you don't remember making.* If you have any doubt whether you've made a pledge or previously contributed, check your records. Be on the alert for invoices claiming you've made a pledge when you know you haven't. Some unscrupulous solicitors use this approach to get your money.
- *Ask how your donation will be distributed.* How much will go to the program you want to support, and how much will cover the charity's administrative costs? If a professional fund-raiser is used, ask how much it will keep.
- *Refuse high-pressure appeals.* Legitimate fund-raisers won't push you to give on the spot.
- *Be wary* of charities offering to send a courier to collect your donation immediately.
- *Consider the costs.* When buying merchandise or tickets for special events, or when receiving free goods in exchange for donating, remember that these items cost money and generally are paid for out of your contribution. Although this can be an effective fund-

raising tool, less money may be available for the charity.

- *Be wary* of guaranteed sweepstakes winnings in exchange for a contribution. You never have to donate anything to be eligible to win.
- *Avoid cash gifts that can be lost or stolen.* For security and tax record purposes, it's best to pay by check. Use the official full name of the charity—not initials—on your check. Avoid solicitors who want to send a courier or use an overnight delivery service to pick up your donation.

"Many charities use your donations wisely. Others may spend much of your contribution on administrative expenses or more fund-raising efforts. Some may misrepresent their fund-raising intentions or solicit for phony causes," the FTC says. ("Charitable Donation$: Give or Take," advisory, Federal Trade Commission, April 1997.) Therefore, before you open your checkbook, check out the charity you're considering with these organizations: Philanthropic Advisory Service, Council of Better Business Bureaus, 4200 Wilson Boulevard, Suite 800, Arlington, VA 22203-1838, (703) 276-0100, www.bbb.org; BBB Wise Giving Alliance, 4200 Wilson Boulevard, Suite 800, Arlington, VA 22203, (703) 276-0100, www.give.org, and American Institute of Philanthropy, 4905 Del Ray Avenue, Suite 300, Bethesda, MD 20814, (301) 913-5200, www.charitywatch.org. In addition, most states require charities to be registered or licensed by the state, so check with your state attorney general or secretary of state.

6.08. Planning Ahead

The mass destruction of Sept. 11 reminded each of us of our mortality. While you're more likely to die in car accident than in a terrorist explosion, the mass-destructive nature of such threats as bioterrorism or nuclear bombs cannot be ignored, particularly if you live or work in a major U.S. city. It, therefore, behooves each one of us to plan ahead for the possibility that we, too, may one day fall victim to terrorism.

- Make out a will and letter of instruction.

Making out a will isn't something most of us care to do, because it brings us face to face with our eventual demise. Dealing with death isn't easy, but having an up-to-date will is important. It will facilitate the distribution of your assets to your loved ones and charities after you're gone.

There are a lot of misconceptions about wills. Some people think because they don't have much money or tangible assets, that a will isn't necessary. They're wrong. Even if the things you leave behind are only of sentimental value, it's best to indicate in advance the persons you'd like to receive them; otherwise, divvying your belongings could cause friction among family members. If you and your spouse own assets jointly, at death, your share will automatically go to the survivor. But what happens to your children if your spouse remarries and fails to designate your share of the assets to them? And what happens if your and your spouse die at the same time? Who will be the guardian of your children? Similarly, people think they can write their own will. Trouble is, such will often don't meet at the necessary legal requirements.

So bite the bullet, schedule an appointment with a lawyer and make out a will. You'll be doing everyone a big favor. And while you're at it, write a letter of instruction covering funeral arrangements and such, and if you've of a mind, make out a living will concerning your medical treatment should you become incapacitated.

- Get fingerprinted; get your blood sampled, and obtain your dental x-rays.

The horrific nature of an act of mass destruction can make identification of remains difficult. Be prudent and get yourself fingerprinted at your local police station or sheriff's office. Ask you doctor to take a blood sample and have to it stored, so you DNA can be checked. Also obtain copies of dental records from your dentist. Planning ahead will reduce the strain on your family should the need for such information ever arise.

- Create a financial plan with the help of an estate planner, lawyer or accountant.

America has developed an "investor class," as economist Larry Kudlow calls it, over the past decade or more, with the explosion in individual retirement accounts, 404(1)k plans, mutual funds and online trading. This means, of course, there's an awful lot of personal savings invested in the stock, bond and money markets, not to mention real estate and collectibles. Should tragedy suddenly befall you, your survivors would be much better off if a financial plan were in place ahead of time that ensured a steady stream of income and kept exposure to taxation as low as possible. In these uncertain times, therefore, it's wise to sit down with financial and legal professionals and plan your estate to meet the goals you'd like to achieve.

- Update, if necessary, the designated beneficiaries of your retirement, savings, bank and investment accounts.

In all likelihood, it has been years since you last looked at the beneficiary designations you made when you opened your various financial accounts. To ensure that your designated beneficiaries are still the correct ones, contact the institutions in which you hold your money and savings and update the designees, if necessary. You should check your Individual Retirement Accounts, 401(k) plans, Keoghs or their equivalents; mutual-fund brokerage accounts, and bank checking and savings accounts.

- Secure adequate life and medical insurance, especially if you travel often.

An accident or act of violence, perpetrated by a terrorist or a common criminal, can take a life at all time and at any age. So you're never too young nor too old to carry life insurance to help meet the needs of your loved ones. It also pays to have adequate heath insurance, especially if you're frequently overseas, but make sure the coverage extends beyond the U.S. borders.

- Keep all tax-related information up to date.

As they say, two things are certain in life: death and taxes. What's odd about taxes, though, is that the government wants them paid even after you're dead. Make sure, therefore, that you keep all information needed for tax-form preparation up to date. That's especially important for the self-employed entrepreneur or small-business owner, who is often the only one who knows what's going on in her business. In the event of your death, you certainly wouldn't want to add the pressures on your spouse or children by forcing them to comb through stacks of papers, unmarked files, and assorted receipts in order to file a tax return.

- Keep paper copies of all bills, receipts, bank accounts, mutual-fund statements, stock and bond holdings and other financial transactions.

In case computerized data get destroyed or become inaccessible, keep copies of all your bills and account statements through the end of the year. These will detail payments toward principal, interest, and other charges, plus any outstanding balance, so you have a record of your account—if there is a computer foul-up. Keep all charge receipts, and check them carefully against the billing statement. Report any discrepancies immediately to the card issuer. Keep canceled checks as proof of payments for recent months. If you bank by computer, download your transaction records before the end of the year and store them on a backup disk. If you haven't saved quarterly reports, get copies of account information from your broker or mutual fund company before year-end.

6.09. Recommended Online Reading

"Bioterrorism," U. S. Food and Drug Administration, www.fda.gov.

"Consumer Education" and "Financial Fraud," American Bankers Association, *www.aba.com*.

"Consumer Information on Bank Deposit Insurance," Federal Deposit Insurance Corp., *www.fdic.gov*.

"Credit and ATM Cards: What To Do If They're Lost or Stolen," Federal Trade Commission, *www.ftc.gov*.

"ID Theft: When Bad Things Happen To Your Good Name," Federal Trade Commission, *www.ftc.gov*.

"Identity Theft: The Crime of the New Millennium," Sean B. Hoar, Assistant United States Attorney, District of Oregon, USA Bulletin, *www.cybercrime.gov/usamarch2001_3.htm*

"Identity Theft: Prevalence and Cost Appear to Be Growing," U.S. General Accounting Office, Report GAO-02-363, March 2002, *www.gao.gov*.

"Facts about: Anthrax, Botulism, Pneumonic Plague, Smallpox," Centers for Disease Control, *www.bt.cdc.gov*.

Chapter 7

How to Protect Your Business and Buildings

"The chief business of the American people is business," President Calvin Coolidge said in 1925. Well, that's as true today as it was then—and it's also one of reasons that the United States has become a target of terrorism. Since the days of the Iranian Revolution of 1979, the U.S. has been dubbed "the Great Satan" by many in the Islamic world. The reason: The U.S. represents progress, modernity, religious, political and cultural freedom, and capitalism—all of which Islamic fundamentalists and extremists oppose. Islamic terrorists attacked the World Trade Center twice—once in 1993 and again 2001—precisely because the towers were symbolic of U.S. economic might.

As long as the threat of Islamic extremism remains, the U.S.—and particularly U.S. companies—can expect to be the target of further assaults. The terrorists will seek to exact costs in terms of lives, money and property. They may even set their sights on U.S. businesses and financial institutions as a means of making money (e.g., hedging in the stock and futures markets ahead of an attack or attempting to steal money through fraudulent schemes or information-systems tampering). In general, though, today's anti-American terrorists want to wreck or, at the very least, disrupt the U.S. economy through direct attacks and intimidation, and they further hope to create a climate of fear in order to destroy public confidence and thus weaken the U.S. not only economically but also politically and socially. They seek, in other words, to destroy the Great Satan. It's imperative, therefore, that American businesses be on guard.

7.01. The Threat Matrix

No company is immune from terrorism. However, because terrorists seek publicity, large, well-known companies are more likely to become targets than are small, lesser known ones. This

Facilities Struck by International Terrorism
Worldwide,1995-2001

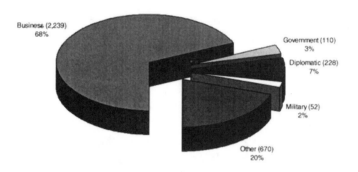

Source: U.S. Department of State

doesn't mean, though, that simply because your company is
small or relatively obscure, that it's out of danger. Terrorists
might, for instance, target the building your firm is housed in,
confuse your company name with that of another, or pick your
name and location at random. Your business might even suffer
collateral damage from a terrorist attack next door. Thus, while
larger firms require the highest level of protection, all businesses, regardless of size or notoriety, should know the basics of
antiterrorism protection, take appropriate preventative measures and institute emergency-response and contingency programs.

The threat matrix for American business follows the lines of
location, type of firm, time-related factors and hierarchy. Companies based in major U.S. cities are at higher risk than those
located elsewhere. In addition, department stores, supermarkets
and shops located in large malls or in high-density areas of
major cities are at greater risk than others. Note, however, that
this could change. If security becomes very tight in major cities,

terrorists might switch to softer targets in the suburbs. Still, the types of businesses most likely to be attacked include transportation (including cargo shipping), financial institutions, infrastructure (especially, electric power, water and communications) and other vital industries (notably, oil refineries, and oil and gas storage depots). Firms whose names are synonymous with "America" could see their foreign operations struck. Because terrorists seek to kill and maim as many people as possible, peak times of business operation also play a part in the threat matrix. Think in terms of rush-hour transportation, winter or summer vacation resorts, and crowded holiday shopping periods. Hierarchy is another consideration. Companies that are symbolic of America are at high risk, as are businesses vital to the U.S. economy. So are firms in industries or sectors that have been attacked before, such as airlines and banks. Money, too, can be a factor, if terrorists think they can steal large sums from a company or its customers.

It's a mistake, however, to become a static thinker. Terrorists sooner or later will break the mold, so expect the unorthodox. The FBI, according to the Associated Press, already has begun planning for the unexpected by "looking over the horizon." A new FBI intelligence unit has thus far warned scuba-diving schools to be wary of suspiciously large equipment purchases or inquiries about potential targets (e.g., ports, dams, water supply or treatment systems, and riverside power plants). Similar warnings have gone out to businesses that supply other materials that terrorists might use, such as fertilizer and chemicals employed in bomb-making. The FBI also has warned banks, Jewish schools and synagogues to be on guard.

In selecting targets, terrorists balance importance against opportunity. A tempting target might be skipped over if security is too tight. Thus, the most vulnerable businesses are those deemed to be high-priority targets with the weakest, most penetrable security. This reinforces our conclusion that terrorism survival is largely a matter of choice. The businesses least likely to be attacked successfully will be those with the best defenses.

7.02. Security Doctrine

Counterterrorism expenditures aren't worth the nickel unless a company adopts a strict philosophy of security. Half-measures don't work. Senior management must believe in security for an antiterrorism program to be effective.

- Security starts at the top.

The most important security guard in a company is its chief executive officer, or CEO. If he's not committed to a philosophy of security, the entire company is at risk. The head of a firm not only controls the budget and guides hiring policy, but his thinking also pervades a company. If he believes in security, other managers will follow—and so will employees. But if he's dismissive of the terrorist threat and as well as the security enhancements, the company will be highly vulnerable to attack. CEOs indeed should take a cue from their Israeli counterparts, who take a hands-on approach to security planning and insist that employees are prepared for any emergency.

Tip The Office of Homeland Security, in conjunction with The Business Roundtable, has established a new communications network to alert CEOs immediately to a terrorist attack and enable them to talk with one another and government officials instantly. Dubbed "CEO COM Link," CEOs must be members of The Business Roundtable and receive approval before they can participate in the program. For information, call The Business Roundtable at 202-872-1260 or go to www.brtable.org.

- Make personnel safety and security your highest priority.

In setting priorities, view security as a pyramid, with the safety and welfare of your personnel at the top. Next comes building security and systems security, including information technology. Finally, make backup systems and contingency planning your base. This structured approach should help in deciding matters of resource allocation, commitment of funds, timing and other corporate policymaking.

The Security Priorities Pyramid

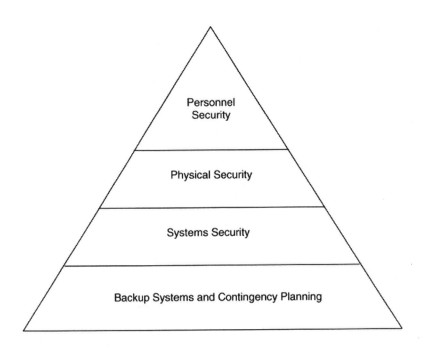

- Don't let cost govern security planning.

Senior executives must be concerned with corporate finances, but too often we've been told by managers, "Just fix the mailroom; we'll get to the rest later." Would they say the same thing about computers or communications? ("Just put computers on the second floor; we'll get to the rest later." Or, "Just hook up the Internet at headquarters; we'll get to the branch offices later.") Of course not. But when it comes to security spending, many business executives suddenly become penny wise and pound foolish. Don't be one of them.

- Hire a qualified corporate security officer.

Nothing beats having a trained and experienced professional in charge of corporate security—and that means more than just hiring a retired policeman. Establish an office of security and put it in the hands of a seasoned professional, well versed in counterterrorism. Consider candidates with backgrounds in government agencies such as the FBI or CIA, or military organizations such as the Defense Intelligence Agency. If your company has a large overseas presence, look for former employees of foreign intelligence services or counterterrorism military officers.

Tip Find someone with an understanding of information technology, because cyberspace threats are likely to grow in the future and you'll need a security chief who can speak the same language as your computer and Internet technicians.

- Be sure your corporate security chief attends state and local terrorism threat briefings.

States and localities are beginning to set up formal procedures for terrorist-related information sharing with businesses in the community. Within a month of the Sept. 11 disaster, New York State, for example, opened an Office of Public Security (www.state.ny.us/security/), which holds closed-door meetings with corporate security chiefs to discuss terrorist threats and responses. Insist that your corporate security director participate in such forums.

- Take advantage of the FBI's National Security Awareness Program.

Knowledge is a key to effective counterterrorism, so take advantage of the information supplied to companies by the FBI. The Awareness of National Security Issues and Response (ANSIR) Program is the FBI's National Security Awareness Program. It's the "public voice" of the FBI for espionage, counterintelligence, counterterrorism, economic espionage, cyber and physical infrastructure protection and all national security issues. The program is designed to provide unclassified national security threat and warning information to U.S. corporate security directors and executives, law enforcement and other government agencies. Information is disseminated nationwide via the ANSIR-Email and ANSIR-FAX networks. Interested U.S. corporate officers should provide their email address, position, company name and address, as well as telephone and fax numbers, to the national ANSIR email address at ansir@leo.gov.An ANSIR coordinator will then contact you.

• Report any hint of trouble to the proper authorities.

The FBI and local law enforcement, among other government agencies, are keenly interested in information that could, when pieced together, reveal an impending terrorist attack. In that regard, you and your company can play an important role by reporting all suspicious activity, no matter how seemingly innocuous, to your local police department or the FBI. FBI field offices, located in 55 major cities throughout the U.S. and in San Juan, Puerto Rico, can be found at www.fbi.gov/contact/fo/fo.htm.

• Tap knowledgeable outside security consultants.

In-house security resources can only go so far in protecting a company because their breath of knowledge and experience is limited. Professional security consultants—such as my own company, Interfor, Inc. (www.interforinc.com or 212-605-0375), which operates in the U.S. and around the world—supply a unique service by double-checking systems, probing for weaknesses and offering solutions. Outside consultants with solid backgrounds in counterterrorism are particularly useful in that they have done this before; they've typically conducted security checks at hundreds of companies and are able to draw on this experience in advising other firms.

• Apply risk-management techniques in counterterrorism policymaking.

"Risk management is a systematic and analytical process that weighs the likelihood that a threat will endanger an asset, individual, or function and identifies actions to reduce the risk and mitigate the consequences of an attack," states the U.S. General Accounting Office in its October 12, 2001 report "Homeland Security: Key Elements of a Risk Management Approach" (GAO-02-150T). "A good risk management approach," it continues, "includes the following three assessments: a threat, a vulnerability, and a criticality. After these assessments have been completed and evaluated, key steps can be taken to better prepare the United States against potential terrorist attacks. Threat assessments alone are insufficient to support the key judgments and decisions that must be made. However, along with vulnerability and criticality assessments, leaders and managers will make better decisions using this risk management approach. If the federal government were to apply this approach universally and if similar approaches were adopted by other segments of society, the United States could more effectively and efficiently prepare in-depth defenses against terrorist acts." For a copy of the report, go to www.gao.gov.

- Institute a notification plan and chains of command.

Emergencies often get out of control because of a lack of timely information and confusion over who's in charge. To avoid these pitfalls, institute a notification program for the central collection of information in a timely manner and create clear chains of command. This combination should make for better decision-making in times of crisis. Be sure, too, that all bases are covered, and build redundancy into the system, so that if someone is unavailable, his responsibilities will be taken over automatically by another, pre-assigned company official.

Tip Equip key personnel with pagers and design "phone trees" (i.e., lists of names and telephone numbers for personnel to call in emergencies; by assigning a limited number of calls to each person, a large number of staff members can be reached in short amount of time) to send out alerts in a speedy fashion.

- Periodically review all security policies and procedures.

Terrorist targets and techniques evolve, so ensure that your security policies and procedures keep pace by conducting periodic reviews. Continuously assess the changing nature of the threat, look for new vulnerabilities at your facilities and in your operations, and conduct checks to verify that all existing security procedures are being followed correctly throughout your enterprise. You might even have teams of specialists probe for weaknesses.

7.03. Personnel Safety

Never forget that your most important corporate assets are your people. Make their safety and security your first priority.

- Educate your workforce in counterterrorism.

Vigilant employees are a company's most valuable counterterrorism tools. The sheer number of eyes and ears helps to reduce the dangers. So educate your labor force—from top to bottom—in antiterrorism. Provide seminars, workshops, training sessions and brochures, explaining to employees what to look for and how to handle emergencies. Deploy suggestion boxes—and reward good ideas.

Tip   Start with the little things to let employees know it's no longer business as usual. For instance, insist that the handwriting on all sign-in and sign-out sheets is legible

- Embed a culture of security within your company.

Use every opportunity to remind employees of the importance of security. The old World War II posters saying, "Loose lips sink ships," actually worked by reminding military personnel, dock workers and civilian defense employees to keep secrets. So consider posters, brochures, training films, email, focus groups and the like. And have senior executives set an example by raising the issue of security at meetings and in everyday discussions.

Total U.S. Targets Attacked by
International Terrorists, 2001

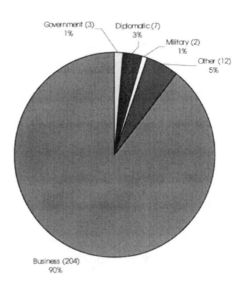

Source: U.S. Department of State

Tip   Instruct employees to treat door access codes and ID badges with the same care they give to protecting their credit cards and bank personal identification numbers (PINs).

• Tell executives, in particular, to vary their daily routines.

Terrorists and other criminals often rely on a person's normal routines to help them carry out their attacks. Sticking with the same schedule and pattern every day lets attackers get their timing down pat. It gives them confidence so that they can lie in wait and target their victim with relative ease. Instruct personnel, particularly executives, to vary their routines. Leave home and work at different times. Drive different routes to work. Don't park in the same spot each and every day. And, if they feel especially vulnerable, tell them to switch cars once and a while.

• Remove VIP signs in company parking lots.

Parking lot signs with the titles or names of a company's senior management are dead giveaways to anyone meaning to do them harm. Indeed, signs of any sort indicating VIP parking pose the same problem. Someone seeking to plant a bomb, fatally disable a vehicle's brakes, or shoot or kidnap a high-level corporate executive can use those signs to select his or her target. Make your executives less vulnerable to attack by ridding your facilities of all parking space indicators.

• Instruct employees in safe methods of business travel at home and abroad.

Our own anecdotal evidence suggests that terrorism remains the hottest topic among business travelers. Most of them offer each other tips by word of mouth. A much more sensible course is to formally instruct your employees in safe methods of business travel, following the recommendations laid out in this book. Don't let your employees feel as if the company abandons them the minute they leave on a trip. Assure them that their travel safety is a corporate concern. Supply employees headed overseas with copies of publications like "Personal Security Guidelines for the American Business Traveler Overseas." Published by the U.S. State Department's Overseas Security Advisory Council, the guide can be downloaded at *www.ds.state.gov/about/publications/osac/personal.html*.

Tip   To protect proprietary information, have your business travelers and foreign-based employees read "Guidelines for Protecting U.S. Business Information Overseas," which outlines the steps to take to protect sensitive information when living, working or travelling abroad. It's at www.ds.state.gov/about/publications/osac/protect.html.

• Take out ransom insurance if your employers travel overseas often.

It makes no sense to be a miser in this age of terrorism and kidnapping for ransom. Consider the plight of Thomas Hargrove, a Texas science writer working in Colombia, who was kidnapped in September 1994 by Revolutionary Armed Forces of Colombia. He was held hostage for 11 months until his family came up with a $500,000 ransom payment. Companies that send their employees overseas frequently shouldn't think twice about taking out ransom insurance policies. (The names of several insurers are listed in an appendix at the back of this book.)

- Know when to hire professional bodyguards.

In November 1986, the president of France's Renault automobile company, Georges Besse, was shot to death in Paris by the French Marxist-Leninist group, Action Directe. Three years later, Deutsche Bank Chairman Alfred Herrhausen was assassinated in Frankfurt, Germany by terrorists with the revolutionary Red Army Faction.

The point is, if you're a target and you don't know about it, the terrorists have got you. So you have to know when to get professional help. It may be that you only require advice on how to protect yourself and what to avoid overseas. Others may need full-time bodyguards. The risk of terrorist attack is greatest for executives of companies viewed as symbols of the United States or any country that's an integral part of the global coalition against terrorism. Terrorists are publicity-seekers. The bigger the name of your company, the higher your position in that company and the better known you are, the greater risk you face.

7.04. Physical Security

Security is determined by the barriers you build. The more sophisticated and extensive the barriers, the harder and longer it will take to get through them. That delay could mean the difference between life and death in a terrorist incident. So think of security as a lock that buys precious time.

- Survey your premises and operations for vulnerabilities and ease of escape.

Terrorists normally conduct surveillance of potential targets before settling on a specific location. They look for openings and weigh the odds of being caught. Most terrorists, apart from suicide bombers, consider escape a key criterion in selecting a target. So, do as the terrorists do. Survey your offices, stores, factories, buildings and operations with an eye toward their vulnerability to attack, and determine how easy it would be for an attacker to evade capture. Then, institute changes to lessen your risk of attack and increase a terrorist's (or a common criminal's) risk of capture.

The Treasury Department's Bureau of Alcohol, Tobacco and Firearms has published an extremely useful guide titled "Bomb Threats and Physical Security Planning" (available online at http://www.atf.treas.gov). Here are a few of its recommendations: Patrol potential hiding places (e.g., stairwells, restrooms and vacant offices). Lock doors to boiler rooms, mailrooms, computer centers, laboratories, switchboards and control rooms. Institute a procedure to account for keys. Keep trash dumpsters under surveillance to prevent the planting of a bomb. Handle combustible materials carefully.

Tip Take similar precautions to prevent burglary and robbery. The Los Angeles Police Department offers some helpful advice under the heading "LAPD Crime Prevention Lesson Plans," which can be found by clicking "Crime Tips" at www.lapd.org.

Caution Don't overlook heating, ventilation and air-conditioning systems. Inspect them for ease of access and the potential for tampering, because biological, chemical or radiological agents could be dispersed throughout a building or set of offices via air ducts. Similarly, recirculated air from a mailroom contaminated with, say, a biological agent could spread disease to other parts of the building.

- Erect concentric rings of defense.

View your security system from the outside in and then erect concentric rings of defense, so that if an outer ring is penetrated, the attackers will be stopped by an inner one. These rings of

U.S. Bombings, Actual and Attempted, 1977-1997

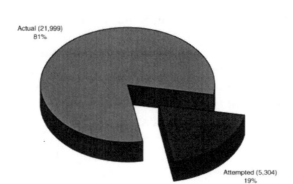

Source: Bureau of Alcohol, Tobacco and Firearms

defense should include physical barriers, such as doors, fencing and lighting, as well as behavioral barriers, such as procedures, routines and employee awareness.

- Install video security and alarm systems.

A good way to determine whether your premises are under surveillance by terrorists or others is to use a closed-circuit video security system, which allows you to spot any repeated appearances of the same suspicious person or persons on or around your property. Video recordings are also very helpful to law enforcement when trying to identify criminal suspects. Silent alarms, connected to your security center, should be deployed on exterior entryways and key interior doors.

Tip   Store recorded videotapes for at least a month before reusing.

- Place crash-proof barriers around points of building entry.

To prevent a car bomber from driving straight into a ground-floor lobby or other point of building entry, install crash-proof barriers. Be careful, however, of the type of barrier you select. For instance, large, concrete floor pots may look attractive, but they are also good places to conceal bombs. Unless such pots are watched 24 hours a day, seven days a week, they're a security liability. Buy solid concrete blocks instead.

Tip Note that specialized engineers and architects can design or retrofit buildings to make them bombproof or bomb resistant.

- Maintain perimeter defenses around large facilities, and pay attention to landscaping.

Fencing, security gates, lighting and even landscaping should all be part of your perimeter defenses around factories and other complexes. Check your property to see if it has places where intruders could hide easily or penetrate perimeter defenses undetected. Keep ground cover, such as hedges, cut low, and leave a gap of several yards between buildings and shrubbery. Also, keep a good distance between parking lots and building walls, for fear of car bombs. The Bureau of Alcohol, Tobacco and Firearms recommends a minimum distance of 300 feet. If that's not possible, have security screen all non-employee drivers and get approval for entry before these cars access the premises. The Royal Canadian Mounted Police's Technical Security Branch offers an excellent discussion of physical security and related matters in a variety of publications that are available online at *www.rcmp-grc.gc.ca/tsb/pubs/index.htm.*

Tip Enclose truck bays and maintain a security presence in shipment areas to prevent building penetration by intruders.

- Reconsider your occupancy of space in a building with public underground parking.

Underground garages in office buildings, particularly in high-risk locales, may become prime terrorist targets. Terrorists would, of course, have to gain entry, so the most vulnerable underground garages are those that are open to the public. It is doubtful that garage attendants or even security personnel would manage to stop terrorists from parking a vehicle loaded with explosions beneath a targeted building. Unless underground parking is restricted to the building's tenants and entry requires opening a locked garage door or the approval of a guard, the building simply isn't safe. If your business occupies space in a building with unrestricted public parking in an underground garage, you ought to consider moving, especially if you're located in a high-risk city or other location. The same holds if your office adjoins an outdoor public parking lot.

Tip   In assessing your risk of terrorist attack, consider your business's proximity to any higher risk targets in neighboring locations, because you could suffer collateral damage.

7.05. Reducing Vulnerabilities

"If you have reason to believe that you are likely to be a terrorist target because of the nature of your business," advises the British Home Office, "you should anticipate that terrorists will do research to work out where your greatest vulnerability is. What material about you is in the public domain? What published facts point to installations or services that are vital to the continuance of business? What might attract attention as a prestige target even though its loss may not mean immediate business collapse? Giving thought to what matters to you, and what is most vulnerable, will enable you to make realistic plans for deterring terrorist attack and minimising [sic] the damage should one occur at or near your premises."

• Know who is in your offices at all times.

Electronic identification cards should be distributed to every employee at all but the smallest of companies and required to be worn at all times. They should be tied into a central computer to provide a real-time accounting of everyone in the building. The only way to accomplish this, though, is to close the loop. In other words, require that ID badges be swiped both upon entering and exiting the building. If there is no notification requirement upon egress, you'll never have a true account of who's actually in the building. The same holds for office temporaries, outside contractors and guests.

Tip   Consider biometric means of identification (e.g., facial or eye recognition systems) if circumstances warrant.

Caution   Don't forget to maintain security at the building's freight entrance.

- Restrict freedom of movement within offices and buildings.

Monitor internal movements within a building or office electronically through the use of surveillance cameras and mini-checkpoints, which needn't be manned but must be tied to your security office. Personnel should be required to swipe an ID card (or provide retinal or facial scans) in order to gain entrance to a floor. On large floors, additional gateways should be established to monitor movement from department to department. If highly sensitive work is conducted at a company, ID badges should limit employee access to those areas in which his physical presence is required. All other areas should be off-limits to non-essential personnel, unless special clearance is given—and that clearance should be time-restricted (i.e., good for, say, only an hour or a day at a time). The idea is to create zones within an office or building so as to limit unrestricted movement. The less freedom a terrorist (or a common criminal) has to move about a building or office, the less able he'll be to get to his target.

- ID check and escort all visitors.

All visitors must be required to sign a logbook and show proper identification. Calls should be made to confirm the appointments before access is permitted. Every visitor should have an escort while in the building. At no time give a visitor a pass that would take them any further than the nearest washroom. Finally, require that each visitor sign out before leaving the building.

Tip   When querying first-time visitors to your facilities, have security ask questions that require full-sentence answers, not just a "yes" or a "no." Such responses tend to reveal a visitor's bona fides.

- Get employees into the habit of questioning unfamiliar faces.

One of the most common means of getting passed check-points, such as keypunch doors, is simply to walk in behind an authorized staff member once the door has been unlocked. Make it a requirement, therefore, for personnel to question anyone unfamiliar who is trying to enter a security door without using their own ID and password. (Again, station cameras at all of these locations so that a suspicious person can be spotted quickly and security personnel sent to the scene promptly.) Further instruct employees to question any unfamiliar person roaming around your offices without an escort.

- Background-check the credentials of all contractors, in-cluding locksmiths.

Don't take anything for granted when allowing outside contractors onto your premises. Check their credentials thoroughly before hiring them. In January 2002, for example, U.S. officials told NBC News that five terrorist suspects in Bosnia were involved in a plot to infiltrate and blow up the U.S. Embassy in Sarajevo. The job reportedly involved embassy insiders. NBC News was told that as part of the well-planned plot, one of the suspects had married the daughter of the Bosnian locksmith who worked for the U.S. Embassy. Over time, the locksmith provided the suspects with keys, codes and combinations to embassy locks and security devices.

- Maintain a list of all persons fired for cause or who have made threats against the company or its employees.

Sadly, many workers and managers have been attacked by former employees and others seeking revenge. It's essential, therefore, to maintain a list of potential threats, including workers and contractors fired for cause and seriously disgruntled clients who have threatened violence. Don't hesitate to contact the police if you believe lives are in danger.

Tip Make sure former employees no longer have password access to your computer systems, keys to offices or company cars. Be sure, too, that they've surrendered all corporate ID badges. Change locks and door codes if you have serious concerns.

- Keep a central file of all hate and threatening mail.

Employees throughout your company should be instructed to forward any hate mail or mailed threats to the director of security, where the items should be tagged, bagged and kept on file for future reference. Contact law enforcement or the FBI in serious cases.

- Sterilize the information you provide about your company.

Terrorists often look for vulnerabilities by using the Internet and other publicly available sources to find information about companies, locations, key facilities, etc. Maps and photographs are particularly useful. Be sure you aren't playing into the terrorists' hands by disseminating information that could be used in target selection and the planning of an attack. Carefully scrutinize all of your published materials, and to the extent possible, sterilize that information by removing key details that could aid a potential attacker. Take an especially close look at the contents of your company's website.

- Check the manifests of any shipments from overseas.

Because of the danger of bomb of various sorts being shipped via container by terrorists overseas, have the manifests for all international shipments sent in advance. Check the contents of shipping containers against the manifest. If a suspicious item is found, evacuate the area and notify security and law enforcement.

- Institute counterterrorism programs at your foreign operations.

Terrorists are out to assault "America" and that includes U.S. business interests located overseas. So don't neglect to institute counterterrorism programs at all of your foreign operations. Maintain open lines of communications, and have your security chief serve as a liaison. Senior management should be notified of and approve all overseas security and contingency plans. Consult "Security Guidelines for American Enterprises Abroad," a compilation of security guidelines for American private-sector executives operating outside the United States. Published by the U.S. State Department's Overseas Security Advisory Council, it can be found at www.ds.state.gov/about/publications/osac/enterprises.html.

7.06. Emergency Preparedness

Traditional emergency plans are insufficient to deal with acts of terror. Relying solely on fire drills just doesn't cut it anymore. Rethink your company's emergency preparations and training with a view toward such terrorist threats as bombings and biological attacks.

- Develop building or office evacuation plans.

For employees to react sensibly in a crisis situation, they ought to have an evacuation plan already down pat. Plan for both complete and partial building evacuations. There should be designated routes of exit and a means of communicating with employees to ensure that they don't run smack into danger. Train marshals, equipped with walkie-talkies or cell phones, to direct the flow of people, and have an evacuation command center that's capable of mobility. (You don't want anyone staying inside a hazardous building.) Consult with local emergency services when devising the plan. For more discussion, see

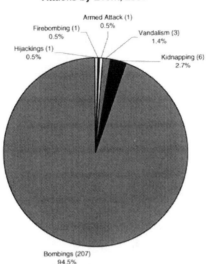

Total Anti-U.S. International Terrorist Attacks by Event, 2001

Armed Attack (1) 0.5%
Firebombing (1) 0.5%
Vandalism (3) 1.4%
Hijackings (1) 0.5%
Kidnapping (6) 2.7%
Bombings (207) 94.5%

Source: U.S. Department of State

the British Home Office's "Bombs: Protecting People and Property—A Handbook for Managers" at www.homeoffice.gov.uk/atoz/terrorists.htm. Also, the Chicago Fire Department offers online an extremely useful "Suggested High Rise Office Building Evacuation Plan" at www.ci.chi.il.us/ Fire/, explaining the roles of floor wardens, floor leaders, searchers, stairwell and elevator monitors, and aides to the handicapped.

Caution Two-way radio communications and cellular telephones should never be used if a bomb is found or suspected, for the transmissions could trigger a detonation.

- Make provisions for evacuating the disabled or elderly.

The U.S. Architectural and Transportation Barriers Compliance Board (a.k.a. Access Board), a federal agency, has designed an emergency evacuation plan to meet the needs of the disabled, including training in the use of evacuation chairs. Go to www.access-board.gov to get a copy of the plan. For more information, contact the Access Board at Suite 1000, 1331 F Street NW, Washington, D.C. 20004-1111, 202-272-0043, 800-872-2253 or 202-272-0080 (TTY 202-272-0082).

- Regularly conduct emergency drills and hold employee seminars.

In this day and age, emergency drills are essential for businesses. These should go beyond mere fire drills and include employee seminars, floor drills and whole building evacuations. The British government offers a useful "Exercise Planners Guide" for "managers, executives, chief officers and others who decide their organization's overall strategy for contingency planning, including training and exercising, to help prioritize the allocation of resources." The guide can be found at www.ukresilience.info/contingencies/cont_bus.htm.

As for seminars, the Oak Ridge National Laboratory insightfully notes in an instructor's manual on chemical warfare that adults "strongly resist learning anything merely because someone says they should" and "will learn only what they feel a need to learn." For tips on holding successful employee seminars, consult "Instructor Guide for Techniques for CSEPP [Chemical Stockpile Emergency Preparedness Program] Instructors," by Edith Jones of the Oak Ridge National Laboratory, which is available at http://emc.ornl.gov/emc/PublicationsMenu.html.

- Have fire marshals review your emergency evacuation systems.

Whether or not you own the building or buildings in which your offices are housed, request a safety inspection from the local fire department. Stress your concern that evacuation routes, such as emergency stairs and fire doors, must be adequate to get your people out in a hurry. Also, have the fire department review your evacuation plans and training procedures, and make any recommended improvements.

- Routinely inspect all fire doors and emergency staircases to ensure they aren't locked or blocked.

Some of the most tragic stories to emerge from the World Trade Centers were those that told of fire doors that were locked. In some cases, the victims could do little more than call their loved ones to say a last goodbye. Don't let that happen at your company. Make it a matter of course to inspect all fire doors to ensure that they are never locked, and have your security personnel regularly transit every emergency route out of your building to make sure there are no bottlenecks or impassable barriers. If that means installing new security devices to prevent theft or trespass, make the investment. Never sacrifice safety just to save a few dollars.

- Develop non-evacuation emergency plans to stay safely indoors.

In some instances, such as attacks with an aerosolized chemical or biological weapon or "dirty bombs" that release radioactive debris, fleeing a building into the contaminated streets would be unwise. Your company, therefore, should also develop plans to keep employees (and customers) within the safety of your building in the event of such an incident. The flow of air from an attack site near your building is your biggest worry. Turn off heating, ventilation and air-conditioning systems, and close all windows and doors. Interior rooms, without any means for air from the outside to seep in, are good places for employees to huddle until rescuers arrive or they're told it's safe to leave the building. ***

Tip To create "safe rooms" into which lethal agents won't penetrate, store thick plastic sheeting and duct tape, and tell workers to fill any keyholes or other large gaps with paper or cloth before taping them over.

- Stockpile emergency supplies and protective masks throughout your building or office.

In case egress from an office is impossible, emergency stockpiles of water and non-perishable food should be stored at several designated locations on every floor. A first-aid kit, cell phone, flashlights, whistles, portable radio and extra batteries also should be stored at these locations. The storage site should *never* be locked. In addition, since infrastructure, notably power plants, are high on the terrorists' list of targets, prudence would dictate installing backup electrical generators. Furthermore, in case of a chemical-biological attack, have plenty of inexpensive N95 facial masks on hand to protect against the inhalation of deadly agents.

Tip Not every company is going to provide employees with emergency equipment, so you could take the opportunity to give your customers pocket-sized flashlights, embossed with your company's name, phone number, etc.

Caution If you receive an unexpected flashlight, be certain you know the sender. The Bureau of Alcohol, Tobacco and Firearms warns that flashlights often are rigged as bombs.

- Adapt the Israeli concept of "protected space," especially at high-risk facilities.

The Israeli Ministry of Defense has long promulgated the concept of "protected space" or protective shelters among the civilian population and businesses. "The Protected Space is a handy, easy-to-reach space capable of providing those staying in it with protection against both conventional and non-conventional weapons for several hours," explains the Israel Home Front Command. Since 1992, every new building or addition to an existing building in Israel has, by law, been equipped with either an Apartment Protected Space or a Floor Protected Space (FPS). Each FPS has a blast door that opens outward, a filtered ventilation system, and emergency lighting, plus a telephone and connections for TV and radio reception. The rooms are stacked one above the other, extending the full height of a building, so that they form one contiguous tower of secure rooms. Sealed openings in the rooms' floors and ceilings

Facilities Struck by International Terrorism Worldwide, 1996-2001

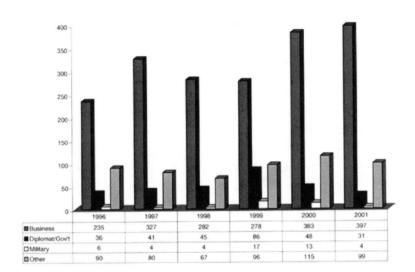

	1996	1997	1998	1999	2000	2001
■ Business	235	327	282	278	383	397
■ Diplomat/Gov't	36	41	45	86	48	31
□ Military	6	4	4	17	13	4
▨ Other	90	80	67	96	115	99

Source: U.S. Department of State

interconnect the FPSs to facilitate escape or rescue. Details can be found at www.idf.il/english/organization/homefront/homefront2.stm.

7.07. Mail Handling

The deadly anthrax letter campaign of 2001 tipped terrorists off to the effectiveness of disseminating lethal biological agents through the mail. It also made the likelihood of similar attacks in the future all but certain. The threat of bioterrorism is greatest for those who handle mail—especially large volumes of mail—as part of their jobs. While these workers deserve special protections, all employees should be tutored in how to properly handle mail, spot suspicious mail and deal with mail-related emergencies. And not to be forgotten, of course, is the ever-present danger of conventional mail bombs.

- Encourage employees, especially mail handlers, to follow hygienic practices.

Washing hands and wrists with antibacterial soap should become a matter of routine, especially after handling mail or returning from out of doors. Washroom soap dispensers should be filled with an antibacterial brand, and signs on antiterrorism hygiene should be posted as reminders. Persons with cuts, scrapes or skin lesions on or near their hands should don disposable gloves before touching mail.

Tip Tell employees never to eat, drink or smoke around mail.

- Establish an enhanced and safe screening process for letters and packages.

Your mailroom is your first line of defense against terrorists who would send bombs or chemical-biological warfare agents by mail, so be sure they're up to the task. Have mailroom personnel properly trained to identify and handle suspicious letters or packages. The Centers for Disease Control and Prevention (CDC) has developed a 15-minute educational video for people who process, sort, or deliver mail. It includes basic information about anthrax, strategies for protecting workers from anthrax exposures, and methods for detecting and responding to a suspicious letter or package. Copies of the video can be ordered from the Public Health Foundation by calling 877-252-1200 or 301-645-7773, faxing 301-843-0159, or going to http://bookstore.phf.org/prod204.htm. The video also can be viewed online at www.bt.cdc.gov.

Tip Consider the purchase of an automated biohazard detection system.

Caution Employees who sort mail on a daily basis are most likely to notice something that is out of the ordinary. Therefore, never use office temporaries in a mailroom. Have trained backups fill in for your regular mail handlers on their days off.

- Follow the CDC's guidelines in your mailrooms and mail processing centers.

The CDC has issued the following "Health Advisory and Interim Recommendations" for protecting workers from exposure to biological agents, such as anthrax, at work sites where mail is processed or handled. (See http://www.bt.cdc.gov/Mail/MailHandlers.asp.) The recommendations cover: 1) engineering controls; 2) administrative controls; 3) housekeeping controls, and 4) personal protective equipment for workers. "These measures," the CDC says, "should be selected on the basis of an initial evaluation of the work site. This evaluation should focus on determining which processes, operations, jobs, or tasks would be most likely to result in an exposure should a contaminated envelope or package enter the work site. Many of these measures (e.g., administrative controls, use of HEPA filter-equipped vacuums, wet-cleaning, use of protective gloves) can be implemented immediately; implementation of others will require additional time and efforts."

The CDC goes on to offer the following advice, reprinted here verbatim:

1. Engineering Controls in Mail-handling/processing Sites

B. anthracis spores can be aerosolized during the operation and maintenance of high-speed, mail-sorting machines, potentially exposing workers and possibly entering heating, ventilation, or air-conditioning (HVAC) systems. Engineering controls can provide the best means of preventing worker exposure to potential aerosolized particles, thereby reducing the risk for inhalational anthrax, the most severe form of the disease. In settings where such machinery is in use, the following engineering controls should be considered:

- An industrial vacuum cleaner equipped with a high-efficiency particulate air (HEPA) filter for cleaning high-speed, mail-sorting machinery
- Local exhaust ventilation at pinch roller areas

- HEPA-filtered exhaust hoods installed in areas where dust is generated (e.g., areas with high-speed, mail-sorting machinery)
- Air curtains (using laminar air flow) installed in areas where large amounts of mail are processed

HEPA filters installed in the building's HVAC systems (if feasible) to capture aerosolized spores. Note: Machinery should not be cleaned using compressed air (i.e., "blow-down/blowoff").

2. Administrative Controls in Mail-handling/processing Sites

Strategies should be developed to limit the number of persons working at or near sites where aerosolized particles may be generated (e.g., mail-sorting machinery, places where mailbags are unloaded or emptied). In addition, restrictions should be in place to limit the number of persons (including support staff and non-employees, e.g., contractors, business visitors) entering areas where aerosolized particles may be generated. This includes contractors, business visitors, and support staff.

3. Housekeeping Controls in Mail-handling/processing Sites

Dry sweeping and dusting should be avoided. Instead, areas should be wet-cleaned and vacuumed with HEPA-equipped vacuum cleaners.

4. Personal Protective Equipment for Workers in Mail-handling/processing Sites

Personal protective equipment for workers in mail-handling/processing work sites must be selected on the basis of the potential for cutaneous or inhalational exposure to *B. anthracis* spores. Handling packages or envelopes may result in cutaneous exposure. In addition, because certain machinery (e.g., electronic mail sorters) can generate aerosolized particles, persons who operate, maintain, or work near such machinery may be exposed through inhalation. Persons who hand sort mail or work at other sites where airborne particles may be generated (e.g., where mailbags are unloaded or emptied) may also be exposed through inhalation.

Recommendations for Workers Who Handle Mail

Protective, impermeable gloves should be worn by all workers who handle mail. In some cases, workers may need to wear cotton gloves under their protective gloves for comfort and to prevent dermatitis. Skin rashes and other dermatological conditions are a potential hazard of wearing gloves. Latex gloves should be avoided because of the risk of developing skin sensitivity or allergy

- Gloves should be provided in a range of sizes to ensure proper fit.
- The choice of glove material (e.g., nitrile, vinyl) should be based on safety, fit, durability, and comfort. Sterile gloves (e.g., surgical gloves) are not necessary.
- Different gloves or layers of gloves may be needed depending on the task, the dexterity required, and the type of protection needed. Protective gloves can be worn under heavier gloves (e.g., leather, heavy cotton) for operations where gloves can easily be torn or if more protection against hand injury is needed.
- For workers involved in situations where a gloved hand presents a hazard (e.g., close to moving machine parts), the risk for potential injury resulting from glove use should be measured against the risk for potential exposure to *B. anthracis*.
- Workers should avoid touching their skin, eyes, or other mucous membranes since contaminated gloves may transfer *B. anthracis* spores to other body sites.

- Workers should consider wearing long-sleeved clothing and long pants to protect exposed skin.
- Gloves and other personal protective clothing and equipment can be discarded in regular trash once they are removed or if they are visibly torn, unless a suspicious piece of mail is recognized and handled. If a suspicious piece of mail is recognized and handled, the worker's protective gear should be handled as potentially contaminated material (See "Guideline For Hand washing And Hospital Environmental Control," 1985, available at http   /www.cdc.gov/ncidod/hip/ guide/handwash.htm
- Hands should be thoroughly washed with soap and water when gloves are removed, before eating, and when replacing torn or worn gloves. Soap and water will wash away most spores that may have contacted the skin; disinfectant solutions are not needed.

Additional Recommendations for Workers Who May Be Exposed through Inhalation

- Persons working with or near machinery capable of generating aerosolized particles (e.g., electronic mail sorters) or at other work sites where such particles may be generated should be fitted with NIOSH-approved respirators that are at least as protective as an N95 respirator.
- Persons working in areas where oil mist from machinery is present should be fitted with respirators equipped with P-type filters.
- Because facial hair interferes with the fit of protective respirators, workers with facial hair (beards and or large moustaches) may require alternative respirators (such as powered air-puri-

fying respirators [PAPRS] with loose-fitting hoods).

- Workers who cannot be fitted properly with a half-mask respirator based on a fit test may require the use of alternative respirators, such as full facepiece, negative-pressure respirators, PAPRs equipped with HEPA filters, or supplied-air respirators. If a worker is medically unable to wear a respirator, the employer should consider reassigning that worker to a job that does not require respiratory protection.
- In addition, the use of disposable aprons or goggles by persons working with or near machinery capable of generating aerosolized particles may provide an extra margin of protection.

In work sites where respirators are worn, a respiratory-protection program that complies with the provisions of OSHA [29 CFR 1910.134] should be in place. Such a program includes provisions for obtaining medical clearance for wearing a respirator and conducting a respirator fit-test to ensure that the respirator fits properly. Without fit testing, persons unknowingly may have poor face seals, allowing aerosols to leak around the mask and be inhaled. (See December 11, 1998, *MMWR*, available at www.cdc.gov/mmwr/preview/mmwrhtml/ 00055954.htm.)

Have employees follow strict procedures to spot suspect mail.

Below is the verbatim text of the CDC's "Updated Information About How to Recognize and Handle a Suspicious Package or Envelope," published Oct. 31, 2001:

Letters containing *Bacillus anthracis* (anthrax) have been received by mail in several areas in the United States. In some instances, anthrax exposures have occurred, with several persons becoming infected. To prevent such exposures and subsequent infection, all persons should learn how to recognize a suspicious package or envelope and take appropriate steps to protect themselves and others.

Identifying Suspicious Packages and Envelopes

Some characteristics of suspicious packages and envelopes include the following:

- Inappropriate or unusual labeling

    - Excessive postage

    - Handwritten or poorly typed addresses

    - Misspellings of common words

    - Strange return address or no return address

    - Incorrect titles or title without a name

    - Not addressed to a specific person

    - Marked with restrictions, such as "Personal," "Confidential," or "Do not x-ray"

    - Marked with any threatening language

    - Postmarked from a city or state that does not match the return address

- Appearance

    - Powdery substance felt through or appearing on the package or envelope

    - Oily stains, discolorations, or odor

    - Lopsided or uneven envelope

    - Excessive packaging material such as masking tape, string, etc.

- Other suspicious signs

    - Excessive weight

- Ticking sound

- Protruding wires or aluminum foil

If a package or envelope appears suspicious, DO NOT OPEN IT.

Handling of Suspicious Packages or Envelopes

- Do not shake or empty the contents of any suspicious package or envelope.
- Do not carry the package or envelope, show it to others or allow others to examine it.
- Put the package or envelope down on a stable surface; do not sniff, touch, taste, or look closely at it or at any contents which may have spilled.
- Alert others in the area about the suspicious package or envelope. Leave the area, close any doors, and take actions to prevent others from entering the area. If possible, shut off the ventilation system.
- WASH hands with soap and water to prevent spreading potentially infectious material to face or skin. Seek additional instructions for exposed or potentially exposed persons.
- If at work, notify a supervisor, a security officer, or a law enforcement official. If at home, contact the local law enforcement agency.
- If possible, create a list of persons who were in the room or area when this suspicious letter or package was recognized and a list of persons who also may have handled this package or letter. Give this list to both the local public health authorities and law enforcement officials.

More information is available at the CDC's bioterrorism site at www.bt.cdc.gov.

- Make sure you employees know what to do if powder is released when handling suspicious mail.

The CDC recommends the following procedures in cases where powder is released from a suspicious package or envelope:

Steps to follow if powder from a suspicious envelope or package has spilled out:

- Do not try to clean up the powder. Cover the spilled contents immediately with anything (clothing, paper, trash can, etc.). Do not remove the covering.
- Leave the room and close the door or section off the area. Ask co-workers and others to leave and keep others from entering.
- Wash your hands with soap and water.
- Do not bring the envelope or package to an emergency department or doctor's office.
- Report the incident to local police or other law enforcement officials. If the incident occurs in the workplace, also notify building security or a supervisor.
- Remove heavily contaminated clothing and other personal items as soon as possible. Place it in a plastic bag or other container that can be sealed. Give the bag of clothing to emergency responders.
- The bag should be labeled clearly with the owner's name, contact telephone number and inventory of the bag's contents.
- Shower with lots of soap and water as soon as possible. Do not use bleach or other disinfectant on your skin.
- Make a list of all people in the room or area, especially those who had actual contact with the powder. Provide the list to law enforcement and public health officials.
- For incidents involving a possibly contaminated letter, the environment in direct contact with the letter or its contents should be decontaminated

with a solution of one part household bleach to 10 parts water following a crime scene investigation. Personal affects may be decontaminated similarly.

In incidents where a biological agent is suspected in the air:

- Turn off local fans or ventilation units in the area.
- Leave the room and close the door or section off the area. Ask co-workers and others to leave and keep others from entering.
- Dial 911 to report the incident to local police and the local FBI field office. If the incident occurs in the workplace, also notify building security or a supervisor.
- Shut down the air handling system.
- Make a list of all people in the room or area. Provide the list to law enforcement and public health officials.
- For incidents involving a possibly contaminated letter, the environment in direct contact with the letter or its contents should be decontaminated with a solution of one part household bleach to 10 parts water following a crime scene investigation. Personal affects may be decontaminated similarly.

Additional information is available at the CDC's bioterrorism site at www.bt.cdc.gov.

- Have a supervisor check into any health complaints that resemble CBW symptoms, especially among mailroom personnel.

If your company receives a letter or package laced with a chemical-biological warfare (CBW) agent that goes undetected, odds are your mailroom personnel will be exposed and could be among the first to show symptoms of disease. Assign a supervisor to look into any health complaints of mail handlers. Also, check with any employee who has taken a sick day to see whether their health problems match any of the signs of exposure to a chemical or biological agent. Supervisors, of course, will need to know the telltale signs of CBW poisoning, so a bit of education will be required. Contact the CDC at www.bt.cdc.gov for guidance.

7.08. Bomb Threats and Explosions

The first thing to know about bombs is that they hardly ever look like bombs. Bombs can be made to resemble anything and often appear innocuous. For example, the bomb that exploded in a busy Hebrew University cafeteria in Jerusalem in July 2002, killing five Americans and two Israelis, was left in a bag on a table and was detonated by a cell phone. Next, err on the side of caution. When in doubt, alert the authorities. Finally, tell employees that if they receive a telephoned bomb threat, stay calm, get as much information as possible from the caller, use the bomb threat checklist underneath their telephones, be attentive to any overheard background sounds or statements, and contact security or the police immediately after the call.

U.S. Bombing Incidents by Target Type, 1977-1997

Target Type	Total	Killed	Injured	Damage ($millions)
Home	9,954	301	1,585	$31.7
Mailbox	6,140	40	94	0.4
Vechicle	6,119	134	579	70.6
Business	5,698	116	1,777	605.9
Educational	1,882	3	506	12.6
Government	1,504	180	782	111.4
Transportation*	773	8	79	1.8
Utility/Energy	572	0	9	14.0
Religious	269	2	9	6.7
Medical	196	0	22	3.8
Police	155	1	19	2.2
Other	2,380	66	663	0.3
Total	35,642	851	6,124	$861.3

*Of the 733 transportation incidents, only 35 involved airports.

Source: Bureau of Alcohol, Tobacco and Firearms

- Keep an eye out for unattended objects and suspicious.

Employees should be alert to any packages, briefcases, luggage, handbags and the like left unattended in the lobby of your building or near the outside of your building, especially in front of large glass windows. Flying glass can be deadly in an explosion. Pay particular attention if someone gingerly places, rather than drops, a package, bag or other item in an unusual place or an out-of-sight spot, like the back of a store shelf or behind plants in a building lobby. Be equally alert to any other suspicious behavior in or near your building. Look for signs of nervousness in the person. Watch to see if he appears to be on the lookout for police or security guards. Be leery of anyone trying—often repeatedly—to enter a locked door or an emergency door. Contact building security or the police, and provide them with a description of the person and the location of the suspicious object.

Tip   Have your building's windows checked by an expert and decide which would benefit from the installation of anti-shatter film or other techniques to reduce injuries in an explosion.

- Take all bomb threats seriously and immediately report them to law enforcement.

Because most bombs are homemade, any caller to your company warning of an imminent explosion could very well be the bomb-maker himself and should be taken seriously. It should go without saying that bombs are nothing to be toyed with by amateurs. Let law enforcement and trained bomb-disposal experts handle things.

- Put a bomb-threat checklist under every office telephone.

The Bureaus of Alcohol, Tobacco and Firearms has compiled the following checklist to use in the event of a telephoned bomb threat. The checklist also can be employed in handling biological or other terrorist threats. A copy of the checklist, contained in a protective paper sleeve or plastic bag, should be placed under every office telephone and at switchboards. All employees should be trained to follow these procedures, explaining to them that the aim is to get as much information from the caller as possible and to write down anything they may overhear. Finally, set up primary and secondary telephone numbers for them to call if they do receive a bomb threat.

• Develop a bomb-incident plan.

We needn't be mere passive victims of bombings or even bomb threats. Advance preparations can alleviate panic and may save lives in the event of a blast. "If there is one point that cannot be overemphasized," says the Bureau of Alcohol, Tobacco and Firearms (ATF), "it is the value of being prepared. Do not allow a bomb incident to catch you by surprise."

The big question is whether or not to evacuate immediately following a bomb threat. The ATF says that initiating a search after a threat is received is "perhaps the most desired approach," because it's "not as disruptive as an immediate evacuation." We, however, recommend this decision be made at the highest level of your company. Have your crisis management team and security officer weigh the pros and cons of immediate evacuation and make recommendations to senior management, on whose shoulders the final decision should rest.

In planning for bomb threats, the ATF recommends the following steps:

Bomb Incident Plan

1. Designate a chain of command.
2. Establish a command center.
3. Decide what primary and alternate communications will be used.
4. Establish clearly how and by whom a bomb threat will be evaluated.
5. Decide what procedures will be followed when a bomb threat is received or device discovered.

Bomb Threat Checklist

Exact time of call: _____

Exact words of caller:

QUESTIONS TO ASK

1. When is the bomb going to explode? _____
2. Where is the bomb? _____
3. What does it look like? _____
4. What kind of bomb is it? _____
5. What will cause it to explode? _____
6. Did you place the bomb? _____
7. Why? _____
8. Where are you calling from? _____
9. What is your address? _____
10. What is your name? _____

CALLER'S VOICE (circle)

Calm	Slow	Crying	Slurred
Stutter	Deep	Loud	Broken
Giggling	Accent	Angry	Rapid
Stressed	Nasal	Lisp	Excited
Disguised	Sincere	Squeaky	Normal

If voice is familiar, whom did it sound like? _____

Were there any background noises? _____

Remarks:

Person receiving call: _____

Telephone number call received at: _____

Date: _____

Report call immediately to _____

Source: Bureau of Alcohol, Tobacco and Firearms

6. Determine to what extent the available bomb squad will assist and at what point the squad will respond.
7. Provide an evacuation plan with enough flexibility to avoid a suspected danger area.
8. Designate search teams.
9. Designate areas to be searched.
10. Establish techniques to be utilized during search.
11. Establish a procedure to report and track progress of the search and a method to lead qualified bomb technicians to a suspicious package.
12. Have a contingency plan available if a bomb should go off.
13. Establish a simple-to-follow procedure for the person receiving the bomb threat.
14. Review your physical security plan in conjunction with the development of your bomb incident plan.

Command Center

1. Designate a primary location and an alternate location.
2. Assign personnel and designate decision-making authority.
3. Establish a method for tracking search teams.
4. Maintain a list of likely target areas.
5. Keep blueprints of floor diagrams in the center.
6. Establish primary and secondary methods of communications. Caution: The use of two-way radios during a search could cause premature detonation of an electric blasting cap.
7. Formulate a plan for establishing a command center if a threat is received after normal business hours.
8. Maintain a roster of all necessary telephone numbers.

For a more detailed discussion, see "Bomb Threats and Physical Security Planning," a pamphlet published by the ATF, which is available online at http://www.atf.treas.gov or through the U.S. Government Printing Office.

U.S. Bombing Damage by Target Type, 1977-1997

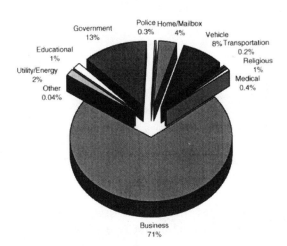

Source: Bureau of Alcohol, Tobacco and Firearms

- Disseminate guidance on what employees should do in a building explosion.

Distribute information to employees on what to do in the event of a building explosion or an attack with chemical or biological weapons. Reprinted here verbatim is guidance from the Federal Emergency Management Agency (www.fema.gov/hazards/terrorism/terrorf.shtm):

DURING: In a building explosion, get out of the building as quickly and calmly as possible. If items are falling off of bookshelves or from the ceiling, get under a sturdy table or desk. If there is a fire:

- Stay low to the floor and exit the building as quickly as possible.
- Cover nose and mouth with a wet cloth.
- When approaching a closed door, use the palm of your hand and forearm to feel the lower, middle and upper parts of the door. If it is not hot, brace

yourself against the door and open it slowly. If it is hot to the touch, do not open the door—seek an alternate escape route.

- Heavy smoke and poisonous gases collect first along the ceiling. Stay below the smoke at all times.

AFTER: If you are trapped in debris:

- Use a flashlight.
- Stay in your area so that you don't kick up dust. Cover your mouth with a handkerchief or clothing.
- Tap on a pipe or wall so that rescuers can hear where you are. Use a whistle if one is available. Shout only as a last resort—shouting can cause a person to inhale dangerous amounts of dust.
- Assisting Victims: Untrained persons should not attempt to rescue people who are inside a collapsed building. Wait for emergency personnel to arrive.
- Follow CDC guidance in attacks with chemical or biological weapons.

Regarding attacks with chemical or biological weapons, the CDC advises:

"Chemical Agents: Chemical agents are poisonous gases, liquids or solids that have toxic effects on people, animals or plants. Most chemical agents cause serious injuries or death. Severity of injuries depends on the type and amount of the chemical agent used, and the duration of exposure. Were a chemical agent attack to occur, authorities would instruct citizens to either seek shelter where they are and seal the premises or evacuate immediately. Exposure to chemical agents can be fatal. Leaving the shelter to rescue or assist victims can be a deadly decision. There is no assistance that the untrained can offer that would likely be of any value to the victims of chemical agents.

"Biological Agents: Biological agents are organisms or toxins that have illness-producing effects on people, livestock and crops. Because biological agents cannot necessarily be detected and may take time to grow and cause a disease, it is almost impossible to know that a biological attack has occurred. If government officials become aware of a biological attack through an informant or warning by terrorists, they would most likely instruct citizens to either seek shelter where they are and seal the premises or evacuate immediately. A person affected by a biological agent requires the immediate attention of professional medical personnel. Some agents are contagious, and victims may need to be quarantined. Also, some medical facilities may not receive victims for fear of contaminating the hospital population."

7.09. Information Systems Security

Information technology (IT) is the lifeblood of modern economies, but as everyone knows, computers and Internet communications are extremely vulnerable to viruses, worms, Trojan horses, denial of service attacks, tampering and the like. This combination of economic importance and systems vulnerability makes IT a tempting target for terrorists.

- Be sure employees follow proper security protocols.

IT security precautions only work if people use them. So be sure that employees follow the proper security protocols, such as password use and the protection of portable computers while traveling. Remind employees to check any new software for viruses before installation and not to store passwords on PF keys. Create an automatic log-off after a computer has gone unused for more than 10 minutes. Distribute, for example, the brochure "Computer Security Awareness," published online by the New York State Office of Technology at www.oft.state.ny.us/security/csa.html, and the Chicago Federal Reserve Bank's "Money $mart" guide to "Safekeeping Web Profiles and Passwords" at www.chicagofed.org.

- Conduct a security check of your IT systems.

The Computer Security Division of the National Institute of Standards and Technology (NIST), a unit of the U.S. Commerce Department, has published a "Security Self-Assessment Guide for Information Technology Systems" to evaluate the security of a particular computer system or group of systems. Although intended for use by government agencies, the guide is a useful tutorial in IT security checks. "Through interpretation of the questionnaire results," it says, "users are able to assess the information technology (IT) security posture for any number of systems within their organization and, in particular, assess the status of the organization's security program plan." The guide available at http://csrc.nist.gov/asset/.

Tip   Carnegie Mellon University's CERT® (Computer Emergency Response Team) Software Engineering Institute has published a guide to help organizations improve the security of their networked computer systems. See "CERT® Security Improvement Modules" at www.cert.org/security-improvement/.

• Make a risk assessment of your IT systems.

IT risk assessment is one of the proactive security measure businesses need to take in this new age of terrorism. The NIST explains how to gauge the likelihood of an IT attack and the resulting impact on an organization in its "Risk Management Guide for Information Technology Systems." The guide outlines a nine-step procedure to conduct a proper IT risk assessment— specifically, system characterization, threat identification, vulnerability identification, control analysis, likelihood determination, impact analysis, risk determination, control recommendations and results documentation. You can download the guide at http://csrc.nist.gov/publications/nistpubs/index.html. For further information, call 301-975-2934 or 301-975-6478.

• Develop the means to detect IT intruders.

According to the Computer Security Institute's "2002 Computer Crime and Security Survey," 90 percent of respondents— mainly large corporations and government agencies—detected

Percentage of World's Internet Population by Region, Q1 2002

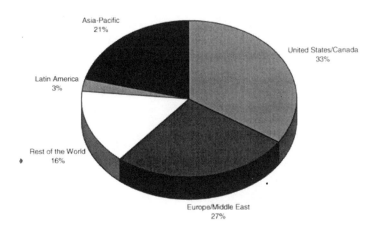

Source: Nielsen//Net Ratings

computer security breaches in the last 12 months and 80 percent acknowledged a resulting financial loss. Nearly $456 million in losses were reported. Clearly, detecting intruders, such as hackers, is important in order to avoid unnecessary costs and to maintain the integrity of your business data and other propriety information. Have qualified professionals install an Intrusion Detection System to stop trouble before it begins. For a further discussion of this topic, see the papers on "CyberStrategies" presented at a New York State Security Conference, April 10-11, 2002, which are located at www.oft.state.ny.us/security/2002secday.htm.

Tip   Encrypt sensitive data, especially customers' credit card numbers.

- Practice IT defense in depth by employing firewalls and backup strategies.

Firewalls are essential these days, given the proliferation of infected emails and websites. But choosing, configuring and maintaining firewalls for a business can be difficult. The NIST, in January 2002, published a set of important recommendations in its "Guidelines on Firewalls and Firewall Policy," available at http://csrc.nist.gov/publications/nistpubs/index.html.

The NIST also issued this key warning: "Firewalls are vulnerable themselves to misconfiguration and failures to apply needed patches or other security enhancements. Accordingly, firewall configuration and administration must be performed carefully and organizations should also stay current on new vulnerabilities and incidents. While a firewall is an organization's first line of defense, organizations should practice a defense in depth strategy, in which layers of firewalls and other security systems are used throughout the network. Most importantly, organizations should strive to maintain all systems in a secure manner and not depend solely on the firewalls to stop security threats. Organizations need backup plans in case the firewall fails."

• Stay abreast of the latest IT vulnerabilities and incidents.

Keeping on top of IT vulnerabilities, new viruses and IT attacks is a vital yet relatively easy chore. Here are some of the more informative online sources that will help to keep your IT team up to date:

- CERT® (Computer Emergency Response Team) Coordination Center, Software Engineering Institute, Carnegie Mellon University, Pittsburgh, PA 15213-3890, 412-268-7090 (24-hour hotline), www.cert.org
- Computer Incident Advisory Capability, U.S. Department of Energy, 925-422-8193, www.ciac.org/ciac/
- Computer Security Resource Center, National Institute of Standards and Technology, 100 Bureau Drive, Mail Stop 8930, Gaithersburg, MD 20899-8930, 301-975-2934 or 301-975-6478, http://csrc.nist.gov/index.html

- Forum of Incident Response and Security Teams, First.Org, Inc., PMB 349, 650 Castro Street, Suite 120, Mountain View, CA 94041, www.first.org
- National Infrastructure Protection Center, J. Edgar Hoover Building, 935 Pennsylvania Avenue, NW, Washington, D.C. 20535-0001, 202-323-3205, www.nipc.gov
- National Institute of Standards and Technology, Vulnerability and Threat Portal (including the current threat level, rated on a scale of 100, and the "Top Ten Vulnerabilities"), 100 Bureau Drive, Stop 3460, Gaithersburg, MD 20899-3460, 301-975-NIST/6478, http://icat.nist.gov/vt_portal.cfm
- New York State Office for Technology, Information Security Department, State Capitol, Empire State Plaza, P.O. Box 2062, Albany, NY 12220, 518-474-0865 or 518-473-2658, www.oft.state.ny.us/security/security.htm
- Overseas Security Advisory Council, Cyber Threat Analysis and News, www.ds-osac.org/edb/cyber/default.cfm
- Symantec Corp. (Norton products), 20330 Stevens Creek Blvd., Cupertino, CA 95014, 408-517-8000, www.symantec.com (with a free online computer security check and virus scan for home users)
- U.S. Department of Justice, Computer Crime and Intellectual Property Section, Criminal Division, 10th & Constitution Ave., NW, John C. Keeney Building, Suite 600, Washington, DC 20530, 202-514-1026, www.cybercrime.gov
- Provide a means of communicating security alerts throughout your company.

Knowledge of a security threat can reduce its impact on a company, so have a mechanism in place to send security alerts instantaneously throughout your enterprise. Similarly, standardize the way employees report incidents to your IT security staff.

Tip Explain the importance of IT security to new hires and office temporaries.

• Ensure your IT security personnel are properly trained.

IT security is an ever-changing challenge, given the new threats that arise on a weekly, if not daily, basis. It's imperative, therefore, to have well-trained IT professionals overseeing your systems—and for them to keep their training up to date. The New York State Office of Technology (www.oft.state.ny.us/security/security.htm) cites the following computer security training programs: The SANS Institute, 866-570-9927 or 540-372-7066, www.sans.org; MIS Training Institute, 508-879-7999, www.misti.com; Computer Security Institute, 415-947-6320, www.gocsi.com; TruSecure's International Computer Security Association, 888-627-2281 or 703-480-8200, www.icsa.net; Information Systems Security Association, Inc., 800-370-4772 or 414-768-8000, www.issa-intl.org, and International Information Systems Security Certification Consortium, Inc., www.isc2.org.

• Be wary of outside IT contractors.

Whenever anyone from outside your company works on your IT systems, you're open to malicious or criminal activity. It's essential, therefore, that you hire only reputable contractors with impeccable credentials. In congressional testimony in 1999, Michael A. Vartis, director of the FBI's National Infrastructure Protection Center, listed a host of dangers. Consider these:

1) Systems maps: By mapping your IT systems, an outside contractor could gain valuable information to sell to the highest bidder.

2) Root access: Contractors often are given the same access privileges as the systems administrator, allowing them to steal or alter information or engage in a denial-of-service attack.

3) Trap doors: By installing trap doors, a contractor could gain access to your systems at a later date through openings they

created.

4) Malicious code: In writing code, someone could place a logic bomb or a time-delayed virus in a system that would later disrupt it.

5) Compromised security: A malicious actor could implant a program to compromise passwords and other aspects of IT system security.

7.10. Contingency and Continuity Planning

The British government warns that "around half of all businesses experiencing a disaster and which have no effective plans for recovery fail within the following 12 months." If you plan ahead for terrorist attacks or other crises and if your employees already know what to do when all goes wrong, your ability to limit the damage—in terms of lives, injures and costs—and to maintain post-crisis business continuity is greatly improved.

- Recognize that contingency and continuity planning works.

Preplanning can make the difference between the survival and demise of your business following a terrorist incident or other disaster. "A few years ago," says a U.K. government handbook, "a terrorist bomb seriously damaged the headquarters of a large insurance company over a spring weekend. By Monday morning furniture, computers, telephones and supplies had been delivered to a relocation address and over 500 staff were at work. This could not have been done without careful planning, which had been tested by exercising, and as a result jobs were preserved and the business continued to flourish." See "How Resilient Is Your Business to Disaster?" at www.ukresilience.info/contingencies/cont_bus.htm.

- Develop IT contingency plans.

Terrororism in the United States by Event, 1980-1999

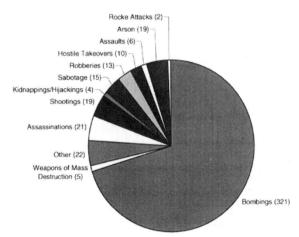

Source: Federal Bureau of Investigation

A business's dependence on IT opens it up to a variety of disruptions, such as power outages, equipment failures and terrorist attacks. IT contingency plans are, therefore, necessary. The NIST, in June 2002, issued an extremely useful guide, covering everything from desktop and portable computers to local area networks and mainframe systems. In "Contingency Planning Guide for Information Technology Systems," it recommends that seven progressive steps be taken: 1) develop a contingency planning statement; 2) conduct a business impact analysis; 3) identify preventive controls; 4) develop recovery strategies; 5) develop an IT contingency plan; 6) plan testing, training and exercises, and 7) plan maintenance. The guide is available at http://csrc.nist.gov/publications/nistpubs/index.html.

• Preplan a crisis communications strategy

To address the concerns of customers, investors, employees and the general public following an attack affecting your company or industry, have a crisis communications strategy in place ahead of time. We suggest taking a look at "The Business Roundtable's Post-9/11 Crisis Communications: Best Practices for Crisis Planning, Prevention and Continuous Improvement," published in June 2002 and available at www.brtable.org. It offers an array of useful advice. "Several Best Practices were reinforced or have emerged due to the events of 9/11 and continuing concerns about terrorism," it says, citing seven steps recommended by communications experts. These are: 1) establish a full-time commitment to crisis management; 2) employ communications techniques to maximize crisis prevention; 3) designate backups; 4) keep vendors and consumers in the loop; 5) address terrorism as a global concern; 6) be sensitive to the communication of risk, and 7) understand the pros and cons of the Web. To which we would add: 8) keep investors and financial analysts in the loop, too.

- Maintain a duplicate directory of employee information at a secure, off-site location.

A duplicate employee directory stored safely at an off-site location could prove essential if you are denied access to your office for security reasons or in the event your office is damaged or destroyed in a terrorist attack. Larger companies could easily store vital employee information electronically at more than one site. A simple and safe approach for small companies would be to save duplicate personnel information on computer disks and then store them—along with printed backup copies—at the homes of senior management or similarly secure sites (e.g., a safety deposit box or a lawyer's office). Keep these records up to date. Similarly, it could prove helpful (especially to law enforcement) to maintain at an off-site location the personnel records of former employees. If your organization teaches students, store their vital statistics at an off-site location and keep the information current.

Tip Also keep duplicates of important business records, contracts, patents and copyrights at a safe, off-site location.

- Maintain a current list of employee emergency contacts.

Require all employees to fill out forms listing the name, address and telephone numbers (both home and office phone numbers) of the person or persons they wished contacted in the event of an emergency—and periodically send out reminders to employees to keep their contact information current.

Tip Encourage employees and management to make out wills.

• Offer employees an option to submit DNA samples and fingerprints.

The tragedy of the World Trade Center attack showed how useful DNA samples and fingerprints can be in identifying remains. Inform your employees that they can voluntarily store samples of their DNA and fingerprints. A caveat, however, is in order: Medical science is showing an ability to discover predisposition to disease and illness in a person's DNA. Some employees may treat an offer to store DNA samples skeptically, thinking (wrongly or rightly) that their company will test the samples for predisposition to illness and then, perhaps, terminate the worker or deny promotion. To put employees' minds at rest, include a written guarantee that the DNA information would only be used by the proper authorities for identification purposes in the event of the employee's death.

• Plan ahead to maintain business continuity following a crisis.

Keeping your business running after a crisis can be difficult. To avoid large losses of revenue and to keep disruptions to a minimum, have a plan in place to maintain continuity. Appoint a Business Continuity Planner as part of your crisis management team. Identify mission-critical operations and key personnel. Look for backup support that already exists at different locations. Maintain a contingency plan that includes: emergency office space, equipped with computers and telephone lines; backup IT systems; emergency phone numbers; allocation of responsibilities to other offices or personnel, and pre-assigned emergency coordinators. Then, keep the plan current, updating it regularly to reflect changes in your business operations and resources.

Tip   The New York State Forum for Information Resource Management offers an online "Business Continuity Health Check" at www.nysfirm.org.

- Get your board of directors' advice on your business continuity plans.

Business continuity management "is different from disaster recovery planning since it is proactive and concentrates on everything that is needed to continue the key business processes, whatever the catastrophe," notes a guide provided online by the British Department of Trade and Industry. Titled "Business Continuity Management—Preventing Chaos in a Crisis" and written by Visor Consultants Ltd. of London, it lists eight steps to take to ensure post-crisis continuity. "In many organisations [sic] the concept of effective and routine Risk Management in parallel with regular Business Continuity Management, should crisis threaten, is being introduced and managed for the first time," it concludes. "However, in the final analysis it is the board of directors who must effect policies to ensure the company is acting responsibly and is suitably prepared to deal with crises." The guide is at *www.dti.gov.uk/mbp/ bpgt/m9ba91001/m9ba910011.html*.

Tip   The British government's official post-Sept. 11 website, U.K. Resilience, has a host of useful links to contingency and continuity planning guides at www.ukresilience.info/contingencies/cont_links.htm.

7.11. Recommended Online Reading

"Bombs: Protecting People and Property—A Handbook for Managers," British Home Office, www.homeoffice.gov.uk/ atoz/terrorists.htm.

"Business Continuity Management—Preventing Chaos in a Crisis," British Department of Trade and Industry and Visor

Consultants Ltd., *www.dti.gov.uk/mbp/bpgt/m9ba91001/
m9ba910011.html*.

"The Business Roundtable's Post-9/11 Crisis Communications:
Best Practices for Crisis Planning, Prevention and Continuous Improvement," The Business Roundtable, June 2002,
www.brtable.org.

"Business Continuity Health Check," New York State Forum for
Information Resource Management, *www.nysfirm.org*.

"Computer Security Awareness," New York State Office of
Technology, *www.oft.state.ny.us/security/csa.html*.

"Contingency Planning Guide for Information Technology Systems," Special Publication SP 800-34, National Institute of
Standards and Technology, Computer Security Resource
Center, June 2002, *http://csrc.nist.gov/publications/nistpubs/index.html*.

"CyberStrategies," New York State Security Conference, Office
for Technology, April 10-11, 2002, *www.oft.state.ny.us/security/2002secday.htm*.

"Expedient Respiratory and Physical Protection: Does a Wet
Towel Work to Prevent Chemical Warfare Vapor Infiltration?" Sorensen, J., and Vogt, B., Oak Ridge National
Laboratory, ORNL/TM-2001/153, 2001, *http://emc.ornl.gov/emc/PublicationsMenu.html*.

"Guidelines for Protecting U.S. Business Information Overseas,"
U.S. State Department, Overseas Security Advisory Council,
www.ds.state.gov/about/publications/osac/protect.html.

"Guidelines on Firewalls and Firewall Policy," Special Publication SP 800-41, National Institute of Standards and Technology, Computer Security Resource Center, January 2002, *http://csrc.nist.gov/publications/nistpubs/index.html*.

"Homeland Security: Key Elements of a Risk Management
Approach," U.S. General Accounting Office (GAO-02-150T),
October 12, 2001, *www.gao.gov*.

"How Do I Know? A Guide to the Selection of Personal
Protective Equipment for Use in Responding to a Release of
Chemical Warfare Agents," Foust, C., Oak Ridge National
Laboratory, ORNL/TM-13343, 1999, *http://emc.ornl.gov/emc/PublicationsMenu.html*.

"How Resilient Is Your Business to Disaster?" British government publication, *www.ukresilience.info/contingencies/cont_bus.htm*.

"Instructor Guide for Techniques for CSEPP [Chemical Stockpile Emergency Preparedness Program] Instructors," Jones, Edith, Oak Ridge National Laboratory, ORNL/M-2102, May 1992, *http://emc.ornl.gov/emc/PublicationsMenu.html*.

"LAPD Crime Prevention Lesson Plans: Burglary Prevention and Robbery Prevention," Los Angeles Police Department (under "Crime Tips"), *www.lapd.org*.

"Personal Security Guidelines for the American Business Traveler Overseas." U.S. State Department, Overseas Security Advisory Council, *www.ds.state.gov/about/publications/osac/personal.html*.

"Physical Security Guides" and "IT Security Guides and Reports," Royal Canadian Mounted Police, Technical Security Branch, *www.rcmp-grc.gc.ca/tsb/pubs/index.htm*.

"Preparing Your Business for the Unthinkable," American Red Cross, *www.redcross.org/pubs/dspubs/terrormat.html*.

"Protected Space /Shelters Guidelines," Israeli Home Front Command, http://www.idf.il/english/organization/homefront/homefront2.stm.

"Risk Management Guide for Information Technology Systems," Special Publication SP 800-30, National Institute of Standards and Technology, Computer Security Resource Center, October 2001, http://csrc.nist.gov/publications/nistpubs/index.html.

"Security Guidelines for American Enterprises Abroad," U.S. State Department, Overseas Security Advisory Council, *www.ds.state.gov/about/publications/osac/*.

"Security Self-Assessment Guide for Information Technology Systems," NIST Special Publication 800-26, National Institute of Standards and Technology, *http://csrc.nist.gov/asset/*.

"Suggested High Rise Office Building Evacuation Plan," Chicago Fire Department, *www.ci.chi.il.us/Fire/*.

"2002 Computer Crime and Security Survey," Computer Security Institute, *www.gocsi.com*.

"Will Duct Tape and Plastic Really Work? Issues Related To
    Expedient Shelter-In-Place," Sorensen, J., and Vogt, B., Oak
    Ridge National Laboratory, ORNL/TM-2001/154, 2001, http://
    emc.ornl.gov/emc/PublicationsMenu.html.

APPENDICES

Appendix A

International Terrorist Groups

At present, there are more than 60 terrorist organizations of significance around the world, and about half of them are considered extremely dangerous and serous threats to the U.S. and its citizens and businesses overseas. Many of the groups are well known, such as Abu Nidal, Hezbollah and Osama bin Laden's Al Qaeda network, while others are obscure, often never heard of outside of their homelands. These include such groups as the Alex Boncayao Brigade, a Philippine urban hit squad, the Army for the Liberation of Rwanda and the Revolutionary United Front in Sri Lanka.

The U.S. government breaks foreign terrorists into two broad groups: 1) designated foreign terrorist organizations (as defined under the Immigration and Nationality Act as amended by the Antiterrorism and Effective Death Penalty Act of 1996), and 2) non-designated yet still active terrorist groups. The official designations have legal implications. It's against the law, for example, for anyone in the U.S. to provide funds or other material support to a designated terrorist organization. Representatives and members of a designated terrorist group can be denied visas or excluded from the United States, and the Department of the Treasury can block the funds of designated organizations.

The following includes the 35 groups currently defined by the U.S. government as "designated foreign terrorist organizations." The descriptions are based largely on U.S. State Department information. ("Patterns of Global Terrorism," U.S. Department of State, May 2002; "Designation of a Foreign Terrorist Organization," statement by Colin L. Powell, U.S. Department of State, Aug. 9, 2002; "Designation of a Foreign Terrorist Organization," statement by Colin L. Powell, U.S. Department of State, Oct. 23, 2002; "Foreign Terrorist Organizations: Fact Sheet," U.S. Department of State, Oct. 23, 2002.)

Abu Nidal: Also known as the Fatah Revolutionary Council, Arab Revolutionary Brigades, Black September and Revolutionary Organization of Socialist Muslims, Abu Nidal is currently based in Iraq but also operates out of Lebanon. It has carried out terrorist attacks in 20 countries, killing or injuring almost 900 persons through the end of 2001. Its targets include the United States, United Kingdom, France, Israel, moderate Palestinians and various Arab countries. Major attacks by Abu Nidal have included the Rome and Vienna airports in December 1985, the Neve Shalom synagogue in Istanbul and the Pan Am flight 73 hijacking in Karachi in September 1986, and the City of Poros day-excursion ship attack in Greece in July 1988. Strength: A few hundred members.

Abu Sayyaf Group (ASG): The ASG, the smallest and most violent of the Islamic separatist groups operating in the southern Philippines, has engaged in bombings, assassinations, kidnappings and extortion. It aims to promote an independent Islamic state in western Mindanao and the Sulu Archipelago in the southern Philippines, which are heavily populated by Muslims. Its first large-scale action was a 1995 raid on the town of Ipil in Mindanao. In 2000, it expanded operations to Malaysia, where it kidnapped more than 30 foreigners, including a U.S. citizen. ASG members have studied or worked in the Middle East and developed ties to the mjuahidin while fighting and training in Afghanistan. In May 2001, the ASG kidnapped three Americans and 17 Filipinos from a tourist resort in Palawan; several of the hostages, including one American, were murdered. Strength: Believed to have a few hundred core fighters, but at least 1,000 others—motivated by the prospect of receiving ransom payments for foreign hostages—allegedly joined in 2000-2001.

Al-Aqsa Martyrs Brigade: An outgrowth of the current Palestinian uprising, or *intifadah* (the word means "shaking" in Arabic), the group aims to drive Israeli soldiers and settlers from the West Bank, Gaza Strip and Jerusalem and to establish a Palestinian state. Al-Aqsa Martyrs Brigade has carried out shootings and suicide operations against Israeli military personnel and civilians and has killed Palestinians who it believed were collaborating with Israel. Although it doesn't necessarily target Americans, at least five U.S. citizens (four of whom held dual Israeli-U.S. citizenship) were killed in the attacks. In January 2002, the group claimed responsibility for the first suicide bombing carried out by a female. Strength: Unknown.

Armed Islamic Group (GIA): GIA, an Islamic extremist group that began its violent activities in 1992, seeks to overthrow the secular Algerian regime and replace it with an Islamic state. Between 1992 and 1998, the GIA conducted a terrorist campaign of civilian massacres, sometimes wiping out entire villages. In 1993, it launched a campaign against foreigners living in Algeria and has killed more than 100, mostly Europeans. Its methods include assassinations, bombings and kidnapping. The GIA hijacked an Air France flight to Algiers in December 1994 and also conducted a series of bombings in France in 1995. Strength: About 200 members.

Asbat al-Ansar: This Sunni group, based in Palestinian refugee camps in Lebanon, is associated with Al Qaeda and follows an extremist interpretation of Islam that justifies violence against civilians. Asbat al-Ansar ("Partisans' League") has carried out several terrorist attacks in Lebanon since it first emerged in the early 1990s, including bombings and assassinations of religious leaders. It raised its profile in 2000 with two dramatic attacks against Lebanese and international targets—notably, a rocket-propelled grenade assault on the Russian Embassy in Beirut. Strength: About 300 fighters.

Aum Shinrikyo ("Supreme Truth"): Also known as Aleph, Aum is a cult that was established in 1987 to take over Japan and then the world. It believes that the end of the world is imminent and that the United States will start World War III with an attack on Japan. In March 1995, Aum members released the chemical nerve agent sarin in the Tokyo subway system, killing 12 persons and injuring up to 6,000. Aum also has attempted to use biological weapons, but the attacks were unsuccessful. Japanese courts have sentenced several of Aum members to death or life imprisonment for the 1995 subway attacks. In July 2001, Russian authorities arrested a group of Russian Aum followers who planned to set off bombs near the Imperial Palace in Tokyo in a plot to free the cult's founder, Shoko Asahara, from jail and smuggle him to Russia. Strength: Estimated at 1,500 to 2,000 persons.

Basque Fatherland and Liberty (ETA): ETA, which stands for Euzkadi Ta Askatasuna, is a Basque separatist group founded in 1959 in hopes of gaining independence for the northern Spanish provinces of Vizcaya, Guipuzcoa, Alava and Navarra and the southwestern French departments of Labourd, Basse-Navarra and Soule. It primarily engages in bombings and the assassination of Spanish officials but conducts kidnappings, robberies and extortion to finance its activities. The group has killed more than 800 persons since the early 1960s. In November 1999, ETA broke a cease-fire and began an assassination and bombing campaign that killed 38 persons and wounded scores more by end-2001. ETA terrorists have been trained in Libya, Lebanon and Nicaragua. Some members have received sanctuary in Cuba, while others reside in South America. ETA also has ties to the Irish Republican Army. Strength: Perhaps in the hundreds.

Communist Party of the Philippines/New People's Army (CPP/NPA): Formed in 1969, these Maoist groups' goal is the overthrow of the Philippine government through protracted guerilla warfare. Founder Jose Maria Sison is believed to direct all CPP and NPA activity from the Netherlands, where he and other members live in self-imposed exile. The NPA, which is the CPP's military wing, opposes any U.S. presence in the Philippines and has killed U.S. citizens there. It also has killed, injured and kidnapped many Philippine citizens, including government officials. Strength: Estimated at over 10,000.

Al-Gama'a al-Islamiyyaor Islamic Group (IG): Active since the late 1970s, this is Egypt's largest militant group. IG's primary goal is the overthrow of the Egyptian government and its replacement with an Islamic state. The group, linked to Osama bin Laden, specializes in armed attacks against Egyptian security and other government officials, Coptic Christians and Egyptian opponents of Islamic extremism. But IG also has called for attacks on foreign tourists, particularly Americans. In November 1997, IG terrorists killed 58 foreign tourists at the Hatshepsut Temple in the Valley of the Kings near Luxor, Egypt. IG claimed responsibility for the attempted assassination of Egyptian President Hosni Mubarak in Ethiopia in June 1995. Its spiritual leader, Shaykh Umar Abd al-Rahman, was sentenced to life in prison in January 1996 for his involvement in the 1993 World Trade Center bombing and remains incarcerated in the United States. The group operates mainly in the Al-Minya, Asyu't, Qina, and Sohaj districts of southern Egypt, but its international presence extends to Afghanistan, Austria, Britain and Yemen. Strength: Unknown.

Hamas: Formed in 1987, Hamas ("Islamic Resistance Movement") is a Palestinian group that aims to use both political and violent means, including terrorism, to establish an Islamic state in place of Israel. Its strength is concentrated in the Gaza Strip and a few areas of the West Bank. Hamas has conducted many attacks, including large-scale suicide bombings, against Israeli civilian and military targets. The group is loosely structured, with some elements working clandestinely and others working openly through mosques and social-service institutions to recruit members, raise money, organize activities and distribute propaganda. It became more active in 2001-2002, claiming numerous attacks against Israeli interests. Strength: An unknown number of hardcore members, with tens of thousands of supporters and sympathizers.

Harakat ul-Mujahidin (HUM): Formerly known as Harakat al-Ansar, HUM is an Islamic militant group based in Pakistan that operates primarily in Kashmir, attacking Indian troops and civilian targets with light and heavy machineguns, assault rifles, mortars, explosives and rockets. HUM leaders in 1998 signed Osama bin Laden's *fatwa*, declaring a "holy war." It's linked to the Kashmiri militant group al-Faran, which kidnapped and later killed five Western tourists in Kashmir in 1995. HUM was involved in the December 2000 hijacking of an Indian airliner. The hijackers negotiated the release of Masood Azhar, an important Harakat ul-Ansar leader imprisoned by India in 1994. Azhar didn't, however, return to the HUM, choosing instead to form the Jaish-e-Mohammed (JEM), a rival and more radical militant group. Strength: Several thousand armed supporters, although a significant number have defected to the JEM since 2000.

Hezbollah: Operating from the Bekaa Valley in Lebanon and the suburbs of Beirut, this radical Shite group, formed in 1982, is dedicated to the overthrow of Israel and is considered among the most dangerous terrorist groups in the world. Hezbollah, meaning "Party of God," has close ties to Iran and Syria and is strongly anti-Western. The group likely was involved in the suicide truck bombings of the U.S. Embassy and Marine barracks in Beirut in October 1983 and the U.S. Embassy annex in Beirut in September 1984. Elements of the group also were responsible for the kidnapping and detention of U.S. and other Western hostages in Lebanon. In South America, Hezbollah attacked the Israeli Embassy in Argentina in 1992 and is a suspect in the 1994 bombing of the Israeli cultural center in Buenos Aires. Hezbollah terrorist attacks in Israel have sought to wreck Middle East peace negotiations. Also known as the Islamic Jihad, Revolutionary Justice Organization, Organization of the Oppressed on Earth and Islamic Jihad for the Liberation of Palestine, Hezbollah maintains terrorist cells in Europe, Africa, North and South America and Asia. Strength: Several thousand supporters and a few hundred terrorist operatives.

Islamic Movement of Uzbekistan (IMU): This coalition of Islamic militants from Uzbekistan and other Central Asian states oppose Uzbekistan's secular regime and hopes to establish an Islamic state. IUM's propaganda also includes anti-Western and anti-Israeli rhetoric. The group is believed to be responsible for numerous car bombings and the abduction of several foreigners, including the kidnapping of four U.S. mountain climbers in 2000 and four Japanese geologists in 1999. IMU operates in Uzbekistan, Tajikistan and Kyrgyzstan and has the support of other Islamic extremist groups in Central and South Asia. Strength: Under 2,000.

Jaish-e-Mohammed (JEM): The Pakistan-based JEM (meaning "Army of Mohammed") is an Islamist group that was founded in 2000 by ultra-fundamentalist Maulana Masood Azhar, who was released from an Indian prison in December 1999 in exchange for 155 hijacked Indian Airlines passengers held hostage in Afghanistan. JEM, which received funding from Osama bin Laden, launched a series of rocket-grenade attacks in

India in 2000. Its supporters are Pakistanis and Kashmiris, as well as Afghans and Arab veterans of the Afghan-Soviet war. The JEM in October 2001 claimed responsibility for a suicide attack on the Jammu and Kashmir legislative assembly building in Srinagar that killed at least 31 persons, but it later denied the claim. The Indian government has implicated the JEM, along with Lashkar-e-Tayyiba, for the December 2001 attack on the Indian Parliament that killed 9 and injured 18. Strength: Several hundred armed supporters.

Japanese Red Army (JRA): Also called the Anti-Imperialist International Brigade, JRA is an international terrorist group that formed in 1970 after breaking away from the Japanese Communist League-Red Army Faction. The JRA's goals are the overthrow of the Japanese government and monarchy; it also seeks to foment worldwide revolution. During the 1970s, the JRA carried out a series of attacks around the world, including the massacre in 1972 at Lod Airport in Israel, two Japanese airliner hijackings and an attempted takeover of the U.S. Embassy in Kuala Lumpur. In April 1988, a JRA operative was arrested on the New Jersey Turnpike after police discovered explosives in his car. He apparently was planning an attack to coincide with the bombing of a USO club in Naples, Italy. The USO bombing killed five persons, including a U.S. servicewoman. The JRA has had close relations with Palestinian terrorists; some JRA members may now be in Syrian-controlled areas of Lebanon. Strength: Down to an estimated half dozen.

Jemaah Islamiya (JI): Founded by Abdullah Sungkar, JI has operated throughout Southeast Asia for years and began targeting U.S. interests in the region in 1997. Its goal is to create a multinational Islamic state, comprising Malaysia, Singapore, Indonesia and the southern Philippines. In December 2001, JI planned to bomb the U.S. Embassy in Singapore; the plot was foiled when authorities arrested 15 JI members. JI has links with Al Qaeda. Strength: Approximately 200 members.

Al-Jihad: Based in Cairo, this Egyptian Islamic extremist group (a.k.a. Egyptian Islamic Jihad, Jihad Group and Islamic Jihad) has been active since the late 1970s and has been a close partner of Osama bin Laden's Al Qaeda organization. The group also may have ties to Iran. Al-Jihad aims to overthrow the Egyptian government and replace it with an Islamic state; it also seeks to attack U.S. and Israeli interests in Egypt and elsewhere. It specializes in armed attacks against high-level Egyptian government officials, including cabinet ministers, as well as car-bombings against U.S. and Egyptian facilities. The original Jihad was responsible for the 1981 assassination of Egyptian President Anwar Sadat. In 1998, a planned Al-Jihad attack on the U.S. Embassy in Albania was thwarted. Al-Jihad's international terrorist network extends to Yemen, Afghanistan, Pakistan, Sudan, Lebanon and the United Kingdom. Strength: Probably several hundred hardcore members.

Kahane Chai (Kach): Its stated goal is to restore the biblical state of Israel. Kach was founded by radical Israeli-American rabbi Meir Kahane; its offshoot, Kahane Chai, was founded by Kahane's son Binyamin following his father's assassination in the United States. The groups were declared to be terrorist organizations by the Israeli Cabinet in 1994. Palestinian gunmen killed Binyamin Kahane and his wife in December 2000 in the West Bank. Strength: Unknown.

Kurdistan Workers' Party (PKK): Founded in 1974 as a Marxist-Leninist group primarily composed of Turkish Kurds, PKK's goal is to establish an independent Kurdish state in southeastern Turkey. In the early 1990s, the PKK moved beyond rural-based insurgent activities to include urban terrorism. At a PKK Congress in January 2000, members claimed the group now would use only political means to achieve its new goal—namely, improved rights for Kurds in Turkey. The PKK's primary targets have been government security forces in Turkey, although it conducted attacks on Turkish diplomatic and commercial facilities in dozens of West European cities in 1993 and again in 1995. In an attempt to damage Turkey's tourist industry, the PKK bombed tourist sites and hotels and kidnapped foreign tourists in the 1990s. It now operates in Turkey, Europe and the Middle East. Strength: Estimated at 4,000 to 5,000.

Lashkar-E-Tayyiba (LT): This is the armed wing of the Pakistan-based religious organization, Markaz-ud-Dawa-wal-Ir-shad (MDI), a Sunni group formed in 1989 in opposition to U.S.

missionaries. Based in Muridke (near Lahore) and Muzaffarabad, LT is one of the three largest and best-trained groups fighting in Kashmir. LT has trained its militants in mobile training camps across Pakistan-administered Kashmir and Afghanistan. It has conducted a number of operations against Indian troops and civilian targets since 1993, including kidnapping and attacks that killed nearly 100 people, mostly Hindu Indians, in 2000. The group claimed responsibility for numerous attacks in 2001, including a January attack on Srinagar airport that killed five Indians along with six militants; an attack on a police station in Srinagar that killed at least eight officers and wounded several others; and an attack in April against Indian border security forces that left at least four dead. The Indian Government publicly implicated LT, along with JEM, for the December 2001 attack on the Indian Parliament building. Strength: Several hundred fighters.

Liberation Tigers of Tamil Eelam (LTTE): Found in 1976, the group seeks to an independent Tamil state and has been engaged in armed conflict with the Sri Lanka government to achieve that end. The Tigers have integrated a battlefield insurgent strategy with a terrorist program that targets not only key personnel in the countryside but also senior Sri Lankan political and military leaders in Colombo and other urban centers. The Tigers are most notorious for their cadre of suicide bombers, the Black Tigers. Political assassinations and bombings are commonplace. The LTTE has refrained from targeting foreign diplomatic and commercial establishments. Strength: Estimated to have 8,000 to 10,000 armed combatants in Sri Lanka, with a core of trained fighters of 3,000 to 6,000

Mujahedin-e Khalq Organization (MEK or MKO): Formed in the 1960s by the college-educated children of Iranian merchants, the MEK sought to counter what it perceived as excessive Western influence during the Shah's regime. Following a philosophy that mixes Marxism and Islam, MEK has developed into the largest and most active armed Iranian dissident group. Its history is studded with anti-Western activity. Recent attacks have focused on the interests of the clerical regime in Iran and abroad. During the 1970s the MEK staged terrorist attacks inside Iran that killed several U.S. military personnel and civilians working on defense projects. It supported the 1979 takeover of the U.S. Embassy in Tehran. In April 1992, it conducted attacks on Iranian embassies in 13 different countries. Since then, it has claimed credit for mortar attacks on government and military buildings in Tehran. Its primary support comes from the Iraqi regime of Saddam Hussein. Strength: Several thousand fighters located on bases scattered throughout Iraq and armed with tanks, infantry fighting vehicles and artillery

National Liberation Army of Colombia (ELN): Operating from the rural and mountainous regions of Colombia, this Marxist insurgent group was formed in 1965 by urban intellectuals inspired by Fidel Castro and Che Guevara. It conducts hundreds of kidnappings for ransom every year, often targeting foreign employees of large corporations, especially in the petroleum industry. ELN frequently assaults energy infrastructure, causing major damage to pipelines and the electric power network. It also has been involved in hijackings, bombings and guerrilla warfare. Strength: Some 3,000 to 5,000 armed combatants.

The Palestine Islamic Jihad (PIJ): Founded by militant Palestinians in the Gaza Strip during the 1970s and now headquartered in Syria, PIJ is committed to the creation of an Islamic Palestinian state and the destruction of Israel through "holy war." Because of its strong support for Israel, the United States has been identified as an enemy of the PIJ. It also opposes moderate Arab governments that it believes have been tainted by Western secularism. PIJ has conducted suicide bombings against Israeli targets in the West Bank, Gaza Strip and Israel. In 2001, it claimed numerous attacks against Israeli interests. Strength: Unknown.

Palestine Liberation Front (PLF): Although splintered into various factions, one PLF group is known for aerial attacks against Israel. The PLF also was responsible for the 1985 attack on the cruise ship *Achille Lauro* and the murder of Leon Klinghoffer, an American citizen. The PLF's pro-Palestinian Liberation Organization (PLO) faction had been based in

Tunisia until the *Achille Lauro* attack; it's now based in Iraq. Strength: Unknown.

Popular Front for the Liberation of Palestine (PFLP): This Marxist-Leninist group was founded in 1967 by George Habash, a member of the Palestinian Liberation Organization (PLO), and committed numerous international terrorist attacks during the 1970s. Since 1978, it has carried out attacks on Israeli and moderate Arab targets. Based in Syria, Lebanon, Israel and the occupied territories, the group opposes Palestinian peace talks with Israel. It stepped up its operational activity in 2001, including the shooting death of Israel's tourism minister in October. Strength: Around 800 members.

Popular Front for the Liberation of Palestine-General Command (PFLP-GC): After splitting from the PFLP in 1968, the General Command faction claimed it wanted to focus more on fighting and less on politics. Violently opposed to Yasser Arafat's PLO and led by a former captain in the Syrian Army, the PFLP-GC is tied closely to both Syria and Iran. The group carried out dozens of attacks in Europe and the Middle East during 1970s and 1980s. Known for cross-border terrorist attacks into Israel using unusual means, such as hot-air balloons and motorized hang gliders, the Damascus-headquartered group's primary focus is now on guerrilla operations in southern Lebanon and small-scale attacks in Israel, West Bank and Gaza Strip. Strength: Several hundred.

Al Qaeda: Established by Osama Bin Laden in the late 1980s, the group was comprised largely of Arabs who fought in Afghanistan against the Soviet invasion. It recruited and trained Sunni Islamic extremists for the Afghan resistance. Its subsequent goal was to establish a pan-Islamic Caliphate throughout the world by working with allied Islamic extremist groups to overthrow regimes it deemed "non-Islamic" and expelling Westerners and non-Muslims from Muslim countries. Al Qaeda members were responsible for the Sept. 11, 2001 attacks on the World Trade Center and the Pentagon, as well the hijacked plane that crashed in Shanksville, Pennsylvania, leaving about 3,000 people dead or missing. It directed the October 2000 attack on the *USS Cole* in the port of Aden, Yemen, killing 17 sailors and injuring another 39. In August 1998, Al Qadea bombed the U.S. embassies in Nairobi, Kenya and Dar es Salaam, Tanzania, killing at least 301 persons and injured more than 5,000. It further was linked to plans to assassinate Pope John Paul II during his visit to Manila in late 1994, to kill President Clinton during a visit to the Philippines in early 1995, to bomb a dozen U.S. trans-Pacific flights in midair in 1995 and to set off a bomb at Los Angeles International Airport in 1999. Al Qaeda also plotted to carry out terrorist operations against U.S. and Israeli tourists visiting Jordan in late 1999, and claims to have shot down U.S. helicopters and killed U.S. servicemen in Somalia in 1993 and to have conducted three bombings that targeted American troops in Yemen in 1992. Strength" Several thousand members and associates.

Real IRA: Also called the True IRA, the Real IRA is an offshoot of the Irish Republican Army (IRA). Formed in 1998 as clandestine armed wing of the 32-County Sovereignty Movement, it's dedicated to removing British forces from Northern Ireland and unifying Ireland. It opposes the IRA cease-fire and Sinn Fein's adoption of the Mitchell principles of democracy and nonviolence. The Real IRA engages in bombings, assassinations, smuggling, extortion and robbery. Its targets include British military forces, police and civilians in Northern Ireland. In London, it bombed the Hammersmith Bridge and launched a rocket attack on the headquarters of Britain's foreign intelligence service (MI6) in 2000 and the headquarters of the British Broadcasting Corp. in 2001. Strength: An estimated 100 to 200 activists.

Revolutionary Armed Forces of Colombia (FARC): Established in 1964 as the military wing of the Colombian Communist Party, the FARC is Colombia's oldest, largest and best-equipped Marxist insurgency. Organized along military lines, FARC has engaged in bombings, murder, kidnapping, extortion and hijacking, as well as guerrilla and conventional military action against Colombian political, military and economic targets. In March 1999, the FARC executed three U.S. human-rights activists on Venezuelan territory after it kidnapped them in Colombia. Foreign citizens often are targets of FARC kidnapping for ransom. FARC has well-documented ties to narcotics traffickers, principally through the provision of armed protection. Its activities extend beyond Colombia to Venezuela, Panama and Ecuador. Strength: About 9,000 to 12,000 armed terrorists.

Revolutionary Nuclei/Cells or Revolutionary People's Struggle (ELA): Formed in 1971 to oppose the military junta that ruled Greece from 1967 to 1974, ELA is a self-described revolutionary, anti-capitalist and anti-imperialist group that has declared its opposition to "imperialist domination, exploitation, and oppression." It's strongly anti-U.S. and seeks the removal of U.S. military forces from Greece. Since 1974, it has conducted bombings against Greek government and economic targets, as well as U.S. military and business facilities, but hasn't claimed an attack since November 2000. Strength: Believed to be small.

Revolutionary Organization 17 November: This Athens-based radical leftist group, formed in 1975, is named for a student uprising in Greece in November 1973 that protested the military regime. The group opposes the Greek establishment, the United States Turkey and NATO. It's committed to the ouster of U.S. bases in Europe and Turkish military forces in Cyprus. It began by assassinating senior U.S. officials and Greek public figures. It then moved on to bombings in the 1980s. Since 1990, it has targeted European Union facilities and foreign firms in Greece, often using rocket attacks. In June 2000, it murdered British Defense Attaché Stephen Saunders. Two years later, a member of the group was injured when a bomb he was handling exploded prematurely; this led to the arrest of at least seven other members, including the group's leader. Strength: Unknown but believed to be small.

Revolutionary People's Liberation Party (DHKP/C): Originally formed in 1978 as Devrimci Sol (or Dev Sol), the group is a splinter faction of the Turkish People's Liberation Party. Renamed in 1994 after factional infighting, it espouses a Marxist ideology and is virulently anti-U.S. and anti-NATO. It finances its activities chiefly through armed robberies and extortion. It assassinated two U.S. military contractors and wounded a U.S. Air Force officer to protest the Gulf war and launched rockets at the U.S. Consulate in Istanbul in 1992. It now conducts attacks in

Turkey, primarily in Istanbul, Ankara, Izmir and Adana, and raises funds in Western Europe. It carried out its first suicide bombings, targeting Turkish police, in 2001. Strength: Unknown.

The Salafist Group for Call and Combat (GSPC): This Algerian splinter faction, formed in 1996, is the most effective group of armed militants inside Algeria. It has gained popular support with a pledge to avoid civilian casualties inside Algeria, even though civilians have, in fact, been attacked. The GSPC attacks government and military targets, primarily in rural areas. Such operations include false roadblocks and assaults on convoys transporting military, police or other government personnel. Strength: Several hundred to several thousand.

Sendero Luminoso or Shining Path (SL): Formed in Peru by a university professor in the late 1960s, SL advocates a militant Maoist doctrine. It became one of the most ruthless terrorist groups in the Western Hemisphere in the 1980s, responsible for the deaths of some 30,000 people. Its stated goal is to destroy existing Peruvian institutions and replace them with a communist peasant revolutionary regime. It also opposes any influence by foreign governments, as well as by other Latin American guerrilla groups, especially the Tupac Amaru Revolutionary Movement. SL also conducts indiscriminate bombing campaigns and selective assassinations. In 2001, the Peruvian National Police thwarted an SL attack against "an American objective," possibly the U.S. Embassy, when they arrested two Lima SL cell members. Strength: About 200 armed militants.

Tupac Amaru Revolutionary Movement (MRTA): This Marxist-Leninist group was formed in 1983 from remnants of the Movement of the Revolutionary Left, a Peruvian insurgency group active in the 1960s. MRTA wants to establish a Marxist regime and to rid Peru of all "imperialist elements" (i.e., primarily U.S. and Japanese influence). Peru's counterterrorism program has diminished the group's ability to carry out attacks; MRTA also has suffered from infighting, the imprisonment or deaths of senior leaders, and loss of leftist support. Previously, it had conducted bombings, kidnappings, ambushes and assassinations. Strength: No more than 100 members.

Umma Tameer-E-Nau (UTN): Founded by Pakistani nuclear scientists with close ties to Osama bin Laden and the former

Taliban regime in Afghanistan, UTN's leader Bashir-ud-Din Mahmood advocated equipping Islamic countries with enriched uranium and weapons-grade plutonium. During repeated visits to Afghanistan, UTN officials met with bin Laden, Al Qaeda leaders and Taliban leader Mullah Omar to discuss the development of chemical, biological and nuclear weapons. During one meeting, a bin Laden associate indicated he had nuclear material and wanted to know how to use it to make a weapon. Mahmood provided information about the infrastructure needed for a nuclear-weapons program. In November 2001, the Taliban left Kabul; workers at UTN's Kabul offices fled with them. Searches of UTN locations in Kabul yielded documents related to nuclear weapons. Strength: Unknown.

United Self-Defense Forces (AUC or Autodefensas Unidas de Colombia): Commonly referred to as *autodefensas* ("self-defense forces"), the AUC is an umbrella paramilitary organization formed in 1997. It says its primary objective is to protect its sponsors from Colombian insurgents. Its supporters are said to include economic elites, drug traffickers and local communities lacking effective government security. Colombian police report that the AUC conducted 804 assassinations, 203 kidnappings and 75 massacres claiming 507 victims in the first 10 months of 2000 alone. AUC forces are strongest in the north and northwest areas of Antioquia, Cordoba, Sucre, Bolivar, Atlantico and Magdalena. Strength: Estimated at 6,000 to 8,000 members.

Recommended Online Reading

"Patterns of Global Terrorism: Background Information on Terrorist Groups," U.S. Department of State, www.state.gov/s/ct/.

Appendix B

A Chronology of Terror

The following chronology, although far from exhaustive, highlights the major events in the history of terrorism and assassination of the past eight decades. It is based on information from a variety of sources, including the Centre for Defence and International Security Studies at Lancaster University in Britain, the U.S. Department of State, the Foreign Ministry of Israel, the Australian Security Intelligence Organisation, the Ministry of Culture of Turkey and The International Policy Institute for Counter-Terrorism, as well as various news sources, including the Associated Press, British Broadcasting Corp., Reuters, **The New York Times** *and* **Washington Post.**

September 16, 1920
Wall Street Bombing: A bomb left in an unattended, horse-drawn wagon explodes at Wall and Broad streets in lower Manhattan, near the New York Stock Exchange and J. P. Morgan & Co., killing three dozen persons and injuring hundreds. Bolsheviks or anarchists are suspected.

February 21, 1931
First Recorded Skyjack Attempt: A group of rebel soldiers approach two American pilots on the ground in Arequipa, Peru and try to force them to fly over Lima, the nation's capital, to drop propaganda leaflets. The pilots refuse; the rebels later end a ten-day standoff.

October 31, 1945
British Forces Attacked in Palestine: Jewish nationalists seeking the end of British rule in Palestine commence a wave of bombings. Jerusalem's King David Hotel, housing British government and military offices, is blown up July 22, 1946, killing 90 and wounding 44. Britain's mandate to rule Palestine, dating from 1922, ends May 15, 1948, and the state of Israel is declared.

January 30, 1948
Mahatma Gandhi Assassinated: While walking to a prayer meeting, Mahatma ("Great Soul") Gandhi is assassinated by a fellow Hindu, who feels Gandhi betrayed the Hindu cause in seeking reconciliation with India's Muslims. Gandhi, an advocate of non-violence, was instrumental in gaining India's independence from Britain in 1947.

June 16, 1948
First In-Air Hijacking: Four Chinese bandits brandish weapons on a Cathay Pacific Catalina flying boat bound from Macao to Hong Kong. The pilot is shot after refusing to follow the hijackers' orders, and the plane crashes, killing 25 aboard.

November 1, 1950
Truman Assassination Attempt: A White House guard is killed and two are wounded by a pair of Puerto Rican nationalists who storm Blair House, opposite the White House, in an attempt on President Harry S. Truman's life. One gunman is killed; the other is wounded.

July 20, 1951
Jordan's King Murdered: King Abdullah of Jordan is assassinated by an Arab extremist as he enters Mosque of Omar in Jerusalem. The assassin and four others are later hanged.

September 11, 1951
Pakistani Premier Assassinated: An Afghan fanatic shoots and kills Pakistani Prime Minister Lisquat Ali Khan at a public gathering Rawalpindi.

October 6, 1951
British Official Ambushed in Malaya: The British High Commissioner in Malaya, Sir Henry Gurney, is killed after his motorcade is ambushed in Pahang by three dozen Communist guerillas; 13 British soldiers also die in the attack. The guerilla leader is killed eight years later by his own men.

March 1, 1954
Gunfire on Capitol Hill: Puerto Rican nationalists open fire from the gallery of the U.S. House of Representatives in Washington, D.C., wounding five congressmen. All four gunmen are arrested and later convicted.

April 1, 1955
Greek Cypriots Bomb British Sites: Seeking the end of British rule, Greek Cypriot EOKA terrorists launch a bombing campaign against British facilities on Cyprus. Cyprus gains its independence in 1960.

December 12, 1957
IRA Attacks British Army Barracks: The Irish Republican Army attacks the British Army barracks at Armagh, Northern Ireland, but are repulsed after a gun battle with guards.

May 1, 1961
First U.S. Aircraft Hijacking: Puerto Rican-born Antuilo Ramierez Ortiz hijacks a National Airlines plane at gunpoint and forces the pilot to fly to Havana, Cuba. Ortiz is granted asylum, but he returns to Miami, Florida, in 1975 and is sentenced to 20 years' imprisonment.

September 9, 1961
France's de Gaulle Escapes Death: In the first of at least 12 assassination attempts, the Organisation Armee Secrete (Secret Army Organization, or OAS) tries to blow up French President Charles de Gaulle in Aube, France, but the roadside device fails to detonate. OAS members, who are former French soldiers protesting any grant of independence to Algeria, machinegun a car carrying de Gaulle in a Paris suburb in 1962; the president again escapes unharmed. Ten other unsuccessful attempts are made on de Gaulle's life over the next three years.

December 16, 1961
ANC Bombings in South Africa: The African National Congress, today South Africa's ruling party, launches an anti-apartheid effort with a bombing campaign against government buildings.

November 22, 1963
President Kennedy Assassinated: President John F. Kennedy is shot and killed while riding in an open motorcade in Dallas, Texas. Lee Harvey Oswald is arrested and charged with the crime and the killing of a Dallas police officer. Oswald himself is killed two days later by Jack Ruby in the basement of the city jail; Ruby dies in prison in 1967.

March 23, 1967
Che Guevara's Exploits in Bolivia: Communist guerillas, led by Cuban revolutionary Ernesto "Che" Guevara, kill six Bolivian soldiers. Seven months later, Guevara and his band are tracked down by government troops and he is killed.

February 21, 1968
U.S. Plane Hijacked to Havana: In the second successful hijacking in U.S. history, a Delta Airlines flight is forced to fly to Havana, Cuba, where the hijacker is given asylum.

April 4, 1968
Martin Luther King, Jr. Killed: U.S. civil-rights leader Martin Luther King, Jr., who was awarded the Nobel Peace Prize in 1964, is assassinated in Memphis, Tennessee. Two months later, James Earl Ray, a petty criminal, is apprehended in London and charged with the killing. Ray enters a guilty plea, which he later recants, and then is convicted of the murder in 1969. He dies in prison in 1998.

June 5, 1968,
Robert F. Kennedy Murdered: U.S. Senator Robert F. Kennedy of New York, brother of the slain president, is assassinated in Los Angeles after winning California's Democratic presidential primary. Sirhan Sirhan, a Jerusalem-born immigrant who came to the U.S. in the 1950s, is apprehended at the scene and later sentenced to life imprisonment.

June 7, 1968
First Basque Separatist Assassination: Basque separatists of the ETA (Euskadi Ta Askatasuna or "Basque Fatherland and Free-

dom"), founded in 1959, assassinate Meliton Manzanas, a secret police chief in San Sebastian, Spain.

July 22, 1968
First Palestinian Terrorist Hijacking: The Popular Front for the Liberation of Palestine carries out its first-ever airplane hijacking, seizing an El Al Boeing 707 in Rome, Italy and diverting it to Algeria; 32 Jewish passengers are held hostage for five weeks.

August 28, 1968
U.S. Ambassador to Guatemala Killed: U.S. Ambassador to Guatemala John Gordon Mein is murdered by a rebel faction when gunmen force his car off the road in Guatemala City and rake the vehicle with gunfire.

December 26, 1968
Palestinians Fire on El Al Plane in Athens: The Popular Front for the Liberation of Palestine machinegun an El Al aircraft at Athens airport in Greece, killing an Israeli. Greek authorities later release two captured terrorists after a Greek plane is hijacked in Beirut, Lebanon. Israeli commandos then raid the Beirut airport, blowing up 13 Arab airliners.

February 18, 1969
El Al Plane Attacked in Zurich: Palestinians attack an El Al aircraft at Zurich airport, Switzerland, killing four people on board; return fire from an Israeli guard kills one of the terrorists.

August 29, 1969
TWA Flight Hijacked by Palestinians: A Trans World Airlines flight is hijacked after taking off from Rome, Italy by members of the Popular Front for the Liberation of Palestine and forced to fly to Damascus, Syria, where all on board are released and a bomb is detonated in the cockpit.

September 3, 1969
U.S. Ambassador to Brazil Kidnapped: The Marxist revolutionary group MR-8 kidnaps U.S. Ambassador to Brazil Charles Burke Elbrick in Rio de Janeiro; Elbrick is freed four days later

after 15 political prisoners are released from jail and flown out of the country.

September 8, 1969
Assaults on Israeli Interests in Europe: Israel's embassies in The Hague, the Netherlands and in Bonn, West Germany, as well as Israel's El Al airline office in Brussels, Belgium, are attacked within minutes of each other with bombs and grenades. Three El Al employees and a customer are injured in the Brussels attack; no one is hurt in the other assaults.

February 21, 1970
Palestinians Down Swiss Airliner: The Popular Front for the Liberation of Palestine blows up a Swiss airliner just after takeoff from Zurich, Switzerland, killing all 47 people aboard.

March 6, 1970
Weather Underground Blast in New York: A townhouse in New York City's Greenwich Village is demolished when three members of the revolutionary Weather Underground accidentally blow themselves up while making bombs.

May 4, 1970
Israeli Consulate in Paraguay Attacked: In Asuncion, Paraguay, two armed Palestinians break into the office of the Israeli Consulate and fire at employees, killing two. The gunmen are apprehended and sentenced to prison.

August 24, 1970
U.S. Army Research Center Bombed: A bomb planted by an anti-Vietnam War group explodes at the University of Wisconsin's Army Math Research Center in Madison, killing a 33-year-old graduate student. Three of four bombers are later convicted.

July 31, 1970
USAID Adviser in Uruguay Abducted: In Montevideo, Uruguay, the Tupamaros terrorist group kidnaps Dan Mitrione, a police adviser with the U.S. Agency for International Development; his body is found ten days later.

May 1970
Baader-Meinhof Gang Formed: Left-wing journalist Ulrike Meinhof helps Andreas Baader break out of a German prison in Berlin, where Baader and his girlfriend Gudrun Ensslin are imprisoned for the 1968 firebombing of a Frankfurt department store. The group goes on to form the Baader-Meinhof Gang. A two-year terrorist rampage throughout Europe follows. The trio is captured in 1972 and later commits suicide in prison in 1976-77.

September 6, 1970
"Skyjack Sunday": Members of the Popular Front for the Liberation of Palestine hijack three planes belonging to TWA, Swissair and British Overseas Airline Co, (BOAC) and divert them to Jordan. An attempt to hijack an El Al flight over England is thwarted. The German, Swiss and British governments accede to the hijackers' demands, and all 400 hostages are freed.

October 10, 1970
Quebec Separatists' Kidnappings: Quebec separatists kidnap Canada's Quebec Cabinet Minister Pierre LaPorte and British diplomat James Cross. LaPorte is murdered but Cross is freed unharmed.

March 1, 1971
Capitol Hill Bombed: A bomb goes off in the Capitol building in Washington, D.C., destroying a restroom and barbershop but injuring no one. The radical Weather Underground claims responsibility.

May 28, 1971
Israeli Consul in Turkey Murdered: In Istanbul, Turkey, Israeli Consul El-Rom is assassinated. The Turkish Liberation Army claims responsibility.

November 28, 1971
Jordanian Premier Assassinated: Jordan's Prime Minister Wasfi Tal is shot and killed by Palestinian Black September terrorists in Cairo, Egypt. A month later, the Jordanian ambassador in

London, England, is shot and wounded by a Black September hit squad.

December 4, 1971
Ulster Unionists Detonate Bomb: The Ulster Volunteer Force (UVF), formed in 1966 to combat Irish nationalism, plants a bomb at a bar in the Catholic area of Belfast, Northern Ireland, killing 15. By the mid-1970s, a vicious UVF unit known as the Shankill Butchers is engaged in horrific sectarian killings.

February 22, 1972
IRA Bombs Officers' Club: An Irish Republican Army bomb attack on the British Parachute Regiment Officers' Mess in Aldershot, England, kills seven.

May 8, 1972
Israelis Storm Hijacked Plane: Israeli commandos storm a hijacked Belgian Sabena airliner at Ben Gurion airport in Israel, killing the four Palestinian Black September terrorists aboard and freeing the hostages. One passenger and five Israeli soldiers are killed.

September 19, 1972:
Israeli London Attaché Killed: An Israeli attaché in London, England is killed when a letter bomb explodes. Black September claims responsibility.

July 21, 1972
Belfast's "Bloody Friday": A total of 19 bombs planted by Irish Republican Army explode within an hour in Belfast, Northern Ireland, killing 11 and injuring 130.

September 5, 1972
Munich Olympic Massacre: Eight Palestinian Black September terrorists seize 11 Israeli athletes in the Olympic Village in Munich, West Germany. In a botched rescue attempt by West German authorities, nine of the hostages and five terrorists are killed.

January 27, 1973
Turkish Consuls Killed in Los Angeles: Turkey's Consul General Mehmet Baydar and Consul Bahadir Demir are murdered in Los Angeles, California by a 78-year-old Armenian American. This attack marks the beginning of a string of attacks on Turkish diplomats around the world.

March 2, 1973
U.S. Ambassador to Sudan Assassinated: U.S. Ambassador to Sudan Cleo A. Noel and other diplomats are assassinated at the Saudi Arabian Embassy in Khartoum by members of the Black September organization.

December 20, 1973
Spanish Prime Minister Killed: Basque Fatherland and Liberty (ETA) terrorists kill Spanish Prime Minister Admiral Luis Carrero Blanco in a bomb attack in Madrid.

May 15, 1974
Israeli Students Taken Hostage: The Popular Front for the Liberation of Palestine raid a high school at Ma'alot, Israel, taking 90 students hostage. When Israeli soldiers storm the school to rescue the youngsters, the gunmen open fire, killing 22 students and wounding dozens more.

October 26, 1974
FALN Bombings in New York: The Armed National Liberation Front (FALN), dedicated to "armed struggle" to "liberate Puerto Rico from United States control," claims credit for five bombings in downtown Manhattan. It also takes responsibility for two earlier blasts in New York and New Jersey. The FALN is ultimately tied to more than 130 bombings in the U.S.

January 24, 1975
Fraunces Tavern Bombing: The Puerto Rican nationalists with the FALN bomb historic Fraunces Tavern near Wall Street, killing four and injuring sixty. George Washington delivered his Farewell Address to his officers at the tavern in 1783.

January 29, 1975
U.S. State Department Bombing: The radical Weather Underground takes responsibility for an explosion at the U.S. Department of State in Washington, D.C.

June 15, 1975
Chicago's Loop Blasts: The Puerto Rican FALN claims credit for two powerful explosions in Chicago's downtown Loop area. Four months later, the group simultaneously detonates bombs in Chicago, New York and Washington, D.C. In November 1976, Chicago police discover an FALN "bomb factory" and identify four group members.

October 22-24, 1975
Turkish Ambassadors Killed in Europe: Turkey's Ambassador to Austria, Danis Tunaligil, is murdered by three gunmen in a raid on the Turkish Embassy in Vienna. Two days later, Turkey's Ambassador to France, Ismail Erez, and his driver die in a Paris ambush. A group calling itself the Armenian Genocide Justice Commandos claims responsibility.

December 2, 1975
Dutch Train Seized by South Moluccans: South Moluccan terrorists seize a train at Beilen, the Netherlands, taking 50 passengers hostage, killing the engineer and executing two passengers in front of television cameras. The terrorists demand Dutch help in regaining independence for their western Pacific islands, which were seized by Indonesia in 1950. The terrorists surrender after a 12-day standoff as police and soldiers raid the train.

December 6, 1975
London's Balcombe Street Siege: British police chase four Irish Republican Army gunmen through London's fashionable West End. Gunfire is exchanged before the IRA members burst into a Balcombe Street flat in northwest London and take a married couple hostage. A six-day siege ends when the hostages are released unharmed and the terrorists surrender to police.

December 29, 1975
LaGuardia Airport Bombing: Nationalists, perhaps Croatians, are suspected of planting a bomb at New York's LaGuardia Airport that kills 11 and injures 75.

June 27, 1976
Entebbe Hostage Crisis: Four members of the German Baader-Meinhof Gang and the Popular Front for the Liberation of Palestine seize an Air France airliner and its 258 passengers, forcing the plane to land at the Entebbe Airport in Uganda. The hijackers free the French crew and most of the passengers but keep some 100 Jewish passengers hostage. Israeli commandos conduct a rescue mission six days later. All the terrorists are killed, as are an Israeli commando and three hostages, one of whom had been hospitalized and was executed by Ugandan President Idi Amin.

September 10, 1976
Croatians Hijack U.S. Plane: Croatian terrorists hijack a TWA flight headed from New York to Paris, France, taking 93 hostages. The hijackers surrender in Paris, but a New York City policeman is killed by a bomb left by the terrorists at Grand Central Station.

October 13, 1977
Palestinians Seize German Airliner: Four Palestinian terrorists hijack a German Lufthansa jet and order it flown to several Middle East destinations over the next four days. After the terrorists kill the pilot, the plane is stormed in Mogadishu, Somalia by German counterterrorist troops and members of British Special Air Services. All 90 hostages are rescued; three terrorists are killed.

February 13, 1978
Blast Disrupts Commonwealth Meeting: In Australia, a bomb explodes outside the Sydney Hilton Hotel, where delegates to the Commonwealth Heads of Government Regional Meeting are staying. The blast kills three people and injures six others.

March 16, 1978

Former Italian Premier Kidnapped: Aldo Moro, a former Italian prime minister and a header of the Christian Democrats, is seized by the Italian Red Brigade, a Marxist terrorist organization. Moro is brutally murdered 55 days later.

May 25, 1978

Unabomber Saga Begins: A package explodes at Northwestern University in Illinois, injuring a campus police officer. Thus begins the 18-year saga of the Unabomber, named for his attacks against universities and airlines. Until his arrest in 1996, the bomber, Theodore Kaczynski, carries out at least 16 bombings that kill three people and injure 29.

March 30, 1979

House of Commons Bombing: Airey Neave, the British Conservative Party's spokesman on Northern Ireland, is killed when a bomb planted under his car explodes outside the House of Commons in London. The Irish National Liberation Army claims responsibility.

June 18 1979

U.S. Gen. Haig Escapes Death: NATO's Supreme Allied Commander for Europe, U.S. Gen. Alexander Haig, escapes assassination after a terrorist bomb explodes under a bridge that his motorcade has just crossed. Germany's Red Army Faction is suspected.

August 27, 1979

Earl Mountbatten Murdered: Earl Louis Mountbatten of Burma, a British admiral and great-grandson of Queen Victoria, is blown up by an Irish Republican Army bomb that destroys his fishing boat off the Irish coast. Two other remote-control bombs kill 18 British troops in Northern Ireland.

November 4, 1979

Iranian Hostage Crisis: After President Jimmy Carter agrees to admit the Shah of Iran into the U.S., Iranian radicals seize the U.S. embassy in Tehran, taking 66 American diplomats hostage.

Thirteen are soon released, but the others are held for 444 days. Their plane is allowed to take off from Tehran immediately after Ronald Reagan is sworn in as president on January 20, 1981.

November 20, 1979
Mecca's Grand Mosque Seized: Two hundred Islamic terrorists seize the Grand Mosque in Mecca, Saudi Arabia, taking hundreds of pilgrims hostage. Saudi and French security forces retake the shrine after an intense battle in which some 250 people are killed and 600 wounded.

March 24, 1980
Archbishop Killed in El Salvador: Catholic Archbishop Oscar Romero is killed by terrorists as he conducts mass at the cathedral in San Salvador, El Salvador.

August 1, 1980
Bologna Rail Station Blast: Rogue elements of Italy's intelligence services are suspected in the bombing of a Bologna train station, which kills 85 people and injures 300.

August 13, 1980
Rash of U.S. Hijackings to Cuba: An Air Florida flight from Key West to Miami is diverted to Cuba by seven Cuban hijackers. Six other U.S. airliners are hijacked to Cuba over the next month. No passengers are harmed.

April 30, 1980
Iran's London Embassy Drama: Six Iraqi-backed Iranians storm the Iranian Embassy in London, England taking 20 hostages. British Special Air Service (SAS) troops recapture the embassy six days later, killing five terrorists and freeing the hostages. Two hostages are killed and two more wounded by the terrorists.

October 26, 1980
Neo-Nazis Bomb Munich Festival: Neo-Nazis bomb a beer festival in Munich, Germany, leaving 13 dead and 72 injured.

December 17, 1980
Turkish Consul Killed in Australia: Turkish Consul-General to Australia, Sarik Ariyak, and a bodyguard are murdered in Sydney by the Justice Commandos of the Armenian Genocide.

March 3, 1980
Sweden's Premier Assassinated: Swedish Prime Minister Olof Palme is shot and killed leaving a Stockholm cinema by a lone gunman, who evades capture.

May 13, 1981
Pope John Paul II Wounded: A Turkish "Grey Wolves" gunman, trained by Middle East terrorist groups and linked to Soviet intelligence, seriously wounds Pope John Paul II in Vatican Square.

March 30, 1981
President Ronald Reagan Shot: John Hinckley, a 25-year-old drifter with a history of psychiatric problems, shoots President Ronald Reagan in the chest outside the Washington Hilton Hotel. Reagan is rushed to a hospital and quickly recovers. White House Press Secretary James Brady is severely wounded in the assassination attempt.

May 16, 1981
Kennedy Airport Bombing: A man is killed when a bomb planted by the Puerto Rican Armed Resistance goes off at New York's John F. Kennedy International Airport.

October 6, 1981
Egyptian President Sadat Assassinated: Soldiers, secretly members of the Takfir Wal-Hajira sect, gun down Egyptian President Anwar Sadat in a reviewing stand at a military parade.

December 4, 1981
Missionaries Murdered in El Salvador: Three American nuns and a lay missionary are found murdered outside San Salvador, El Salvador, victims of a extremist death squad.

December 17, 1981
U.S. Army General Kidnapped: U.S. Army Major General James L. Dozier and wife are kidnapped by the Italian Red Brigade in Verone, Italy. Dozier is deputy chief of staff of the allied land forces for Southern Europe. The couple is released 42 days later.

February 28, 1982
Wall Street Bombings: Four powerful bombs detonate in front of financial institutions in New York's Wall Street district. The FALN claims credit in a five-page communiqué. Another New York bombing follows in September.

July 20, 1982
IRA London Parks Bombings: Two Irish Republic Army bombs in London's Hyde and Regent's parks kill 11 British soldiers and injure 51 people.

September 14, 1982
Lebanon's President-Elect Assassinated: Lebanon's President-elect Bashir Gemayel is assassinated by a car bomb that explodes outside his party's Beirut headquarters.

December 31, 1982
New Year's Eve Bombings in New York: Puerto Rican FALN terrorists plant several bombs in New York City on New Year's Eve. Two explosions rock federal courthouses in lower Manhattan and Brooklyn. Another bomb, outside police headquarters, maims an officer. Two detectives are severely injured in a fourth explosion near the federal courthouse at Foley Square in lower Manhattan.

April 18, 1983
Bombing of U.S. Embassy in Beirut: A suicide bomber attacks the U.S. Embassy in Beirut, Lebanon, killing 63 people and injuring 120. The Islamic Jihad claims responsibility.

May 25, 1983
U.S. Navy Officer Killed in El Salvador: A U.S. Navy officer is

assassinated by the Farabundo Marti National Liberation Front in El Salvador.

October 9, 1983
North Korean Hit Squad in Burma: North Korean agents blow up a delegation from South Korea in Rangoon, Burma, killing 21 persons and injuring 48.

October 23, 1983
U.S. Marine Barracks Bombed in Beirut: Simultaneous suicide truck-bomb attacks are made on U.S. and French compounds in Beirut, Lebanon. A 12,000-pound bomb destroys the U.S. compound, killing 242 Marines, while a 400-pound device destroys the French base and kills 58 French troops. Islamic Jihad claims responsibility.

November 7, 1983
U.S. Senate Bombed: A bomb explodes near the Senate Republican Cloak Room on Capitol Hill in Washington, D.C. No one is injured. A group calling itself the Armed Resistance Unit claims responsibility, saying the bombing was a response to U.S. military action in Grenada. Three women later plead guilty to the attack and are sentenced to 5 to 20 years in prison.

November 15, 1983
U.S. Naval Officer Assassinated in Greece: A U.S. Navy officer is shot by the November 17 terrorist group in Athens, Greece, while his car is stopped at a traffic light.

December 17, 1983
London's Harrods Bombed: London's famed Harrods department store is rocked by an Irish Republican Army car bomb that kills two policemen and three civilians,

March 16, 1984
U.S. Envoy Kidnapped in Beirut: The Islamic Jihad kidnaps and later murders U.S. Embassy Political Officer William Buckley in Beirut, Lebanon. Buckley is the CIA's Beirut station chief. After

desperate efforts to rescue him fail, Buckley is assassinated following torture.

April 12, 1984
Bombing in Spain Kills U.S. Soldiers: Eighteen U.S. servicemen are killed and 83 others are wounded in a bomb attack on a restaurant near a U.S. Air Force Base in Torrejon, Spain. Hezbollah claims responsibility.

April 17, 1984
Libyan Embassy Drama in London: British security forces surround the Libyan People's Bureau in London after a police-woman is killed by small-arms fire coming from inside the embassy. After British citizens in Libya are threatened, the U.K. government grants the embassy staff unfettered diplomatic passage to Tripoli. No one is arrested for the murder.

June 5, 1984
India's Golden Temple Seized: Sikh terrorists occupy the Golden Temple in Amritsar, India. One hundred people die when Indian security forces retake the holy shrine.

October 12, 1984
Britain's Thatcher Escapes Death: British Prime Minister Margaret Thatcher and her cabinet escape assassination in an Irish Republican Army bomb attack on the Grand Hotel, Brighton, England, where the Conservative Party Congress is being held. Five people are killed and 30 injured in the attack, which destroys the front of the hotel.

October 31, 1984
Indira Gandhi of India Assassinated: Indian Prime Minister Indira Gandhi is gunned down by her own Sikh bodyguards in Delhi, India. Nearly 3,000 people die in the ensuing riots.

February 7, 1985
U.S. Officials in Mexico Kidnapped: Under the orders of narcotrafficker Rafael Cero Quintero, Drug Enforcement Ad-

ministration agent Enrique Camarena Salazar and his pilot are kidnapped, tortured, and executed.

March 16, 1985
U.S. Journalist Kidnapped in Beirut: American journalist Terry Anderson is kidnapped in Beirut, Lebanon, by Iranian-backed Islamic radicals. He is released in December 1991.

June 6, 1985
U.S. Academics Seized in Beirut: Thomas Sutherland, a professor at American University in Beirut, Lebanon, is kidnapped by Islamic terrorists. Later, in September 1986, another American University professor in Beirut, Joseph Cicippio, also is seized by Iranian-backed terrorists. Both men are released in late 1991.

June 14, 1985
TWA Hijacking Leaves U.S. Sailor Dead: A Trans World Airlines flight en route from Athens, Greece, to Rome, Italy, is hijacked by two Lebanese Hezbollah terrorists and force to fly to Beirut. Eight crew and 145 passengers are held for 17 days. An American passenger, U.S. Navy Diver Robert Stethem, is murdered, his body dumped on the tarmac of Beirut International Airport. Flying twice to Algiers, the aircraft returns to Beirut after Israel releases 435 Lebanese and Palestinian prisoners. Three of the Shiite gunmen are on the White House's October 10, 2001 "The List of Most Wanted Terrorists."

June 23, 1985
Air India Bombing: A suitcase bomb destroys Air India Flight 182 over the Atlantic, killing all 329 people aboard. Both Sikh and Kashmiri terrorists are blamed for the attack. Two cargo handlers, meanwhile, are killed at Tokyo airport in Japan, when another Sikh bomb explodes in an Air Canada aircraft bound for India.

September 30, 1985
Soviet Diplomats Kidnapped in Beirut: In Beirut, Lebanon, Sunni terrorists kidnapped four Soviet diplomats. One is killed, but three are later released.

October 7, 1985
Achille Lauro Hijacking: Four Palestinian Liberation Front (PLF) terrorists hijack the Italian cruise ship *Achille Lauro*, carrying more than 400 passengers and crew, in the Mediterranean. The hijackers demand Israel free 50 Palestinian prisoners. The terrorists kill a disabled American tourist, 69-year-old Leon Klinghoffer, and throw his body overboard with his wheelchair. The hijackers surrender after two days in exchange for a pledge of safe passage to Egypt, but when an Egyptian jet tries to fly the hijackers to freedom, U.S. Navy F-14 fighters intercept it and force it to land in Sicily. The terrorists are taken into custody.

November 13, 1985
Bogota's Palace of Justice Debacle: Leftist M-19 terrorists seize the Palace of Justice in Bogota, Colombia, taking a hundred hostages, including several judges. The terrorists and most of the hostages are killed when the Colombian Army storms the building.

December 27, 1985
Rome and Vienna Airports Attacked: Sixteen people are killed and more than 100 are wounded when Abu Nidal terrorists launch suicide assaults with guns and grenades on passenger terminals at airports in Rome, Italy, and Vienna, Austria.

March 30, 1986
TWA Aircraft Bombed in Greece: A Palestinian splinter group detonated a bomb as TWA Flight 840 approached Athens Airport, killing four U.S. citizens.

April 5, 1986
Berlin Disco Bombing and Raid on Libya: Two U.S. soldiers are killed and 79 U.S. servicemen are injured in a Libyan bomb attack on a nightclub in West Berlin, West Germany. In retaliation, U.S. military jets bomb targets in and around Tripoli and Benghazi. On April 17, the bodies of American librarian Peter Kilburn and two Britons are found near Beirut, Lebanon; the three are slain in apparent retaliation for the U.S. raid on Libya.

September 5, 1986
Pan Am Jet Seized in Pakistan: Arab terrorists seize a Pan American Airways jetliner in Pakistan, killing 17 hostages and wounding 127 others before Pakistani forces storm the plane.

September 14, 1986
Korean Airport Blast: North Korean agents detonate an explosive device at Seoul's Kimpo Airport, killing five persons and injuring 29.

November 17, 1986
France's Renault Chief Shot: The president of France's state-owned Renault automobile company, Georges Besse, is shot to death in Paris by the French Marxist-Leninist group, Action Directe.

January 10, 1987
British Envoy Disappears in Beirut: British church envoy Terry Waite disappears in Beirut, Lebanon while on a mission to secure the release of Western hostages held by Iranian-backed terrorists. Waite is freed in November 1991.

November 29, 1987
Korean Airliner Downed: North Korean agents plant a bomb aboard Korean Air Lines Flight 858, which originated in Abu Dhabi, United Arab Emirates and stopped over in Baghdad, Iraq on its way to Bangkok, Thailand. The plane disappears from radar over the sea near Burma (Myanmar); 115 passengers and crew are lost.

December 26, 1987
American Hangout in Spain Bombed: Catalan separatists bomb a Barcelona, Spain bar frequented by U.S. servicemen, killing an American citizen.

February 17, 1988
U.S. Peacekeeper Murdered in Lebanon: U.S. Marine Corps Lt. Col. William Higgins is kidnapped and murdered by the Iranian-backed Hezbollah group while serving with the United

Nations Truce Supervisory Organization (UNTSO) in southern Lebanon.

April 14, 1988
Naples USO Club Bombed: The Organization of Jihad Brigades detonates a car bomb outside a United Service Organization (USO) Club in Naples, Italy, killing an American sailor.

June 28, 1988
U.S. Diplomat in Athens Killed: The U.S. Embassy's Defense Attaché in Greece is killed when a car bomb explodes outside his Athens home.

December 21, 1988
Pan Am 103 Explodes over Scotland: Pan American Airlines Flight 103 is blown up over Lockerbie, Scotland. All 259 people on board are killed when a bomb explodes at a height of 30,000 feet, raining debris down on the Scottish town, where 11 residents also perish.

April 21, 1989
U.S. Army Officer Murdered in Manila: The Communist New People's Army assassinates Col. James Rowe in Manila, the Philippines. In September, the group kills two U.S. defense contractors.

November 30, 1989
German Banker Killed by Assassins: The Red Army assassinated Deutsche Bank Chairman Alfred Herrhausen in Frankfurt, Germany.

May 13, 1990
U.S. Soldiers Killed in the Philippines: The military wing of the Communist Party of the Philippines, the New People's Army, kills two U.S. Air Force personnel near Clark Air Force Base.

February 7, 1991
IRA Mortars Hit 10 Downing Street: The Irish Republican Army attacks British Prime Minister John Major's 10 Downing Street

residence, near Parliament in London, with homemade mortars launched from a van parked nearby. No one is injured; the terrorists escape.

May 21, 1991
Rajiv Gandhi Assassinated: Indian Congress Party leader and former Prime Minister Rajiv Gandhi are assassinated in a bomb blast while campaigning near Madras. He had been swept into office in a landslide in 1984 after his mother's assassination.

March 17, 1992
Israeli Embassy Blast in Argentina: Hezbollah claims responsibility for a blast that levels the Israeli Embassy in Buenos Aires, Argentina, killing 29 and wounding 242.

May 2, 1992
Islamic Jihad Attacks Eilat: A tourist is killed in an Islamic Jihad attack on the Israeli Red Sea resort of Eilat. Two terrorists are killed and one is captured.

January 31, 1993
U.S. Missionaries Abducted: The Revolutionary Armed Forces of Colombia snatch three U.S. missionaries in the eastern Panamanian village of Púcuro, near the Colombia border. In 2001, based on guerrilla testimony, the three men are declared dead after it's determined they were shot by their captors in 1996 as Colombian troops closed in.

December 6, 1992
India's Ayodhya Mosque Destroyed: Hindu radicals tear down an ancient Muslim mosque in the city of Ayodhya, setting off deadly riots between India's Hindu majority and Muslim minority.

February 26, 1993
World Trade Center Bombing: The World Trade Center in New York City is badly damaged when a car bomb planted by Islamic terrorists explodes in an underground garage. The bomb leaves six people dead and 1,000 injured. Followers of Umar Abd al-

Rahman, an Egyptian cleric preaching in the New York area, carry out the attack.

April 14, 1993
Iraqis Attempt to Kill President Bush: The Iraqi intelligence service attempt to assassinate former U.S. President George Bush during a visit to Kuwait. The U.S. launches a cruise-missile attack on the Iraqi capital Baghdad two months later in retaliation.

April 24, 1993
Bomb Rips London Financial District: An IRA truck bomb devastates the Bishopsgate area of London's financial district, killing one, injuring 44 and causing $1.5 billion in damage.

May 1, 1993
Sri Lanka's President Assassinated: Sri Lankan President Ranasingle Premadasa is blown up by a Tamil Tiger suicide bomber.

February 25, 1994
Hebron Massacre: Jewish extremist and U.S. citizen Baruch Goldstein machineguns Moslem worshippers at a mosque in West Bank town of Hebron, killing 29 and wounding about 150.

March 9-10, 1994
London's Heathrow Airport Attacked: In a period of 30 hours, the IRA launches a series of mortar attacks on London's Heathrow Airport, paralyzing British air traffic. No one is hurt.

April 6, 1994
Hamas Revenge Bombing: A member of Hamas carries out a suicide car-bombing at a bus stop in the northern Israeli town of Afula. Eight people are killed and more than 50 are wounded.
Rwandan President Killed: Rwanda's President Juvenel Habyarimana is killed when his aircraft shot down by a surface-to-air missile while approaching Kigali airport, Rwanda

April 13, 1994
Israeli Bus Station Blast: A suicide bomber attacks the central

bus station in Hadera, north of Tel Aviv, Israel, killings five and injuring thirty. Hamas takes credit for the attack.

June 14, 1994
Chechens Take 1,000 Hostages: Chechen rebels take 1,000 hostages at Budennovsk, Russia, and 150 are killed in a rescue attempt by the Russian Army. The Chechens are later allowed to escape in return for the freedom of the remaining hostages.

July 26, 1994
Israeli Embassy Explosion in London: A bomb detonates outside the Israeli Embassy in London, England, injuring 14. Twelve hours later, a second bomb explodes, injuring four at the offices of an Israeli charity in north London. Islamic terrorists are suspected.

September 23, 1994
U.S. Writer Held Hostage in Colombia: Revolutionary Armed Forces of Colombia rebels kidnap a Texas science writer working in Colombia, Thomas Hargrove, and hold him for 11 months until a $500,000 ransom is paid.

October 19, 1994
Tel Aviv Shopping District Blast: A Hamas suicide bomber sets off an explosion on a bus traveling through the heart of Tel Aviv's shopping district. The blast kills 22 people and wounds 42 others.

November 12, 1994
Suicide Bicyclist Attacks Gaza Checkpoint: A Hamas suicide bomber riding a bicycle detonates an explosion at an Israeli Army checkpoint near the Netzarim settlement in Gaza. Three Israeli soldiers are killed, 11 others are wounded.

December 24, 1994
Air France Hijackers Target Eiffel Tower: Four members of the Algerian terrorist group Armed Islamic Group, dressed as airport officials, seize Paris-bound Air France Flight 8969, carrying 227 passengers and crew, as the jumbo jet prepares to

depart Algiers. One passenger is killed immediately by the hijackers, who intend to crash the plane into the Eiffel Tower in the heart of Paris. After landing in Marseilles, France, for refueling. French commandos storm the plane, killing the four terrorists and safely rescuing the remaining passengers and crew.

March 8, 1995
Attack on U.S. Diplomats in Pakistan: Two unidentified gunmen kill two U.S. diplomats and wounded a third in Karachi, Pakistan.

March 20, 1995
Japanese Subway Nerve-Gas Attacks: Twelve persons are killed and 5,700 are injured in a Sarin nerve-gas attack at a crowded subway station in the center of Tokyo, Japan. A similar attack occurs nearly simultaneously in the Yokohama subway system. The Aum Shinrikyu cult is found to be behind the attacks, in which containers of gas were placed in subway stations and trains. Several cult members are later sentenced to death or life in prison.

April 9, 1995
American Tourist Killed in Israel: An Islamic Jihad suicide bomber drives his explosive-laden van into in a military convoy in Gaza, killing seven Israeli soldiers and an American tourist. Two hours later, a Hamas suicide bomber attacks an Israeli convoy near Netzarim, blowing up a police jeep but killing only himself. More than 50 people are wounded in the two attacks.

April 19, 1995
Oklahoma City Bombing: Extremists Timothy McVeigh and Terry Nichols destroy the Alfred P. Murrah Federal Building in Oklahoma City with a massive truck bomb that kills 166 and injures hundreds more. At the time, it's the largest terrorist attack ever on U.S. soil.

August 21, 1995
Jerusalem Bus Attack: A Hamas suicide bomber detonates a

bomb on a bus in Jerusalem's northern neighborhood of Ramat Eshkol, killing four people and injuring more than 100. Among the dead is an American teacher.

September 13, 1995
Attack on U.S. Embassy in Moscow: A rocket-propelled grenade is fired through the window of the U.S. Embassy in Moscow, ostensibly in retaliation for U.S. strikes on Serb positions in Bosnia.

November 2, 1995
Gaza Buses Rocked by Explosions: Two suicide bombers detonate explosions a minute apart near two buses in Gaza. Eleven Israelis are lightly wounded in the first attack, none in the second. The attacks are believed to come in retaliation for the October 26 assassination of Islamic Jihad leader Fathi Shakaki in Malta. Islamic Jihad claims responsibility for both attacks.

November 4, 1995
Israel's Prime Minister Assassinated: Prime Minister Yitzhak Rabin of Israel is assassinated by a lone gunman after speaking to a crowd of 50,000 gathered at Tel Aviv's King's Square for a Saturday night peace rally. The assassin, an Israeli law student, confesses to the killing.

November 13, 1995
Saudi Military Installation Attack: The Islamic Movement of Change planted a bomb in a Riyadh military compound that kills one U.S. citizen, several foreign national employees of the U.S. Government, and more than 40 others.

November 19, 1995
Egyptian Embassy Attack: A suicide bomber drove a vehicle into the Egyptian Embassy compound in Islamabad, Pakistan, killing at least 16 and injuring 60 persons. Three militant Islamic groups claim responsibility.

January 9, 1996
Chechens Seize 3,000 Civilians: Nine Chechen rebels seize 3,000 civilians in Kizlyar, Dagestan, to protest at the Russian occupation of their homeland. A Russian rescue effort turns into a bloody battle, with the security forces using artillery and attack helicopters. Hundreds of civilians are killed; most of the Chechens escape.

January 31, 1996
Bomb Injures 1,400 Sri Lankans: Sri Lanka's Tamil Tiger guerillas detonate a massive car bomb in the heart of Columbo's business district, killing eight persons and injuring 1,400. Security forces intercept other suicide bombers, preventing further carnage.

February 15, 1996
Athens Embassy Attack: Unidentified assailants fired a rocket at the U.S. embassy compound in Athens, causing minor damage to three diplomatic vehicles and some surrounding buildings. Circumstances of the attack suggested it is an operation carried out by the 17 November group.

February 16, 1996
IRA End Cease-Fire: The Irish Republican Army ends an 18-month cease-fire, exploding a massive bomb in London's Docklands district. Two people are killed and scores are injured.

February 26, 1996
Jerusalem Bus Attack: In Jerusalem, a suicide bomber blows up a bus, killing 26 persons and injuring 80; three Americans are killed and three injured.

March 4, 1996
Dizengoff Center Bombing: Hamas and the Palestine Islamic Jihad (PIJ) both claimed responsibility for a bombing outside of Tel Aviv's largest shopping mall that kills 20 persons and injures 75 others, including two U.S. citizens.

May 13, 1996
West Bank Attack: Arab gunmen opened fire on a bus and a group of Yeshiva students near the Bet El settlement, killing a dual U.S.-Israeli citizen and wounding three Israelis. No one claimed responsibility for the attack, but Hamas is suspected.

June 15, 1996
U.K. Shopping Center Bombing: An Irish Republican Army truck bomb detonates at a Manchester, England shopping center, wounding 206 persons.

June 25, 1996
Khobar Towers Bombing in Saudi Arabia: A fuel truck carrying a bomb exploded outside the U.S. military's Khobar Towers housing facility in Dhahran, Saudi Arabia, killing 19 U.S. military personnel and wounding 515 persons. Several Islamic groups claim responsibility.

July 20, 1996
Basque Airport Bombing: A bomb explodes at Tarragona International Airport in Reus, Spain, wounding 35 persons. The Basque Fatherland and Liberty (ETA) organization is suspected.

July 27, 1996
Atlanta's Olympic Park Bombing: A bomb detonates in Centennial Olympic Park in Atlanta, Georgia, where as many as 70,000 people are gathered to celebrate the Summer Olympics. A woman dies, and 110 people are wounded. In 1998, authorities charge Eric Robert Rudolph with the bombing, as well as two double bombings in the Atlanta area that injured 60.

August 1, 1996
Archbishop of Oran Killed: A bomb goes off at the home of the French Archbishop of Oran, Algeria, following a meeting with the French Foreign Minister. The blast kills the Archbishop and his chauffeur The Algerian Armed Islamic Group is suspected.

August 17, 1996
Missionaries Kidnapped in Sudan: Sudan People's Liberation

Army rebels kidnap six missionaries, including an American, in Mapourdit. The hostages are freed 11 days later.

October 1, 1996
Assassination of South Korean Consul: In Vladivostok, Russia, assassins kill a South Korean consul near his home. No one claims responsibility, but North Korean agents are suspected.

November 23, 1996
Hijacked Jet Runs Out of Fuel: An Ethiopian Airways jet is hijacked en route from Addis Adaba to Nairobi, Kenya, and diverted to Australia. It runs out of fuel and crashes into the Indian Ocean, killing 123 people, and 52 people survive, including two hijackers.

December 3, 1996
Paris Subway Explosion: A bomb explodes aboard a Paris subway train as it arrives at the Port Royal station, killing four and injuring 86. No one claims responsibility, but Algerian extremists are suspected.

December 17, 1996
Hundreds Held Hostage in Peru: The Tupac Amaru Revolutionary Movement takes several hundred people hostage at a party given at the Japanese Ambassador's residence in Lima, Peru. Among the hostages are several U.S. officials, foreign ambassadors and other diplomats, Peruvian officials and Japanese businessmen. The terrorists soon release most of the hostages but keep dozens of Peruvians and Japanese until April 22, 1997, when security forces retake the building.

February 23, 1997
Empire State Building Sniper: A Palestinian gunman opens fire on tourists on the observation deck of the Empire State Building in New York City, killing a Danish national and wounding several other people before turning the gun on himself.

July 12, 1997
Havana Hotel Explosions: Bombs rock the Hotel Nacional and

the Hotel Capri in Havana, Cuba, injuring three people. A previously unknown group calling itself the Military Liberation Union claims responsibility.

July 30, 1997
Jerusalem Market Blast: Two Palestinian militants blow themselves up and kill 16 shoppers at the Mahane Yehuda open-air market in Jerusalem. Hamas and Islamic Jihad claim credit. On September 4, three Islamic suicide bombers detonate explosives in Jerusalem's Ben Yehuda pedestrian mall, killing five shoppers and wounding 200.

November 12, 1997
U.S. Businessmen Killed in Pakistan: Two unidentified gunmen kill four U.S. auditors and their Pakistani driver as they left the Sheraton Hotel in Karachi, Pakistani. The Islami Inqilabi Council, or Islamic Revolutionary Council, claims responsibility.

November 17, 1997
Luxor Tourists Slaughtered in Egypt: Members of Egypt's largest militant group, Al-Gama'a al-Islamiyya (or Islamic Group), gun down 58 foreign tourists and four Egyptians and wound 26 others at the Hatshepsut Temple in the Valley of the Kings near Luxor.

January 29, 1998
First Fatal U.S. Clinic Bombing: In the first fatal abortion-clinic bombing in the U.S., an explosion kills a security guard and injures a nurse in Birmingham, Alabama.

August 1, 1998
IRA's Banbridge Bombing: A 500-pound car bomb planted by the Real IRA, a dissident Irish republican group, explodes in Banbridge, Northern Ireland, injuring 35 persons and damaging at least 200 homes.

August 7, 1998
U.S. Embassy Blasts in East Africa: A bomb goes off at the rear entrance of the U.S. embassy in Nairobi, Kenya, killing 291

people, including 12 Americans; more than 5,000 people are injured. Another bomb detonates outside the U.S. embassy in Dar es Salaam, Tanzania, killing 10 and wounding 77, including one U.S. citizen. Both embassy buildings are extensively damaged. The Clinton administration says Osama bin Laden is responsible.

August 15, 1998
IRA's Omagh Bombing: A 500-pound car bomb planted by the Real IRA in the central shopping district of Omagh, Northern Ireland, kills 29 and injures 330.

October 18, 1998
Colombian Pipeline Bombing: The Colombian National Liberation Army (ELN) sets off a bomb near the Ocensa pipeline in Antioquia Province, killing 71 persons and injuring 100 others. The pipeline is jointly owned by the Colombian national oil company, Ecopetrol, and a consortium of U.S., French, British and Canadian companies.

November 15, 1998
Colombians Take American Boy: Armed Colombian assailants follow a U.S. businessman home in Cundinamarca Province and kidnap his 11-year-old son. A $1 million ransom is demanded. The boy is freed two months later.

February 25, 1999
Americans Murdered in Colombia: Revolutionary Armed Forces of Colombia (FARC) abduct three U.S. citizens working for the Hawaii-based Pacific Cultural Conservancy International. On March 4, the bodies of the three victims are found in Venezuela, just north of the Colombian border. In April 2002, the U.S. government indicted FARC and six of its members in connection with the slayings.

March 1, 1999
Hutus Pounce on Tourists: Some 150 armed Hutu rebels attack three tourist camps in Uganda, killing four Ugandans and abducting more than a dozen tourists, including three U.S.

citizens. Two of the Americans and six other hostages are later killed.

August 31—September 13, 1999
Russia Hit by Bombing Wave: Hundreds of Russians are killed and many more are injured in four bombings just days apart. First, a powerful blast rips through a Moscow shopping center near the Kremlin, killing one person. Next, a car bomb detonates outside army officers' apartments in the southern republic of Dagestan, killing more than 60 people. Days later, a massive explosion destroys a nine-story apartment building in Moscow, taking the lives of at least 93 persons. Finally, around 150 residents die when a large bomb wrecks another Moscow apartment building. Islamic militants are suspected in the bombings.

December 14, 1999
LAX Millennium Bombing Foiled: An Algerian, Ahmed Ressam, is arrested while attempting to cross into Washington State from Canada with a car-full of explosives. He intends to bomb Los Angeles International Airport (LAX) on the eve of the 2000 millennium celebration. He later testifies that he received money and training at terrorist camps in Afghanistan run by Osama bin Laden.

December 24, 1999
India Airlines Hijacking: Five militants hijack an Indian Airlines plane, carrying 189 people en route to New Delhi, and force it to land in Kandahar, Afghanistan, where the hijackers demand freedom for a Pakistani cleric and several Kashmiri separatists held in Indian jails. The plane and passengers are released a week later.

May 1, 2000
U.N. Peacekeepers Killed in Sierra Leone: In Sierra Leone, the Revolutionary United Front (RUF), hoping to force out United Nations' peacekeepers, kill five U.N. soldiers and kidnap 500 others, most of whom are later released. The RUF also is

believed responsible for shooting down a U.N. helicopter, killing two foreign journalists, including an American.

June 8, 2000
U.K. Diplomat Ambushed in Greece: In Athens, Greece, two gunmen kill British Defense Attaché Stephen Saunders in an ambush. The Revolutionary Organization 17 November, a radical leftist group, claims responsibility.

August 9, 2000
Bomb Kills Moscow Pedestrians: A pedestrian underpass in Moscow, packed with commuters and shoppers, is rocked by a bomb that kills eight and injures 50 others.

September 16, 2000
Russian Apartment Building Blast: A truck explodes outside a nine-story apartment building in the southern Russian city of Volgodonsk, killing 17 people. Islamic militants are suspected.

September 21, 2000
Rocket Hits British Spy Headquarters: Dissident Irish republicans are suspected of using a Russian-built anti-tank weapon to launch a rocket attack on the headquarters of Britain's foreign intelligence service (MI6) in London. No one is injured.

October 7, 2000
Joseph's Tomb Ransacked: Crowds of Palestinians ransack a Jewish religious shrine in the West Bank known as Joseph's Tomb following the breakdown of the Israeli-Palestinian peace process. The attack caps a week of violence, marking the beginning of the latest Palestinian armed uprising, or *intifada.* Palestinians blame Ariel Sharon's September 28, 2000 visit to a disputed Jerusalem site, the Temple Mount or al-Haram al-Sharif, for the violence; Sharon is later elected Israeli Prime Minister in 2001.

October 1, 2000
Church Bombing in Tajikistan: Nine worshipers are killed and 70 injured when a bomb explodes at Sonmin Grace Church in

Dushanbe, Tajikistan. Local authorities arrest 12 church leaders as suspects, asking some of them to deny their faith in exchange for release. All are eventually let go, and three Islamic extremists are arrested for the bombing.

October 12, 2000

Attack on *USS Cole*: In the port of Aden, Yemen, a small dingy carrying explosives rams the destroyer *USS Cole*, killing 17 sailors and injuring 39. Supporters of Osama bin Laden are suspected.

Helicopter Hijacked in Ecuador: In Ecuador, a group of armed kidnappers, led by former members of the Colombian Popular Liberation Army (EPL), take 10 employees of the Spanish energy consortium REPSOL hostage. In January 2001, the kidnappers murder an American hostage, Ronald Sander. The remaining hostages are released February 23 after the oil companies pay a $13 million ransom.

November 2, 2000

Explosion Rocks Jerusalem Mall: Two Israelis are killed by a powerful car bomb at central Jerusalem's Mahane Yehuda market, a frequent target of terrorist attacks. On November 22, two more Israelis are killed and 55 wounded by a car bomb in northern town of Hadera. On December 28, an explosion on a bus near Tel Aviv wounds 13.

January 16, 2001

Mujahideen Storm Indian Airport: A six-man suicide squad of the militant Lashkar-e-Tayyba group attempt to seize India's Srinagar airport. All six terrorists are killed by security forces; two civilians and two security officers also are killed in the exchange of gunfire.

March 4, 2001

BBC Studios Bombed: Security officers are attempting a controlled explosion of a Real IRA car bomb when it explodes outside the British Broadcasting Corp.'s Television Centre in London. BBC staff had already been evacuated. Approximately 20 years before, on March 1, 1981, IRA icon Bobby Sands began a

66-day hunger strike that resulted in his death; nine other prisoners also died in the hunger strike.

March 9, 2001
Basque Separatist Bombing: Two policemen are killed by the explosion of a car bomb planted in Hernani, Spain by Basque separatists.

May 26, 2001
Hostages Taken in the Philippines: In Palawan, the Abu Sayaaf Group (ASG) kidnaps 20 persons, including three Americans, from a Philippine beach resort. A month later, ASG behead one of the Americans; several Filipinos also are murdered. U.S. missionary Martin Burnham and a Filipina nurse are killed during a rescue operation by Philippine troops on June 7, 2002; Burnham's wife Gracia is rescued.

June 1, 2001
Tel-Aviv Nightclub Bombing: A suicide bomb attack on a Tel Aviv disco leaves 21 people dead and more than 100 others injured. Islamic Jihad claims responsibility.

August 9, 2001
Jerusalem Restaurant Bombing: A suicide bomber shatters a busy Jerusalem pizza restaurant, killing 15 people and wounding 90. Hamas admits responsibility. Three days later, another suicide bomber attacks a restaurant near Haifa, Israel, killing himself and injuring 20.

September 11, 2001
World Trade Center and Pentagon Attacks: Two hijacked airliners slam into the Twin Towers of New York's World Trade Center. The Pentagon is struck by a third hijacked plane. A fourth hijacked aircraft, apparently bound for Washington, D.C. crashes into a field in Pennsylvania. Some 3,000 people are killed all told. Osama bin Laden's Al Qaeda network is held responsible, and the United States commences a war against terrorism. After forming the Global Coalition Against Terrorism, the U.S. launches air attacks and ground assaults against Al Qaeda

terrorist camps in Afghanistan; the terrorists are routed and the Taliban government is ousted from power.

October 5, 2001
First U.S. Anthrax Letter Fatality: A 63-year-old photo editor for a Florida publisher dies from inhalation anthrax; anthrax spores later are found in the building in which he worked. By the end of November, two Washington postal workers, a woman in New York and another in Connecticut also die of the rare disease. More than a dozen other cases of anthrax exposure are confirmed. Anthrax is discovered in letters sent to journalists in New York and members of Congress. No one claims responsibility.

October 17, 2001
Israeli Minister Assassinated: Israeli Tourism Minister Rechavam Zeevi is assassinated by gunmen affiliated with the Popular Front for the Liberation of Palestine.

December 1-2, 2001
Four Bombs Rock Israel: Two suicide bombers detonate nail-filled explosives near a crowded Zion Square shopping complex in Jerusalem, killing 11 Israelis and wounding 180. A car bomb, timed to explode as rescue workers arrive, rocks the area 10 minutes, but no injuries are reported. Twelve hours later, a fourth bomb rips through a bus in the Israeli port city of Haifa, killing 15 persons and injuring more than 100 others. Islamic Jihad claims responsibility for the attacks.

December 12, 2001
Israeli Bus Bombed: Palestinian militants detonate bombs underneath a bus in the West Bank and gun down the fleeing passengers, killing 10 Israelis and injuring 30. Hamas claims responsibility. Minutes after the bus attack, two Hamas suicide bombers hurl themselves against two cars outside an Israeli settlement in Gaza, killing themselves and injuring four others.

December 13, 2001
Indian Parliament Attacked: At least five gunmen storm the

Indian Parliament in New Delhi, killing seven people with grenades, AK-47 rifles and a human bomb. Security forces kill the attackers during a 90-minute gun battle.

December 22, 2001
Shoe Bomber Subdued: Flight attendants and passengers on American Airlines Flight 63, en route from Paris, France to Miami, Florida, subdue a British citizen with alleged ties to Al Qaeda after he attempts to ignite plastic explosives contained in his shoes. The diverted jetliner lands safely in Boston, Massachusetts, where the suspect is taken into custody.

January 17, 2002
Attack on Israeli Banquet: A Palestinian gunman opens fire on a banquet in Hadera in northern Israel, killing six persons and injuring 30 before police shot him. The Al Aqsa Brigades, a militia linked to Yasser Arafat's Fatah movement, claims responsibility.

January 25-27, 2002
First Palestinian Woman Bomber: A female suicide bomber touches off an explosion in Jerusalem's central shopping district, killing herself and an elderly man and wounding 113 others, including a survivor of the Sept. 11 World Trade Center collapse. Two days earlier, a Palestinian gunman raked the same area with gunfire, killing two and injuring 20 before being shot by police.

March 2-4, 2002
New Wave of Attacks in Israel: In three days, a Palestinian suicide bomber kills 10 Israelis in Jerusalem; a sniper guns down seven Israeli soldiers and three civilians at a West Bank checkpoint; another sniper kills an Israeli soldier near the Gaza Strip, and a Palestinian gunman opens fire in a Tel Aviv restaurant, killing three persons. More than 300 Israelis and 900 Palestinians have been killed since the latest Palestinian uprising began in September 2000.

March 3, 2002
Colombian Rebels Execute Senator: FARC, Colombia's largest
rebel group, is suspected in the execution-style slaying of three
persons, including a Senator and her chauffeur-bodyguard,
whose bodies are found along a road, 25 miles west of Bogota.

March 4, 2002
Spanish Stock Exchange Bomb: Police deactivate a 33-pound
bomb planted in the Bilboa Stock Exchange, 200 miles south of
Madrid, after receiving a telephone warning naming the Basque
separatist group ETA.

March 17, 2002
Pakistan Church Attack: Grenades explode in a packed Protes-
tant church in Islamabad, killing five worshippers - including an
American woman and her daughter - and wounding 45 others,
in an attack aimed at Pakistan's foreign community.

March 20, 2002
U.S. Embassy Bombing in Peru: Just three days before President
George Bush is scheduled to visit Peru, a car bomb explodes
outside the U.S. Embassy in Lima, killing at least nine persons
and injuring dozens in a late night attack. Shining Path rebels
are suspected.

March 26-April 1, 2002
Suicide Bombers Besiege Israel: In the course of a week, three
Israelis are injured in a car blast in Jerusalem; 28 persons
celebrating Passover at a hotel in the resort town of Netanya die
in an explosion; 30 diners are wounded in a bomb blast at a Tel
Aviv restaurant; 14 Jews and Arabs are killed in the bombing of
a Haifa restaurant, and a policewoman is injured by a suicide
bomber in Jerusalem.

April 11, 2002
Blast Hits Tunisian Synagogue: A natural gas-laden tanker truck
slams into a wall surrounding an ancient synagogue on the
Tunisian island of Djerba; the explosion kills 16 persons,
including 11 German nationals. Terrorism is suspected.

April 21, 2002
Philippine Town Bombings: Three explosions rock the southern Philippine city of General Santos, killing 14 and injuring 45. The Abu Sayyaf Group claims responsibility.

May 7, 2002
Pool Hall Blast in Israel: A pool hall popular with Israeli teenagers is bombed in Rishon Letzion, south of Tel Aviv killing 15 persons and injuring about 60 others.

May 8, 2002
Pakistan Bus Attack: Sixteen persons, including 11 French nationals, are killed and 20 more are injured when an explosives-packed car slams into a bus heading from the airport to a Karachi hotel. Muslim extremists are later arrested in conjunction with the attack.

May 9, 2002
Russian Parade Bombed: In a Russian town near Chechnya, a remote-controlled bomb shattered a Victory Day parade, killing more than 40 people and injuring 150 others. Officials blamed Islamic extremists.

June 5 and June 18-19, 2002
Israeli Buses Struck: An Islamic militant detonated a car bomb alongside a crowded bus in northern Israel, killing 16 passengers and wounding dozens. Less than two weeks later, a Palestinian suicide bomber aboard a rush-hour bus in Jerusalem kills 19 passengers and injures more than 50 others. A day later, seven Israelis die and 35 are injured in a suicide attack on an East Jerusalem bus stop. In the first six months of 2002, Palestinian suicide bombers kill more than 200 Israelis and wound hundreds more.

June 14, 2002
U.S. Consulate Targeted in Karachi: A suicide driver slams his explosives-filled vehicle into a concrete barrier in front of the U.S. Consulate in Karachi, setting off an explosion that kills 12

Pakistanis and injures 45. Muslim extremists are later arrested in the case.

July 16-17, 2002

Palestinian Ambush and Bombing: Palestinians disguised as Israeli soldiers stage an elaborate ambush, detonating a bomb to halt a West Bank bus and then fire on fleeing passengers; seven persons are killed and 14 wounded. A day later in Tel Aviv, dual suicide bombers blow themselves up seconds apart, leaving three Israelis dead and more than 40 wounded.

July 31, 2002

Hebrew University Blast: A lunchtime bomb explosion in a crowded Hebrew University cafeteria in Jerusalem kills seven persons, five of them Americans, and wounds more than 80 others. Hamas claims responsibility.

August 4, 2002

Israeli Bus Bomb: A Palestinian suicide bomber blows up a rush-hour bus in northern Israel, killing nine passengers and wounding 60 others. Hamas takes responsibility.

Spanish Car Bomb: A car bomb explodes in front of a military police barracks, killing two civilian bystanders and injuring 25 others, in the southern resort town of Santa Pola. Basque separatists with the ETA are suspected.

August 5, 2002

Gunmen Storm Pakistan School: Four gunmen burst into a Christian school in Muree, Pakistan trying to force their way into buildings where 150 Australian, European and American children of missionaries had taken refuge. Six people are killed, and three are injured. None of the students is hurt. It's the sixth attack on Western interests in Pakistan since the start of the year.

Pilgrims in Kashmir Ambushed: Suspected Islamic militants attack a group of Hindu pilgrims in Kashmir with grenades and automatic weapons, killing eight and wounding 27.

August 7, 2002
Colombian Inauguration Shelling: Mortar shells fired by suspected FARC rebels rock Colombia's president palace and parliament building in Bogota moments before the swearing in of President Alvaro Uribe. Nineteen people are killed, and dozens are wounded.

August 9, 2002
Grenades Hit Pakistan Hospital: In the third attack in a week on Christians in Pakistan, militants hurl grenades at churchgoers on the grounds of a Presbyterian hospital in Taxila, 25 miles northwest of Islamabad, killing three nurses and injuring two dozen others.

September 25, 2002
Indian Temple Siege: Two suspected Islamic militants storm a Hindu temple in Gandhinagar, India, killing 31 people and injuring many more before being shot dead by Indian troops.

October 2, 2002
Sniper Terrifies D.C. Suburbs: A three-week shooting spree begins in suburban Maryland and extends to Washington, D.C. and Virginia, leaving ten persons dead and four wounded. Police later apprehend two suspects.

October 12, 2002
Bali Nightclub Blast: A massive explosion destroys a jammed nightclub on the Indonesian resort island of Bali, killing nearly 200 people, many of them Australian and other foreign tourists. An arrested suspect tells police that the blast was intended to kill not Australians but Americans, and the U.S. links the plot to the Al Qaeda terrorist network.

October 23, 2002
Moscow Theater Takeover: Chechen rebels seize a crowded Moscow theater, taking some 800 people hostage and threatening to set off explosives unless their demands are met. About 120 hostages and 50 rebels die after Russian special forces use a

"sleeping gas" as they storm the building, ending the three-day siege.

October 28, 2002
U.S. Diplomat Killed in Jordan: USAID officer Laurence Foley is assassinated as he left his home in the Jordanian capital of Amman.

November 26, 2002
Attacks in Kenya and Israel: In synchronized attacks on Israeli tourists in Kenya, bombers strike a resort hotel in the coastal city of Mombassa, killing 12 persons, and minutes later two missiles narrowly miss an Israeli jetliner during takeoff from the local airport. In northern Israel, two gunmen fire on passengers at a bus terminal and voters at a nearby polling station, killing six and injuring dozens more.

December 27, 2002
Car Bombs Hit Chechen Capital: Two vehicles packed with 1.5 tons of TNT crash into the courtyard of the Russian government headquarters in the Chechen capital of Grozny, killing at least 61 persons and wounding more than 100 others.

December 30, 2002
American Missionaries Slain in Yemen: A suspected Islamic militant armed with a semiautomatic rifle opens fire on American missionaries operating a Southern Baptist hospital in the town of Jibla in southern Yemen, killing three and wounding another.

January 5, 2003
Bombers Strike Tel Aviv: Two suicide bombers blow themselves up just seconds apart in downtown Tel Aviv, killing 23 persons and injuring 100 more in the deadliest attack against Israel in 10 months.

Recommended Online Reading:

"International Terrorism: Terror Attack Database," The International Policy Institute for Counter-Terrorism, http://www.ict.org.il/

"Patterns of Global Terrorism: 2000-2001," Bureau of Public Affairs, U.S. Department of State, www.state.gov/s/ct/.

"Patterns of Global Terrorism: 1995-1999," Office of the Coordinator of Counterterrorism, U.S. Department of State, www.state.gov/www/global/terrorism/annual_reports.html.

"Recent Terrorism Events: Background and Context," Congressional Quarterly (CQ) Press, www.cqpress.com.

"Significant Terrorist Incidents, 1961-2001," Office of the Historian, Bureau of Public Affairs, U.S. Department of State, www.state.gov.

"Terrorism," Centre for Defence and International Security Studies, Lancaster University, United Kingdom, www.cdiss.org/terror.htm.

"Terrorism," Dudley Knox Library, Naval Postgraduate School, Monterey, California, http://web.nps.navy.mil/~library/terrorism.htm

Appendix C

Where to Get Help and Information

The following is a selection of sources for assistance and information relating to matters discussed in this book. The listings are grouped according to subject and are intended for reference purposes only. They should not be construed as an endorsement of a product or service, and they are not a guarantee of quality. Consumers are responsible for their own purchasing decisions and should exercise care. No liability shall attach to the author or publisher of this book. Note: In most cases, Web addresses have been abbreviated, leaving out the standard http:// prefix.

Air Ambulances, Medical Evacuations and Medical Escorts

U.S.-based International Services: Many of the U.S.-based services below accept collect calls from overseas and many of the toll-free telephone numbers work anywhere in North America and the Caribbean.

Advanced Air Ambulance, Miami, Fl; tel.800-633-3590, 305-232-7700 or 305-599-1100; fax 305-232-7734; www.flyambu.com.

Aero National, Inc., Washington, Penn., 800-245-9987 or 412-228-8000; www.aeronational.com

Air Ambulance America, Austin, Tex.; tel. 800-222-3564 or 512-479-8000; www.airambulance.com.

Air Ambulance Network, Tarpon Springs, Fl.; tel. 800-327-1966or 727-934-3999; fax 727-937-0276; www.airambulancenetwork.com.

Air Ambulance Professionals, Fort Lauderdale, Fl.; tel. 800-752-4195 or 954-491-0555; www.airambulanceprof.com.

AirEvac, Phoenix, Ariz.; tel. 800-421-6111 or 800-321-9522; www.airevac.com

Air Response, Inc., Denver, Col., Clearwater, Fl. and Scotia, N.Y.; tel. 800-631-6565 or 303-858-9967, fax 888-631-6565 or 303-858-9968; www.airresponse.net.

American Jet International, Houston, Tex.; tel. 888-435-9254 or 713-641-9700; www.iflyaji.com.

Care Flight International, Inc., Clearwater, Florida; tel. 800-282-6878 or 727-530-7972; www.careflight.com.

Critical Care Medflight, Lawrenceville, Ga.; tel. 800-426-6557 or 770-513-9148; fax: (770) 513-0249; www.criticalcaremedflight.com.

Global Care, Inc., Alpharetta, Ga.; tel. 800-860-1111; www.globalems.com.

International Association for Medical Assistance to Travellers, 417 Center Street, Lewiston, NY 14092, 716-754-4883 or 40 Regal Rd., Guelph Ontario, Canada N1K 1B5, 519-836-0102, www.iamat.org

International SOS Assistance, Philadelphia, Penn., 800-523-8930, 215-244 1500 or 215-245 4707; www.internationalsos.com.

Med Escort International, Inc., Allentown, Penn.; tel. 800-255-7182 or 610-791-3111; fax 610-791-9189; www.medescort.com.

Medex Assistance Corp., Timonium, Md.; tel. 888-MEDEX-00, 800-537-2029 or 410-453-6300; fax 410-453-6301; www.medexassist.com.

Medjet International, Inc., Birmingham, Al.; tel. 800-356-2161 or 205-592-4460; www.medjet.com.

Medway Air Ambulance, Lawrenceville, Ga.; tel. 800-233-0655 or 770-934-2080; www.medwayair.com.

Mercy Medical Airlift (a charitable organization), Manassas, Va.; tel. 800-296-1217 or 703-361-1191; www.patienttravel.org.

National Air Ambulance, Ft. Lauderdale, Fl.; tel.800-327-3710 or 305-525-5538; www.nationaljets.com.

Travel Care International, Inc., Eagle River, Wis.; tel. 800-524-7633 or 715-479-8881; www.travel-care.com.

Worldwide Assistance Services, Inc. (a unit of Paris-based Europ Assistance), Washington, DC, 800-777-8710 or 703-204-1897, www.worldwideassistance.com

Foreign-based International Services:

Austria: Austrian Air Ambulance, Vienna; tel. 43-1-40-144; fax 43-1-40 155' www.oafa.com. Tyrol Air Ambulance, Innsbruck' tel. 43-512-22-422; www.taa.at.

Canada: SkyService, Toronto/Montreal; tel. 800-463-3482; 514-497-7000; www.skyservice.com.
China: Medex Assistance Corp. (U.S.-based), Beijing; tel. 86-10-6465-1264; fax 86-10-6465-1269; www.medexassist.com.
Finland: Euro-Flite Ltd., Helsinki/Vantaa' tel. 358-9-870-2544; fax 358-9-870-2507; www.jetflite.fi.
France: Medic'Air, Paris; tel. 33-1-41-72-1414; http://medicair.starnet.fr/.
Germany: German Air Rescue (DRF), Filderstadt; tel. 49-711-70-10-70; www.drf.de.
Singapore: International SOS Pte Ltd., Singapore; tel. (65) 338 2311 or (65) 338 7800; www.internationalsos.com.
South Africa: Medex Assistance Corp. (U.S.-based), Capetown; tel. 021-726-351; fax 021-751-478; www.medexassist.com.
Thailand: Siam Land Flying Co. Ltd., Bangkok, tel. 011-662-535-6784; fax 011-662-535-4355; www.executivewings.com.
United Kingdom: International SOS Assistance (UK) Ltd., London, England; tel. 44 (0)20 8762 8000 or 44 (0)20 8762 8008; www.internationalsos.com. Medex Assistance Corp. (U.S.-based), Brighton, England; tel. 44-1273-22-3002; fax 44-1273-22-3003; www.medexassist.com.

Airline Links and Phone Numbers

Federal Aviation Administration, www.faa.gov/airlineinfo.htm

Airport Links—U.S. and Foreign

Federal Aviation Administration, www.faa.gov/airportinfo.htm

Air Travel—Consumer Complaints, Protection and Reports

Aviation Consumer Protection Division, U.S. Department of Transportation, Room 4107, C-75, Washington, DC 20590,

202-366-2220 (TTY 202-366-0511), www.dot.gov/airconsumer/
index.htm
Federal Aviation Administration, 800 Independence Avenue
SW, Washington, DC 20591, 800-255-1111, www.faa.gov
Office of Aviation Enforcement and Proceedings, U.S. Depart-
ment of Transportation, 400 Seventh Street, SW, Room 4107,
Washington,   DC   20590,   www.dot.gov/airconsumer/
index1.htm

Air Travel—Flight Delays

Air Traffic Control System Command Center, Federal Aviation
Administration, www.fly.faa.gov

Air Travel Safety and Security

Aviation Safety Alliance, 1301 Pennsylvania Ave. NW, Suite
1100,   Washington,   DC   20004,   202-626-4104,
www.aviationsafetyalliance.org
Federal Aviation Administration, 800 Independence Avenue
SW, Washington, DC 20591, Consumer Safety and Security
Complaints, 800-255-1111, www.faa.gov
Federal Aviation Administration, Flight Standards Service, International Aviation Safety Assessment Program (IASA),
www.faa.gov/apa/iasa.htm
Federal Aviation Administration, Office of Civil Aviation Security, Criminal Acts Against Civil Aviation, http://cas.faa.gov/
crimacts/iacs.html
National Transportation Safety Board, 490 L'Enfant Plaza, SW,
Washington, D.C., 20594, 202-314-6000, www.ntsb.gov/avia-
tion/aviation.htm

Air Travel Safety—Foreign Airlines

Aviation Safety Assessment Program, Federal Aviation Administration, 800-322-7873, 800-255-1111, www.faa.gov/apa/iasa.htm

Air Travel Security and Baggage Guidelines

Federal Aviation Administration, Information Hotline (normal business hours), 800-322-7873, www.faa.gov
Transportation Security Administration, 400 Seventh St. SW, Washington, DC 20590, 866-289-9673, www.tsa.gov

Air Travel Statistics

U.S. Department of Transportation, Bureau of Transportation Statistics, www.bts.gov

Air Travel Warnings—U.S. and Abroad

U.S. Department of Transportation, Travel Advisory Line, 800-221-0673
U.S. Department of State, Travel Hotline, 202-647-5225

Air Travel—Weather Information

National Oceanic and Atmospheric Administration, National Weather Service, www.nws.noaa.gov

Arson

Bureau of Alcohol, Tobacco and Firearms, Arson & Explosives
    Division, 800 K St. NW, Room 680, Washington, DC 20001,
    800-461-8841 or 202-927-7930, www.atf.treas.gov
U.S. Fire Administration, 16825 S. Seton Ave., Emmitsburg, MD
    21727, 301-447-1000, Fax: 301-447-1052, www.usfa.fema.gov

Bank Deposit Insurance Check

Federal Deposit Insurance Corp., 550 17th Street NW, Washing-
    ton, DC 20429, 877-275-3342 or 202-942-3147, www2.fdic.gov/
    edie/

Bank Fraud

Federal Deposit Insurance Corp., 550 17th Street, NW, Washing-
    ton, DC 20429-9990, 800-759-6596 or 877-275-3342,
    www.fdic.gov
Federal Reserve Board, 20th St. and Constitution Ave., NW,
    Washington, DC 20551, 202-452-3000,
    www.federalreserve.gov

Bioterrorism and Chemical Warfare

American College of Emergency Physicians, 1125 Executive
    Circle, Irving, TX 75038-2522, 800-798-1822, www.acep.org
American Council on Science & Health, 1995 Broadway, Second
    Floor, New York, NY 10023-5860, 212-362-7044, www.acsh.org
Center for Nonproliferation Studies, Monterey Institute of
    International Studies, 460 Pierce Street, Monterey, CA 93940,
    831-647-4154, http://cns.miis.edu
Centers for Disease Control and Prevention, Emergency Re-
    sponse Hotline (24 hours): 770-488-7100, 1600 Clifton Rd.,

Atlanta, GA 30333, General Information: 800-311-3435, 888-246-2675 or 404-639-0385, www.bt.cdc.gov

Federal Emergency Management Agency, 500 C St. SW, Washington, DC 20472, 202-566-1600, www.fema.gov

Federation of American Scientists, 1717 K St. NW, Suite 209, Washington, DC 20036, 202-546-3300, www.fas.org

Food and Drug Administration, 5600 Fishers Lane, Rockville, Maryland 20857, 888-463-6332, www.fda.gov

Food Contamination Hotline, U.S. Department of Agriculture, 800-535-4555, www.usda.gov

Israeli Defense Forces, Home Front Command, www.idf.il/english/organization/homefront/index.stm

John Hopkins University, Center for Civilian Biodefense Strategies, 410-223-1667, www.hopkins-biodefense.org

MedlinePlus, U.S. National Library of Medicine, http:// www.nlm.nih.gov/medlineplus/biologicalandchemical weapons.html

Oak Ridge National Laboratory, P.O. Box 2008, Oak Ridge, TN 37831, 865-574-4160, http://emc.ornl.gov/emc/PublicationsMenu.html

Public Health Foundation, 1220 L Street NW, Suite 350, Washington, DC 20005, 202-898-5600, www.phf.org

State Public Health Agencies Directory and Hotlines, www.statepublichealth.org

U.S. Environmental Protection Agency, Environmental Emergency Hotline: 800-424-8802, 1200 Pennsylvania Avenue, NW, Washington, DC, 20460, 215-814-5000, www.epa.gov

Virtual Naval Hospital™, U.S. Navy Bureau of Medicine and Surgery and The University of Iowa, www.vnh.org

Bombs

Bureau of Alcohol, Tobacco and Firearms, Arson & Explosives Division, 800 K St. NW, Room 680, Washington, DC 20001, 800-461-8841 or 202-927-7930, www.atf.treas.gov

Federal Bureau of Investigation, J. Edgar Hoover Building, 935 Pennsylvania Avenue, NW, Washington, D.C. 20535-0001, 202-324-3000 , www.fbi.gov

British Terrorism-Related Websites

Defense Ministry, www.operations.mod.uk
Emergency Newsroom, www.ukonline.gov.uk
Foreign & Commonwealth Office, www.fco.gov.uk
Foreign Travel Advisories, www.fco.gov.uk/travel
News Coordination Center, www.ukresilience.info
Prime Minister's Office, www.pm.gov.uk
Scotland Yard, Metropolitan Police, www.met.police.uk

Building Security

Bureau of Alcohol, Tobacco and Firearms, Arson & Explosives
    Division, 800 K St. NW, Room 680, Washington, DC 20001,
    800-461-8841 or 202-927-7930, www.atf.treas.gov
Royal Canadian Mounted Police, Technical Security Branch,
    613-991-9497, www.rcmp-grc.gc.ca/tsb/

Cell Phones—International

Cellhire USA LLC , 45 Broadway, 20th Floor, New York, NY
    10006, 866 CH ONLINE, Fax: 212 376 7383, www.cellhire.com
InTouch USA, 800-872-7626, Int'l: 1-703-222-7161, Fax: 1-703-222-
    9597, www.intouchusa.com
Japan Cell Phone Rentals, JCR Corporation, P.O. Box 15915,
    Honolulu, HI 96830, 800.611.7374, 808-924-5339, 808-922-8655,
    www.jcrcorp.com
Planetfone, 101 Convention Center Drive, Suite 700, Las Vegas,
    Nevada   89109,   888-988-4777,   Fax: 888-388-4800,
    www.planetfone.com
Rent Cell, 2625 Piedmont Road, Suite 56-170, Atlanta, GA 30324,
    800-404-3093,   404-467-4508,   Fax: 810-454-1990,
    www.rentcell.com
TravelCell, 877-235-5746, www.travelcell.com

Travelers Telecom, 17141 Ventura Blvd Suite 204, Encino, CA
    91316,   800-736-8123,   818-325-2820,   Fax   818-325-2828,
    www.travtel.com
VoiceStream, 800-937-8997, 505 998 3793, Fax: 800 998 3666,
    www.voicestream.com

CEO Security Services

Awareness of National Security Issues and Response, Federal
    Bureau of Investigation, email: ansir@leo.gov
CEO COM Link, Business Roundtable/Office of Homeland
    Security, 202-872-1260, www.brtable.org
Interfor, Inc., Corporate Security, World Headquarters, 575
    Madison Avenue, Suite 1006, New York, NY 10022, 212-605-
    0375, www.interforinc.com

Charity Information and Verification

American Institute of Philanthropy, 4905 Del Ray Avenue, Suite
    300,   Bethesda,   MD   20814,   301-913-5200,
    www.charitywatch.org
BBB Wise Giving Alliance, 4200 Wilson Boulevard, Suite 800,
    Arlington, VA 22203, 703-276-0100, www.give.org
Philanthropic Advisory Service, Council of Better Business
    Bureaus, 4200 Wilson Boulevard, Suite 800, Arlington, VA
    22203-1838, 703-276-0100, www.bbb.org

Check Theft/Fraud

CrossCheck, 707-586-0551, www.cross-check.com
Equifax Check Systems, 800-437-5120, www.equifax.com
International Check Services, 800-526-5380, www.intlcheck.com
National Check Fraud Service, 843-571-2143, www.ckfraud.org
National Processing Company, 800-255-1157, www.npc.net

SCAN (Shared Check Authorization Network), 800-262-7771, www.scanassist.com

TeleCheck, 800 710-9898 or 800 927-0188, www.telecheck.com

U.S. Postal Inspection Service, 800-ASK-USPS, www.usps.com/postalinspectors/welcome.htm

Coping with Terrorism—Adults and Children

American Academy of Child and Adolescent Psychiatry, 3615 Wisconsin Ave., NW, Washington, D.C. 20016-3007, 202-966-7300, www.aacap.org

American Medical Association, 515 N. State Street, Chicago, IL 60610, 312-464-5000, www.ama-assn.org

American Psychiatric Association, 1400 K Street NW, Washington, DC 20005, 888-357-7924, www.psych.org

National Center for PTSD (Post-Traumatic Stress Disorder), 802-296-6300, www.ncptsd.org

National Institute of Mental Health, 6001 Executive Boulevard, Rm. 8184, MSC 9663, Bethesda, MD 20892-9663, 301-443-4513, www.nimh.nih.gov

U.S. Department of Transportation, Aviation Consumer Protection Division, Room 4107, C-75, Washington, DC 20590, 24-hour complaint line: 202-366-2220 (TTY 202-366-0511), or go to www.dot.gov/airconsumer/

U.S. Veterans Administration, Mental Health and Behavioral Sciences Services, 810 Vermont Avenue, N.W., Room 915, Washington, DC 20410, 800-827-1000, www.va.gov

Credit Card Fraud, Loss or Theft

Equifax, P.O. Box 740241, Atlanta, GA 30374, 800-525-6285 www.equifax.com

Federal Trade Commission, Consumer Response Center, 600 Pennsylvania Avenue, NW, Washington, DC 20580, 877-382-4357, www.ftc.gov

MasterCard, 800-MC-ASSIST or 636-722-7111 (international collect calls accepted), www.mastercard.com

TransUnion, Fraud Victim Assistance Division, P.O. Box 6790, Fullerton, CA 92634, 800) 680-7289, 800-680-7289, www.tuc.com

U.S. Postal Inspection Service, 800-ASK-USPS, www.usps.com/postalinspectors/welcome.htm

Visa Card, 800-847-2911 or 410-581-9994 (international collect calls accepted), http://usa.visa.com

Credit Cards (Pre-approved)—Opt Out

Main Opt-Out Number: 888-5OPTOUT (or 888-567-8688).
Equifax, 800-525-6285, www.equifax.com
Experian, 888-397-3742; www.experian.com
TransUnion, 800-680-7289, www.transunion.com

Credit Reports

Equifax, P.O. Box 740241, Atlanta, GA 30374, 800-685-1111, www.equifax.com

Experian, P.O. Box 949, Allen TX 75013-0949, 888-397-3742, www.experian.com

TransUnion, 760 Sproul Road, P.O. Box 390, Springfield, PA 19064-0390, (800) 916-8800, www.tuc.com

Crisis Assistance—Families of U.S. Citizens Overseas

U.S. Department of State, Office of American Citizens Services and Crisis Management, 202-647-5225, or U.S. Department of State Operations Center Task Force, 202-647-0900, http://travel.state.gov/crisismg.html

Cyberterrorism and Computer/Internet/Information Security

CERT® (Computer Emergency Response Team) Coordination Center, Software Engineering Institute, Carnegie Mellon University, Pittsburgh, PA 15213-3890, 412-268-7090 (24-hour hotline), www.cert.org

Computer Incident Advisory Capability, U.S. Department of Energy, 925-422-8193, www.ciac.org/ciac/

Computer Security Resource Center, National Institute of Standards and Technology, 100 Bureau Drive, Mail Stop 8930, Gaithersburg, MD 20899-8930, 301-975-2934 or 301-975-6478, http://csrc.nist.gov/index.html

Forum of Incident Response and Security Teams, First.Org, Inc., PMB 349, 650 Castro Street, Suite 120, Mountain View, CA 94041, www.first.org

National Infrastructure Protection Center, J. Edgar Hoover Building, 935 Pennsylvania Avenue, NW, Washington, D.C. 20535-0001, 202-323-3205, www.nipc.gov

National Institute of Standards and Technology, Vulnerability and Threat Portal, 100 Bureau Drive, Stop 3460, Gaithersburg, MD 20899-3460, 301-975-NIST/6478, http://icat.nist.gov/vt_portal.cfm

New York State Office for Technology, Information Security Department, State Capitol, Empire State Plaza, P.O. Box 2062, Albany, NY 12220, 518-474-0865 or 518-473-2658, www.oft.state.ny.us/security/security.htm

Overseas Security Advisory Council, Cyber Threat Analysis and News, www.ds-osac.org/edb/cyber/default.cfm

Symantec Corp. (Norton products), 20330 Stevens Creek Blvd., Cupertino, CA 95014, 408-517-8000, www.symantec.com (free online computer security check and virus scan for home users)

U.S. Department of Justice, Computer Crime and Intellectual Property Section, Criminal Division, 10th & Constitution Ave., NW, John C. Keeney Building, Suite 600, Washington, DC 20530, 202- 514-1026, www.cybercrime.gov

Deaths Abroad—U.S. Citizens

U.S. Department of State, Office of American Citizens Services and Crisis Management, 202-647-5225, http://travel.state.gov/crisismg.html

Disaster Relief

American Red Cross, 430 17th Street, NW, Washington, DC 20006, 877-272-7337, www.redcross.org
Federal Emergency Management Agency, 500 C Street SW, Washington, D.C. 20472, 800-462-9029, www.fema.gov

Elderly and Disabled Assistance

AARP (formerly the American Association of Retired Persons), 601 E St., NW, Washington, DC 20049, 800-424-3410, www.aarp.org
American Red Cross, 430 17th Street, NW, Washington, DC 20006, 877 272 7337, www.redcross.org
Federal Emergency Management Agency, 500 C Street SW, Washington, D.C. 20472, 800-462-9029, www.fema.gov
Transportation Security Administration, 400 Seventh Street SW, Washington, DC 20590, 866-289-9673, www.tsa.gov
U.S. Architectural and Transportation Barriers Compliance Board (a.k.a. Access Board), Suite 1000, 1331 F Street NW, Washington, D.C. 20004-1111, 800-872-2253 or 202-272-0080 (TTY 800-993-2822 or 202-272-0082), www.access-board.gov.
U.S. Fire Administration, Federal Emergency Management Agency, www.usfa.fema.gov

Fire Safety

Chicago Fire Department, Public Education Section, 1010 South Clinton St., Chicago, Illinois 60607, 312-747-6691/92, www.ci.chi.il.us/Fire/

Hotel-Motel Fire Safety Database, U.S. Fire Administration, Federal Emergency Management Agency, www.usfa.fema.gov/hotel/search.cfm

Los Angeles Fire Department, 200 North Main Street Los Angeles, California 90012, 213-485-5971, www.lafd.org

New York City Fire Department, Office of Fire Safety Education, 718-999-2343/44, www.nyc.gov/html/fdny/html/safety/fire-safety.html

U.S. Fire Administration, 16825 S. Seton Ave., Emmitsburg, MD 21727, 301-447-1000, www.usfa.fema.gov

First Aid

American Association of Poison Control Centers, Poisoning Emergencies: 800-222-1222, 3201, New Mexico Avenue, Suite 310, Washington, DC 20016, General Information: 202-362-7217, www.aapcc.org

American College of Emergency Physicians, 1125 Executive Circle, Irving, TX 75038-2522, 800.798.1822, www.acep.org

American Red Cross, 430 17th Street, NW, Washington, DC 20006, 877 272 7337, www.redcross.org/pubs/

Virtual Naval Hospital™, U.S. Navy Bureau of Medicine and Surgery and The University of Iowa, First Aid Manual for Soldiers, U.S Department of the Army Manual, www.vnh.org/FirstAidForSoldiers/fm2111.html

Food Contamination and Safety

Food and Drug Administration, Center for Food Safety and Applied Nutrition, Emergency Hotline: 301-443-1240, 200 C Street SW, Washington, DC 20204, Genera Information: 800-532-4440, www.fda.gov

FoodSafety.gov (U.S. government gateway to food safety information), www.foodsafety.gov.

U.S. Department of Agriculture, Food Safety and Inspection Service, Washington, D.C. 20250, www.fsis.usda.gov

U.S. Department of Agriculture/Food and Drug Administration, Foodborne Illness Education Information Center; Meat and Poultry Hotline 800-535-4555, www.fsis.usda.gov

Identity Protection Services

Credit Manager (Credit Expert), P.O. Box 310, Blue Ridge Summit, PA 17214, 800-787-6864, www.creditexpert.com

Equifax Credit Watch, P.O. Box 740241, Atlanta, GA 30374, 800-685-1111, www.equifax.com

Identity Guard, P.O. Box 222455, Chantilly, VA 20153-2455, 800-214-4791, www.identityguard.com

Identity Theft

Federal Trade Commission, Identity Theft Clearinghouse, 600 Pennsylvania Avenue, NW, Washington, DC 20580, 877-438-4338 or 877-FTC-HELP, www.consumer.gov/idtheft/victim.htm

Identity Theft Resource Center, P.O. Box 26833, San Diego CA 92196, 858-693-7935, www.idtheftcenter.org

National Association of Attorneys General, 750 First Street, NE, Suite 1100, Washington, DC 20002, 202-326-6000, Fax: 202-408-7014, www.naag.org

Project Money $mart, Federal Reserve Bank of Chicago, 230 South LaSalle Street, Chicago, Illinois 60604-1413, 312-322-5322, www.chicagofed.org

Social Security Administration, SSA Fraud Hotline, P.O. Box 17768, Baltimore MD 21235, 800-269-0271 or 800-772-1213, www.ssa.gov

U.S. Government Identity Theft Website, Federal Trade Commission, www.consumer.gov/idtheft/index.html

U.S. Postal Inspection Service, 800-ASK-USPS, www.usps.com/postalinspectors/welcome.htm

Information Technology Training

Computer Security Institute, 415-947-6320, www.gocsi.com
Information Systems Security Association, Inc., 800-370-4772 or
    414-768-8000, www.issa-intl.org
International Information Systems Security Certification Con-
    sortium, Inc., www.isc2.org
MIS Training Institute, 508-879-7999, www.misti.com
SANS Institute, 866-570-9927 or 540-372-7066, www.sans.org
TruSecure, International Computer Security Association, 888-
    627-2281 or 703-480-8200, www.icsa.net

Insurance—Identity Theft

Travelers, New York; tel. 888-695-4635; www.travelerspc.com/
    personal/equote/theft/.

Insurance—Kidnap/Ransom/Extortion

Aon (Canada), Toronto; tel. 416-868-5500; www.aon.ca.
Chubb Group of Insurance Companies, Warren, New Jersey;
    908-903-2000; www.chubb.com/businesses/dfi/kidnap.html.
Kemper Insurance Companies, Kemper Financial Insurance
    Solutions, New York, N.Y.; toll-free 1-877-KEMPER-6 or 646-
    710-7000; www.fis.kemperinsurance.com/kidnap.asp.

Insurance—Travel

Access America, Inc., Richmond, VA, 800-284-8300,
    www.accessamerica.com
ASA, Inc., International Health Insurance, Phoenix, AZ, 888-
    ASA-8288, www.asaincor.com
AXA Assistance, Bethesda, MD, 301-214-8200, www.axa-assis-
    tance-usa.com

Clements International, Washington, DC, 800-872-0067 or 202-872-0060, www.clements.com

Global Alert!, Van Nuys, CA, 800-423-3632, www.globalalerttravel.com

Health Care Global, Wallach & Co. Middleburg, VA, 800-237-6615, 540-687-3166 or 540-281-9500, www.wallach.com

Highway To Health, Fairfax, VA, 888-243-2358, http://highwayto-health.com

International Medical Group, Indianapolis, IN, 800-628-4664 or 317-655-4500, www.imglobal.com

MEDEX International, Timonium, MD, 800-732-5309, www.medexassist.com

MultiNational Underwriters, Inc., Indianapolis, IN, 800-605-2282, www.mnui.com

Petersen International Underwriters, Inc., Valencia, CA, 800-345-8816, www.piu.org

Travelex, Omaha, NE, 800-228-9792, www.travelex-insurance.com

Travel Guard, Noel Group, Stevens Point, WI, 800-826-1300, www.noelgroup.com

Travel Insurance Services, Walnut Creek, CA, 800-937-1387 or 925-932-1387, www.travelinsure.com

Unicard Travel Association, Overland Park, KS, 800-501-0352, www.unicard.com

Internet/Telemarketing Fraud

Equifax Fraud Alert, P.O. Box 740241, Atlanta, GA 30374, 888-766-0008, www.equifax.com

Federal Trade Commission, 600 Pennsylvania Avenue, NW, Washington, DC 20580, 877-FTC-HELP, www.ftc.gov

Internet Fraud Complaint Center (a partnership between the Federal Bureau of Investigation and the National White Collar Crime Center), www1.ifccfbi.gov

National Fraud Information Center, P.O. Box 65868, Washington, DC 20035, 800-876-7060, www.fraud.org

Junk Mail—Opt Out

Direct Marketing Association, Mail Preference Service, Box 643, Carmel, NY 10512, www.the-dma.org

Mail Fraud and Theft

U.S. Postal Inspection Service, 800-ASK-USPS, www.usps.com/postalinspectors/welcome.htm

Mail Handling

Centers for Disease Control and Prevention, Emergency Response Hotline (24 hours): 770-488-7100, 1600 Clifton Rd., Atlanta, GA 30333, General Information: 800-311-3435, 888-246-2675 or 404-639-0385, www.cdc.gov
Public Health Foundation, 1220 L Street NW, Suite 350, Washington, DC 20005, 202-898-5600, www.phf.org
U.S. Postal Service, Mail Security, 800-ASK-USPS, www.usps.com

News

U.S.-based news services and newspapers
ABC News, www.abcnews.go.com
Associated Press, http://wire.ap.org
CBS News, www.cbsnews.com
CNN, www.cnn.com
Fox News, www.foxnews.com
Los Angeles Times, www.latimes.com
NBC News, www.msnbc.com
New York Times, www.nytimes.com
Voice of America, www.voa.gov
Wall Street Journal, www.wsj.com

Washington Post, www.washingtonpost.com

Foreign.-based news services and newspapers
Agence France-Presse, www.afp.com
British Broadcasting, www.bbc.co.uk
Financial Times, www.ft.com
Reuters, www.reuters.com
Russia's Pravda, http://english.pravda.ru/

Directories of online newspapers:
Kidon Media Link, www.kidon.com/media-link/usa.shtml
Newslink, http://newslink.org
Directories of radio and TV stations:
    Kidon Media Link, www.kidon.com/media-link/usa.shtml
NewsDirectory.com, www.newsdirectory.com
    Newslink, http://newslink.org
    Radio-Locator, www.radio-locator.com
Online translator of foreign-language news and websites:
    AltaVista's Babelfish, http://world.altavista.com

Nuclear Hazards/Accidents/Weapons and Radiation

American Council on Science & Health, 1995 Broadway, Second
    Floor, New York, NY 10023-5860, 212-362-7044, www.acsh.org
Center for Nonproliferation Studies, Monterey Institute of
    International Studies, 460 Pierce Street, Monterey, CA 93940,
    831-647-4154, http://cns.miis.edu
Federal Emergency Management Agency, 500 C Street SW,
    Washington, D.C. 20472, 800-462-9029, www.fema.gov/haz-
    ards/nuclear/
Federation of American Scientists, 1717 K St. NW, Suite 209,
    Washington, DC 20036, 202-546-3300, www.fas.org
Radiation Emergency Assistance Center, Oak Ridge Institute for
    Science and Education, P.O. Box 117, MS 39, Oak Ridge, TN
    37831-0117, 865 576 3131, www.orau.gov/reacts/intro.htm
U.S. Nuclear Regulatory Commission (including potassium
    iodide information), Washington, D.C. 20555, 800-368-5642 or
    301-415-8200, www.nrc.gov/what-we-do/radiation.html

Report Terrorist/Suspicious/Criminal Activity

Federal Bureau of Investigation, J. Edgar Hoover Building, 935 Pennsylvania Ave. NW, Washington, D.C. 20535-0001, 202-324-3000, www.fbi.gov (local FBI office locator at www.fbi.gov/contact/fo/fo.htm)

National Infrastructure Protection Center, NIPC Watch and Warning Unit, 202-323-3205 or 888-585-9078, J. Edgar Hoover Building, 935 Pennsylvania Ave. NW, Washington, D.C. 20535-0001, nipc.watch@fbi.gov or www.nipc.gov/incident/cirr.htm

Royal Canadian Mounted Police (phone number and department locator), www.rcmp-grc.gc.ca

U.S. Nuclear Regulatory Commission, Nuclear Incident Hotline: 301-816-5100, Washington, D.C. 20555, 800-368-5642 or 301-415-8200, www.nrc.gov

Sexual Assault Prevention

National Crime Prevention Council, 1000 Connecticut Avenue, NW, 13th Floor, Washington, DC 20036, 202-466-6272, www.ncpc.org

U.S. State Department, Bureau of Diplomatic Security, http://ds.state.gov

Smoke Hoods

Air Security International, 713-430-7300, www.airsecurity.com

Brookdale International Systems, 800-459-3822, 604-324-3822, www.evac-u8.com, www.smokehood.com

Social Security Fraud

Social Security Administration, SSA Fraud Hotline, P.O. Box 17768, Baltimore MD 21235, 800-269-0271 or 800-772-1213, www.ssa.gov

Telemarketing—Opt Out

Direct Marketing Association, Telephone Preference Service, Box 643, Carmel, NY 10512, www.the-dma.org

Terrorism Background Information

Brookings Institution, 1775 Massachusetts Ave. NW, Washington DC 20036, 202-797-6000, www.brook.edu

Cato Institute, 1000 Massachusetts Avenue, NW, Washington D.C. 20001-5403, 202-842-0200, www.cato.org

Center for Strategic and International Studies, Homeland Defense, 1800 K Street, NW, Suite 400, Washington, DC 20006, 202-887-0200, www.csis.org/burke/hd/index.htm

Centre for Defence and International Security Studies, Department of Politics and International Relations, Cartmel College, Lancaster University, Lancaster, LA1 4YL, United Kingdom, + 44 (0)1524 594 261, www.cdiss.org/terror.htm

Council on Foreign Relations, The Harold Pratt House, 58 East 68th Street, New York, NY 10021, 212-434-9400, www.cfr.org

Dudley Knox Library, Naval Postgraduate School, 411 Dyer Rd., Monterey, CA 93943, http://web.nps.navy.mil/~library/terrorism.htm

Heritage Foundation, 214 Massachusetts Ave. NE, Washington D.C. 20002-4999, 202-546-4400, www.heritage.org

Hoover Institution, Stanford University, Stanford, CA 94305-6010, 877-466-8374 or 650-723-1754, www-hoover.stanford.edu

International Policy Institute for Counter-Terrorism, Interdisciplinary Center Herzlia, P.O. Box 167, Herzlia, 46150, Israel, Fax: 972-9-9513073, http://www.ict.org.il/

RAND, 1700 Main Street, P.O. Box 2138, Santa Monica, CA 90407-2138, 310-393-0411, www.rand.org

U.S. Central Intelligence Agency, Washington, D.C. 20505, 703-482-0623, www.odci.gov/terrorism/

U.S. Defense Department, The Pentagon, Washington, DC 20301, www.dod.gov
U.S. State Department, 2201 C Street NW, Washington, DC 20520, 202-647-4000, www.state.gov

Terrorism Warnings (Online)

Australian Department of Foreign Affairs and Trade, www.dfat.gov.au
Australian Embassy, Washington, D.C., www.austemb.org
Australian Federal Government, www.fed.gov.au
Australian Prime Minister's Office, www.pm.gov.au
British Foreign & Commonwealth Office, www.fco.gov.uk
British Home Office, www.homeoffice.gov.uk
British Prime Minister's Office, www.pm.gov.uk
Canadian Government Homepage, http://canada.gc.ca
Centers for Disease Control and Prevention, www.cdc.gov
Royal Canadian Mounted Police, www.rcmp-grc.gc.ca
Scotland Yard (London Metropolitan Police), www.met.police.uk
U.K. Resilience (U.K. government antiterrorism clearinghouse), www.ukresilience.info
U.S. Central Intelligence Agency, www.cia.gov
U.S. Defense Department, www.defenselink.mil or www.dod.gov
U.S. Federal Bureau of Investigation, www.fbi.gov
U.S. FirstGov (U.S. government information gateway), www.firstgov.gov
U.S. Office of Homeland Security, www.whitehouse.gov/home-land/
U.S. State Department, www.state.gov

Travel Emergencies

Canadian Department of Foreign Affairs, Canadian citizens overseas can call collect 613-996-8885; for calls originating in

Canada or the U.S. use 800-267-6788 or 613-944-6788, www.voyage.gc.ca

International Association for Medical Assistance to Travellers, 417 Center Street, Lewiston, NY 14092, 716-754-4883 or 40 Regal Rd., Guelph Ontario, Canada N1K 1B5, 519-836-0102, www.iamat.org

U.S. Department of State, U.S. Citizens and Families Helplines (including cases of arrest abroad): 888-407-4747, 202-647-5225, 317-472-2328 or 202-647-4000, www.state.gov

Travel Warnings

British Foreign & Commonwealth Office, Foreign Travel Advisories, 020-7008-0232/0233, www.fco.gov.uk/travel

Canadian Department of Foreign Affairs, Foreign Travel Advisories, www.voyage.gc.ca or www.voyage.gc.ca/destinations/menu_e.htm

Federal Aviation Administration, 800-221-0673, www.faa.gov

U.S. Department of State, Travel Hotline, 202-647-5225, www.state.gov

Travelers' Health

American Society of Tropical Medicine and Hygiene, 60 Revere Drive, Suite 500, Northbrook, IL 60062, 847-480-9592, www.astmh.org

Centers for Disease Control and Prevention, Travelers' Health Information, 1600 Clifton Rd., Atlanta, GA 30333, 877-FYI-TRIP, www.cdc.gov/travel

International Association for Medical Assistance to Travellers, 417 Center Street, Lewiston, NY 14092, 716-754-4883 or 40 Regal Rd., Guelph Ontario, Canada N1K 1B5, 519-836-0102, www.iamat.org

International Society of Travel Medicine, P.O. Box 871089, Stone Mountain, GA, 30087-0028, 770-736-7060, www.istm.org

Public Health Resources: State Health Departments, Centers for Disease Control and Prevention, www.cdc.gov/mmwr/international/relres.html.

Travel Health Online, www.tripprep.com

U.S. Border Crossings Wait Times

U.S. Customs Service, Travel Information, www.customs.gov

U.S. Customs Regulations

U.S. Customs Service, Traveler Information, www.customs.gov

U.S. Embassies and Consulates

Directories of U.S. Embassies and Consulates worldwide, http://travel.state.gov/links.html or http://usembassy.state.gov

Afghanistan, Bebe Mahro (Airport) Road, Kabul. Note: Embassy services to U.S. citizens in Afghanistan are severely limited. The U.S. Embassy in Islamabad, Pakistan is providing most consular services to American citizens until further notice.

Albania: Tirana, Rruga Elbasanit 103; tel. (355)(42) 32875 or (355)(42) 47285; fax (355)(42) 74957; www.usemb-tirana.rpo.at.

Algeria: Algiers, 4 Chemin Cheikh Bachir El-Ibrahimi, B.P. 549 (Alger-gare) 16000; tel. [213] (21) 691-425/255/186; fax [213] (21) 69-39-79.

Andorra: Madrid, Serrano 75; tel. (34)(91) 587-2200; fax (34)(91) 587-2303; www.embusa.es. U.S. Consulate, Barcelona, Paseo Reina Elisenda 23-25; tel. (34)(93) 280-2227; fax (34)(93) 205-5206; www.embusa.es/ircbarna/ircbarcen.html.

Angola: Luanda, Rua Houari Boumedienne #32, C.P. 6468; tel. (244)(2) 445-481, 447-028, 446-224, 445-727; fax (244)(2) 446-924; http://usembassy.state.gov/angola/.

Anguilla: Contact U.S. Embassy in Barbados.

Antigua and Barbuda: Contact U.S. Embassy in Barbados, or U.S. Consular Agent in Antigua, Bluff House, Pigeon Point, English Harbour; tel. (268) 463-6531; fax (268) 460-1569.

Argentina: Buenos Aires, Avenida Colombia 4300; tel. (54)(11) 5777-4533 or (54)(11) 4514-1830; fax (54)(11) 5777-4240; http://usembassy.state.gov/posts/ar1/wwwh0100.html.

Armenia: Yerevan, 18 General Bagramian St.; tel. 011 (3741) 151-551; fax 011 (3741) 151-550; www.arminco.com/embusa/.

Aruba: Contact U.S. Consulate in Curaçao.

Australia: Canberra, Moonah Place, Yarralumla ACT 2600; tel. (02) 6214-5970 or (61)(2) 6214-5600, fax (61)(2) 6273-3191; www.usis-australia.gov. U.S. Consulates: Sydney, Level 59, MLC Centre, 19-29 Martin Place; tel. (61)(2) 9373-9200; fax (61)(2) 9373-9184; www.usis-australia.gov/sydney/. Melbourne, 553 St. Kilda Rd.; tel. (61)(3) 9526-5900; fax (61)(3) 9525-0769; http://usembassy-australia.state.gov/melbourne/. Perth: Level 13, 16 St. Georges Terrace; tel. (61)(8) 9231-9400; fax (61)(8) 9231-9444; http://usembassy-australia.state.gov/perth/.

Austria: Vienna, Boltzmanngasse 16, Ninth District; tel. (43)(1) 31339; fax 512 58 35; http://www.usembassy-vienna.at/. Consular Agency, Salzburg: Alter Markt 1; tel. (43)(662) 84-8776.

Azerbaijan: Baku, Prospect Azadlig 83; tel. (9-9412) 98-03-35, 36, or 37; (9-9412) 90-66-71; www.usembassybaku.org.

Bahamas: Nassau, 42 Queen St.; tel. (242) 322-1181; after hours (242) 328-2206; fax (242) 356-7174; http://usembassy.state.gov/nassau.

Bahrain: Manama, Bldg. 979, Road No. 3119, Zinj District (next to Al Ahli Sports Club); tel. 973-273-300; fax 973-256-242; hotline 973-255-048; www.usembassy.com.bh.

Bangladesh: Dhaka, Diplomatic Enclave, Madani Avenue, Baridhara; tel. (880-2) 882-3805, (880-2) 882-4700 ext. 2610, or (880-2) 882-4700; fax (880-2) 882-4449; www.usembassy-dhaka.org.

Barbados: Bridgetown, American Life Insurance Co. (ALICO) Building, Cheapside; tel. (246) 431-0225; fax (246) 431-0179; http://usembassy.state.gov/posts/bb1/wwwhmain.html.

Belarus: Minsk, 46 Starovilenskaya Ulitsa; tel. (375) 172-10-12-83 or 234-77-61; fax (375) 172-76-88-62; www.usis.minsk.by.

Belgium: Brussels, 27 Boulevard du Regent; tel. (011-32) 2-508-2111 from U.S., or 02-508-2111 in Belgium; fax 02-511-2725; www.usembassy.be.

Belize: Belize City, Gabourel Lane and Hutson St.; tel. 011 (501) 2-77161/62/63.

Benin: Cotonou, Rue Caporal Anani Bernard; tel. (229) 30-06-50, 30-05-13, or 30-17-92; fax (229) 30-14-39 or 30-19-74; http://usembassy.state.gov/benin/.

Bermuda: Devonshire, Crown Hill, 16 Middle Rd.; tel. 1-441-295-1342, after hours 1-441-235-3828. http://usembassy.state.gov/posts/bb1/wwwhmain.html.

Bhutan: Contact U.S. Embassy in New Delhi, India.

Bolivia: La Paz, 2780 Avenida Arce; tel. (591) 2-433-812; after hours (591) 2-430-251; fax (591) 2-433-854; www.megalink.com/usemblapaz/.

Bosnia and Herzegovina: Sarajevo, Alipasina 43; tel. (387)(33) 445-700; after hours (387)(33) 445-700; fax (387)(33) 659-722; www.usis.com.ba.

Botswana: Gaborone, Embassy Drive, Government Enclave; tel. (267) 353-982; after hours (267) 357-111; fax (267) 356-947; http://usembassy.state.gov/botswana/.

Brazil: Brasilia, Avenida das Nacoes, Lote 3; tel. 011-55-61-321-7272, after hours 011-55-61-321-8230; www.embaixada-americana.org.br. Consulates: Recife, Rua Goncalves Maia 163; tel. 011-55-81-3421-2441, after hours 011-55-3421-2641. Rio de Janeiro: Avenida Presidente Wilson 147; tel. 011-55-21-2292-7117, after hours 011-55-21-2220-0489; www.consulado-americano-rio.org.br. Sao Paulo, Rua Padre Joao Manoel 933; tel. 011-55-11-3081-6511, after hours 011-55-113064-6355; www.consuladoamericanosp.org.br.

Britain: See United Kingdom.

British Virgin Islands: Contact U.S. Embassy in Barbados.

British West Indies: Look under island name for information.

Brunei: Bandar Seri Begawan, 3rd floor, Teck Guan Plaza, Jalan Sultan PSC 470 (BSB); tel. (673)(2)229-670; after hours (673)(8) 730-691; fax (673)(2)225-293; http://amembbsb@brunet.bn.

Bulgaria: Sofia, 1 Saborna St. (formerly 1 a. Stamboliyski boulevard); tel. (359)(2) 937-5100; fax (359)(2) 981-8977. U.S.

Consolates: Sofia, Kapitan Andreev St.; tel. (359)(2) 963-2022; fax (359)(2) 963-2859; http://www.usembassy.bg.

Burkina Faso: Contact the U.S. Consular in Ouagadougou, Avenue John F. Kennedy; tel. (226) 30-67-23/24/25; fax (226) 31-23-68.

Burma (Myanmar): Rangoon, 581 Merchant Street; tel. (95-1) 282055 and (95-1) 282182; fax (95-1) 256018.

Burundi: Bujumbura Avenue des Etats-Unis; tel. (257) 223-454; fax (257) 222-926.

Cambodia: Phnom Penh, no. 16, Street 228 (between streets 51 and 63); tel. (855-23) 216-436 or 218-931; after hours (855-23) 216-805; fax (855-23)-216-437.

Cameroon: Yaounde, Rue Nachtigal; tel. (237) 23-40-14; fax (237) 23-07-53. Douala, (237) 42-53-31; fax (237) 42-77-90.

Canada: Ottawa, Ontario, 490 Sussex Drive; tel. (613) 238-5335; fax (613) 688-3082; www.usembassycanada.gov. Calgary, Alberta, Suite 1050, 615 Macleod Trail SE; tel. (403) 266-8962; after hours (403) 228-8900; fax (403) 264-6630. Consulates: Alberta, Manitoba, Saskatchewan and the Northwest Territories, excluding Nunavut. Halifax, Nova Scotia, Suite 910, Cogswell Tower, Scotia Square; tel. (902) 429-2480; after hours (902) 429-2485; fax (902) 423-6861. Consulars: New Brunswick, Newfoundland, Nova Scotia, Prince Edward Island and the islands of Saint Pierre and Miquelon. Montreal, Quebec, 1155 St. Alexander St.; tel. (514) 398-9695; after hours (514) 981-5059; fax (514) 398-0702. Consulars: Southwestern Quebec with the exception of the six counties served by the U.S. Embassy in Ottawa. Quebec City, Quebec, 2 Place Terrace Duffer in; tel. (418) 692-2095; after hours (418) 692-2096; fax (418) 692-4640. Consular: Abita-West, Abita-East, St. Maurice, Trois-Rivieres, Nicolet, Wolfe, Frontenac, all other counties to the north or east within the province of Quebec, and Nunavut, Toronto, Ontario, 360 University Avenue; tel. (416) 595-1700; after hours (416) 201-4100; fax (416) 595-5466. Consulars: Ontario except the six counties served by the U.S. Embassy in Ottawa. Vancouver, British Columbia, 1095 West Pender St.; tel. (604) 685-4311; fax (604) 685-7175.

Cape Verde: Praia, Rua Baillie M. Macedo 81; tel. (238) 61-56-16 or 17; fax (238) 61-13-55, and to obtain updated information on travel and security in Cape Verde.

Cayman Islands. Contact U.S. Embassy in Jamaica, or the Consular Agency in George Town, Grand Cayman, at Adventure Travel, Seven-Mile Beach; tel. (345) 946-1611; fax (345) 945-1811.

Central African Republic: Bangui, Avenue David Dacko; tel. (236) 61-02-00; after hours (236) 61-34-56 or 61-69-14; fax (236) 61-44-94.

Chad: N'Djamena, Avenue Felix Ebque; tel. (235) 51-62-11, 51-70-09, 51-77-59, 51-90-52, 51-92-18 and 51-92-33; fax (235) 51-56-54.

Chile: Santiago, Avenida Andres Bello 2800; tel. (56-2) 335-6550 or 232-2600; after hours (56-2) 330-3321; fax (56-2) 330-3005; www.usembassy.cl.

China: Beijing, 2 Xiu Shui Dong Jie; tel. (86-10) 6532-3431, 6532-3831; after hours (86-10) 6532-1910; fax (86-10) 6532-4153, 6532-3178; www.usembassy-china.org.cn. Chengdu, No. 4, Lingshiguan Road, Section 4; tel. (86-28) 558-3992, 555-3119; fax (86-28) 558-3520; after hours (86-0) 13708001422. Guangzhou, No. 1 South Shamian Street; tel. (86-20) 8188-8911 ext. 255 or (86-20) 8186-2418; after hours (86-0) 13902203169; fax (86-20) 8186-2341. Shanghai, 1469 Huaihai Zhonglu; tel. (86-21) 6433-6880; after hours (86-21) 6433-3936; fax (86-21) 6433-4122, 6471-1148. Shenyang, No. 52, 14th Wei Road; tel. (86-24) 2322-1198, 2322-0368; after hours (86-0) 13704019790; fax (86-24) 2322-2374.

Colombia: Bogota, Avenida El Dorado and Carrera 50; tel. (011-57-1) 315-0811; after hours 315-2109/2110; fax (011-57-1) 315-2196/2197; http://usembassy.state.gov/bogota. Consulates: Barranquilla, Calle 77B, No. 57-141, Piso 5, Centro Empresarial Las Americas; tel. (011-57-5) 353-2001; fax (011-57-5) 353-5216; conagent@metrotel.net.co.

Comoros: Port Louis, Mauritius, Rogers house, fourth floor, John F. Kennedy Street, Port Louis, Mauritius; tel. (230) 202-4400 and 208-2347; fax (230) 202-4401 and 208-9534; www.usembassymauritius.mu. Or contact the liaison representative in Moroni, Quartier Oasis, POB 720; tel. (269) 73-00-11; fax (269) 73-00-12.

Republic of Congo: Kinshasa, 310 Avenue des Aviateurs; tel. 243-88-43608.

Costa Rica: Pavas, San Jose; tel. (506) 220-3050; after hours (506) 220-3127; http://usembassy.or.cr.

Cote d'Ivoire: Abidjan, 5 Rue Jesse Owens; tel. (225) 20-21-09-79; fax (225) 20-22-45-23.

Croatia: Zagreb, Andrije Hebranga 2; tel. (385)(1) 455-5500; after hours (385)(1) 455-5281 or (385)(91)455-2384; www.usembassy.hr.

Cuba: Havana, Calzada between L and M Streets, Vedado; tel. (537) 33-3551 through 33-3559; after hours 33-3026 or 66-2302.

Curaçao: Willemstad, J.B. Gorsiraweg #1; tel. 011-599-9-461-3066; fax 011-599-9-461-6489; after hours 011-599-9-560-6870; cgcuracao@interneeds.net.

Cyprus: Nicosia, Metochiou and Ploutarchou St.; tel. (357)(2) 776-400; www.americanembassy.org.cy.

Czech Republic: Prague, Trziste 15; tel. (420) (2) 5753-0663; after hours (420) (2) 5753-2716; www.usembassy.cz.

Democratic Republic of the Congo (formerly Zaire): Kinshasa, 310 Avenue des Aviateurs; tel. 243-88-43608 or 243-88-43608, extension 2164/2376 or 243-88-46859 or 44609; fax 243-88-00228, 43467 or 03276.

Denmark, Greenland and the (Faroe) Islands: Copenhagen, Dag Hammarskjolds Alle 24; tel. (45) 35-55-31-44; after (45) 35-55-92-70; fax (45) 35-43-02-23; www.usembassy.dk.

Djibouti: Djibouti City, Plateau du Serpent, Boulevard Marechal Joffre; tel. (253) 35-39-95; after hours (253) 35-13-43; fax (253) 35-39-40; http://usembassy.state.gov/posts/dj1/wwwhindex.html.

Dominica: Bridgetown, American Life Insurance (ALICO) building, Cheapside; tel. 1-246-431-0225; fax 1-246-431-0179; http://usembassy.state.gov/posts/bb1/wwwhcons.html.

Dominican Republic: Santo Domingo, Calle Cesar Nicolas Penson and Calle Leopoldo Navarro; tel. (809) 221-2171; after hours (809) 221-8100. Consulars: Puerto Plata, Calle Beller 51, 2nd floor, office 6; tel. (809) 586-4204.

East Timor: Contact U.S. Embassy in Indonesia.

Ecuador (Galapagos Islands): Quito, Avenida 12 de Octubre and Avenida Patria; tel. (011-593-2) 256-2890, extension 4510; after hours 256-1749; fax (011-593-2) 256-1524; www.usembassy.org.ec. Consulars: Guayaquil, 9 de Octubre and Garcia Moreno; tel. (011-593-4) 232-3570; after hours 232-1152; fax (011-593-4) 232-0904.

Egypt: Garden City, Cairo, 5 Latin America St.; tel. (20)(2) 795-7371; fax (20)(2) 797-2472; www.usembassy.egnet.net.

El Salvador: San Salvador, Final Boulevard Santa Elena; tel. 011-503-278-4444; www.usinfo.org.sv.

England: See United Kingdom.

Equatorial Guinea: Yaounde, Cameroon, Rue Nachtigal; tel. 237-23-40-14; fax 237-23-07-53. Douala; tel. 237-42-53-31; fax 237-42-77-90.

Eritrea: Asmara, Franklin Roosevelt Street; tel. (291-1)12-00-04; fax (291-1)12-75-84.

Estonia: Tallinn, Kentmanni 20; tel. (372) 668-8100; after hours from U.S. (011)(372)509-2129 or 0-509-2129 from Estonia; fax (372) 668-8267; www.usemb.ee.

Ethiopia: Addis Ababa, Entoto Avenue; tel. [251] (1) 550-666, extension 316/336; after hours [251] (1) 552-558; fax [251] (1) 551-094; www.telecom.net.et/~usemb-et.

Fiji: Suva, 31 Loftus St.; tel. (679) 314-466; fax (679) 302-267.

Finland: Helsinki, Itainen Puistotie 14B; tel. 358-9-171931; after hours 358-9-605414; fax 358-9-652057; www.usembassy.fi.

France: Paris, 2, rue St. Florentin; tel. 011/33/1-43 12 22 22 or 01-43 12 22 22; fax 01-42 61 61 40; www.amb-usa.fr. Marseilles, 12, Blvd Paul Peytal; tel. 011/33/4-91 54 92 00; fax 011/33/4-91 55 09 47. Strasbourg,15 Avenue d'Alsace; tel. 011/33/3-88 35 31 04; fax 011/33/3-88 24 06 95.

French Guiana: Contact the U.S. Embassy in Suriname.

French Polynesia (Tahiti): Contact the U.S. Embassy in Fiji.

French West Indies: Contact the U.S. Embassy in Barbados.

Gabon: Libreville, Boulevard de la Mer; tel. (241) 76-20-03/4 or 74-34-92.

The Gambia: Fajara, Kairaba Avenue; tel. (220) 392856, 392858 or 391971; fax (220) 392475

Georgia: Tbilisi, 25 Atoneli St.; tel. (995)(32)98-99-67 or (995)(32)98-99-68, fax (995)(32)93-37-59; www.georgia.net.ge/ usembassy.

Germany: Berlin, Neustaedtische Kirchstrasse 4-5; tel. (49)(30) 238-5174 or 8305-0. Consulates: Clayallee 170; tel. (49)(30) 832-9233; fax (49)(30) 8305-1215. Düsseldorf, Willi-Becker-Allee 10; tel. (49)(211)788-8927; fax (49)(211)788-8938. Frankfurt, Siesmayerstrasse 21; tel. (49)(69) 75350; fax (49)(69) 7535-2304. Hamburg, Alsterufer 27/28; tel. (49)(40) 4117-1351; fax (49)(40) 44-30-04. Leipzig, Wilhelm-Seyfferth-Strasse 4; tel. (49)(341) 213-8418; fax (49)(341) 21384-17 (emergency services only). Munich, Koeniginstrasse 5; tel. (49)(89) 2888-0; fax (49)(89) 280-9998. Bremen, Bremen World Trade Center, Birkenstrasse 15; tel. (49)(421) 301-5860; fax (49)(421)301-5861.

Ghana: Acca, Ring Road East; tel. (233-21) 775-347 or 48; fax (233-21) 775-747; www.usembassy.state.gov/ghana/.

Greece: Athens, 91 Vasilissis Sophias Boulevard; tel. (30)(1) 721-2951. Consulate: Thessaloniki, Plateia Commercial Center, 43 Tsimiski Street, 7th floor; tel. (30)(31) 242-905; http:// www.usisathens.gr.

Greenland: See the U.S. Embassy in Denmark.

Grenada: Lance aux Epines, "Green Building;" tel. 1-473-444-1173/4/5/6; fax 1-473-444-4820; www.spiceisle.com.

Guadeloupe: See the U.S. Embassy in Barbados.

Guatemala: Guatemala City, Avenida La Reforma 7-01, Zone 10; tel. (502) 331-1541; after hours (502) 331-8904; fax (502) 331-0564; http://usembassy.state.gov/guatemala/.

Guinea: Conakry, 2nd Blvd. and 9th Ave.; tel. (224) 41-15-20/21/ 23; fax (224) 41-15-22; www.eti-bull.net/usembassy/.

Guinea-Bissau: The U.S. Embassy remains closed. Consulate: Dakar, Senegal, Avenue Jean XXIII; tel. (221)823-4296; fax (221)822-5903; consulardakar@state.gov.

Guyana: Georgetown, 100 Young and Duke Streets; tel. 011-592-225-4900 through 54909; after hours 011-592-226-2614 or 226-8298 or 227-7868 leave a message for pager number 6516; fax 011-592-225-8497.

Haiti: Port-au-Prince, Harry Truman Blvd.; tel. (509) 22-0200, 22-0354, 23-0955 or 22-0269; fax (509) 23-1641; http://usembassy.state.gov/haiti. Connsulate: Port-au-Prince, Rue Oswald Durand; tel. (509) 23-7011; fax (509) 23-1641.

Honduras: Tegucigalpa, Avenida La Paz; tel. 011-504-236-9320 or 011-504-238-5114; fax 011-504-238-4357; www.usmission.hn. Consulate: San Pedro Sula, Banco Atlantida Building 8th floor; tel. 011-504-558-1580; www.usmission.hn.

Hong Kong: Central, Hong Kong, 26 Garden Road; tel. (852) 2523-9011; fax (852) 2845-4845; www.usconsulate.org.hk/.

Hungary: Budapest, v. 1054 Budapest, Szabadsag Ter 12; tel. (36-1) 475-4400; after hours (36-1) 475-4703/4929; fax (36-1) 475-4188/4113; www.usis.hu/consular.htm.

Iceland: Reykjavik, Laufasvegur 21; tel. (354) 562-9100; fax (354) 562-9118.

India: New Delhi, Shanti Path, Chanakyapuri; tel. (91)(11)419-8000, fax(91)(11)419-0017; http://usembassy.state.gov/posts/in1/wwwhmain.html. Consulates: Calcutta, 5/1 Ho Chi Minh Sarani, 700071, tel. (91)(033) 282-3611/3615; http://usembassy.state.gov/calcutta/. Chennai (Madras), Mount Rd.; tel. (91)(44) 827-3040 or 811-2000; fax (91)(44) 827-2020; http://usembassy.state.gov/chennai/. Mumbia (Bombay), Lincoln House, 78 Bhulabhai Desai Rd.; tel. (91)(22) 363-3611; fax (91)(22) 363-0350; http://usembassy.state.gov/mumbai/.

Indonesia: Jakarta, Medan Merdeka Selatan 5; tel. (62)(21)3435-9000; fax (62)(21)3435-9922. www.usembassyjakarta.org. Consulates: Surabaya, Jalan Raya Dr., Sutomo 33; tel. (62)(31) 567-2287/8; fax (62)(31)567-4492; consularsuraba@state.gov. Bali, Jalan Hayam Wuruk 188; tel. (62)(361)233-605; fax (62)(31) 222-426; amcobali@indo.net.id.

Iran: Contac the U.S. Embassy in Switzerland.

Iraq: Contact the U.S. Embassy in Poland.

Ireland: Dublin, 42 Elgin Road, Ballsbridge; tel. (353)(1)668-7122; after hours (353)(1)668-9612/9464; fax (353)(1) 668-9946; www.usembassy.ie/.

Israel, the West Bank and Gaza: Tel Aviv, 71 Hayarkon St.; tel. (972)(3) 519-7575; after hours (972)(3) 519-7551; fax (972)(3) 516-4390; http://consular.usembassy-israel.org.il. Consulates: Jerusalem, 27 Nablus Road; tel. (972)(2) 622-7200; after hours (972)(2) 622-7250; fax (972)(2) 627-2233; www.uscongen-jerusalem.org. Haifa, 26 Ben Gurion Boulevard; tel. (972)(4) 853-1470.

Italy: Rome, Via Veneto 119a; tel. 24 hours (39) 06-46741, fax (39) 06-4674-2217. U.S. Consulates: Florence, at Lungarno Amerigo Vespucci 38; tel. 39-055-239-8276/7/8/9 or 39-055-217-605; fax 39-055-284-088.Milan at Via Principe Amedeo 2/10; tel. 39-02-290-351; fax 39-02-290-35-273. Naples, at Piazza della Repubblica: tel. 39-081-583-8111; fax 39-081-761-1804.

Jamaica: Kingston, Life of Jamaica Building, 16 Oxford Rd.; tel. (876) 935-6044; fax (876) 935-6018; http://usembassy.state.gov/kingston/.

Japan: Tokyo, 1-10-5 Akasaka; tel. 81-3-3224-5000; after hours 81-3-3224-5168; fax 81-3-3224-5856; http://usembassy.state.gov/tokyo/. Osaka-Kobe, 2-11-5 Nishitenma, Kita-ku; tel. 81-6-6315-5900; after hours 0990-526-160; fax 81-6-6315-5914. 81-6-6315-5900; http://synapse.senri-i.or.jp/amcon/. Naha, 2564 Nishihara, Urasoe; tel. 81-98-876-4211; fax 81-98-876-4243; http://usembassy.state.gov/naha/. Sapporo, Kita 1-Jo Nishi 28-chome, Chuo-ku; tel. 81-11-641-1115; fax 81-11-643-1283; http://usembassy.state.gov/sapporo/. Fokuoka, 2-5-26 Ohori, Chuo-ku; tel. 81-92-751-9331; fax 81-92-713-9222; http://usembassy.state.gov/fukuoka/. Nagoya, Nishiki SIS Building 6th Floor, 3-10-33; tel. 81-52-203-4011; fax 81-52-201-4612; http://usembassy.state.gov/nagoya/.

Jordan: Amman, Abdoun; tel. [962](6) 592-0101; after hours [962](6) 592-0120; fax 592-4102; www.usembassy-amman.org.jo.

Kazakhstan: Almaty, 99/97A Furmanova Street; tel. 7-3272-63-39-21; after hour 7-3272-50-76-27; fax 7-3272-50-62-69; consular-almaty@state.gov.

Kenya: Nairobi, Mombasa Road; tel. (254) (2) 537-800; after hours (254) (2) 537-809; fax (254) (2) 537-810.

Kiribati: Majuro, Republic of the Marshall Islands; tel. (692) 247-4011; fax (692) 247-4012.

Kuwait: Bayan, Al-Masjid Al-Aqsa Street, Plot 14, Block 14; tel. 965-539-5307 or 539-5308; after hours 965-538-2097; www.usembassy.gov.kw.

Kyrgyz Republic: Bishkek, 171 Prospect Mira; tel. 996-312-551-241; fax 996-312-551-264.

Laos: Vientiane, Thanon Bartholonie (aka Rue Bartholonie, near
   Tat Dam); tel. (856-21) 212-581, 212-582, 212-585; after hours
   (856-20) 502-016; fax (856-21) 251-624; http://usembas-
   sy.state.gov/laos/.
Latvia: Riga, Raina Boulevard 7; tel. (371) 703-6200; fax (371) 782-
   0047; http://www.usis.bkc.lv/embassy/.
Lebanon: Antelias; tel. [961] (4) 542-600, 543-600, 544-310, 544-
   130,   and   544-140;   fax   [961]   (4)   544-209;
   www.usembassy.com.lb/.
Lesotho: Maseru West, 254 Kingsway; tel. 266-312-666.
Liberia: Monrovia, 111 United Nations Drive; tel. (231) 226-370;
   fax (231) 226-154.
Libya: Contact the U.S. Embassy in Belgium.
Liechtenstein: Contact the U.S. Embassy in Switzerland.
Lithuania: Vilnius, 2600 Akmenu 6, tel. (370-2) 665500; fax (370-2)
   665510; www.usembassy.lt.
Luxembourg: Luxembourg City, 22 Boulevard Emmanuel Ser-
   vais;   tel.   (352)   46-01-23;   fax   (352)   46-19-39;
   www.amembassy.lu.
Macau: Contact the U.S. Consulate General in Hong Kong.
Macedonia (Former Yugoslav Republic of): Skopje, Ilindenska
   bb; tel. (389) (2) 116-180; fax (389) (2) 213-767; http://usembas-
   sy.mpt.com.mk.
Madagascar: Antananarivo, 14-16 Rue Rainitovo; tel. [261] (20)
   22-212-57; fax [261] (20) 22-345-39.
Malawi: Lilongwe, Area 40, City Center; tel. (265) 773-166, 773-
   342 and 773-367; fax (265) 770-471.
Malaysia: Kuala Lumpur, 376 Jalan Tun Razak; tel. (60-3)2168-
   5000; fax (60-3)242-2207; http://usembassymalaysia.org.my/.
Maldives: Contact the U.S. Embassy in Sri Lanka.
Mali: Bamako, Rue Rochester NY and Rue Mohamed V; tel. (223)
   22-38-33; fax (223) 22-37-12.
Malta: Valletta, third floor of Development House, St. Anne St.;
   tel.   (356)   235-960;   fax   (356)   243-229;
   U.S.Embassy@kemmunet.net.mt.
**Marshall Islands: Located on the ocean-side of the island's
   road, near the Church of the Latter-Day Saints and Gibson's
   Express, "Long Island;" tel. (692) 247-4011; fax (692) 247-4012;
   http://usembassy.state.gov/majuro/.

Martinique: Contact the U.S. Embassy in Barbados.

Mauritania: Nouakchott, between the Presidency building and the Spanish Embassy; tel. (222) 25-26-60, 25-26-63, 25-11-41, or 25-11-45; fax (222) 25-15-92.

Mauritius: Port Louis, Rogers House (fourth floor) on John F. Kennedy St.; tel. (230) 208-2347 or 202-4400; fax (230) 208-9534; www.usembassymauritius.com.

Mexico: Mexico City, Paseo de la Reforma 305, Colonia Cuauhtemoc; tel. 011-525-080-2000 or 5-080-2000; ccs@usembassy.net.mx. Consulates: Ciudad Juarez, Avenida Lopez Mateos 924-N; tel. (52)(1) 611-3000. Guadalajara, Progreso 175; tel. (52)(3) 825-2998. Monterrey, Avenida Constitucion 411; tel. (52)(8) 345-2120. Tijuana, Tapachula 96; tel. (52)(6) 681-7400. Hermosillio, Avenida Monterrey 141; tel. (52)(6) 217-2375. Matamoros, Avenida Primera 2002; tel. (52)(8) 812-4402. Merida, Paseo Montejo 453; tel. (52)(9) 925-5011. Nogales, Calle San Jose; tel. (52)(6) 313-4820. Nuevo Laredo; Calle Allende 3330, Col. Jardin; tel. (52)(8) 714-0512. Acapulco, Hotel Continental Plaza, Costera Miguel Aleman 121—Local 14; tel. (52)(7) 484-03-00 or (52)(7) 469-0556. Cabo San Lucas, Blvd. Marina y Pedregal No. 1, Local No. 3, Zona Centro; tel. (52)(1) 143-3566. Cancun, Plaza Caracol Two, Third Level, No. 320-323, Boulevard Kukulcan, km. 8.5, Zona Hotelera; tel. (52)(9) 883-0272. Cozumel, Plaza Villa Mar in the Main Square—El Centro, 2nd floor right rear, Locale No. 8, Avenida Juarez and 5th Ave. Norte; tel. (52)(9) 872-4574. Ixtapa/Zihuatanejo, Local 9, Plaza Ambiente; tel. (52)(7) 553-2100. Mazatlan, Hotel Playa Mazatlan, Rodolfo T. Loaiza No. 202, Zona Dorada; tel. (52)(6) 916-5889. Oaxaca, Macedonio Alcala No. 407, Interior 20; tel. (52)(9) 514-3054 (52)(9) 516-2853. Puerto Vallarta, Edif. Vallarta, Plaza Zaragoza 160-Piso 2 Int-18; tel. (52)(3) 222-0069. San Luis Potosi, Edificio "Las Terrazas," Avenida Venustiano Carranza 2076-41; tel. (52)(4) 811-7802. San Miguel de Allende, Dr. Hernandez Macias No. 72; tel. (52)(4)152-2357 or (52)(4)152-0068.

Micronesia: Kolonia, Kasalehlie St.; tel. (691) 320-2187; fax (691) 320-2186.

Moldova: Chisinau, Strada Alexei Mateevici 103; tel. (373)(2) 23-37-72; after hours (373)(2) 23-73-45.

Monaco: See the U.S. Embassy of France.

Mongolia: Ulaanbaatar, Micro Region 11, Big Ring Road; tel. (976)-1-329-095; www.us-mongolia.com.

Montserrat: Contact U.S. Embassy in Barbados.

Morocco: Rabat, 2 Avenue de Marrakech; tel. (212)(37) 76-2265. Consulates: Casablanca, 8 Boulevard Moulay Youssef; tel. (212)(22) 26-45-50; fax (212)(22) 20-41-27; www.usembassy-morocco.org.ma/.

Mozambique: Maputo, 193 Avenida Kenneth Kaunda; tel. (258-1) 49-27-97; after hours (258-1) 49-07-23; fax (258-1) 49-01-14; consularmaputo@state.gov.

Namibia: Windhoek, 14 Lossen St.; tel. (264-61) 22-1061; fax (264-61) 22-9792.

Nauru: Contact the U.S. Embassy in Fiji.

Nepal: Kathmandu, Pani Pokhari; tel. (977) (1) 411179; fax (977) (1) 419963; www.south-asia.com/USA.

Netherlands: The Hague, at Lange Voorhout 102; tel. (31)(20) 310-9209. Consulates: Amsterdam, Museumplein 19; tel. (31)(20) 664-5661, (31)(20) 679-0321, or (31)(20) 575-5309; after hours (31)(70) 310-9499; www.usemb.nl.

Netherlands Antilles: Contact the U.S. Embassy in Curacao.

New Caledonia: Contact the U.S. Embassy in Fiji.

New Zealand: Wellington, 29 Fitzherbert Terrace; tel. (64-4) 472-2068; fax (64-4) 471-2380. Consulates: Auckland, fourth floor, Yorkshire General Building, Corner of Shortland and O'Connell St.; tel. (64-9) 303-2724; fax (64-9) 366-0870; http://homepages.ihug.co.nz/~amcongen/.

Nicaragua: Managua, Kilometer 41/2 (4.5) Carretera Sur; tel. (505) 266-6010 or 268-0123; after hours (505) 266-6038; fax (505) 266-9943; http://usembassy.state.gov/managua.

Niger: Niamey, Rue des Ambassades; tel. (227) 72-26-61, 72-26-62, 72-26-63, 71-26-64; fax (227) 73-31-67 or 72-31-46; USEMB@INTNET.NE.

Nigeria: Abuja, 9 Mambilla, Maitama District; tel. [234](9) 523-0916. Consulates: Lagos, 2 Walter Carrington Crescent; tel. 011 [234] (1) 261-1215; after hours 011 [234] (1) 261-1414 or 0195 or 0078 or 0139 or 6477; Lagoscons2@state.gov.

North Korea: Contact the U.S. Embassy in Beijing, China.

Northern Ireland: See United Kingdom.

Norway: Oslo, Drammensveien 18; tel. (47) 22-44-85-50; fax (47) 22-56-27-51; www.usa.no.

Oman: Muscat, Jameat A'Duwal Al Arabiya St.; tel. (968) 698-989; fax (968) 699-189; www.usa.gov.om/.

Pakistan: Islamabad, Diplomatic Enclave, Ramna 5; tel. (92-51) 2080-0000; fax (92-51) 822-632; www.usembassy.state.gov/islamabad or www.usembassy.state.gov/pakistan. Consulates: Karachi, 8 Abdullah Haroon Road; tel. (92-21) 568-5170; after hours 92-21-568-1606; fax (92-21) 568-0496; www.usembassy.state.gov/pakistan or www.usembasy.state.gov/posts/pk2/wwwhamcn.html. Lahore, 50-Empress Road; tel. (92-42) 636-5530; fax (92-42) 636-5177; http://usconsulate-lahore.org.pk/. Peshawar, 11 Hospital Road; tel. (92-91) 279-801 through 803; fax (92-91) 276-712; http://brain.net.pk/~consul/.

Palau: Koror; tel. (680) 488-2920; fax (680) 488-2911.

Panama: Panama City, Balboa Ave. 39th St.; tel. 011-507-207-7000/7030; after hours 011-507-207-7000; fax 011-507-207-7278; www.orbi.net/usispan/.

Papua New Guinea: Port Moresby, Douglas St.; tel. (675) 321-1455; fax (675) 321-1593; consularportmoresby@state.gov.

Paraguay: Asuncion, 1776 Mariscal Lopez Avenue; tel. (011-595-21) 213-715; usconsulasuncion@hotmail.com.

Peru: Monterrico, Avenida Encalada, Block Seventeen; tel. (51-1) 434-3000; after hours (51-1) 434-3032; fax (51-1) 434-3065 or 434-3037; http://usembassy.state.gov/lima. Consulates: Cusco, Binational Center (Instituto Cultural Peruana Norte Americano, ICPNA) at Avenida Tullumayo 125; tel. (51-8) 24-51-02; fax (51-8) 23-35-41; consagentcuzco@terra.com.pe.

Philippines: Manila, located at 1201 Roxas Boulevard, Manila City; tel. (63-2) 523-1001; fax (63-2) 522-3242; http://usembassy.state.gov/posts/rp1/wwwh3004.html. Consulates: Cebu, third floor, PCI Bank, Gorordo Ave.; tel. (63-32) 231-1261.

Poland: Warsaw, Aleje Ujazdowskie 29/31; tel. (48)(22) 628-3041; fax (48)(22) 625-0289; after hours (48)(22) 625-0055. Consulates: Krakow, Ulica Stolarska 9; tel. (48)(12) 429-6655; fax

(48)(12) 421-8292; after hours 0601-483-348. Poznan, Ulica Paderewskiego 7; tel. (48)(61) 851-8516; fax (48)(61) 851-8966.

Portugal: Lisbon, Avenida das Forças Armadas,Sete Rios; tel. (351)(21) 727-3300; fax (351)(21) 726-9109; ww.american-embassy.pt. Consulates: Ponta Delgada, Avenida D. Henrique; tel. (351)(96) 282216/7/8/9. Funchal, Madeira, Rua Tentente Coronel Sarmento,Ed; tel. (351)(29) 174-3429 fax (351)(29) 174-3808.

Qatar: Doha, 22nd February St.; tel. (974) 488-4176; after hours (974) 553-1085; www.usembassy.org.qa.

Romania: Strada Tudor Arghezi 7-9; tel. (40) 1-210-4042; after hours (40) 1-210-0149. Consulates: Strada Filipescu no. 26 (formerly Strada Snagov); tel. (40) 1-210-4042; fax (40) 1 211-3360. Cluj-Napoca, Universitatii 7-9, Etaj 1; tel. (40) 64-193-815.

Russia: Moscow, Novinskiy Bulvar 19/23; tel. (7) (095) 728-5000; fax (7) (095) 728-5084; http://usembassy.state.gov/moscow/. Consulates: St. Petersburg: Ulitsa Furshtadskaya 15; tel (7-812) 275-1701; fax (7-812) 110-7022; after hours (7-812) 274-8692; http://usembassy.state.gov/stpetersburg/. Vladivostok, Ulitsa Pushkinskaya 32; tel. (7) (4232) 30-00-70; fax (7)(4232) 30-00-91; after hours; (7) (4232) 26-84-58 or (7) (4232) 21-52-90; http://usembassy.state.gov/vladivostok/. Yekaterinburg, Number 15, Gogol St. (Ulitsa Gogolya); tel. (7-3432) 62-98-88 or (7-3432) 564-744; fax (7-3432) 564-515; after hours (8)(29) 05-15-06; www.uscgyekat.ur.ru.

Rwanda: Kigali, Boulevard de la Revolution; tel. 250-505601/505602/505603; fax 250-72128.

Samoa: Apia, in the John Williams Building, fifth floor, Beach Rd; tel. (685) 21-631; fax (685) 22-030; http://travel.state.gov/samoa.html.

Sao Tome and Principe: Contact the U.S. Embassy in Gabon.

Saudi Arabia: Riyadh, Collector Rd. M, Riyadh Diplomatic Quarter; tel. (966) (1) 488-3800; fax (966) (1) 488-7275. Consulates: Dhahran, tel. (966) (3) 330-3200; fax (966) (3) 330-0464. Jeddah, Palestine Rd.; tel. (966) (2) 667-0080; fax (966) (2) 669-3078 or 669-3098.

Senegal: Dakar, Avenue Jean XXIII; tel. (221) 822-4599; after hours (221) 823-4604.

Seychelles: Contact the U.S. Embassy in Mauritius.

Sierra Leone: Freetown, the corner of Walpole and Siaka Stevens St.; tel. (232)(22) 226-481; fax (232)(22) 225-471.

Singapore: 27 Napier Road; tel. [65] 476-9100; after hours [65] 476-9100; fax [65]476-9340; www.usembassysingapore.org.sg.

Slovak Republic: Hviezdoslavovo nam. 4; tel. (421)(7) 5443 0861, (421)(7) 5443 3338; fax (421)(7) 5441 8861; www.usis.sk.

Slovenia: Ljubljana, Presernova 31; tel. (386)(1) 200-5500; fax (386)(1) 200-5535; www.usembassy.si.

Solomon Islands: Contact the U.S. Embassy in Papua New Guinea.

Somalia: Nairobi, Kenya, Mombasa Road (for the northeastern and southern regions of Somalia); tel. (254)(2)537-800; after hours (254)(2)537-809. Or contact the U.S. Embassy in Djibouti (for the northwest).

South Africa: Pretoria, 877 Pretorius St. Arcadia; tel. (27-12) 342-1048; fax (27-12) 342-5504. Consulates: Johannesburg, No. 1 River Street (corner of River and Riviera Road); tel. (27-11) 644-8000; fax (27-11) 646-6916. Cape Town, Broadway Industries Center; tel. (27-21) 421-4280; fax (27-21) 425-3014. Durban, Durban Bay House, 29th floor, 333 Smith Street; tel. (27-31) 304-4737; fax (27-31) 301-0265.

South Korea: Seoul, 82 Sejong-Ro Chongro-Ku; tel. (82-2) 397-4114; fax (82-2) 738-8845; http://usembassy.state.gov/seoul.

Spain: Madrid, Serrano 75; tel. (34)(91) 587-2200; fax (34)(91) 587-2303; www.embusa.es. Consulates: Barcelona, Paseo Reina Elisenda 23-25; tel. (34)(93) 280-2227; fax (34)(93) 205-5206; www.embusa.es/ircbarna/ircbarcen.html.

Sri Lanka: Colombo, 210 Galle Road, Colombo 3; tel. (94)(1) 448-007; after hours (94)(1) 447-601; fax (94)-(1)-436-943; http:// usembassy.state.gov/srilanka.

St. Kitts and Nevis: Contact the U.S. Embassy in Barbados.

St. Lucia: Contact the U.S. Embassy in Barbados.

Sudan: Khartoum, Sharia Ali Abdul Latif; tel. (249)(11) 774-700 and 774-611; fax 774-137. Cairo; tel. (20)(2) 795-7371; http:// usembassy.egnet.net/sudan.htm.

Suriname: Paramaribo, Dr. Sophie Redmonstraat 129; tel. (011)(597) 472-900; after hours (011)(597) 088-0338.

Swaziland: Mbabane, Central Bank Building on Warner St.; tel. (268) 404-6441/5; fax (268) 404-5959.

Sweden: Stockholm, Dag Hammarskjoldsvag 31; tel. (46)(8) 783-5300; fax (46)(8) 660-5879; after hours (46)(8) 783-5310; www.usemb.se.

Switzerland: Bern, Jubilaeumstrasse 93; tel. (41)(31) 357-7011; after hours (41)(31) 357-7218; fax (41)(31) 357-7280; www.us-embassy.ch. Consulates: Zurich, American Center of Zurich, Dufourstrasse 101; tel. (41)(1) 422-2566; fax (41) (1) 383-9814. Geneva, Rue Versonnex, 1207; tel. (41)(22) 840-5160; fax (41)(22) 840-5162.

Syria: Damascus, Abu Roumaneh, al-Mansur St. No. 2; tel. [963] (11) 333-2814, 332-0783, 333-0788, and 333-3232; fax [963] (11) 331-9678.

Taiwan: Taipei, No.7 Lane 134, Hsin Yi Rd. Section 3; tel. (886-2) 2709-2000; after hours (886-2) 2709-2013; fax (886-2) 2709-0908. Kaohsiung, No. 2 Chung Cheng 3rd Rd., 5th Floor; tel. (886-7) 238-7744; fax (886-7) 238-5237; aitam-cit@mail.ait.org.tw.

Tajikistan: Almaty, 99/97A Furmanov St.; tel. 7(3272) 63-39-05. Dushanbe, 10 Pavola St.; tel. 011 (992)(372) 21-03-48/50/52; fax 011 (992)(372) 21-03-62.

Tanzania (Zanzibar): Dar es Saleem, 140 Msese Road, Kinondoni District St.; tel. (255)[22] 266-6010 through 5; fax (255)[22] 266-7285; consulardx@state.gov.

Thailand: Bangkok, 95 Wireless Rd.; (66-2) 205-4000; tel. (66-2) 205-4049; fax (66-2) 205-4103; www.usa.or.th. Chiang Mai, 387 Wichayanond Rd.; tel. (66-53) 252-629; fax (66-53) 252-633.

Togo: Lome, Rue Kouenou and Rue Tokmake (formerly known as Rue Pelletier Caventou and Rue Vauban); tel. (228) 21-29-92; after hours (228) 21-29-93; fax (228) 21-79-52.

Tonga: Contact the U.S. Embassy in Fiji.

Trinidad and Tobago: Port-of-Spain, 15 Queen's Park West; tel. 1-868-622-6371; fax 1-868-628-5462.

Tunisia: Tunis, 144 Avenue de la Liberte, 1002 Tunis-Belvedere; tel. (216) 71-782-566 extension 4430; fax (216) 71-788-923; http://usembassy.state.gov/posts/ts1/wwwhmain.html.

Turkey: Ankara, 110 Ataturk Blvd.; tel. (90)(312) 468-6110; fax (90)(312) 467-0019; www.usemb-ankara.org.tr. Consulates:

Istanbul, 104-108 Mesrutiyet Caddesi, Tepebasi; tel. (90)(212) 251-3602; fax (90)(212) 252-7851; www.usisist.org.tr. Adana, the corner of Vali Yolu and Ataturk Caddesi; tel. (90)(322) 459-1551; fax (90)(322) 457-6591. Izmir, Kazim Dirik Caddesi 13/8; tel. (90)(232) 441-0072/2203; fax (90)(232) 441-2373.

Turkmenistan: Ashgabat, 9 Pushkin St., off Maqtymquly St.; tel. 993-12-35-00-45; fax 993-12-51-13-05; www.usemb-ashgabat.rpo.at.

Turks and Caicos: Contact U.S. Embassy in Bahamas.

Tuvalu: Contact the U.S. Embassy in Fiji

Uganda: Kampala, Gaba Rd.; tel. 256-41-234-142; fax 256-41-258-451; uscons@infocom.co.ug.

Ukraine: Kiev, 10 Vulitsa Yuria Kotsubinskoho; tel. (380) (44) 490-4000; after hours 240-0856; fax 244-7350; www.usemb.kiev.ua.

United Arab Emirates: Abu Dhabi, 11th St.; tel. (971) (2) 443-6691; after hours (971) (2) 443-4457; fax (971) (2) 443-5786; www.usembabu.gov.ae. Consulates: Dubai, 21st floor of the Dubai World Trade Center; tel. (971) (4) 331-3115; fax (971) (4) 331-6935.

United Kingdom and Gibraltar (England, Wales, Scotland, Northern Ireland): London, 24 Grosvenor Square; tel. 0207-499-9000 or 011-44-207-499-9000; fax 0207-495-5012 or 011-44-207-495-5012; www.usembassy.org.uk. Consulates: Edinburgh, 3 Regent Terrace; tel. 0131-556-8315 or 011-44-131-556-8315; after hours 0131-260-6495 or 011-44-131-260-6495; fax 0131-557-6023 or 011-44-131-557-6023; www.usembassy.org.uk/scotland. Belfast, 14 Queen St.; tel. 01232-328-239 or 011-44-1232-328-239; after hours 01232-241-279 or 011-44-1232-661-629; fax 01232-248-482 or 011-44-1232-248-482.

Uruguay: Montevideo, Lauro Muller 1776; tel. (598)(2) 408-7777; fax (598)(2)408-4110 or -8611; www.embeeuu.gub.uy/.

Uzbekistan: Tashkent, Ulitsa Chilanzarskaya, 82; tel. (998 71) 120-5450; fax (998 71) 120 6335; www.usis.uz/wwwhcon.htm.

Vanuatu: Contact the U.S. Embassy in Papua New Guinea.

Venezuela: Caracas, Calle Suapure and Calle F, Colinas de Valle Arriba; tel. (011)(58)(2) 975-6411; after hours (011)(58)(2) 975-

9821; fax (011)(58)(2) 975-8991; http://usembassy.state.gov/ca-
racas/. Consulates: Maracaibo, Centro Venezolano Americano del Zulia (CEVAZ), Calle 63 No. 3E-60; tel. (011)(58)(61)
91-1436 or 91-1880.

Vietnam: Hanoi, 6 Ngoc Khanh, Ba Dinh District; tel. (84-4) 831-
4590; after hours (84-4) 772-1500; fax (84-4) 831-4578; http://
usembassy.state.gov/vietnam/. Consulates: Ho Chi Minh
City, 4 Le Duan, District 1; tel. (84-8) 822-9433; fax (84-8) 822-
9434; www.uscongenhcmc.org.

Yemen: Sanaa, Dhahr Himyar Zone, Sheraton Hotel District; tel.
(967) (1) 303-155, extension 118, 265 or 266; fax (967) (1) 303-
175.

Yugoslavia, Federal Republic of: Belgrade, 48 Kneza Milosa St.;
tel. (381) (11) 646-924; or (381) (11) 645-655. Kosovo; tel. (873-
762-029-525).

Zaire: See Democratic Republic of Congo.

Zambia: Lusaka, the corner of Independence and United Nations Ave.; tel. (260-1) 250-955 or 250-230; after hours (260-1)
252-234; fax (260-1) 252-225.

Zimbabwe: Harare, 172 Herbert Chitepo Ave.; tel. (263-4) 250-
593/4; after hours (263-4) 250-595; fax (263-4) 722-618 and 796-
488.

U.S. Passport Information

U.S. State Department, National Passport Information Center,
telephone billing fees are charged for calls to 900-225-5674,
Visa, MasterCard and American Express credit holders can
charge calls to 888-362-8668, http://travel.state.gov/pass-
port_services.html

Victims of Terrorism/Crime

Office for Victims of Crime, U.S. Department of Justice, 800-627-
6872, www.ojp.usdoj.gov/ovc/

Terrorism Victim Hotline, 800-331-0075, U.S. Department of Justice

Visa Services

U.S. State Department, 202-663-1225, http://travel.state.gov/visa_services.html

Water Security

U.S. Environmental Protection Agency, Environmental Emergency Hotline: 800-424-8802, 1200 Pennsylvania Avenue, NW, Washington, DC, 20460, 215-814-5000, www.epa.gov

Index

[References are to pages and appendices.]

S